1864 PROSPECT OF COLLEGE AND VILLAGE

Aldren A. Watson 1964

TO SHARE OUR DARTMOUTH HERITAGE WITH YOU

THE COLLEGE ON THE HILL

A voyce crieth in the wildernesse, Prepare ye the way of the Lord; make streight in the desert a path for our God.

THE COLLEGE ON THE HILL

A Dartmouth Chronicle

EDITED BY

RALPH NADING HILL

Dartmouth Publications
Hanover · New Hampshire

Library of Congress Card no. 64-16542

COMPOSITION BY THE VERMONT PRINTING COMPANY
AND PRINTING BY THE MERIDEN GRAVURE COMPANY

Table of Contents

List of Illustrations

A DARTMOUTH CHRONICLE

Dartmouth on Purpose:
A Foreword

JOHN SLOAN DICKEY

THE Dartmouth venture chronicled here has been adventurous but not haphazard. Assuredly, there is much that is varied and unpredictable in any educational venture. And the higher the education, the more unpredictable it sometimes seems to get, especially to those steadying the ladder on the ground. But unpredictable and contrary as it may be, higher education is a creation of men's purposes.

Purpose is the fundamental continuity in any living thing. A perceptive student of human institutions, H. J. W. Hetherington, remarked that a "purposeless institution is hard to imagine." Having in mind that a live institution literally grows its own purposefulness, he cautioned us that "we do not understand any institution until we look at its history."

Certain it is that no institution, especially a college, ever grew great except "on purpose" in a sense of both direction and determination. Dartmouth, as this story reveals, has been an extraordinarily purposeful institution. From the historic Charter itself, through the title chosen by President-Emeritus Hopkins for his papers, *This Our Purpose,* a strong avowal of purpose has guided the life of this College.

It is perhaps too little remembered that George the Third was not solely concerned with "spreading Christian Knowledge among the Savages" when on December 13, 1769, he granted the Dartmouth Charter, as he so majestically put it, "of our special grace certain knowledge and mere motion." A major purpose of His Majesty and his Governor, John Wentworth, and particularly of those who were competing for the new institution with promised land, was "also that the best means of Education be established in our Province of New Hampshire."

The Charter is heedful of Wheelock's plan "for carrying on the great design among the Indians," but one cannot ponder the far-sighted scope of this remarkable document without realizing that its authors were perhaps even more mindful of the larger, more enduring need in the new land for that "best means of education." The life-giving power of the Royal Charter called forth the erection of a college

by the name of Dartmouth College for the education and instruction of Youth of the Indian Tribes in this Land in reading, writing & all parts of Learning which shall appear necessary and expedient for civilizing & christianizing Children of Pagans as well as in all liberal Arts and Sciences; and also of English Youth and any others.

These purposeful words have weathered well. The mission of "civilizing and christianizing" has changed with the times — and with the "Pagans." As the Indians disappeared from Hanover Plain a more than ample supply of customers has been forthcoming from that wonderfully embracing group specified in the Charter simply as "any others." The purposes of the Charter endure in meaning and relevance because today as two centuries ago they bespeak the fulfillment of man and the enjoyment of his life through an unbounded learning.

The purposes set forth in the Charter speak for themselves, but after two-hundred years of life so does the institution itself. Its daily life proclaims what it is. Even though a large part of its purpose is the past made present, there is no escaping the fact that the purpose of an institution is also the course which those at the helm at any particular time are pursuing.

We need not dwell on the fact that the helm of a modern college is not at all as single-minded an operation as the nautical figure may suggest. Nonetheless the president is perforce the spokesman for the helm and however many share in setting the course it is unlikely that there is much institutional sense of purpose where the president is unable or unwilling to speak to it. As I have learned my way into the Dartmouth presidency and as the postwar period became its own new era, speaking to the purpose of the institution has loomed larger for me both as a necessity of the job and as a perplexity. The difficulty is that the College seen in its entirety is always more varied and more ongoing than it ever seems when put to words.

An educational enterprise at its best is always in the process of becoming rather than a finished thing ready for its official portrait. At no point is it ever precisely what it was or will be simply because it personifies the precept commended to the Class of 1956 by Detlev Bronk at a memorably wet commencement: "it is better to travel than to arrive." It is in this sense of the ongoing college that I speak here of Dartmouth's purpose.

Nothing characterizes the American liberal arts college more than the comprehensiveness of the education it seeks to provide. The Dartmouth Charter enjoined on the College nothing less than "education and instruction . . . in reading, writing & all parts of Learning . . . for civilizing & christianizing . . . as well as in all liberal Arts and Sciences." Translated into a faculty and curriculum for American society in the latter half of the twentieth century that is quite an order, but in truth it is an order which Dartmouth and other comparable colleges still seek to fill.

> It is also my firm belief that this Institution will so attach the Indians to the British Interest that it will prevent more Incursions & ravages upon the Peasantry in those remote Countries than the best Regiment of Troops that could be raised. – Gov. John Wentworth, 1770.

The uniqueness of the historic cultural college, whether existing independently or as the core of a university, is its corporate commitment to provide a higher education which in all essential ways prepares a man for the meaningful enjoyment of life.

Before speaking about the components of such an educational experience I ought to explain the importance I attach to the "corporate" quality of this commitment on the part of the College. I regard this commitment on the part of the institution, its sense of institutional purpose, if you will, as the central orienting force of the entire enterprise. An educational enterprise with this orientation is perforce more than merely a housing and feeding facility supporting the personal purposes of scholars and students. An institution with a purpose that focuses on helping the student learn his way toward total fulfillment, finds that this purpose is itself a powerful orienting factor in the educational experience of the undergraduate. The quality of an institution's concern or lack of concern for him is more often than not a factor in how the undergraduate learns to take himself. We do well not to be misled by his manifest resistance to other people's purposes; he is more responsive to the purpose of the place than he knows. It is an influence which permeates his own purposes both then and later. It is the unique contribution of the institution, *per se,* to the individual educational experience because it furnishes the cohesion and coherence which make the total educational experience at such a college significantly greater than its parts.

If you've listened to the talk of those who make their careers in higher education or glanced at what passes for the literature about it, you know that there are at least as many ways to describe the elements of a college education as there are talks and books — and, of course, committee reports — on the subject. This can be disconcerting until we realize that, aside from the inevitable instances of thin thought lacquered over with thick words, most of the variations reflect fashions in terminology or individuality in approach and emphasis.

I find it useful to break the institutional purpose of a college into four abiding concerns which for my fun and your remembering I put in this alliterative order: competence, conscience, capacity for commitment and comprehensive awareness. I speak of "abiding concerns" because these are basic educational aims which a purposeful college should always have on its mind. I also want to be clear that I do not regard them as watertight categories in the life and work of the campus. Naturally enough not all activities of the college bear equally on each of these concerns; there must be a measure of specialized attention in all kinds of learning. The essential thing is that the institution in its corporate integrity should feel responsible to each of its undergraduates for making the best contribution education can make toward the individual's fulfillment in each of these areas of concern.

The development of intellectual competence is by all odds "the first among equals" in the concerns of a college. It is not that man lives by brains alone but simply that intellectual work is the prime business of any enterprise of higher education. It is the one thing a college is best suited to do, the thing it ought to do best and certainly must do well if it is to be a good college in any respect.

There is, of course, nothing new about this proposition. It is only when we apply it to the requirements of contemporary society that we sense the new imperatives it has laid on the college and its constituencies, especially on the student and his teacher.

Dartmouth and other leading colleges operate today under the challenge — and burden — of knowing that for the first time both the security of the nation and the well-being of our society are decisively dependent on the quality of our higher education. We are so accustomed to thinking of "going to college" as merely a matter of personal advantage that it is hard for us to grasp how drastically decisive higher education has suddenly become for our society.

[4]

As to the future, we can only be sure that we have reached the point in man's ability to breed knowledge where *accelerated* change in all things, not merely change, must be regarded as the normal condition of life. This circumstance naturally enough has had its first great impact on those enterprises whose business is the production and distribution of knowledge.

It is an axiom of business that nothing more surely dooms an enterprise than obsolescence. No enterprise is more susceptible to this kind of trouble than one that specializes in accelerating the rate at which its own stock in trade — knowledge — becomes obsolete. Indeed, the accelerating rate at which knowledge is being made obsolete is probably the most fundamental factor distinguishing today's college from yesterday's.

The growing realization that knowledge is a process and not a fixed thing has sharpened the relevance of the ancient principle that education only produces an educated person if it creates an ongoing learner. A diploma (whether writ in Latin or English!) will no longer mask this truth.

The higher this kind of education goes the more "ongoing" must be the teacher himself as a learner. It is not merely that otherwise the subject matter he teaches becomes obsolete; more seriously he is fatally deficient in the abiding essential of all great teaching — the example he sets.

> The site for Dartmouth College was not determined by any private interest, or to favor any party on earth, but the Redeemer's. – Eleazar Wheelock, 1771.

Today's Dartmouth student must not only be prepared for the adult life of an ongoing learner, but increasingly he must also be specifically prepared for going on as a student to the specialized work of graduate education. Modern knowledge in all walks of life, not merely as formerly only in the so-called learned professions, requires a professional level of competence in any man who aspires to live and work at the leadership levels of American society. The preparation of an intellectual competence that will pass current in the quality markets of our competitive society requires a first-rate person doing first-rate work at both the undergraduate and graduate levels of higher education.

In sheerest outline this is why upwards of 80 per cent of Dartmouth's graduates must today be prepared to go on to advanced study. It is why Dartmouth has a faculty of teacher-scholars. It is why these men require first-rate tools of learning and the opportunity to carry on their own professional development hand-in-hand with their teaching. It is why Dartmouth's new educational program (the so-called three-course, three-term plan) in both structure and spirit seeks to extend the student's experience with independence in learning. It is why the work at a first-rate modern college is what it is — demanding. All of this and more is why Dartmouth has the *sine qua non* of a preeminent college, a student body able and willing to be worthy of it all.

Before going on to the other purposeful concerns of the college I mentioned earlier, it might be well to conclude these observations on the College's concern for intellectual competence with a word about those segments of Dartmouth where perforce the purpose of the institution is sharply focused on the development of advanced professional competence. I refer to Dartmouth's three associated schools: The Dartmouth Medical School, The Thayer School of Engineering, The Amos Tuck School of Business Administration, and the graduate programs being offered by a number of the College departments at the Master's level and since 1962 for the Ph.D. degree.

Most newcomers to a knowledge of Dartmouth, on learning of these graduate-level programs involving between 300 and 400 students, quickly ask in some amazement, "But then you *are* a university?" And from time to time one meets a person who seems to find it disconcerting that such an institution is still proudly a college by name and primary commitment at a time when most college presidents preside over universities. These occasions usually lead to a few words about the Dartmouth College Case and the bad name it gave to the word "university" in these parts a hundred and fifty years ago, but they also remind us that this institution, with its staunch championship of the undergraduate college as the stronghold of liberal learning in America, has done the reality of its full-length portrait less than justice.

Each of the three associated schools has been a notable pioneer in its field of professional education. The Medical School is today the third oldest of American medical schools and in recent years has served as the pioneering prototype on which a half dozen or more new basic-science medical schools have been patterned. Almost a hundred years ago The Thayer School was a leader in establishing liberal learning as a foundation for advanced engineering education. In 1900 Dartmouth created the first graduate school of business in her Tuck School.

These graduate schools make their way today in three highly competitive areas of professional learning. At the same time each maintains an extraordinarily close, mutually rewarding relationship to the total life and work of Dartmouth; each is an essential part of Dartmouth's response to the growing need in American higher education for a more advantageous relationship between the purposes of liberal and professional education.

The refounding of the Dartmouth Medical School under the leadership of Dr. S. Marsh Tenney between 1957 and 1962 and the ensuing development of the Gilman Bio-Medical Center is a vivid instance of of Dartmouth's unusual, perhaps unique, potential for collaboration between undergraduate, professional, and graduate education. In addition to doubling the enrollment of the Medical School, increasing its full-time faculty ten times and sponsored research support nearly two hundred times, creating totally new teaching, research, and library facilities for both the Medical School and the College's Department of Biological Sciences, this collaborative effort initiated Dartmouth's first interdisciplinary graduate program at the Ph.D. level in molecular biology.

At the same time and in response to a similar initiative by the Department of Mathematics, a new Ph.D. program in mathematics was undertaken. Although the Ph.D. degree is not as unprecedented at Dartmouth as some imagined — it was authorized seventy years earlier and eight degrees were granted — it is fair to say that these and similar programs both directly and indirectly are a part of Dartmouth's total response to today's demand for a greater output of intellectual competence from our enterprises of higher education.

It ought not to escape the record that in both of these instances the objective was not simply to produce more Ph.D.'s, but rather to develop projects with special significance having particular appropriateness for Dartmouth. The current focus of medicine and the life sciences on molecular subjects plus the potential at Dartmouth for an unusually intimate collaborative approach met these requisites in molecular biology. In the case of mathematics, a strong group of teacher-scholars was able and anxious to do something about the critical shortage in college teaching of men and women with first-rate, modern mathematical training.

Both programs were closely related to the research interests of the faculty members involved and there can be no doubt that in many instances the undergraduate teaching of these teacher-scholars was stimulated and strengthened by their participation in these programs. Indeed, in a number of instances, fine teachers were thereby actually

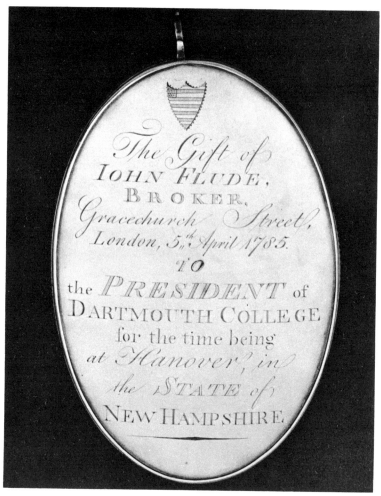

recruited or retained who otherwise would have been lost to under-graduate teaching at Dartmouth.

One needs only to observe the disappearance or decline of the college as a coherent institutional core at many universities to be made aware that research activity and graduate programs can cause trouble for un-dergraduate education. But there is impressive evidence in other institu-tions and in our own experience that research work and selective grad-uate programs need not detract from undergraduate education. The groves of academe have their own temptations to waywardness but the growing criticism of the "non-teachers" by their brethren in the higher education community suggests to me that most faculty members still find teaching first-rate undergraduates the most fundamental, and for many the most rewarding, work in higher education.

[8]

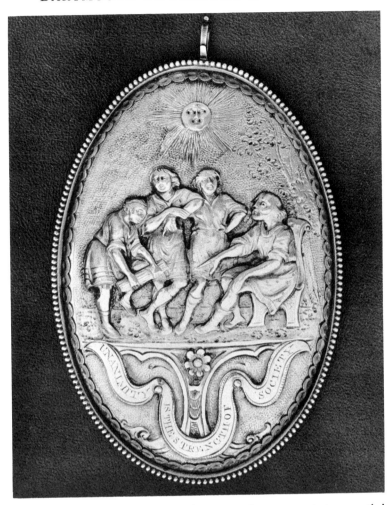

By no means all teacher-scholars need or want to participate in graduate programs. One needs only to observe today as in the past the scholarly and creative activity of some of our finest teachers to see the truth of this. We have had little if any evidence at Dartmouth of a "flight from undergraduate teaching" and even if, as some believe, such a tendency is in fact spreading throughout the academic community, I still have confidence that the Dartmouth faculty's pride in good teaching and its commitment to liberal learning will be more than a match for this malaise. Certainly, in today's world, an institution of Dartmouth's size and character could not prosper, let alone find preeminence, in a doctrinaire rejection of research activity and graduate offerings. The way forward must be a positive one that seeks through judgment and planning to have these needful academic functions under-

[9]

taken selectively, for the right reasons and with genuinely responsible regard for the overall purposes and welfare of the institution.

It is significant that in authorizing the new doctoral programs the Trustees laid down the principles that new, outside financing be secured, that candidates possess academic qualifications comparable to candidates in first-rate programs elsewhere, that all candidates previously have had a liberal education, and that during their professional study at Dartmouth they should have opportunities for continuing experience with the work and enjoyment of liberal learning.

Dartmouth's explicit concern that her candidates for the Ph.D. degree should continue and extend their experience with the liberating arts is rare, if not unique, in American graduate education. It reflects the depth of her institution-wide commitment to liberal learning and it reminds this chronicler that he has yet to say a word about the place of conscience, commitment, and comprehensiveness as rightful concerns of the college purpose in undergraduate education.

I chose the word "conscience" because it speaks to both moral and religious sensitivity, and especially because it bespeaks individuality. For me it is broad and flexible enough to be compatible with the modern educational experience and yet sufficiently focused and tenacious to foster in the individual a growth of personal responsibility toward other men and God or "just the universe," if somehow or other that capacious phrase seems preferable. Conscience is not intended as a substitute for thought or belief; it is at most an expanding promise to oneself to be kept by going beyond self in thought, action, and belief.

The William Jewett Tucker Foundation, established by the Dartmouth Trustees in 1951, is designed in purpose and in the person of its dean to witness and further the abiding concern of the corporate College that the growth of conscience should be part of the Dartmouth experience.

This effort to unite an ancient concern and contemporary circumstance stands on the considered resolve of the Trustees that today's college cannot commit itself in these matters to much more — or to much less — than the conviction that good and evil exist, that it is an educated man's duty to know and choose the good, and that it is part of Dartmouth's work to prepare men to make that choice.

The distance between concern and accomplishment in the field of morals is surely a distance that has not been shortened by modern life. I doubt that this gap has actually widened since the "good old days," but our perplexity is certainly more manifest and if I am to single out one area where I think today's college has its greatest difficulty in holding onto a sense of comprehensive purpose with confidence, I have no hesitation in saying it is here. The reasons, of course, are as old as man's nature and as contemporary as his latest fashionable folly — both of which between eighteen and twenty-two are likely to be conspicuously irresistible.

There are sincere and knowledgeable people who counsel the modern college to stay clear of a concern with conscience lest through confusion and frustration it impair its primary mission to the intellect. There is something to be said for the secular college "cutting its losses" in this area. Having progressively given up the earlier forms of this concern, e.g., preacher presidents, religious requirements, and most puritanical proscriptions, perhaps the time has come for the college to give up this concern in its entirety.

Dartmouth, as I have said, has not done this. Rather we have committed this College to the search for new approaches which while appropriate to contemporary circumstance will serve the cause of conscience in the life and work of a modern campus. It has seemed to us that to do otherwise would ultimately limit the central concern of liberal learning with what men are, expose the College to education's greatest danger — the creation of power without corresponding restraint and responsibility in its use, and leave the product of such an education without one of the ingredients necessary to a life of high accomplishment.

The weight of this last consideration was brought home to me, as I hope it may be to you, by one of Dr. Tucker's most memorable statements to the Dartmouth undergraduates of his day, in which he bracketed conscience and commitment — he called it "heart," saying, "Do not expect that you will make any lasting or very strong impression on the world through intellectual power without the use of an equal amount of conscience and heart."

As with some other truths, I got my first real feel of the role of commitment in the affairs of men when I came up against highly intelligent individuals who simply did not have it. They could sustain neither effort nor loyalty in a large or difficult undertaking and, needless to say, neither could they generate effort or loyalty in their associates. Their competence was bounded by frustration; they were expert but not much else.

Recognizing, as we should, that a capacity for commitment is a complex, highly subjective quality and that its learning and its manifestation vary with individuals, I still would testify from experience with five generations of undergraduates that its development is possible and peculiarly appropriate as a part of the educational experience of today's undergraduate.

I say "development" because I doubt that a deep-seated quality of this nature is often learned in college unless it was planted in the personality much earlier. And I say "peculiarly appropriate" to the experience of today's undergraduate because what I have seen suggests to me that he increasingly comes from a background and works in an intellectual climate that produces rather little experience with the discipline of commitment.

Take that elementary quality of commitment we call a capacity for hard work. Earlier, in a dominantly rural and home-oriented America, learning the "meaning of work" and other experiences with commitment were more a part of family life than can be the case in the urban — or suburban — life of an affluent society. Today the hard work of study in school and college is often the first significant experience many a college youth has with this discipline of life. And yet he has even this experience in a climate which at home and at college is socially as permissive as he can make it, and intellectually is, inevitably and properly, much more concerned with developing his critical and creative capacities than his capacity for commitment.

Here again the teaching-by-example done by a first-rate teacher-scholar is perhaps the single most meaningful educational experience with commitment an undergraduate can have. It must be the heart of a good college education. Even the least responsive student does not entirely escape this influence in the course of four years of college regardless of what he says and thinks at the time. On the other hand this ought not to be the whole of the college experience for anyone; for the majority of our students it is not and cannot be. This then is where the teacher is supplemented by the corporate concern of the college that each student may have a variety of opportunities for learning his individual way toward that mature capacity for commitment which Dr. Tucker called "heart."

This is why I have always regarded the "business" of undergraduate learning at Dartmouth as embracing both the curricular and the extra-curricular and it is why I believe that the educational experience of many undergraduates is significantly enriched by their participation in intercollegiate athletics and other campus enterprises where the outcome is theirs to win or lose, to make or break.

[12]

It has been a commonplace in college folklore that some students become overly involved in extracurricular activities. It is not as generally recognized, however, that these things seize undergraduates, when they do, just because the activity in question has something that all education should have — it is *real* to the point where it involves the student totally, pride and all. There is far less danger today than in the past that any large number of undergraduates will permit themselves to be pulled under by extracurricular activities. The academic pace at a college such as Dartmouth prevents it and, indeed, actually enhances the value of the extracurricular activity to the student who is strengthened by the choices he is forced to make, the confidence he acquires in managing himself in several roles, and the satisfaction he earns from learning to matter to something other than himself. It is out of that kind of learning, in class and out, that the sinews of conscience and commitment grow strong.

If tangible proof is desired that a college in its totality, including such factors of institutional character as place, heritage, and comprehensive purpose, can in fact make a difference on the commitment side of a man's learning, there is probably no better example to cite than Dartmouth. Since the days of Daniel Webster the dedication of men to the cause of this College has been proverbial. And it is no mere coincidence, I think, that more often than not the college graduate who is most closely identified with the welfare of his or her institution is also the person to whom the larger community turns for the leadership of other causes that matter.

This side of learning may be somewhat out of fashion in American higher education, but until that distant day when knowledge is self-executing my bet will be on the college that purposefully finds a place in its life and work for the growth of its students in conscience and commitment.

> Yet, my dear friend, let me say to you, be comforted. . . . Neither can falsehood and malice finally prevail against truth. For a time it afflicts, and humbles our hopes; it no doubt calls for our prudence, perseverance . . . but I hope and trust we are founded too deeply for the causeless blasts of malice. – Gov. John Wentworth to Eleazar Wheelock, 1774.

Competence, conscience, commitment, taken together and seriously, these three concerns assure a comprehensive purpose for any college. And yet I suggest that the modern college, if it is to offer an educational experience which truly prepares an undergraduate for a life-time of on-going self-liberation, must reserve a special place within its institutional sense of purpose for the concern I call comprehensive awareness. Is there, in fact, any characteristic of a liberally educated person more basic and constant than his capacity for being aware of anything which contributes to the meaningful enjoyment of his life? He may, of course, be aware and still pass it by, but that is something else again. The point here simply is that if he has not learned to push out the borders of his awareness he has little or no chance of liberating himself from the en-thrallment of a narrowly conceived, mean, and meagerly shared existence.

Since the adoption of the so-called Richardson curriculum in 1924, Dartmouth has relied on a variety of devices to protect the scope of the academic experience of her undergraduates. The most basic device has been the distributive requirements for the A.B. degree which assure that every student will have some acquaintance with each of the three main divisions of today's liberal learning — the humanities, the sciences, and the social sciences. In addition to this strategic principle the same aim of breadth has been served by such generally prescribed offerings as the earlier freshman courses in Citizenship and Evolution, today's General Reading Program, and the Great Issues course for seniors.

All generally prescribed programs have something wrong with them, ranging from a student's congenital resistance to any requirement, to the reluctance of many faculty members to commit themselves for long to unspecialized undertakings of this nature. And yet those of us who have both studied and taught in such programs, and then had the op-portunity to observe their impact on thousands of individuals, as well as on the institution as a whole, particularly its sense of corporate pur-pose, have no doubt whatsoever that the balance is strongly in favor of the dedicated effort required. Perhaps nothing has given me greater con-fidence in Dartmouth's pursuit of preeminence in undergraduate edu-cation than the willingness of some of our strongest faculty members to put this kind of effort into such programs. Such teaching bespeaks more meaningfully than any presidential words the reality of this College's sense of institutional purpose.

In spite of all that has been done in these and other ways to protect the comprehensiveness of the undergraduate educational experience, developments of the past twenty-five years have put this side of organ-ized liberal learning under mounting pressure. On the one hand there is the circumstance, mentioned earlier, that our increasingly professional society, with its accelerating rate of obsolescence in all fields of knowledge, requires a deeper and more intensive education to create the kind of competence that is necessary at the leadership levels of life. This is a condition of life and an educational imperative that neither the college nor its customers can escape except by stopping the world while they get off. Inevitably this condition of life will be reflected in the strategy of the curriculum, in the content of specific courses and in the approach of the teacher to both his subject and his teaching. The total emphasis is inevitably more toward concentration than comprehensiveness.

Even with the reassurance that today's liberally educated man must be a person who has penetrated some field far enough to have the kind of respect for all fields that comes with knowing how little is known in his own, and that the mastery of any subject can itself be a form of liberation, I still am clear that the liberal arts college cannot simply say "so be it" and walk away from its historic concern for exposing its product to the broadest possible range of significant human experience in both time and place.

A decision to reject comprehensiveness as an aim of the college might well accelerate the inward orientation of all academic departments to the ultimate intellectual disadvantage of each. There is probably no more useful lesson than this to be learned from the intellectual incest which earlier characterized and limited professional education in such fields as medicine and law. The more professional any field of study becomes the greater is its need for hybrid vigor. Such a narrowing of the college purpose at this particular time would mean weakening that greater part of education which, as Mr. Justice Holmes once put it, "begins when what is called your education is over." I refer, of course, to the fact that one of the great, perhaps the greatest, liberating missions of the historic cultural college has been to sensitize its product, perhaps more aptly, to make him "sticky" with awareness for those later experiences which over the course of a lifetime can add up to an education.

Any weakening in the preparation of today's college graduate for this side of his ensuing education would come at the very moment when, on a front fully as critical as that of competence, education is faced with an equally unprecedented circumstance of life. We are fond of talking about the "explosion of knowledge," and in the sciences and technology it is a terribly apt figure. But there has also been another kind of explosion in the world of learning which for the responsible citizenry of our time is nothing less than an "explosion of relevance." Areas of the world which were formerly "out-of-the-way," or at least out of our way, and the experiences of others which only a generation ago were regarded as irrelevant to American daily life are suddenly and solidly of front-page consequence.

To put it bluntly, our ignorance of others has become relevant to us. Manifestly, this challenge to the universality of a liberating education cannot be met by prescribing for everyone courses on India, Indonesia, China, Japan, the Soviet Union, Latin America, Africa, or even Canada, and the American Negro!

> Such extravagances of youth will happen, among numbers, in any society; nor can any be expected in this world where the folly and passions of inexperienced young men will not require correction. – Gov. John Wentworth, 1774.

Specialized offerings of this sort, of course, are increasingly available at colleges such as Dartmouth whose size and strength make this kind of curricular coverage both possible and necessary. Even so the range of these specialties must be kept within practical bounds. At best the number of these courses that can be taken by any substantial part of the student body is limited. Their presence in the curriculum probably has its greatest impact on the college as a whole through the witness they bear and the increased "awareness" in the climate of the campus which teacher-scholars and visiting lecturers in these fields create.

We must accept, I think, the prospect that pre-professional preparation will preempt an increasingly larger portion of the classroom schedule and the study hours of the ablest portion of America's college population. But I see no way for the college to meet its responsibility for preparing men to "live and learn" comprehensively other than by purposefully and strategically permeating the undergraduate experience, in the classroom and outside, with opportunities for the student to become aware of significant human experience that of itself he cannot "take" in the form and depth of a course on the subject. If in this way the college can help the undergraduate to become more comprehensively aware, as in other ways he is made more deeply aware and "professionally" competent, we can then count on another unprecedented circumstance of modern life to take up where the college leaves off and "see him through."

That other unprecedented circumstance is the infinitely improved and expanded opportunities in modern adult life for upgrading awareness into knowledge, understanding, and enjoyment. International news services and cultural exchanges, national newspapers, quality periodicals, paperback books, television and radio, travel, music, theater, the fine arts, and adult education projects in all fields, all of these and more are available as never before to the alert adult who has learned to want them.

It might also be noted that many of us in higher education have been singularly slow to take full account of this fundamental change in planning what today's college can best do to prepare its products to be lifetime learners in this kind of a world. It is sadly true that our liberal arts colleges have done a poorer job preparing men to be ongoing learners in their lives than in their vocations. Too often I fear this underwater side of the iceberg of liberal learning has not had the attention it deserves simply because it has had little reality for a professor whose life and work are *both* spent deep in an atmosphere of liberal learning. He has not lived in any ivory tower, but the inevitability of his daily personal involvement in a community of liberal learning is very, very different from the business and professional lives of most college graduates.

This concern for building a better "follow-through" onto their Dartmouth education, along with our aim to give all seniors a common and comprehensive adult learning experience, led to the establishment of the Great Issues course. Through the special purposes and procedures of this project we have sought to give all our men in their last year of classroom liberal learning some experience in applying that learning to the circumstances of life, using so far as practicable the forms and resources of adult living rather than those of the academic regimen. Perhaps the deepest satisfaction I have known as a teacher-administrator is the witness borne by the thousands of young alumni with whom I shared these Dartmouth years that the Great Issues experience made a difference in the quality of their "follow-through."

Two other recent responses to our concern for comprehensiveness in the Dartmouth experience illustrate the strategic, institution-wide fronts on which a sense of college purpose can form and operate. As I mentioned above one of the radically altered circumstances of life that liberal learning must reckon with is the "explosion of relevance." Today's liberally educated man must ponder a world with which his formal education has simply not yet caught up. Manifestly only a small part of this new relevance coming from the less familiar so-called "non-western" cultures can be packaged in traditional courses and jammed into an already bulging curriculum.

Recognizing the need for a more strategic response to this imperative, Dartmouth in 1963, with the assistance of a sizable grant from the Ford Foundation, undertook to explore the possibility that the principle of comparative study might be used more widely by teacher-scholars, particularly in the humanities and the social sciences, to cross-fertilize their own scholarly work, and as a means for broadening the reach of their teaching in established courses. The Comparative Studies program is being developed over a five-year period, but already participating faculty members see significant promise for enlarging teaching horizons and quickening the undergraduate learning experience.

It is no secret within the American academic community that compared with the humanities and the social sciences, particularly the former, the sciences have been "off to the races" — and the moon. Some might even add, "with money to burn." This is not the place to explain or appraise this fundamental phenomenon in our society, but it is in order to say that few knowledgeable educators, whatever their own predilections may be, would deal with it by putting a curb on science. Dartmouth is rightfully proud of the vitality of her sciences; her aim is to see other fields, like June, "bustin' out all over." The busting out comes man by man, but the over-all purposes and programs of the institution are also an essential part of it. In addition to its strategic bearing on the aim of comprehensiveness, the Comparative Studies project is tangible evidence of the search at Dartmouth for programs which will open fresh, significant opportunities within the social sciences and the humanities both for the development of the individual teacher-scholar and for the kind of collaborative pioneering that is peculiarly appropriate to these fields.

The humanities have probably wanted most for attention on the contemporary American campus. The opportunity for a genuinely creative response at Dartmouth and in the Hanover community was long handicapped by miserably inadequate facilities for music and theater. The opportunity for the other arts to play their proper role in the life and work of a liberal arts campus was likewise limited. The creative and performing arts are not, of course, the whole of the humanities but they are the heartland where man's understanding of his lot has found its most moving and meaningful expression. Embracing as they do the essence of man's knowledge of woe and joy and beauty in all times and all places, they provide perhaps the most significant

[18]

experience a person can have with the unbounded comprehensiveness of liberal learning. Since November, 1962, the Hopkins Center, Dartmouth's uniquely comprehensive educational facility, has brought this experience in greater degree than ever before into the awareness or the daily work of every Dartmouth student.

The uniqueness of the Center is the planned interrelationship of the instructional, the creative, the cultural, and the community activities of a residential college. Each of several dozen facilities focuses on its own prime function, but it is the combination itself, the concept of a genuinely educational center, that has created a new vitality and cohesiveness in the Dartmouth experience. As a modern Agora in this community of higher education its influence pervades the life and work of the College and, indeed, has reached out to the larger community of liberal learning. It testifies that high competence and comprehensive awareness can enjoy each others' company within the educational experience of a purposeful college.

*　　*　　*　　*　　*

In 1819, in the famed Dartmouth College Case, the great Chief Justice of the Supreme Court of the United States, John Marshall, in upholding the integrity and independence of this institution spoke of the properties of life conferred on the College by its Charter, saying, "Among the most important are immortality and . . . individuality."

The truth of these prophetic words is the burden of this chronicle and the promise of tomorrow's Dartmouth.

The Historic College

RALPH NADING HILL

A SEASONED observer of the College once remarked to President Ernest Martin Hopkins that no one can understand Dartmouth unless he recognizes that it is a religion. The word "spirit" suggests as much and explains as little, yet this intangible has always been the impelling element in the Dartmouth organism.

Professor Edwin D. Sanborn wrote long ago that the College was endowed alike by heredity and environment and that "There is something in being part of an adventure that has hewn its way into a wilderness at first physical and later symbolical to accomplish an exalted purpose." Calling Dartmouth a "spiritual romance," President William Jewett Tucker discovered a very great advantage "in the well-nigh unrivaled possession of an originating spirit at once creative, adventurous and charged with spiritual power." Professor Charles D. Adams considered that three elements are to be found in a college at its best: a ruling idea, a body of traditions, and a strong personality.

President Hopkins wrote that out of a small New England village comes a mental and emotional stimulus and that there is "much in the cultural environment, in the close-knit fellowship of human associations." Hanover, the Place, has been made much of by President John Sloan Dickey as the dwelling "of the spirits of the men who over the years built the College." Time and again in the long history of the Hanover Plain anything unaccounted for has been attributed to the "Dartmouth spirit." "It came with the Dartmouth spirit," wrote Professor Sanborn, "and that which is born of the Spirit is spirit."

The ninth of America's Colonial institutions of higher learning and the last to receive its charter from the Crown of England, Dartmouth is the only college that has graduated a class every year since 1771. It is the

[21]

only college to have survived a divisive blow so nearly mortal and so far reaching in its effects as the Dartmouth College Case, renowned in the history of American Constitutional law. Its strength and character are rooted in its twenty-decade struggle toward pre-eminence; its spirit comes from environment and heredity. Eleazar Wheelock clearly considered that his founding of Dartmouth was a Divine mission. Only in the energy that arises in a crusade can one account for the survival of the College before and after the Revolution.

In the public view and in that of the thirty-odd thousand living alumni of Dartmouth, Wheelock has tended to pass out of history into folklore by way of Richard Hovey's poems and Walter Humphrey's Thayer Hall murals, in which the College's founder is presented as a merry squire. Even in Joseph Steward's posthumous portrait he appears amiable and passively contented in academic surroundings that bear no resemblance to the early Hanover clearing with its stumps, its smoky cabins, and plain frame houses. But Wheelock was rarely contented. He could be amiable and seems to have been quite patient; yet often, as he trudged forward under his heavy burden, he was fretful, dictatorial, and peevish.

The role assigned to him in Hovey's celebrated song as the purveyor of five hundred gallons of rum into the wilderness is almost pure fiction: one of Wheelock's chief concerns was keeping students out of local taverns. "As for the *five hundred* gallons . . . ," states James Dow McCallum in his biography of Wheelock, "all that can be said is that they fill the exigencies of the meter much better than the cramped space of an eighteenth century vehicle wending its slow way from Lebanon, Connecticut, to Hanover." Yet the passing of two centuries has not distorted the view of Eleazar Wheelock's contemporaries, friend or foe, that he was a commanding personality. His stature seems indeed to have grown, and this despite the failure of his foremost aim in life: the Christian education of the American Indian.

He was born in Windham, Connecticut, on April 22, 1711, the son of Ralph, a prosperous farmer; the grandson of Captain Eleazar, a cavalry commander in the French and Indian Wars; and the great-grandson of Ralph, an English divine who in 1637 found Massachusetts an asylum for his Nonconformist views. Through his mother, Eleazar was the descendant of prominent Connecticut citizens. Few details survive of his youth other than his attendance at Yale and subsequent study of theology. In 1734 he became pastor of the Second Parish of Lebanon, Connecticut, and within a year married a young widow with three children, Mrs. Sarah Maltby. Before her death in 1746 she bore him six children, three of whom did not survive infancy. Five more children resulted from Wheelock's second marriage to Mary Brinsmead, but this large household was able to subsist on properties Eleazar inherited from his family and from his first wife, and on those acquired through his second, together with his professional income and revenue from his farms.

Young Wheelock had a fair complexion, was of middle stature and stood erect and dignified. In the eyes of his contemporary and friend, Benjamin Trumbull, he appeared as a "gentleman of comely figure, of a mild and winning aspect; his voice smooth and harmonious, — *the best by far I have ever heard.*" President Stiles of Yale thought him tolerably well educated (as well he might, for Eleazar had been graduated from Yale with honors in 1733) but did not understand how a man with such "small literary furniture" could achieve distinction. Stiles thought him "piously sweet" with an air of the religious politician. The hard transactions of his later life scarcely bear out this assessment, nor do Wheelock's letters, which the Dartmouth historian, Leon Burr Richardson, has described as "models of tact, suavely worded, accommodating in nonessentials, but rocklike in their firmness when matters which he deemed fundamental were in question."

Early in his preaching Wheelock was seized by the Great Awakening, a religious virus carrying feverish concern over the fate of the soul to all New England and dividing Calvinists into the damned and redeemed. Led by Jonathan Edwards and George Whitefield, a small band of evangelists converted some twenty-five to fifty thousand people. In the front echelon was Eleazar Wheelock, who in the year 1741 was said to have preached five hundred sermons, "close and pungent and yet winning beyond almost all comparison, so that his audience would be melted even into tears before they were aware of it," according to Trumbull. Wheelock was not considered an extremist. Nonetheless he was a "New Light," was branded as such by the conservative clergy and carried this opprobrium or distinction with him the rest of his life. It was the evangelist in him that led to his Indian School in Connecticut and later to Dartmouth College.

An extremely potent but relatively inconspicuous force in the struggle for empire in America were the Protestant denominations in England and Scotland seeking to spread the gospel in the western wilderness, thus to offset the successes of the French Jesuit priests in carrying Catholicism to the American Indian. The country able to win the

allegiance of the Indians might ultimately gain the huge prize of North America. Provincial gifts of valuable grants of land in New England townships to the Society for the Propagation of the Gospel were one way of forwarding the aims of the King and the Church of England. Another was sending missionaries to indoctrinate Indians with English and Christian ideals.

At the height of the revival Wheelock's brother-in-law, John Davenport, had made a Christian of a young Connecticut Mohegan named Samson Occom, whose father had died and whose mother appealed to Eleazar Wheelock for help in preparing him for college. Always hard-pressed for funds to support his family Wheelock had augmented his income by instructing English boys, but the twenty-year-old Occom seems to have become, in 1743, his first Indian pupil. When Occom's weak eyes forced him to give up his studies four years later he became a schoolteacher in New London and subsequently a preacher and schoolmaster to the Montauk tribe on the eastern tip of Long Island. By fishing and hunting, by moving to the planting grounds in summer and the woods in winter, by making wooden spoons, cedar pails, and churns and by binding books he managed to raise a large family and conduct his missionary work as well.

Wheelock was immensely pleased. He began to visualize a language and missionary school for Indian and white students in the heart of the Colonies, far removed from the distractions of tribal life which in the past had thwarted missionaries in the field. Wandering tribes of eastern Algonquins, wasted by war and poverty, were his first concern, and when, in 1754, he received two young Delawares who had come two hundred miles on foot, the Lebanon residents shared his interest and sympathy. The following year he received £500 from them, and from a wealthy Mansfield farmer, Colonel Joshua More, an equivalent gift in land and buildings adjoining Wheelock's own property. This became More's (later Moor's) Indian Charity School, a pioneering enterprise. That it was able to gain a reputation in such difficult times, and that ten years later it could still be in existence with twenty-nine Indian and eight white boys in attendance, all of whom were on charity, was owing purely to Wheelock's persistence in the face of the most disheartening reverses.

In the decade after the opening of the school Colonel More, its benefactor, died. During the late 1750's France and England were waging their furious, climactic battles for empire. Interest in helping educate Algonquins, who were allied with France and were raiding English colonies, had expired. Wheelock was unable to obtain a charter for his school either from the King or from the Connecticut legislature. In 1762 the governor of the province of New Hampshire, Benning Wentworth, vetoed a bill passed by the assembly to grant Moor's School £250—probably because the Governor was an adherent of the Anglican Church and Wheelock was a Congregationalist. At this time, however, the Massachusetts General Assembly made grants to Wheelock from a fund established for Indian education. The English Company for Propagation of the Gospel in New England, which was without Anglican Church affiliations, continued its smaller grants. At the same time the Society in Scotland for Propagating Christian Knowledge, with Presbyterian associations, interested itself in the missionary producing potentials of Moor's School. However, the head of the Boston board held the revivalists in contempt, blocking Wheelock whenever he could.

Although Wheelock was long obliged to draw on his own income for the support of his charity students, his perennial and far-ranging appeals were occasionally answered. George Whitefield, his revivalist mentor and friend, found some generous contributors on a preaching tour of England and Scotland. Benedict Arnold turned over to Moor's School a large part of the profits of one of his seafaring expeditions. Benjamin Franklin raised £120 and John Phillips, founder of Exeter Academy, gave £100. People in the immediate neighborhood contributed clothing and their own labor.

Prospects for the school changed following the rout of the French and Algonquins by the British, the Continentals, and the Iroquois in 1759. Naturally Wheelock's sympathies were with the British; but in his, if not in the public outlook, it seemed to make little difference whether Moor's School received a French Algonquin or a British Iroquois. With the defeat of the French there was no longer the urgency on the part of England to win the Indians to the King's cause, although warlike tribes remained in the west and missionary work was still regarded as important. Wheelock turned his attention to the Six Nations of the Iroquois Confederacy. Competing with each other for the sponsorship of his expeditions to the Six Nations were the English and Scottish societies, and Wheelock was hard pressed as a go-between seeking funds. He would allay their suspicions only to find them aroused again over false rumors and petty complaints. When hostilities among the Iroquois broke out, all that Wheelock received in his collection basket after a sermon calling for missionary funds was a bullet and a gun flint.

Problems within the school, perhaps the most vexing of all, are revealed in a letter from Wheelock to George Whitefield in 1761.

None know, nor can any, without Experience, Well conceive of, the Difficulty of Educating an Indian. They would soon kill themselves with Eating and Sloth, if constant care were not exercised for them — at least the first year. They are used to set upon the Ground, and it is as natural for them as a seat to our Children — they are not wont to have any Cloaths but what they wear, nor will they, without much Pains, be brot to take Care of any, — They are used to a Sordid Manner of Dress and love it as well as our Children to be clean. They are not used to any Regular Government, the Sad Consequences of which you may a little guess at. They are used to live from Hand to Mouth (so we Speak) and have no care for Futurity, they have never been used to the Furniture of an English House and dont know but that a Wineglass-is as strong as a Handiron. Our Language when they Seem to have got it is not their Mother Tongue, and they cannot receive nor communicate in that as in their own. . . .

Trying to prevent young Indians from falling prey to rum and other notorious vices by removing them to his school was admirable but visionary, for Wheelock reckoned neither with heredity nor the added problems that an utter change of environment brought to his young charges. Yet hope and faith always arose to stay the hand of the Devil, and the hinterlands continued to feel the vibrations of a crusade.

Perhaps the brightest ornament of Wheelock's labors, other than Occom, was Samuel Kirkland, a white student who went from Moor's School to Princeton and then into missionary work with the Senecas and Oneidas.

I fear I have seen my best Days for Hardships and an Indian Life [he wrote Wheelock] a little-over-straining brings an old Pain in my Breast: Am not able to carry a Pack of moderate Size . . . without spitting Blood. Yet in the main I have enjoyed usual Health through many Fatigues. Blessed be God, I am not discouraged; I am willing to wear out sooner or later, if only it may be in the Cause of my Divine Master.

Kirkland lived to become an important negotiator for Congress, and in 1793 founded, on land given him by Indians and the state of New York, an academy which became Hamilton College. He married a niece of Wheelock. His son became president of Harvard for nearly two decades.

Fruitful by any standards were the labors of some of Wheelock's Indian missionaries, whose fascinating letters and journals tell of sacrifice and privation, of temptation, failure, and sometimes triumph. Pathetic in terms of Wheelock's grand design, they are a part of an honorable chapter in the dishonorable book of the white man's relations with the Indians.

Wheelock in the pursuit of his purpose found himself increasingly pressed for funds. He was able, with the aid of Occom and a Norwich minister, Nathaniel Whitaker, to raise nearly £300 in Boston and Portsmouth in 1765. He made such an impression on the New Hampshire Assembly that Governor Benning Wentworth, who had previously turned him down, offered five hundred acres of land should he decide to move Moor's School to New Hampshire. It had long been clear that he was going to have to move it somewhere, for he wanted a charter and had not yet succeeded in obtaining one from Connecticut. He had in mind an expanded school for missionaries, interpreters, schoolmasters, and others in the heart of a large area divided into townships, of which one in three would be reserved for Indians. Through Sir William Johnson, superintendent of Indian affairs, he

tried long and in vain to secure a grant in northern Pennsylvania. Sir William wrote discouragingly of the Indians' mistrust of Yankees for wanting too much land. The more cogent reason that Sir William favored Episcopal missionaries in his sphere of influence was later apparent. Wheelock could only dream of affluence for his school and of a free principality to place it in.

George Whitefield had once suggested that an Indian preacher's presence in England might help; again in 1764 Wheelock learned from across the water that an "Indian minister in England might get a Bushel of Money for the School." He dared send his valued apostle, Samson Occom. Now in his forties, this star pupil had become a seasoned minister, dignified yet unassuming, his round bronze face wearing a bright intellectual expression. Preaching between three and four hundred sermons in England and Scotland during the course of two and a half years, Occom became a public figure (and so, through him, did Wheelock, in whose honor a widely sung hymn called *Lebanon* was composed). With Nathaniel Whitaker, his companion abroad, Occom raised eleven thousand pounds, greater, it is said, than any amount secured in England and Scotland by any other American educational institution before the Revolution.

That this could be accomplished by Dissenters at the very portals of the official church seems unfathomable. Probably it could not have been done without the help of prominent Englishmen, notably William Legge, Second Earl of Dartmouth, the scion of an illustrious family. Born in 1731 he became at the age of thirty-four Lord of Trade and Plantations. Subsequently he was Secretary of State for the Colonies and finally Lord Privy Seal and Lord Steward of the Household to King George the Third. Because of his enlightened views of the Colonies and their problems he enjoyed unprecedented confidence at home and abroad at a time when relations with America were deteriorating. Whitefield called him "a Christian Lord and an UnCommon one." A torchbearer for the Great Awakening in England, he was an admirer of Whitefield, and therefore of Occom and Wheelock. He became president of the London board of trustees for the handling of funds for Moor's School and secured from the King a gift of £200.

An equally interesting and generous friend of the Indian school was a London commoner named John Thornton, who grew up in a household of great wealth gained in trade. "Though he was frugal and exact in his personal expenses," wrote Frederick Chase, the Dartmouth historian, "the stories of his princely benevolence read like a fairy tale. Once he offered a struggling young merchant £10,000 without security. Again, by the stroke of a pen he placed the humble proprietor of a small property in Ireland in affluence." A handsome young American then in England was a third key figure in the future of Dartmouth College: John Wentworth, just appointed Royal Governor of New Hampshire in the place of his Uncle Benning, who had fallen into disfavor in that frontier province. The youthful governor expressed his interest by contributing twenty-one pounds.

When Occom and Whitaker set sail for America in 1768 the eleven thousand pounds remained at interest in England and Scotland, a situation (particularly in the case of the canny and frugal Scottish trustees) that was to cause almost as much wringing of hands in the woods of New Hampshire, and elicit as many memorials, missives, recriminations, and countercharges as the Dartmouth College Case. At the moment College affairs seemed more hopeful although, sadly, Occom and Wheelock had a falling out over the expenses of the former's family, and his affiliations with a cause he had served so well ended.

Although Moor's School was now potentially well off (which is to say that its founder was well off, since he was responsible for drawing on the money raised abroad), Wheelock was nearing sixty and too

[29]

many unfavorable forces were at work outside Moor's School. In 1768 the attendance began to decline; an Oneida arrived in Lebanon and took home all the students of that tribe, so that the next year only three Indians were left. Wheelock was becoming thoroughly discouraged, not about the value of missionary work but about the way he was conducting it. It was clear to him that he must concentrate on preparing white students for the field as roving missionaries; he could say conclusively that removing Indians from their tribes to his school had failed.

The most melancholy part of the account I have to relate, and which has occasioned me the greatest weight of sorrow, has been the bad conduct and behaviour of such as have been educated here after they have left the school. . . . The current is too strong, and is tenfold more so by reason of the united force of such wicked dealers as are making great gain to themselves by the swift destruction of the poor savages; and by this means the progress of this design has been retarded. . . . I don't hear of more than half who have preserved their characters unstain'd. . . . And six of those who did preserve a good character are now dead.

Wheelock's resilient will served him now, as it had in the past and would in the future, to rebuild out of the ashes of fifteen years' labor.

Such had become his reputation as an unselfish man of high purpose that renewed efforts toward moving his school brought promising solicitations from many quarters. As has been noted, it had for some years been his wish to move Moor's School out of settled Connecticut, although Hebron and Lebanon had offered him £1000, and £800, respectively, to remain. Pennsylvania was no longer a potential, but in New York Province Albany had promised six-and-a-half acres of land and a sixteen-room house. The governor of Massachusetts was willing to charter a college and to grant two thousand acres in Pittsfield. Another Massachusetts offer came from Stockbridge, but Wheelock was wary of the "jealous and envious eye" of the Boston clergy, should he locate in Massachusetts.

New Hampshire was the most inviting possibility. The offer of former Governor Benning Wentworth of five hundred acres of land still stood. American-born John Wentworth, the new governor, whom Timothy Dwight described as "a man of sound understanding, refined taste, enlarged views, and a dignified spirit," was proving himself equally the servant of the King, and of all his people. At home in genteel and aristocratic Portsmouth, he loved the wild forests to the west and warmly respected the various faiths and interests of the pioneers who streamed into them from southern New England after the French and Indian Wars. Naturally he hoped Wheelock would establish a Church of England college in New Hampshire, but when the latter stood firm against the Bishop of London as a member of the Board of Trustees during negotiations for a charter, Wentworth cheerfully acquiesced. Nor did he insist on his original request that he have control of funds and that three provincial officers be members of the Board. He offered the college, moreover, the grant of a whole township.

Wheelock chose New Hampshire in April, 1769, but it was not until December 13 that Governor Wentworth's seal was affixed to the charter. Generously specifying a great range of rights and privileges, it was considered at the time to be the most liberal possessed by any similar institution in America.

The upper valley of the Connecticut River and the pine-covered New Hampshire Grants west to Lake Champlain were mountains removed from the restraints of parliaments and clerics. Only recently had this sternly beautiful country been freed from the threat of invasion from French Canada: Sir Jeffrey Amherst had, after generations of bloodshed, driven the French off Lake Champlain and out of the walls of Quebec. A college on the banks of the northern Connecticut would

[31]

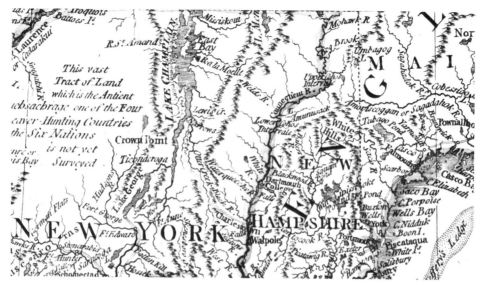

likely be near the entrance to the military road Amherst had cut through the mountains from the river to Lake Champlain. Canadian remnants of the once great Algonquin nation, long under the tutelage of French priests, would not be too far removed from an English mission in that region of the Connecticut Valley. These and other considerations were weighed by Wheelock as he pondered a site.

For a time the upland plain of Haverhill opposite the Connecticut's great Ox-Bow captured his imagination. Northeast of this town was Landaff, granted to the College by Wentworth in January, 1770, the obvious choice of the Governor. But on Wheelock's arrival in New Hampshire in June he found a seemingly straightforward decision to be painfully complex. Because of the obvious enhancement of land values, should their towns be selected, a covey of speculators and agents descended to exert what pressure they could. Governor Wentworth said he could not approve a location where ownership in land rested in the hands of a few; he owned parts of many towns himself, but he was not going to consult his own interests.

During an eight-week inspection tour of various sites Wheelock apparently spent only three days (June 8-11) in Hanover and Lebanon, where thirty-three hundred acres were available in one large tract. Not a single clearing broke the dark plateau of soaring pines beneath which, to the west, the steeply sloping banks of the Connecticut drew sufficiently near together to afford a bridge. Wheelock must have been impressed, for on July fifth in Portsmouth it was announced that Hanover had been chosen. Immediately thereafter a cry of anguish went up from speculators interested in other localities — a babble still to be heard a year later. "The great clamour in the country (and that by which great numbers are prejudiced) is that I'm wholly in a plan to aggrandize and enrich myself and family," despaired Wheelock. The reverberations reached the trustees of the funds raised in England. Even George Whitefield, until he learned better, was persuaded to believe that Wheelock had bought for himself a great farm to be improved with missionary funds from England and Scotland.

While the complaints of the speculators were as reprehensible as they were unfounded, there was some justice in the fears of the English and Scottish trustees that the money Wheelock planned to spend in New Hampshire would go for purposes other than that for which it was raised: an Indian missionary school. In view of his disappointing experience in Connecticut, Wheelock now had in mind primarily a college for whites who would go out among the Indians as roving missionaries. His design was the same as if Indians were to be brought to the school: indeed Indians *were* presently brought to Hanover and it was they who helped to save for Dartmouth funds that might otherwise have been sacrificed. Nevertheless, many abroad, among them Lord Dartmouth, for whom the College was named, lost interest because of what they considered a perversion of the original plan. Only the skillful diplomacy of a voice crying in the wilderness saved these vital resources for the daring migration to New Hampshire.

> What gives me concern is that the College affairs are in so perplexed a situation. The obstacles to its prosperity appear so many and of such a nature that without a wonderful interposition of Providence what hopes can we entertain of their removal? – John Phillips, 1779.

The trek from Lebanon to Hanover began early in August, less than a month after Wheelock had returned from his scouting trip. That he did not suffer from the rigors of corduroy road and blazed trail seems remarkable for a man of fifty-nine, who only a year previously had written: "I have been in a bad state of Health and in my own Opinion and in the opinion of my Friends very near the End of my Race, but through the pure Mercy of God . . . I have now More hope of recovering a comfortable State of Health than I had for many years past." He put behind him the comfort and reassurance of a settled community, he left his Connecticut farms (which were worth more than his debts but could not then be sold except at a sacrifice), and now he established himself on the Hanover Plain with thirty to fifty men trying to wrest from the ancient forest of pines, some of them said to be as tall as 270 feet, a place to build shelters.

They let the trees lie where they fell in a six-acre clearing sixty rods from the river, cut paths around them, and then with adze and axe (but without stone, brick, glass, or nails) put up a temporary log hut near the later site of Silsby Hall. They dug two dry wells; a third at some distance produced water, so they had to dismantle the log hut and move it to a new site (to the west of what is now Thornton and to the north of the present Reed). There they set to work on a one-story, 40 by 32 dwelling for Wheelock and a two-story, 80 by 32 all-purpose building with eighteen rooms, including a kitchen, "academy" and sleeping quarters for the students. (The larger building was on the southeast corner of the Green and faced east, its longer dimension running north and south. Wheelock's dwelling, immediately to the northeast, faced south. The well is now under the sidewalk next to the road near the southwest corner of Reed Hall.)

Madame Wheelock had not received a letter telling of the delay in developing the new site and in mid-September had departed from Lebanon. Relationships had become strained there, and she had been glad to set out in the fine English coach or "chariot" that John Thornton had given Wheelock two years previously. Jabez Bingham, Eleazar's nephew, drove a load of goods which included a barrel of rum, a "cag" of wine, some apple brandy, a gross of pipes, and a hundred pounds of tobacco. Among the charity students on foot was an Indian boy who resented having to drive the cows. Bezaleel Woodward, Wheelock's son-in-law, arrived by way of Boston with another contingent.

It was near the close of day; [he wrote] there was scanty room in the Doctor's shanty for the shelter of those who were on the ground, and none for us who had just arrived. All constructed for a temporary residence a tent of crotched stakes and poles covered with boughs. It was soon ready, and we camped down wrapped in our blankets, and for a time slept very comfortably. During the night, however, a storm arose of high wind and pelting rain. Our tent came down and buried us in its ruins. After mutual inquiries, we found no one injured, and as the storm raged with unabated fury, we resolved to abide the issue as we were, and wait for the day. When fair weather returned, we made more substantial booths for our protection until better accommodations could be provided.

Wheelock's comments about the arduous weeks after his family and students had arrived, but before the two larger buildings had become habitable at the second site, reflected a new and thriving optimism:

[34]

I housed my stuff, with my wife and the females of my family, in my hutt. My sons and students made booths and beds of hemlock boughs; and in this situation we continued about a month, till the 29th day of October, when I removed with my family into my house. And though the season had been cold, with storms of rain and snow . . . yet by the pure mercy of God the season changed for the better in every respect . . . till my house was made warm and comfortable, a school-house built, and so many rooms in the College made quite comfortable as were sufficient for the students which were with me, in which they find the pleasure and profit of such a solitude.

Wheelock's optimism seems to have arisen from a sense of physical well-being in the clear air of the north country. Temporarily, at least, he had exchanged the frustrations of missionary politics and religious polemics for a very active command on the frontier.

By the end of 1771 forty-eight acres had been cleared of felled pines that covered the ground to a depth of five feet. Too green to burn, they were cut up and left in piles or, as soon as the heavy stumps had been pulled, were dragged to the river. There was a controversy over logs that should have been marked with the King's broad arrow for use as masts and spars for the Royal Navy, but instead bore the College mark — placed there, Wheelock asserted, by unscrupulous persons cutting timber unlawfully. Although Governor Wentworth later interceded in its behalf, the College was fined by His Majesty's Massachusetts agents, who had intercepted the logs down the Connecticut.

While the first winter had been relatively mild, the second brought deep snow. On still cold nights the cries of hungry wild animals could be heard around the cattle and sheep pens. Supplies for the College family had to be brought from as far away as two hundred miles. Fodder for the horses and cows came fifty miles by oxen. The next spring Wheelock was dickering for potatoes, hay, beans, feathers, nails, hogs, and a good cook. He wanted a barn and needed malt, bake, and wash houses. These were built in 1772. (The barn, 55 by 40 feet, was near the northwest corner of the Green.) By the end of 1773 he had cleared two hundred acres, had planted most of them with hay and grain, and had fenced in about two thousand acres of woodland to restrain his horses, his seven yoke of oxen, and twenty cows. He had also built himself a good house (on the present site of Reed Hall), for the roof over the garret of his temporary one-story dwelling had leaked on his paper as he wrote. The ever-generous John Thornton of London supplied the money, and fourteen men the labor. The frame of timbers was so heavy that when it was pushed up, one side at a time, the effort forced blood from the nostrils of some of the men. Two stories high with a gambrel roof, the structure housed Wheelock's family and a number of the students. He was pleased to report that eleven dwellings had now taken the place of the "horrid wilderness," that his energetic compatriots were gathering the Indian harvest, were counting bricks he had bought in Lyme, were hauling dirt and digging limestone.

As soon as he had moved into his new house, his former one-story dwelling (which had replaced his first log hut) became, with a thirty-foot addition to the west, the College Hall and commons, the chapel and meetinghouse. The eastern end contained the kitchen and commons, and the western two-thirds of the building became one large room entered from the south, with an aisle down the center and seats for students and townspeople to the right and left, respectively. The platform was made of basswood planks. This expanded building was half the College. The larger structure to the southwest, housing many of the eighty students, the two-room preparatory department or academy on the ground floor and one-room library on the second, was the remainder. Harshly treated by nature, this building annually heaved and sank with the frost. Its outer deterioration was subsequently restrained with reddish-brown paint. Wheelock had always regarded these as temporary buildings to be replaced by brick and stone structures at the earliest moment, but neither time nor resources enabled him to give much thought to the future.

He had to secure, and with more difficulty retain, bakers, brewers, cooks, and dairymen. He must find a blacksmith for the growing community, and someone to make potash. He had to "gather" a church, which he did in January, 1771, with a membership of twenty-seven. He was of course the supervisor of curriculum, the court of last resort for the students and, as justice of the peace, the principal authority in the village. Or so he had calculated until the forces of Evil, embodied in the local tavern keepers, arose to plague him. One John Sargeant on the other side of the river was resentful because the Governor had ignored him as proprietor of the ferry by awarding a franchise to the College in 1772. Not only did he continue to run his ferry but saw to it that students who called at his tavern were well fortified. There was a similar hostelry near the falls in Lebanon. But the worst was that of John Payne in the northwest part of the village. He had received a license through the influence of a Portsmouth sheriff named Sympson, who thought he had been slighted by Wheelock at the first Commencement. Payne sold liquor indiscriminately to white and Indian students, and even to Wheelock's sons, much to the anguish and despair of the President, who never quite managed to get Payne's license revoked at Portsmouth.

The punch bowl also seems to have overflowed in other directions and never more freely than at Commencement, a ceremony that Wheelock must have learned to dread. The first came in August, 1771. Governor Wentworth, with a retinue of some sixty persons, arrived from Portsmouth to witness the rough-hewn ceremonies on a stage of boards in the open air. John Wheelock, the President's son, was among the four graduates. The diplomas could not be signed because not enough Trustees were in attendance for a quorum. Chase remarks that one of the Indians, "scorning the stage, spoke — in his native language, no doubt — from an overhanging pine." An ox was roasted on the Green and rum was served to the multitudes according to the custom of the day. In appreciation of Wheelock's exertions the Governor sent him from Portsmouth what was to become one of the College's prized heirlooms, a beautiful silver punch bowl weighing forty-nine ounces and inscribed as follows:

His Excellency, John Wentworth, Esq., governor of the Province of New Hampshire and those Friends who accompanied him to Dartmouth College the first Commencement 1771 in Testimony of their gratitude and good wishes present this to the Rev. Eleazar Wheelock D.D. President and to his Successors in that office.

This inspiring gift met its antidote in the chief cook, who was so far gone as to be unable to provide for the guests. The Portsmouth gentry could testify that the fare was inferior to that to which they were accustomed. Wheelock made the best showing he could in the circumstances: his new home had not yet been built. He explained that he had but one tablecloth, a gift from a generous lady in Connecticut.

The ceremonies in 1772 were dignified and elaborate, but again the hogshead of rum which the Governor provided to wash down the roasted ox proved too much for the cooks, and Wheelock was hard pressed to feed the many guests. At the Commencement of 1773 George Jaffrey presented the College with its fine seal. The candidates fittingly received degrees before the Governor in Wheelock's unfinished house. For the third time, however, the cooks defaulted. In the preceding March Wheelock had recorded his hope that "Providence designs to deliver us from the plague of unskilfull, deceitful, and unfaithful cooks, two of whom Mr. Woodward has lately *ordered to the whipping-post* for stealing."

While the subject of unpalatable food has recurred over the years with the monotony of a metronome, never since the Revolution has it provoked such a crisis. In 1774 a student smuggled out a sample of bread for exhibit in Portsmouth. Governor Wentworth performed what he confessed was "the strict duty of friendship" in calling Wheelock's attention to the quality of food, which he had heard was neither wholesome nor plentiful, so that the students were "thereby unhealthy and debilitated, their constitution impaired, and their friends and parents highly disgusted."

Wheelock replied:

Everything has been done that was doable for the comfort & health of the Scholars. As to their diet I have plenty of Good Pork, Beef, fresh meat all the winter and as often since as it co'd be had. They have had wheat or Indian puddings & butter or sauce as often as they pleased excepting a few days we were out of Butter and it could not be had. We have had a fullness of sugar & molasses, chocolate and tea when it could be had . . . they have had pea, rye or wheat coffee. They have not had a fullness of milk. My cows had the horn distemper this spring, & some died & others almost as good as dead. I have sent to Connecticut for more. They have had for sauce peas, potatoes cabage & turnips (in the season of them) & plenty of greens the best that this country affords. Several sorts of food they reject with an outcry such as peas & pork cooked by the best skill of our country. Fresh meat broth they wholly refuse nor have the cooks dared to offer it to them more than two or three times for the twelve months past and then it raised a hideous clamor. Sometimes the cooks have made mistakes and the scholars have not been dealt with as they ought to have been. Last week there was a gross mistake made, the pudden was not well salted. Upon the clamor I went over to see & found that part of the pudden was too fresh & the other part too salt. The cook told me her salt was too coarse and the pudden not sufficiently stirred after the salt was put in which she readily confessed about through very great hurry. . . .

The Trustees considered the matter at the Commencement of 1774 and found complaints about the food unjustified, except that for a few days some beef was served which, though edible, had become somewhat tainted.

One of those who commented on the food problem was the eminent New Hampshire historian Jeremy Belknap, a guest at the Commencement of 1774. He saw Wheelock's beechwood log house, "the first sprout of the College," and observed that the library, while small, had some good books in it. There were two eighteen-inch globes and a good solar microscope. He thought that the President was making too much of what he fancied were the College's enemies, that it "is constantly spoken of as in a state of victory over them, which serves to keep alive a spirit that I think ought to be discouraged." Wheelock was indeed inclined to attribute all good fortune "to the Smiles of Heaven" or to "the Pure Mercy of God" and misfortune, if not to the most Evil of all, at least to those who had consorted with him.

> I have brought my Alma Mater to this presence, that, if she must fall, she may fall in her robes and with dignity. – Daniel Webster, 1818.

In resisting the temptation to magnify flaws in their subjects, let historians remember the Indian supplication that judgment not be passed upon another until one has walked in his moccasins. No president in the Wheelock Succession has ever carried a heavier load. The College was then a single heartbeat, one strong traveler on a road filled with stumbling blocks.

Money problems, theoretically, were not as pressing as they had been in Connecticut, but Wheelock expended more energy trying to draw on the English and Scottish funds than Occom and Whitaker did in raising them. The Trustees abroad were adamant in their criticism that funds intended for the schooling of Indians were being spent for whites. In associating Moor's School with the newly established College in Han-

Path to River

Lane to Burying Yard

THE CAMPUS 1775

1. John Payne Tavern
2. Bezaleel Woodward House
3. Malt House
4. College Barn
5. William Winton, mason
6. Comfort Seaver, carpenter
7. Captain Storrs Tavern
8. Blacksmith Shop
9. Commons Hall
10. Log Hut
11. Old College
12. Wheelock Mansion House
13. Well
14. Dr. John Crane
15. Jabez Bingham, farmer

Watson (AW) 64

over, Wheelock had promised that a suitable number of Indians would continue to be admitted; that the foreign funds would be devoted strictly to them and that no buildings would be erected at the expense of the fund except those needed for the Indian School. A distinction was of course hard to make when there were only two buildings for both institutions.

The English Trustees relented, and finally in the course of four years allowed the entire principal of their fund to be spent. Prior to the Revolution, John Thornton privately advanced an additional thousand pounds. Without these resources Dartmouth would have foundered. Wheelock was thwarted, however, by the tight-fisted Presbyterian Trustees of the Scottish Fund, who cited his *Narrative* of 1771 as evidence of the futility of educating Indians. They were jealous that the College was falling under the domination of Anglicans in London and Wentworth's coterie in New Hampshire. Although the Governor promised to break any man's commission who proved unfriendly to Dartmouth, his liberal outlook was circumscribed by that of Portsmouth Anglicans who begrudged the rising Congregationalist influence in the Connecticut Valley.

For four years following his arrival in New Hampshire, Wheelock had begged the New Hampshire legislators for an appropriation for the erection of a "College": failing in that he asked permission to raise the money through a lottery. The assembly would not grant it. The College was rich in land, but land neither earned money to pay bills nor produced much if sold. Indeed, Wheelock had to send men sixty miles to clear the College grant at Landaff to prevent forfeiture of the charter. Of the 40,000 acres that Dartmouth owned in New Hampshire and the incipient Republic of Vermont to the west, only the 3,000 on the Hanover Plain were of immediate value because settlement was making them so.

Partly through his tenacious missionary spirit and partly through the hope of gaining support from the Scottish Fund, Wheelock was teaching twenty-one Indians in Hanover in 1774. In 1771 he had tried to renew his relationship with the Iroquois by sending David Avery to the Six Nations. Avery remained at Oneida a year but was unable to recruit new students. John Mathews and Abraham Simons, two Indian pupils, were unsuccessful on a journey to the Tuscaroras, and a third mission in 1772 to the Indians of the Ohio likewise failed. Canadian tribes, however, produced ten students that year and there were eight others from miscellaneous sources, in addition to ten young Indian children under Wheelock's care. The Revolution ruined what had been pain-fully achieved. Yet there is this to be said of Wheelock's final effort in behalf of the Indians: their warpaths never crossed Hanover. Whether or not they approved of missionary schools, whether or not they took up arms with the British against the Americans, they remembered the Reverend Doctor as an unselfish friend. Many of the tribes of the Six Nations indeed remained neutral through the war because of the diplomacy of Wheelock's former students, some of them agents of Congress.

The Revolution was a baneful drought to a seedling enterprise still

taking root. All sustenance from England was cut off. Wrenched away were some of the best friends of the College. Wheelock was distraught over the plight of John Wentworth, whose interest in the people of New Hampshire and loyalty to the College transcended all the controversies of the day, but whose withdrawal from the province ·he had governed so fairly and well was inevitable. Broken irrevocably were the ties with London's magnanimous benefactor, John Thornton, and with the London Company for Propagation of the Gospel. All the soul-searching of a minister of the Gospel about the unholy specter of war, all the painful rationalizing about political philosophies were now added to the physical dangers and practical uncertainties of keeping the College alive. Rumors, of course, gained credence that Wheelock was a Tory. This a free-spirited religious dissenter could never have been. He proved his firm devotion to the cause of freedom — but primarily, as always, maintained his passionate attachment to Dartmouth College, whose achievements and aims he placed above any civil or international catastrophe.

At the outset of the War he was more desperately in need of funds than ever and sought them from every conceivable source. He implored those indebted to him or to the College to meet their obligations. He tried to sell or mortgage his Connecticut farms. He asked for a loan from the legislature of Connecticut and tried to raise a subscription in Massachusetts. He asked William Morris of Philadelphia for a loan of £500. Sylvanus Ripley, a graduate of the Class of 1771, a missionary and tutor, wrote: "Atlas formerly sustained the Heavens, so [Wheelock] bears upon his shoulders the weight of this College. We Tutors only steady it a little & keep it from tumbling off." When, during Burgoyne's campaign up Lake Champlain in 1777, the hinterlands were thrown into confusion and alarm, Wheelock wrote the Council of Safety, meeting in Windsor, Vermont, that he looked to God for direction and for arms and ammunition to protect Dartmouth College! The previous year, after the American retreat from the invasion of Canada, he had applied to the commanding generals of the northern armies and the Committee on Indian Affairs for a grant to help support the College. On the grounds of the Committee report that Dartmouth was "conciliating the friendship of the Canadian Indians, or at least of preventing hostilities from them in some measure" it received $500 from Congress. Ragged and anemic as it was — at intervals almost without food — Dartmouth survived the war without ever closing its doors, an accomplishment of no other college. Although Wheelock described himself in 1777 as in a "Broken State of Health" he was still forging ahead.

With all of the problems clamoring at his doorstep during the war it is hard to believe that he could have found the energy to engage in politics, but he was so engaged, and deeply. In part he initiated his new role and in part he fell heir to it. Since 1740 the government of New Hampshire had been dominated by the royal governor and the satellites around him who guided the politics of the assembly, enforced the laws through his Council, and took pains to ensure that the destiny of the province remained in their hands. This was accomplished chiefly through laws stipulating that any member of the assembly must own property with a value of at least £300, and that those districts or counties paying the most taxes were privileged to elect the most representatives. Naturally these edicts did not appeal to the poor settlers who streamed into the northern Connecticut Valley at the end of the French and Indian Wars. The Revolution did not remove the obnoxious laws, and the people of the Connecticut Valley clamored in vain for a proper voice at Exeter (which had replaced Portsmouth as the capital).

Love, peace, joy in God reign triumphant — the only discourse now in fashion when students visit one another's rooms is of the Kingdom of Heaven, and it would be a reproach to anyone if he should introduce any thing frothy, vain, trifling or unprofitable into the conversation. – Eleazar Wheelock, 1778.

In 1776 Hanover, Canaan, and Cardigan displayed their independence by refusing to choose representatives to the assembly. Among the architects of what became known as the College Party were Wheelock (still hopeful of a large domain with the College at its center), and his son-in-law, Bezaleel Woodward. In July, 1776, eleven towns along the Connecticut met in Hanover to voice their grievances. Six months later they were all refusing to pay taxes or participate in the government at Exeter. So successful was the College Party in its strategy that it gathered into its orbit five more towns. In 1778 all sixteen voted to secede from New Hampshire and join the new Republic of Vermont. So it was that Dartmouth became a Vermont college, and Wheelock a Vermont justice of the peace.

Having remade the boundary between Vermont and New Hampshire, the College Party began to visualize a whole new state carved out

[45]

of both sides of the Connecticut Valley with Dresden, as the College district of Hanover was now called, the center and capital. This would require wooing all the New Hampshire towns east to the White Mountains and all the Vermont towns west to the Green Mountains. It would entail doing battle with the celebrated Ethan Allen, who with his brother Ira had forged a new republic out of the crucible of conflicting land claims in the mountains and valleys between the Connecticut and Lake Champlain.

All is safe and certain. The Chief Justice delivered an opinion this morning, in our favor, on all the points. – Daniel Webster, 1819.

Long having claimed this country, the government of New Hampshire had been chartering, granting, and settling it. New York, with equally strong designs and claims, had been moving in from the west. The Allens, at the head of the so-called Bennington Party, had become a third power by buying great tracts for a pittance, by organizing an independent republic to support the settlers who had received grants under New Hampshire, and by raising a militia, the illustrious Green Mountain Boys, to keep out the partisans of New York. When in 1778 the College Party in Dresden grafted the sixteen New Hampshire towns onto Vermont, the political situation in the one-year-old Green Mountain Republic was this: the Allens hoped Congress would make Vermont a state, thus recognizing their republic as a separate entity. They regarded the sixteen towns as an embarrassment of riches, for unless they renounced them they were afraid that Congress would refuse to recognize any of Vermont's claims against New York. There were other over- and under-tones in this intricate border operetta; but the decision of the Allens was that they must get clear of the College Party, whom Ethan called "a Petulent, Pettefoging, Scribbling sort of Gentry, that will Keep any Government in hot water till they are thoroughly brought under by Exertions of Authority." Accordingly Vermont disowned the sixteen towns in February, 1779. The indignant College Party was not to be upstaged that easily; and as it turned out, these were but the opening scenes in the border wars. They comprised, however, all the political events in which the ebbing energies of Eleazar Wheelock allowed him to engage.

For some time he had been aware that he was nearing the end of a race whose burdens had grown progressively heavier. In 1777 he became involved in a most unpleasant controversy with the citizens of Hanover over the relatively insignificant matter of inoculations for smallpox. The question of whether infected students and townspeople should be quarantined in the College mills at Mink Brook precipitated an argument so vehement that Wheelock engaged in correspondence about the possible removal of the College to New York. But these were the overtures of a tired and desperate man. So poor was the College that it could not have moved to Lyme or Norwich; so impoverished were the students, particularly those on charity, that they had nothing to wear. Wheelock's testimony of April, 1778, would be ludicrous, were it not so pathetic:

My family & School are in want of Cloathing . . . we have cut up all the Sheets Table Cloths under beds Towels &c which could be spared in the House, to cover their nakedness, and have now Scarce a whole linnen garment in the house and most of them Such as you would not think worth taking from the floor unless for a papermill.

The College seemed to have fallen "under the Righteous Frowns of heaven. . . ." Thus he accounted for the long cold winter of 1778-79 and for the death of many of his cattle owing to a shortage of fodder. There were complications on the farms, there was trouble with the students over the food and with Tavernkeeper and Town Surveyor John Payne, who knocked down the College gates over the highway every time Wheelock erected them. The Doctor could hardly be blamed for invoking ecclesiastical authority to charge those who disagreed with him with transgressions of moral law. In the depression of illness and age he saw the cause of a lifetime, a good cause, a noble cause, sinking under adversity and he was too sick to sustain it. He had asthma, he had a disease of the skin, and early in 1779 he was seized with epilepsy. On March 29 he wrote his old friend, Dr. Whitaker:

I have been a long time in a very low state and my case of late has been esteemed desperate by my Physicians but, by the pure mercy of God, I am so far reviv'd as to be able unassisted more than by my staff to walk from my bed to the fire and back again and to sit in my chair near half my time.

When he could no longer walk, he directed that he be carried into the chapel to conduct the service. And when his strength would not permit that, the students gathered at his house to hear the word of God. He died on April 24, 1779, in the sixty-ninth year of his age. A large gathering accompanied him to his grave among the pines of the cemetery a few rods from his precious College. His stone bears these fitting words:

BY THE GOSPEL HE SUBDUED THE FEROCITY
OF THE SAVAGE AND TO THE CIVILIZED HE
OPENED NEW PATHS OF SCIENCE
TRAVELER
GO IF YOU CAN AND DESERVE
THE SUBLIME REWARD OF SUCH MERIT

*   *   *   *   *

After the last words of praise and supplication had been spoken by his brother-in-law, Benjamin Pomeroy, who had journeyed the long way from Connecticut for the memorial service, the question remained: would the College die too? Eleazar Wheelock's will left no doubt, if any there had been, that it was a family enterprise. He would have been the last to claim that he *owned* the College, but its finances had become so involved with his own that they were almost inseparable.

Conditioned as we have become to laws governing private, charitable corporations we can with difficulty conceive of an institution whose charter gave the President the personal privilege of naming his successor. Wheelock's attempt to untangle personal and College debts and credits in his will through the gift to his family of a large amount of property certainly gave substance to charges of a family dynasty on the part of those who had accumulated grievances of one kind or another. He left each of his two daughters in Hanover one hundred acres, and each of his four sons two hundred acres of prime village land. Two other daughters received his house in Connecticut. He bequeathed his Hanover dwelling to his son John, together with an obligation to care for his mother. He directed that from the interest on £1,700, which the College owed him, £50 should go to care for his son Ralph, now a hopeless epileptic (but originally his choice as his sucessor), and the remainder to his widow; and that after their deaths the principal was to go to the College. The buildings, including the mills, the land they stood on, and the site for the new hall he had been trying to build were left to the College. So many factors governed the making of his will that it cannot properly be judged in retrospect. The most important provision was that naming his son John as his successor.

According to the *Reminiscences of Professor Shurtleff* young John Wheelock "was in physique tall and very spare but was exceedingly muscular. His nose was a perfect quadrant. He was extremely neat in

[48]

his dress, and always wore small clothes with knee buckles, and a cocked hat. He was a ready talker, profuse in words, but not always forcible ones." George Ticknor, the celebrated Boston scholar, who as a youth lived in the John Wheelock house, wrote that the President was "stiff and stately. He read constantly, sat up late and got up early. He talked very gravely, and slow, with a falsetto voice. Mr. Webster could imitate him perfectly. . . . I saw a great deal of him, from 1802 to 1816 . . . but never felt the smallest degree of familiarity with him, nor do I believe that any of the students or young men did." Ticknor recalled that the Wheelock household "cookery was detestable" and that he hated to come down to dinner. The fine furnishings of the house, the linen sheets and pillow cases trimmed with lace, he recalled, were in marked contrast to the cuisine. They had been brought to Hanover by Wheelock's wife, the daughter of a former governor of the island of St. Thomas.

As a lieutenant colonel on the staffs of Generals Gates and Stark in the late wars, John Wheelock had been characterized as competent, though casual and debonair. His attempt to affect the dignified and studious demeanor of a college president at the much too tender age of twenty-five (the youngest man, it is said, ever to achieve this office) was wholehearted but less than successful. Leon Burr Richardson has observed that "his powers of assimilation were slight compared with his powers of acquisition, and his learning savored of pedantry rather than of real scholarship." He labored mightily on an unwieldy tome called *Philosophical History of the Advancement of Nations with an Inquiry into the Causes of their Rise and Decline,* which fortunately found no publisher.

The pretentious vocabulary which filled his addresses, intended to impress the students, sometimes had the opposite effect, as when after visiting a medical lecture, he declaimed in chapel, "Oh Lord, we thank Thee for the oxygen gas, for the hydrogen gas, for the mephitic gas; we thank Thee for all the gases. And we thank Thee for the cerebrum, for the cerebellum, for the medulla oblongata." But these overcompensations for the deficiencies of youth were partly balanced by his eager devotion to the College. He was a resourceful administrator and, although the students never really liked him, a respected disciplinarian. For some months he had been hesitant to assume the presidency, and his brother-in-law, Bezaleel Woodward, had shouldered the burden. While struggling as treasurer with a debt larger than all of the assets of the College and coping with the strains of the Revolution, this faithful lieutenant of the elder Wheelock was still waging the war of the fluctuating boundary between New Hampshire and Vermont.

When the Green Mountain Republic had expelled the sixteen New Hampshire towns in 1799, thus dashing the College Party's hopes for an independent state in the Connecticut Valley with the College district (Dresden) as the capital, Woodward was stirred to new stratagems. Like the tributaries of the Connecticut the interests of Vermont and New Hampshire valley towns flowed together. The Dresden party was able to rekindle the sympathies of neighboring Vermont towns, which were as disaffected with the leadership of the Bennington Party of the Allens as the western border towns of New Hampshire were with the government at Exeter. As the result of much intrigue ten Vermont towns seceded and joined New Hampshire. With this added territory the College Party calculated that it could bend the Exeter legislature to its will. In 1781, however, much to the consternation of Dresden, the Green Mountain Boys resumed the offensive, not only retrieving their own land but admitting to Vermont a much-enlarged block of territory east of the Connecticut, a total of thirty-four New Hampshire towns. For ten months Dartmouth was again a Vermont college; again Dresden entertained the hope of becoming capital, if not of a separate independent state, at least of the newly enlarged Republic of Vermont. This final union was terminated by General Washington, who advised Governor Chittenden that if he returned the New Hampshire towns (and those of New York that Vermont had at the same time grafted to its western border), Congress might admit the Green Mountain Republic to the Union. Vermont followed the advice of the Father of His Country; the College Party disbanded; and Bezaleel Woodward appeared in Exeter as the chastened representative of Hanover.

In 1780 the Revolution had reduced the number of students to about forty, three of whom were Indians on charity. The Continental currency had depreciated. The crops had failed. The only recourse was the sacrifice of land at a fraction of its potential value. Had the College possessed a clear title to all the property it was presumed to own, sufficient revenue to place it on a sound footing might have been assured. But the grant of the town of Landaff turned out to be a crushing liability. After the College had spent large sums developing it according to the terms of Governor Wentworth's charter of 1770, settlers who claimed title under a previous grant and speculators in league with political enemies of the College succeeded in spiriting away the whole township. Dartmouth's loss was estimated at $10,000. Through the exertions of Captain Ebenezer Webster, father of Daniel, and old General John Sullivan, who arose from a terminal illness to make a spirited plea in the legislature, the College later received partial recompense in the award of a second grant on the headwaters of the Connecticut River. In 1785, six years before he established his own university in Burlington, Ira Allen, architect with his brother Ethan of the Republic of Vermont, persuaded his legislature to grant Dartmouth 43,000 acres in what became the town of Wheelock. John Phillips gave 4,000 additional acres in the town of Grafton. The College's crucial need for cash was met through the immediate sale of portions of these properties.

Having resolved meanwhile to try his hand at foreign solicitation, John Wheelock set sail for Europe in 1783 with an imposing parchment intended to introduce him abroad. It was signed by General Washington, the Secretary of War, Governors, members of Congress, and others. (Very nearly the equal, in terms of autograph value, of the founding papers of the Republic, the document reposes in the archives of Baker Library.) Wheelock's reception in France was sympathetic and in the Netherlands he secured donations through the Prince of Orange; but the climate in England was bleak. While the Earl of Dart-

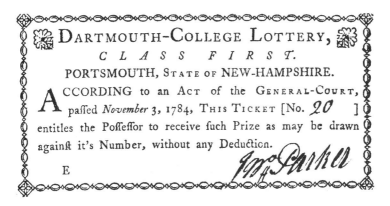

mouth expressed his pleasure in the integrity and accomplishments of the elder Wheelock, neither he nor other Englishmen were interested in making further contributions to a college in Revolutionary America. Wheelock obtained little more than the promise of a telescope and an air pump.

The ship in which he embarked for Boston in 1783 was stripped of her canvas in a series of storms and was wrecked off Cape Cod on the second of January, 1784. Forty passengers managed to escape with their lives; but their possessions, including John Wheelock's strong box filled with papers worth, he claimed, £5,000 to the College, were lost. Thus his expedition ended in costly failure.

At home the College's money crisis seemed to have eased through the sale of lands, although its buildings were in a wretched state and there were no funds to replace them. A vigorous campaign was accordingly undertaken by the President and members of his family. While a lottery sanctioned by the legislature was unsuccessful, a canvass of the neighboring towns produced the surprising sum of nearly $9,000. Thus in 1784, on a site prepared by the elder Wheelock eleven years previously, work began on a building 175 feet long and 52 feet wide, reputedly the largest of its kind in New England. The original plans called for three stories of brick. Wood was substituted owing to its moderate cost and its abundance in proximity to the new College sawmill. Constructed of longitudinal sills of hand-hewn Etna pine fifteen inches square and 75 feet long, roof cords 50 feet long, and uprights of tough oak, the frame was finished in 1786. The raising by a great force from the hinterlands required ten days that summer and was an awesome spectacle of muscle power. During the following year the frame was covered over and, although little joiner work had been done inside, the Commencement exercises in September of 1787 were held on a stage in the vast interior. When spectators climbed the sides of the speakers' platform half way through the services, it collapsed with a groan, and the dignitaries "had to look for themselves in one place and their wigs in another."

The work went forward, with chimney bricks from Hanover and Lebanon, lime from Lebanon and Cavendish, Vermont, nails from Grafton and Rowley, Massachusetts, door handles from the Hanover blacksmith. In 1791, after seven years of labor and backbreaking financial sacrifice, "The College" was finished. Nearly four decades were to pass before it became known as Dartmouth Hall, but from the day of the first lecture and from the first night that students slept in its barren and drafty chambers this noble building became the center and soul of the Hanover Plain. On the ground floor three east-west corridors, all with doors at each end, were bisected by a transverse hall, also with outside doors north and south. The rooms were numerous and small, but many were necessary to serve the diverse functions of dormitory, classroom, and social center. The College library was there (opened one hour every two weeks), as were also a special room for the "philosophical apparatus" obtained by John Wheelock abroad, and a museum of curiosities containing, in the words of Professor Francis Childs, "a stuffed zebra which the students loved to purloin and transport to the belfry or the stage of the College chapel." There were rooms for the literary societies, the Social Friends and the United Fraternity. Only the Commons and chapel were elsewhere.

As the result late in 1789 of a so-called "nocturnal visitation" in which the students demolished the badly rotted former hall and meeting room, the Trustees voted to build a chapel southwest of Dartmouth Hall (partly in front of the later site of Thornton Hall). Fifty feet in length from east to west and thirty-six in width with a hip roof, it was completed in the late summer of 1790; a notoriously cheerless building in the opinion of the students. The following year a new Commons Hall was built, and in 1795 the community erected the meeting house at the northwest corner of the Green. In no case was money available for these buildings — it was always an accessory after the fact. Lands were sold or some other expedient was devised by the hard-driven president and treasurer.

As had his father, Wheelock looked covetously at the old £2,500 lodestone of the Scottish Fund, held inviolate all these years by its zealous Trustees. Since the war Moor's Indian Charity School had become an academy for paying white students. No funds were available for charity scholars either Indian or white, although a number had been maintained until 1785, long after the English Fund had become exhausted. Through soothing overtures on his trip to Europe, followed by solemn affidavits about proper bookkeeping and courteous assurances about the separateness and integrity of the missionary school, John Wheelock in 1785 actually extracted from the wily Scots £625 in partial payment for the support of the Indians during his father's administration. In 1791 he obtained £658 more. In 1800 Moor's School again began to receive Indians in small numbers and the Scottish Fund henceforth honored drafts in their behalf. In view of his father's futile efforts, this was no small accomplishment on the part of John Wheelock. With the inauguration of Governor John Taylor Gilman in the chapel, and the meeting of the legislature in Hanover in 1795, the long years of friction with the state government temporarily ended. The ensuing era was one of relative well-being. A series of official lotteries brought in over $3,-600. Receipts from student enrollment rose markedly. During the last ten years of the eighteenth century Dartmouth graduated 362 students, Harvard 394, Yale 295, and Princeton 240. A notable landmark in the same decade was the establishment at Dartmouth of what was then the fourth medical school in the United States.

Its founder, Nathan Smith, a native of Massachusetts, had seemed

[53]

destined for a life as a farmer. His interest in medicine was aroused through his assistance by chance at an operation. Following a year of preparatory schooling and an apprenticeship, he attended Harvard Medical School. Upon his graduation he settled down to a highly successful practice in Cornish, New Hampshire. The Dartmouth Medical School was founded in 1797, and Smith was installed, two years later, in the north end of Dartmouth Hall. During his sixteen years in Hanover he occupied, according to a successor, Oliver Wendell Holmes, not a chair but a whole settee of medicine. His students followed him on horseback from the classroom into the hinterlands, and in dimly-lighted farm bedrooms shared the other dimensions of his work as practitioner and investigator. Smith gave land in Hanover for a separate medical school and wrested from the legislature the money for a building. When well past middle age, after he had left Dartmouth, he pioneered further in the establishment of three more medical schools at Yale, Bowdoin, and the University of Vermont, thus becoming the patron saint of his profession in New England.

By the turn of the century Dartmouth had survived three decades perilously beset by poverty and war. No one could have conceived of a worse crisis. Yet its makings were in evidence as early as 1793, when Judge Nathaniel Niles of West Fairlee, Vermont, was elected to the Board of Trustees. Versatile, self-reliant, contentious, Niles was the image of the Vermont independent. He had been graduated from Princeton; he had been a member of the Vermont legislature, a judge of the state supreme court, a representative in Congress, a presidential elector; he had invented a machine for making wire; he had studied medicine and metaphysics and considered himself a poet. Perhaps Jefferson's statement that he was the ablest man he had ever known had something to do with their compatible political philosophies, for Niles was a crusading Democrat. In his insistence upon more representative conduct of the College church affairs lay the root of his aversion to John Wheelock.

To characterize Wheelock's Board of Trustees as Congregationalist would be to oversimplify. Wheelock held fast to Presbyterian principles of polity, which placed church government in the hands of the elders, while Niles's banner proclaimed pure democracy in the conduct of church affairs. Following the Revolution, New Hampshire Congregationalists had achieved what the Portsmouth Episcopalians previously coveted — in effect a connection between church and state. The inhabitants of each town or parish were required by law to support the Congregationalist minister. This was a part of what Judge Niles (whose own Vermont constitution decreed absolute religious freedom) was fighting. He could not abide Wheelock's patriarchal views, reflected also in his concept of the role of the college president as an authority aided and abetted, but not governed, by the Board of Trustees. John Wheelock indignantly reciprocated Niles's aversion, but there was no way he could get him off the Board.

The feud became endemic. Niles began an investigation in the Vermont legislature of the validity of the grant to the College of the town of Wheelock, and particularly of the way the president was handling annual revenue from leases in the town. According to the charter half was to go to Dartmouth and half to Moor's School. Niles claimed that Wheelock, without conferring with anyone, had taken half of the an-

nual income himself. Fortunately for Dartmouth the Vermont legislature dismissed a petition to declare the charter of the town of Wheelock invalid; for as time went on, the rents from these 23,000 acres in Vermont comprised one-half of the permanent funds of the College and Moor's School. Without them the latter could not have continued after the Scottish Fund had ceased to support the school. Niles, however, was implacable, and more than any other individual except Wheelock himself was responsible for the rising tensions among members of the board. Richardson observes that when the College was small, poor, and without much prestige, the Trustees were content to agree with the President on almost every issue; but now that it was on a level with other eastern universities they began to take a proprietary view of their responsibilities.

In 1796 Judge Niles succeeded in persuading the Board to appoint the Reverend Charles Backus, a Connecticut Congregationalist, to the Phillips Professorship of Theology. By sending David McClure to dissuade Backus from accepting, Wheelock was able to checkmate the indignant Niles. To fill the role of preacher to the College the Trustees in 1804 named the Reverend Roswell Shurtleff. The townspeople desired that he become their minister also, and that John Smith, Professor of Languages and a minion of John Wheelock, relinquish his post as minister of the College Church. Through the clever stratagem of rounding up some Hartford, Vermont, Presbyterian members who had not attended services in Hanover for years, the President was able to outvote the local constituency, with the result that Smith and Shurtleff were named co-pastors of the church. This greatly inflamed many of the Hanover members, and in consequence they withdrew from the Church of Christ at Dartmouth College to form in 1810 the Church of Christ in the Vicinity of Dartmouth College, with Shurtleff as their minister.

Wheelock made this intolerable affront to his prestige a prime issue to the Board of Trustees. However, they did not choose to take sides and tried earnestly to act as conciliators. When their patience ran out the moderates began to swing to the opposition headed by Judge Niles. The towering figures who composed the Board in the early 1800's were not to be dismissed as mere ciphers. Among them was Elijah Paine, whose voice, it is said, could be heard distinctly for three-quarters of a mile — a Phi Beta Kappa student at Harvard, an early settler in Vermont, a judge of its supreme court and of the Federal District Court, a farmer and manufacturer, a man, like Judge Niles, of formidable versatility. Another Vermonter, the scholarly Charles Marsh, was a prominent Federalist, as were Judge Timothy Farrar, Thomas Thompson, New Hampshire representative and senator, and Peter Olcott, a lieutenant governor of Vermont, a friend of Webster, and the father of Mills Olcott, long the most accomplished and persuasive citizen of Hanover. When the College was torn in two these were some of the giants who guided its destiny.

With the death of Peter Olcott and that, in 1809, of Professor John Smith, control of the Board was irrevocably lost by Wheelock. Thenceforth only his adversaries were elected. As Wheelock's status descended in the succeeding years, his obstinacy ascended until, it is said, the Board would have dismissed him, had the College not owed him so much money. Unable to get his way even in the appointment of faculty members, the President began to draw up artillery on the larger battleground of the state capital. In 1815 he asked the legislature to investigate the College. The following year an anonymous pamphlet called *Sketches of the History of Dartmouth College and Moor's Charity School . . . ,* undoubtedly from his pen, charged that among other high-handed actions the Dartmouth Trustees were withholding money due the President and misappropriating the Phillips and other funds. This of course stirred to a ferment the political ingredients in the Dartmouth conflict. A new Wheelock petition asking for an investigation was granted by the legislature.

In June, 1815, William Plumer, a Democrat destined to become Governor the following year, used the religious schism in the College as a point of departure for urging the separation of church and state and the enactment of laws permitting incorporation of all denominations. The assembly acted, and the Congregational church soon lost its favored status.

When the College case entered the public domain, the religious and political alignments of the Board of Trustees became blurred. Congregationalism was synonymous with Federalism; but since the latter was dying in New Hampshire, John Wheelock's opportunity to recapture control lay with the Baptist, Methodist, and nonsectarian Democrats. The Congregationalist Trustees, who had been fighting the patriarchal domination of the Board by one man, found themselves in the peculiar position of maintaining the Board's status in the face of an oncoming attempt by Presbyterian Wheelock and Democrats of alien faiths to pack it. The political and religious factors in the controversy were, however, exterior to the immediate struggle on the Hanover Plain for control of the Board of Trustees.

[59]

At the Commencement of 1815, citing principally the pamphlet which Wheelock had circulated against them, the Trustees removed him from office. This startling action had the effect of raising him in public esteem as a martyr and, as Federalist friends of the Board had feared, of bringing on a political hurricane in the state election of 1816. The Democrats rallied to Wheelock and embraced his cause as theirs. The campaign was one of the stormiest in the history of New Hampshire, with partisans hurling such epithets as "infidels," "French Jacobins," "the gangrened persecutors of President Wheelock," and "the infuriated bigots of popism in the dark ages."

Following their overwhelming victory the Democrats set about paying their political debt to Wheelock for having provided the dominant issue. Since the report of the legislative committee to investigate the College contained little to recommend the causes either of Wheelock or of Governor Plumer, who had campaigned to reform the College, the investigation was conveniently sidetracked with the assertion that a defective charter was the true basis of Dartmouth's troubles. Ignoring requests of the Trustees for a hearing, the assembly passed on June 26 a new law changing the name of the College to Dartmouth University and increasing the number of Trustees from twelve to twenty-one, the nine new members to be appointed by the Governor and council. A twenty-five-member Board of Overseers headed by the principal officers of the state was given the power to confirm or annul any decision of the Board of Trustees.

The first meeting of the Trustees of Dartmouth University, held at the Commencement of 1816, was a fiasco. The Governor was unable to obtain a quorum, and no one in the College was successful in finding a key to the room where the new Board was scheduled to meet. It finally assembled in Concord in February, 1817, to elect as President of Dartmouth University the ailing but triumphant John Wheelock, who displayed his pleasure by forgiving part of the College's indebtedness to him and bestowing upon the new corporation five farms in Vermont and two houses in Hanover.

Adamantly holding the College's defenses against the aggressions of the Governor and assembly was President Francis Brown of the class of 1805, a native of Yarmouth, Maine, elected by the old Board in 1815 when Wheelock was deposed. While the University was successful in breaking into the buildings and substituting new locks, it had more difficulty with the College's human property. Restricted though their classes were to a building called Rowley Hall, most of the students rallied around President Brown. A reaction to the callous and un-principled methods of the legislature was bringing him the sympathy of the public also.

It was thus in an atmosphere of less than unqualified victory that John Wheelock died in April of 1817. Both institutions joined hands to do him homage, but it was already clear to the College that his performance had on balance been more hurtful than constructive. As Benjamin Franklin Sanborn said: "[Eleazar] Wheelock was a mixed, though strong character; his son . . . had the mixture without the strength." He possessed neither the selfless good will, nor the missionary spirit of his father. His relationships (even with his brothers, who became estranged over money and land matters) were laden with controversy at a time when diplomacy and quiet consolidation were vital to a still frail institution. Upon his death John Wheelock was found to be the richest man in New Hampshire, with an estate worth as much as $100,000. In addition to his earlier gift he left Dartmouth University 745 acres in Hanover and Lebanon, three other Hanover lots with their buildings, and large tracts in Grantham, New Hampshire, and in the Vermont townships of Washington, Sterling, and Sharon. If the cause of Dartmouth University did not prevail, these bequests were to go to the Presbyterian Church for the benefit of the Princeton Theological Seminary!

In June, William Allen, John Wheelock's son-in-law, became president of Dartmouth University. He must have done so with misgivings, for the new corporation had become the defendant in a suit filed by the Trustees of Dartmouth College against William Woodward, its former clerk and treasurer. The son of Bezaleel and the nephew of John Wheelock, Woodward had refused to surrender to the College its charter, seal, trustee records, and accounts. Little did anyone foresee that this action would result in a decision by the United States Supreme Court that was to become a cornerstone in American jurisprudence.

The suit was first entered in the Court of Common Pleas of Grafton County, but since the judge of this court was William Woodward himself, it was carried to the Superior Court at Haverhill and later at Exeter. The College retained Daniel Webster of the Class of 1801, Jeremiah Smith, and Jeremiah Mason, all natives of New Hampshire, all Federalists, all with commanding regional reputations and with profound respect for each other. Years later Webster remarked of Mason, with whom he had tangled in Portsmouth early in his career: "If I were asked who is the greatest lawyer I ever met, I should name

John Marshall, but if you took me by the throat and forced a real opinion, I would have to say, Jeremiah Mason." As for Webster, Mason said of their first encounter in a courtroom: "He broke upon me like a thunder storm in July, sudden, portentous, sweeping all before it."

The case was heard in May and September of 1817. The pith of Smith's and Mason's arguments was that the action of the legislature in abolishing the old corporation and substituting a new one was beyond the scope of its powers; that no vested right could be transferred except by agency of a court of justice; that while legislatures had some control over public corporations, those privately established were free in the management of their property and affairs; that private charitable corporations were in this category, dependent as they were on private funds; and that the Constitution of the United States directed that no state should pass a law impairing the obligations of contracts. Webster concluded for the plaintiff in a two-hour argument which was said to be the equal of his later illustrious defense of the College in Washington. John M. Shirley, in *Dartmouth College Causes and the Supreme Court of the United States,* says of Webster's Exeter argument that

Tradition and old letters point to the one conclusion: if not the greatest it was one of the most brilliant efforts of his life and produced a most extraordinary effect. He closed with the "Caesar in the Senate House" peroration which was so much admired by Professor Goodrich and others when he recited it at Washington and the court was generally in tears.

The defense was represented by George Sullivan, attorney general of New Hampshire, and Ichabod Bartlett, who maintained that the old corporation was not abolished by the 1816 act of the legislature, but enlarged or extended. Dartmouth, they maintained, was not a private corporation in that its activities were public in character and it was hence subject to public control. It seemed to those present, particularly to friends of the College, that the lawyers for the defense had made a poor showing in contrast to Mason, Smith and Webster, but Webster shrewdly deduced that it would be strange indeed if Governor Plumer's court should refuse to execute laws he had promoted.

When the court decided for the University the defeated but determined College asked Webster to appeal to the United States Supreme Court. The case of the Trustees vs. Woodward, The Church of Christ at Dartmouth College vs. The Church of Christ in the Vicinity of Dartmouth College, the College vs. the University, the Governor and legislature of New Hampshire vs. the College, the Democrats vs. the Federal-

ists, the populists vs. the conservatives — for it was all this and more —
was heard in Washington on March 10, 1818. The capitol having been
partially razed by the British in the War of 1812, the Supreme Court
was sitting in a "mean apartment of moderate size in the North Wing."
His five-hour argument earned the thirty-six-year-old Webster a national reputation. As printed the address contains the cogent reasoning
but not the eloquence and impassioned pleading that made such an
effect on the spectators, and indeed upon the Justices. Posterity is

[63]

dependent upon the memory of Professor Chauncey Goodrich of Yale, who had been present, and whose recollections were faithfully set down by Rufus Choate:

Mr. Webster entered upon his argument in the calm tone of easy and dignified conversation. His matter was so completely at his command that he scarcely looked at his brief, but went on for more than four hours with a statement so luminous, and a chain of reasoning so easy to be understood, and yet approaching so nearly to absolute demonstration, that he seemed to carry with him every man of his audience without the slightest effort or weariness on either side. It was hardly *eloquence,* in the strict sense of the term; it was pure reason. Now and then, for a sentence or two, his eye flashed and his voice swelled into a bolder note, as he uttered some emphatic thought; but he instantly fell back into the tone of earnest conversation, which ran throughout the great body of his speech. . . .

I observed that Judge Story, at the opening of the case, had prepared himself, pen in hand, as if to take copious minutes. Hour after hour I saw him fixed in the same attitude, but, so far as I could perceive, with not a note on his paper. The argument closed, and *I could not discover that he had taken a single note.* . . .

The argument ended. Mr. Webster stood for some moments silent before the Court, while every eye was fixed intently upon him. At length, addressing the Chief Justice, Marshall, he proceeded thus: —

'*This, Sir, is my case!* It is the case, not merely of that humble institution, it is the case of every College in our land. It is more. It is the case of every eleemosynary institution throughout our country — of all those great charities founded by the piety of our ancestors to alleviate human misery, and scatter blessings along the pathway of life. It is more! It is, in some sense, the case of every man among us who has property of which he may be stripped, for the question is simply this: Shall our State Legislatures be allowed to take *that* which is not their own, to turn it from its original use, and apply it to such ends or purposes as they, in their discretion, shall see fit!

'Sir, you may destroy this little Institution; it is weak; it is in your hands! I know it is one of the lesser lights in the literary horizon of our country. You may put it out. But if you do so, you must carry through your work! You must extinguish, one after another, all those great lights of science which, for more than a century, have thrown their radiance over our land!

'It is, Sir, as I have said, a small College. And yet, *there are those who love it—*'

Here the feelings which he had thus far succeeded in keeping down, broke forth. His lips quivered; his firm cheeks trembled with emotion; his eyes were filled with tears, his voice choked, and he seemed struggling to the utmost simply to gain that mastery over himself which might save him from an unmanly burst of feeling. I will not attempt to give you the few broken words of tenderness in which he went on to speak of his attachment to the College. The whole seemed to be mingled throughout with the recollections of father, mother, brother, and all the trials and privations through which he had made his way into life. Every one saw that it was wholly unpremeditated, a pressure on his heart, which sought relief in words and tears.

The court room during these two or three minutes presented an extraordinary spectacle. Chief Justice Marshall, with his tall and gaunt figure bent over as if to catch the slightest whisper, the deep furrows of his cheek expanded with emotion, and eyes suffused with tears; Mr. Justice Washington at his side, with his small and emaciated frame and countenance more like marble than I ever saw on any other human being. . . .

Mr. Webster had now recovered his composure, and fixing his keen eye on the Chief Justice, said, in that deep tone with which he sometimes thrilled the heart of an audience:—

'Sir, I know not how others may feel,' (glancing at the opponents of the College before him,) 'but, for myself, when I see my alma mater surrounded, like Caesar in the senate house, by those who are reiterating stab upon stab, I would not, for this right hand, have her turn to me, and say, *Et tu quoque, mi fili! And thou too, my son!*'

He sat down. There was a deathlike stillness throughout the room for some moments; every one seemed to be slowly recovering himself, and coming gradually back to his ordinary range of thought and feeling.

It was not until February 2, 1819, in an atmosphere turbulent with political cross currents, that the Supreme Court of the United States reversed the decision of the New Hampshire Superior Court. In the words of Chancellor James Kent this judgment "did more than any other single act proceeding from the authority of the United States to throw an impregnable barrier around all rights and franchises derived from the grant of government, and to give solidity and inviolability to literary, charitable, religious and commercial institutions of our Country."

> Our College cause will be known to our children's children. Let us take care that the rogues shall not be ashamed of their grandfathers. – Daniel Webster, 1819.

On the day of the epochal decision Webster, offering his congratulations to President Brown, wrote that he felt a load removed from his shoulders much heavier than he had been accustomed to bear. Congressman Joseph Hopkinson, a colleague of Webster in the case, wrote the same day of a triumph *"broad and deep over legislative despotism and party violence for the future. . . .* I would have an inscription over the door of your building. 'Founded by Eleazar Wheelock, Refounded by Daniel Webster.' "

*   *   *   *   *

Four harrowing years had passed since Francis Brown, at the age of thirty-one, had taken the reins of the College. John Aiken of the Class of 1819 recalled him as "singularly dignified and commanding, one of the noblest specimens of manhood that my eyes ever beheld. . . . His large full blue eyes and genial beaming face invited confidence, yet his whole expression was so sagacious and so penetrating that no student ever dreamed of deceiving him, or presumed on unbecoming familiarity with him. . . . We all took delight in pleasing him, for we both loved and honored him." So fully did he grasp the Dartmouth College Case in every detail that Jeremiah Mason said he could have argued it in court with distinction. Hamilton College asked him to become its president at twice the salary he was receiving at Dartmouth, but he remained devotedly in Hanover.

The presence of Daniel Webster and Rufus Choate helped to make the Commencement of 1819 one of the most memorable in the history of the College. The University had been rich through the munificence of John Wheelock, but the University was no more. The impoverished College was rich in the security bequeathed by the high court. President Brown, however, was dying. Sixty-four years later (on March 16, 1883) Joseph Emery wrote in *The Dartmouth* of a characteristic act of solicitude on the part of Webster for the ailing President. At the Commencement meeting of the Trustees and faculty Webster advised Dr. Brown to go South as a possible treatment for his tuberculosis. Brown replied that this might be wise but that he was poor and unable to bear the expense. Having just received $500 from the Trustees, presumably in connection with his defense of the College, Webster endorsed it over to President Brown, saying, "That will help you, sir." Dr. Brown did go South but, failing to improve, returned to Hanover in June, 1820, in an even more critical condition. Moved to tears, he declined a student demonstration of welcome, saying that he "had need of pall bearers rather than a triumphal procession and was coming to

his home prepared to die." The third President in the Wheelock Succession lingered for a month and on July 27 passed away.

The Reverend Daniel Dana of the Class of 1788, a minister in Newburyport, Massachusetts, found the problems of the College too trying for a preacher from a quiet pastorate and resigned the presidency after being in office less than a year. He was followed by the Reverend Bennett Tyler of South Britain, Connecticut, who made progress in his six-year administration, but who also found the accumulated problems overwhelming and resigned in August, 1828. Dartmouth was a small college and there were indeed those who loved it; but many, notably the officers and legislators of the state whose ears had been boxed by the Supreme Court, did not. Strongly partisan Democrats sent their sons elsewhere to college. In 1820 Dartmouth owed back salaries of more than $4,000, and twice that to the heirs of John Wheelock as the result of a court action. With a total debt of $16,500 the College was unable to embark on a construction program or even maintain the buildings it had. Without the timely help of a citizen of Orford, John B. Wheeler, who gave a thousand dollars during the court struggle, and the subsequent contributions of others, Dartmouth would probably have closed its doors. Although, during the 1820's, the enrollment recovered its former level of 150, tuition scarcely paid the bills: the students from the upland farms of the North Country were even poorer than the College.

Yet during these hard-scrabble decades there was a richness of spirit, born of common hardship, that was making uncommon men of the sons of Dartmouth. Of the 1,177 graduates under Eleazar and John Wheelock nine out of ten entered law, medicine, theology, or teaching. In a tabulation of their accomplishments Leon Burr Richardson discovered that "three were members of the President's cabinet, eight were members of the Senate, and thirty-seven were members of the national House of Representatives. Ten were governors of states . . . one . . . was a justice of the United States Supreme Court, fifteen were judges of state courts of the highest jurisdiction, and sixty-nine presided over lower courts." Daniel Webster, of course, heads Professor Richardson's list. Then comes Jesse Appleton, 1792, who

became the second president of Bowdoin, succeeding Joseph McKeen, 1774, a product of the College under the elder Wheelock. Zephaniah Swift Moore, 1793, was president of Williams and afterwards the first president of Amherst. Philander Chase, 1796, carried the standard of Episcopacy across the Alleghanies, was successively Bishop of Ohio and of Illinois and founder of Kenyon and Jubilee Colleges. Sylvanus Thayer, 1807, was the real father of West Point and established the Thayer School of Civil Engineering. In the same class was George Ticknor, first professor of modern languages at Harvard . . . and a potent influence in the social and intellectual life of Boston at a time when that region was preeminent as a literary center. . . . Levi Woodbury [1809] at twenty-five judge of the highest court of the state, later Governor of New Hampshire, twice member of the Senate of the United States, Secretary of the Navy from 1831 to 1834, Justice of the United States Supreme Court from 1845 to his death in 1851. . . . [Congressman] Thaddeus Stevens [1814] for a limited period occupied a position of power such as few men have held in the history of the nation. . . .

Such was the evangelistic background of the College that among the most interesting graduates of the early nineteenth century were the ministers and missionaries. As a result of a lifelong interest in the ancestors of the Indian race, Solomon Spaulding, 1785, a student of divinity, wrote a fictitious history called *The Manuscript Found,* said to have been the source of the Mormon Bible. A Vermonter of the Class of 1813, Albert B. Carrington, was one of the few who journeyed to Utah with Brigham Young on his scouting expedition. As one of the twelve Mormon apostles he became a pioneer statesman of the church and territory. John Humphrey Noyes of the Class of 1830 founded in Putney, Vermont, and later at Oneida, New York, his controversial Perfectionist experiment with its doctrine of complex or "plural" marriage, described by George Bernard Shaw as "one of those chance attempts at Superman which occur from time to time in spite of the interference of man's blundering institutions."

I wish the College may live to the third and fourth and tenth century. I hope it will live as long as there is an American nation, and that will be to the end of all time. – William Tecumseh Sherman, 1869.

Other graduates were putting their marks on widely varying professions. Fred Lewis Pattee considered Thomas Green Fessenden of the Class of 1796 the first real American humorist. At the age of thirty-six Dr. Amos Twitchell, 1802, became the first to perform the operation of tying the carotid artery, thus saving the life of a man wounded by gunshot. Samuel Lorenzo Knapp, 1804, is said to have been the first historian of American literature. Captain Alden Partridge, 1806, an early superintendent of West Point and founder of Norwich University, has been given credit for being the first exemplifier in America of the elective system in a liberal education, and at the same time of a citizenry well prepared to take up arms so that they would be in a position of "awing-down their would-be foes." Of John Ledyard, the Marco Polo of the Class of 1776, and of many other independent and adventurous graduates of the early nineteenth century it can be said that theirs also was the Dartmouth spirit.

In August, 1828, the Board of Trustees elected as the sixth President, the Reverend Nathan Lord, a graduate of Bowdoin, formerly a teacher at Exeter and later pastor of the Congregational church at Amherst, New Hampshire. His affiliation with Dartmouth had been as a member of the Board of Trustees since 1821. Strong in physique, in mind, and sense of purpose, he more nearly approached the ideal than had any of his predecessors since Eleazar Wheelock. Part of his appeal to students was his repute as a runner, jumper, and skater, and part, no doubt, was his forthright character, a model of exemplary conduct. With his high forehead, penetrating blue eyes, and ample square jaw he appeared to David Cross, 1841, "like some prophet of the Old Testament."

Alpheus B. Crosby, 1853, recalled that a dressing down in the President's study was to be avoided at all costs.

The chair of the culprit being so arranged as to flood his face with light, Doctor Lord, with his face in shadow, and his eyes impenetrably concealed by green glasses, sat there, at once a Rhadamanthus and a Sphinx. Then there was an ominous silence for a few moments, at the expiration of which the candidate for discipline was informed that "certain facts have come to the knowledge of the Faculty" and he would be invited to vary the monotony of existence by telling the truth. No victim of the Inquisition ever dreaded the thumbscrew or the rack more than the college malefactor feared this scathing interview with Doctor Lord.

He affected the green glasses, it is said, to hide the twinkle in his eyes, for he confessed that "things ludicrous are apt to set me off beyond propriety." In chapel the glasses were useful as camouflage. While appearing to read from the Bible he was actually reciting from memory, his eyes all the while wandering from aisle to aisle to detect improprieties among the students. He was effective in emergencies, as when he stemmed a mass withdrawal of the students from College in 1830 with the words: "Go, young gentlemen, if you wish; we can bear to see our seats vacated but not our laws violated." If the ringing command: "Disperse, young Gentlemen, disperse!" did not end a riot, he waded in with his cane, landing hard blows in every direction.

Brain of the New World! What a task is thine! – Walt Whitman, Hanover, 1872.

Intellectual curiosity and astuteness in administration were also combined in President Lord's makeup. Responding to the College's critical need for new facilities he succeeded, by contributing the last $440 himself, in reaching the goal of $50,000 in a general solicitation. The tangible results were Thornton Hall and Wentworth Hall, the impressive three-story Greek Revival companions on either side of Dartmouth Hall. Responsible for their chaste and balanced proportions was Ammi B. Young, architect of the Boston Customs House and the Vermont State capitol. Through the bequest of the Honorable William Reed in 1837 Young designed a third distinctive building in the same tradition. A fourth, on the present site of Rollins Chapel, would have completed the symmetry of the Old Row, had it not been for a depression that unfortunately outlived the classical revival in architecture. The museum, art gallery, the College and literary society libraries were moved out of Dartmouth Hall to the ground floor of Reed Hall, which they shared with classrooms. The upper stories became a dormitory. Two floors in the center of Dartmouth Hall had given way to a single large chapel with austere wooden benches sacred to none.

Among other changes on the campus during the long administration of Nathan Lord was the removal of Eleazar Wheelock's mansion house from the campus to its present site on West Wheelock Street (where it later served the town as the Howe Library), and the erection in 1852 of a small brick observatory, the gift of Dr. George C. Shattuck of the Class of 1803. In 1851 Abiel Chandler, a native of New Hampshire and prominent Boston businessman, left $50,000 for the founding of a scientific department, whose building stood on the west side of the Green next to Crosby Hall until 1936. Like most of his predecessors the President was unable to tempt the New Hampshire legislature to appropriate funds for buildings or any other purpose. The slender private endowment thus rose very slowly to $214,000 at the outset of the Civil War. Through Dr. Lord's efforts the first modest alumni association was established in 1855, frankly "with reference to the more effectual raising of money."

In view of the fact that as late as 1840 rents from the Vermont town of Wheelock comprised one-third of the College's operating income, Dartmouth owed its survival as much or more to the Green Mountain State grant as to those in New Hampshire. Journeying to Wheelock Dr. Lord would set up a temporary office in the old brick hotel to greet the tenant farmers in person and to receive their rents. As those down on their luck filed past, caps in hand, to explain why they could not pay, the President excused, encouraged, or rebuked them as circumstances warranted. On Sunday he always preached in the local church. His affairs in good order after several days' work, he would start for Hanover in a carriage or on horseback, leading a caravan of wagons of grain or of livestock which he had accepted in lieu of rent. If the rule of the College was authoritarian it was benevolent: the President promised that if a Wheelock boy fitted himself for Dartmouth he would not have to pay tuition.

Increasing enrollment of course had a salutary effect upon the finances of the College, but various influences caused it to fluctuate

[71]

A VIEW OF DA

[72]

OUTH COLLEGE BUILDINGS.

Ammi B. Young Archt.

Lebanon N.H.

dramatically. In 1835-36 it was 186. Five years later it had risen to 341. In 1845-46 it dropped to 179, then began a gradual recovery to 275 in the fall of 1860. Early in the Lord administration the percentage of students from New Hampshire was 74.6 and that from Vermont and New Hampshire 84.3 of the total. With the coming of the railroads in the 1840's the proportion of northern New Englanders began more than a century of decline. From one to five Indians were in attendance under the auspices of the old Scottish Fund from 1826 to 1849, when Moor's School was closed. Thereafter, until late in the nineteenth century, the presence of a few northern and western Indians on Scottish Fund scholarships reminded the College of its original mission.

Although the texture of the student body was essentially homespun during the Lord administration, descriptions of Commencements during the 1830's do not suggest that the atmosphere was insulated from the immediate environs or the outside world. Very early on the morning of graduation day throngs of outlanders in all kinds of conveyances took to the roads leading to Hanover and converged upon the Green, which by noon was choked with people, tents and booths dispensing nicknacks, candy, hard cider, hard patent medicines, and hard liquor.

I was sorry to see such a host of peddlars, gamblers, drunkards and shows [wrote a newspaper correspondent in 1833]. I was never more astonished than to see at such an anniversary and at such a place the unaccountable degree of immorality and vice. I should think that there were in sight of one another thirty places of gambling. During the performances in the meeting house the vociferations of a dozen auctioneers were to be distinctly heard in the house.

The contrast between the boisterous Green and the solemn meeting house must have seemed bizarre indeed in 1838 when Ralph Waldo Emerson, in an address considered by Thomas Carlyle to be one of Emerson's noblest, exhorted the graduating class to resist the low influences that would assail them.

. . . You will hear, that the first duty is to get land and money, place and name. "What is this Truth you seek? What is this Beauty?" men will ask, with derision. If, nevertheless, God have called any of you to explore truth and beauty, be bold, be firm, be true. When you shall say, "As others do, so will I. I renounce, I am sorry for it, my early visions; I must eat the good of the land, and let learning and romantic expectations go, until a more convenient season;" — then dies the man in you; then once more perish the buds of art, and poetry, and science, as they have died already in a thousand men. The

[74]

hour of that choice is the crisis of your history; and see that you hold yourself fast by the intellect. Feel that it is this domineering temper of the sensual world, that creates the extreme need of the priests of science; and that it is the office and right of the intellect to make and not take its estimate. . . . Be content with a little light, so it be your own. Explore, and explore, and explore. Be neither chided nor flattered out of your position of perpetual inquiry. . . . Why should you renounce your right to traverse the starlit deserts of truth, for the premature comforts of an acre, house, and barn? Truth also has its roof, and bed, and board. Make yourselves necessary to the world, and mankind will give you bread, and if not store of it, yet such as shall not take away your property in all men's possessions, in all men's affections in art, in nature, and in hope.

At the equally memorable Commencement of 1853 Rufus Choate gave his ringing eulogy of Webster before an audience that packed the meeting house. Forty-two years later in *The Dartmouth* Charles Caverno wrote that he stood

during the delivery of that eulogy in one of the windows on the west side of the church most of the time with one foot on the window sill and one on the railing of a pew. Other students were wedged into the window as tight as we could be. Outside, a farmer looking man had got a narrow plank and fastened one end of it against the chapel and the other lay on the window sill. The man lay prone on it. It was an uncomfortable position, for it slanted down toward the chapel rather steeply. He meant to see and hear Choate. . . .

Certain opinions courageously and unswervingly maintained by President Lord but not by the faculty, the alumni, or the outside world, assured the survival of Dartmouth's and indeed northern New England's, heritage of contention and waywardness. Dr. Lord thought that "ambition and emulation are selfish principles, that they are consequently immoral and ought not to be appealed to in a private or public discipline. . . ." He considered that the system of honors and prizes exalted the attainment of knowledge at the expense of both virtue and wisdom, in the scramble of competition. Consequently in 1835 he decreed that every senior, not a chosen few, would speak at Commencement. The ennui arising from an almost endless parade of orations resulted presently in the selection of speakers by drawing lots. Throughout his administration, however, the President held fast to the rule that there would be no competing for prizes or prize scholarships, this in the face of protests from the faculty and from the alumni to the Board of Trustees that something had to be done to re-introduce "intellectual and moral excitement" into the system.

[75]

A far greater bone of contention, one that ultimately led to Dr. Lord's resignation, was his philosophy about slaveholding. It is said that his early views were Abolitionist and that he attended the first anti-slavery convention in Philadelphia, but that following a visit to the South he changed his mind. His was a literal interpretation of the Bible; he felt that slavery was condoned therein, and by God's law. The more heated the issue became in the North and the more violently the Abolitionists and most of the clergy denounced slaveholding, the more adamantly Nathan Lord clung to his Fundamentalist views. He spelled them out in a pamphlet that went into four editions and aroused great feeling against the College — although of course the views of the College were not those of Dr. Lord. In some respects he was far more liberal in his outlook than some of the most incendiary Abolitionist leaders. In Troy, New York, at the ordination of a Negro preacher, he was the only white minister present.

> Students visiting West Lebanon will please take notice that Prof. Hiram Orcutt has been appointed special policeman, and henceforth all persons caught treaspassing on the grounds of Tilden Female Seminary, will be seized and held trial by that officer. – *The Dartmouth,* 1878.

As the controversy passed the point of tolerance his position collided head-on with that of prominent alumni such as Amos Tuck, 1835, for nine years a Trustee, a leading Abolitionist and a founder of the Republican Party. While Jeremiah Marston of the Class of 1843, a large slaveholder in Missouri, would agree with President Lord, certainly Marston's brother, Gilman, 1837, a prominent Abolitionist and general in the Union Army, could not; nor Colonel Franklin A. Haskell, 1854 (author of the illustrious narrative of the Battle of Gettysburg), killed in combat shortly before his promotion to brigadier general; nor George W. Brown, 1831, Mayor of Baltimore, who escorted the harassed Sixth Massachusetts Regiment through his city armed only with an umbrella; nor John Hutchinson, 1853, expelled from the first legislature of Kansas and twice arrested because of his antislavery views.

In 1863 the conference of Congregational Churches in Merrimack County asked the Trustees that Dr. Lord, however great his services had been to Dartmouth, be removed from the presidency. Although their views about slavery strongly coincided with those of the ministers, the Trustees were unwilling to request the resignation of so true a servant of the College. They did, however, adopt resolutions in support of the war and against the institution of slavery. After presenting a

forthright memorial in which he declared he felt no obligation "to surrender my moral and constitutional right and Christian liberty . . . ,
nor to submit to any censure nor consent to any condition such as are
implied in the aforesaid action of the Board," Dr. Lord tendered his
resignation and ended his stewardship of three-and-a-half decades.

The circumstances of his retirement were regretful but amicable.
At the Commencement of 1864 the Trustees awarded him an honorary
degree — the degree that Abraham Lincoln might otherwise have received. At the previous Commencement Dr. Lord had cast the deciding
vote against such an award to the Great Emancipator. With Dr. Lord
himself receiving a degree at the Commencement of 1864 the Trustees
could not very well award one to President Lincoln on the same occasion, and the next year the President was dead.

Held by a less respected and beloved man Nathan Lord's views on
slavery would have cast a shadow over the remainder of his life. Not so
with the ex-President, who held no bitterness against anyone, and

[77]

against whom no rancor remained after the scars of the War had healed. He had educated eight boys among his ten children at Dartmouth and met their expenses out of a salary never more than $1,600 a year. Since he had nothing when he resigned, his friends presented him with a purse in the form of an annuity which supported him comfortably in a house at the north end of the Green until he died at the age of seventy-seven.

> . . . most people of sense appear to be well satisfied that there is a propriety in not herding young men and women together in our great public institutions of learning. – *The Dartmouth*, 1879.

A graduate of the Class of 1874 recalled the seventh President of Dartmouth as "a pen-and-ink portrait in black and white" — an apt portrayal of all Dartmouth's preacher-presidents, but one that particularly suited Asa Dodge Smith with his well-brushed silk hat and long coat. "Even the shirt studs and cuff links attached to the immaculate linen were black, and his pale face and white hair were in striking contrast with his black coat," the graduate wrote. "In conversation he was somewhat formal, and at times his language was florid and flattering, which no doubt was due to his long pastorate in a metropolitan church, where a clergyman's influence and popularity are more or less dependent upon saying pleasant things to members of the congregation. He was, however, a man of strong sympathetic nature, whose great purpose in life was to make the world better and happier."

Another student, Francis E. Clark, 1873, founder of the Christian Endeavor Society, remembered "one of the warmest hearts that ever beat in a president's bosom" and an interview during which President Smith dropped to his knees and prayed that Clark might give his life to the ministry. His prayer answered, the President preached the sermon when Clark was ordained in Portland, Maine. Although Dr. Smith was said to display his large vocabulary through the use of words that to most of his listeners were unfamiliar, he was a compelling speaker out of the pulpit and in. No doubt his twenty-nine year friendship with men of wealth in his New York congregation was not the least of the reasons that recommended him for the presidency, since the inflation of the Civil War had made even more acute the College's chronic shortage of capital.

Dr. Smith was still an erect and vigorous figure when at the age of fifty-nine he began his administration of thirteen years. Of a $100,000 fund-raising goal established by the Trustees the President himself obtained over $28,000 shortly after taking office. Another $20,000 re-

sulted from a general subscription over the course of four years. Despite the failure of a later campaign to raise $200,000, the number of scholarships was increased from 42 to 103 and several significant bequests were received. Richard Fletcher of Boston left $100,000 and Tappan Wentworth, a Lowell, Massachusetts, lawyer, a large bequest appraised at $276,000, with the stipulation that it not be used until it reached half a million through appreciation. Although the endowment was doubled and tuition from a somewhat larger enrollment was raised from $51 to $90, operating losses of $90,000 were added to the debt of the College during Dr. Smith's administration.

Growth, or lack of it, was not however to be judged entirely by profit and loss statements and balance sheets, particularly if the College's associated schools are considered. After falling off during the

Civil War, attendance at the Medical School recovered and surpassed its former levels to reach 100 in 1879. However far its scientific program seemed to diverge from that of the classical curriculum, the Chandler School was gaining in endowment and enrollment. Similarly divergent in purpose was the Agricultural School, founded in 1866 as the result of the Morrill Land Grant Act assigning public lands for the support of such schools in each state. Although Dartmouth, in the words of Richardson, was still not "in good odor" with the New Hampshire authorities owing to the bitter vestiges of the College Case and the position Dr. Lord had taken during the Civil War, the state decided to establish its agricultural school in Hanover as an adjunct of the College (albeit with a separate board of trustees). The new establishment opened in 1868. Two years later the community was treated to the rare spectacle of the arrival on a special train of the Governor and most of the legislature for the laying of the cornerstone of a new and separate building. Upon its completion Victorian Culver Hall was considered the most imposing edifice in New Hampshire. Although its mansard roof was destined to shelter the Agricultural College for only a little more than two decades, no one then doubted that the new tenant would remain permanently.

> In these latter days there has developed a theory called evolution. I have thoroughly and critically examined this theory and find it is absolutely false. – Samuel Colcord Bartlett, 1895.

The opening of Thayer School in 1871 was a permanent milestone of the Smith administration. As superintendent and architect of West Point from 1817 to 1833 and builder during three decades of the fortifications in Boston Harbor, General Sylvanus Thayer, 1807, provided leadership as well as an endowment of $70,000 for his engineering school in Hanover.

Not the least development of the Smith administration was the growth of regional alumni associations in Boston, New York, Washington, Chicago, Missouri, Cincinnati, Lowell, and Manchester, and along with it alumni determination to exert influence in the immediate affairs of the College. During these years there seems to have been little interest either on the part of alumni, administration, or students in coeducation. A trustee committee appointed to weigh the matter never reported nor, so far as is known, even convened.

The most memorable event testifying to the College's sheer ability to endure was the observance in 1869 of the one-hundredth anniversary of the granting of its charter. All divisive influences of the past vanished in the triumphant gathering of the far-flung clan of Dartmouth at Commencement on the twenty-first of July. Inside Yale's graciously loaned tent, 205 by 85 feet and capable of holding an immense throng, a great stage was covered with flags and bunting. An even larger temporary wooden building on the northeast side of the Green was fitted up as a restaurant with enough tables to seat 1,200 at one time. One hundred army tents, loaned by the state, served as dormitories east of Dartmouth Hall.

The morning of the twenty-first dawned clear. As early as nine o'clock a great concourse of people overflowed the town to witness a procession of

Undergraduates in the order of their classes, then the Germania Band, then the President of the College, the Governor of the State and his Aides, the Honorable Board of Trustees, the Faculty and Executive Officers of the College, the Chief Justice of the United States, the Judges of the Supreme Court of New Hampshire and other States, Senators and Representatives in Congress, the Army and Navy, Invited Guests of the College and distinguished Strangers, the Alumni in order of the Classes, beginning with the Class of 1804, and ending with the Class of 1868.

Passing in front of the church and the white houses north of the Green where ailing ex-President Lord sat at his window, all of the marchers removed their hats in respect for the man under whom thirty-five classes had received their degrees. The high point of the ceremonies was the oratory in the mammoth tent on the afternoon of the twenty-second. The first address, that of United States Chief Justice Salmon P. Chase, Dartmouth, 1826, was followed by the reading of a poem by the vice-president of the Association of Alumni. At this point, in the testimony of William H. Duncan of the Class of 1830, official recorder of the ceremonies, a rumbling of thunder was heard.

Then came a few scattering drops of water pattering upon the roof of the tent, but soon the winds blew, and the rain descended and fell upon the roof, as if the very windows of heaven had been opened. There followed such a scene as no tongue, nor pen, nor pencil can describe. . . . Judge Barrett with the true pluck of an ETHAN ALLEN stood by his colors and the more the wind blew and the storm raged, the louder he read his poetry. He seemed to read as if there were something in the poetry to halt the wind and still the raging of the tempest. But the elements were too much. . . . He was obliged

[81]

to cease, and with a slouched hat and dripping gown fled the stage, and when you looked for him, he was not to be found. . . .

But he was not alone in his misery. The manly and stately form of the Chief Justice, the President of the College, Reverend Doctors of Divinity, were all in the same condition — they all stood drenched and dripping, like fountains in the rain. Even General SHERMAN had to succumb, once in his life, and seek the protection of an umbrella. Some huddled under umbrellas, some held benches over their heads, and some crept beneath the platform.

But what can we say of the ladies? They entered the tent that afternoon arrayed as beautifully as the lilies of the field. . . . They entered rejoicing in their taste and beauty, — they left like dripping Naiads . . . their faces limp and soiled, their coiffeurs crushed — their trimmings departed — their rich silks stained and ruined. . . . The storm passed over and Judge BARRETT came forward and finished reading the poem.

Thus well or disastrously, depending upon the point of view of the legion of spectators, did the storm of 1869 earn among all Commencement thunderstorms past and present a reputation as historic as the proceedings themselves.

There was no silver lining in the cloud that darkened the last years of the administration of Asa Dodge Smith. Upon the death of Daniel Blaisdell, for forty years treasurer of the College and of the Dartmouth Savings Bank, it was discovered that the financial affairs of the College had been deplorably managed, and that there was a shortage of

$40,000. Through the heirs of Blaisdell about half of the loss was recovered. So disheartening were these circumstances and a sudden decline in the enrollment in the fall of 1876 that the President fell ill and lived less than eight months after his resignation in December.

Samuel Colcord Bartlett, the eighth President in the Wheelock Succession, was a native of New Hampshire, a graduate of the College and a Congregational minister. Unlike Dr. Smith he was a student; he had taught philosophy and Biblical literature for many years in Chicago. He had either been unrealistic or badly advised in his expectation that he would not become enveloped in fund-raising and administrative work. Sharply awakened to these priorities immediately after his inauguration in 1877, he did quite well by them in an otherwise cyclonic administration of fifteen years. He ministered to the College's chronic operating deficits and, with the help of windfall bequests, increased the endowment to over a million dollars. He built a Romanesque chapel named for its donor, Edward Rollins (who, sadly, died in Hanover shortly after the dedication in 1885). He constructed a 130,000-volume library building, Wilson Hall. Following the destruction of the Dartmouth Hotel in the great Main Street fire of 1887 he built the Wheelock House, whose construction and planning so strongly reflected a limited budget that it had almost immediately to be made over. It was nevertheless the College's own hotel and it stands today as part of the Hanover Inn. He acquired several other buildings, including the Professor Noyes dwelling as a residence for himself and his successors. He built a baseball cage and for an athletic field secured thirty acres of land that the Agricultural College had been using as an experimental farm. He landscaped the College Park and created the outdoor amphitheater known as the Bema, in which generations of seniors received their degrees. As a symbol to replace the Old Pine, attacked by lightning in 1887 and by a windstorm five years later, he arranged that successive classes build portions of a medieval tower on Observatory Hill, which they did to the last course of stone in 1895. Besides these contributions he was responsible for progressive innovations within the curriculum, for the raising of faculty salaries, and the addition of thirty scholarships.

His quick and clever mind was acknowledged by all: his accomplishments were plainly to be seen, and his rapier tongue plainly to be heard. His sorties against the faculty, the officers of the associated schools and the alumni — and theirs against him — seemed likely to annihilate the College. When, in an open faculty meeting, a reticent professor asked for further information on a subject under discussion, the President snapped: "I am surprised you do not understand the matter. I thought I had explained it two or three times so that a person of ordinary ability or ordinary comprehension might understand it." Thus he gained the hostility of two-thirds of the faculty and much of the town. The ultimate reaction of the dissident professors was a carefully devised plan which they hoped would force the President out of office. He retaliated by attempting to persuade the Board of Trustees to fire them. Caught in the middle, as in John Wheelock's day, they tabled the matter, thus preparing the battleground for new skirmishes. So tense was the atmosphere in 1890 that the Governor wrote: "There is always something in Hanover to keep us in a flurry, and the slightest thing stirs the whole college."

The sallies of the President against the entrance requirements of Chandler School and its financial dependence upon the College were really caused, its defenders said, by his contempt for scientific education. He forbade the professors of the College to teach in Chandler over fifty hours each year, stipulating that half of their Chandler income would go to the College treasury. This further embittered the classical faculty and weakened Chandler School, which depended upon the teaching staff of the College. The dispute brought to the hands of the Trustees a memorial from over one hundred graduates of Chandler protesting the President's plan for lowering the entrance requirements, obviously with an eye to making its whole program seem ridiculous.

The Medical School seems to have escaped the presidential stiletto, but the Agricultural College shared the plight of Chandler. The President chose Commencement as an occasion to extol the College curriculum and demean that of the Agricultural School as being suited for "highway surveyors, selectmen and, perhaps, members of the legislature." The enraged faculty and students of the school survived this affront but their relationship with the College became markedly strained and tentative. From time to time overtures were made toward removal of the school from Hanover. In 1890 Benjamin Thompson left it $400,000 with the stipulation that it be removed to Durham. The legislature accepted both the bequest and the condition, and in 1892 the Agricultural School departed for Durham, where it has evolved into the University of New Hampshire.

The alumni of Dartmouth have always been noted for their proprietary concern for the College and for their lack of reticence in making their criticisms known, but it is doubtful that matters ever again reach such an impasse that the President actually stands trial for alleged malfeasance in office. That is what happened in the Bartlett regime.

As early as 1881 the Trustees had received from thirty-one members of the New York alumni association a communication expressing their fear that the rumored activities of the President would impair the growth of the College and alienate the alumni. That same year, with their diplomas safely in hand, forty-four of the sixty-one members of the graduating class called for Dr. Bartlett's removal from office. The newspapers of course diligently reported every detail of what promised to be still another galvanic controversy at Dartmouth. In the vanguard of the editorial critics of Dr. Bartlett was Charles R. Miller of the Class of 1872, who had just become editor of *The New York Times*.

As the result of mounting pressure, the Trustees appointed an investigative committee to consider allegations that the President was habitually insolent, discourteous and dictatorial; that he had stifled all free and independent discussion of College matters; that he had ignored and usurped the functions of faculties of various departments; that he had imperiled the influence of the faculty with the students and endeavored to bring certain members into disgrace in the eyes of the students and the public; that he had exerted his influence to impair and diminish the prosperity of the different departments of the College; that in his public official relations he had used language to humiliate and disgrace the students; that he had so far lost the confidence of the members of the faculty that out of a total membership of twenty-three, sixteen openly expressed their belief that his resignation should be secured. In June the "trial" (it was not an official court but resembled one in every aspect) began with three lawyers including the U. S. District Attorney of New York and the leader of the bar of that state representing the irate alumni, and with two prominent Northcountry advocates defending Dr. Bartlett. The President seems to have conducted himself with his usual incisiveness and even with enthusiasm. Some of his methods in administration may have been heavy-handed; there had been some honest errors in judgment, but reports that the faculty was against him were exaggerated. In the face of his artful self-defense the charges rather melted away. In its final report to the Trustees the investigating committee pointed to the manifest improvements during the Bartlett regime and called for peace. The editors of the student yearbook declared in 1883:

Charges of the gravest character have been made against our president; and, while we would not pass judgment upon them, we deplore the fact that the

trustees have deemed it best to do likewise and rendered a verdict like that of the Irish jury who said: "We find the accused not guilty, but advise him not to do it any more."

Whatever the truth of the other charges against Dr. Bartlett, it is clear that he was no diplomat in a position that called for massive diplomacy. Yet for the very reason that he could always be counted on to go them one better, many of the students regarded him with awe and respect. There is the historic anecdote about a donkey being led by seniors to the platform in the old Dartmouth Hall chapel prior to rhetorical exercises. Upon his arrival Dr. Bartlett regarded the donkey amicably, then taking the list of speakers announced: "As I call the names you may come up and stand beside your brother and declaim." (In a second version the President is said to have remarked calmly:

[86]

"Excuse me, gentlemen, I did not know you were holding a class meeting," and departed.) On another occasion, when the students placed an outhouse at the chapel entrance, Dr. Bartlett reproved them for having moved their "own ancestral halls" to College property.

In the view of William H. Ham, 1897, the President belonged in the front rank of that procession of "characters" which the town of Hanover and the Dartmouth faculty have so long and liberally supplied.

I remember him with his erect posture, wearing a Prince Albert coat and white tie and high silk hat, walking with a gold-headed cane past the campus, his personal Negro servant rolling his bicycle which he recently had learned to ride. When they arrived at the new athletic field, he passed his cane to his servant and mounted the bicycle and rode around the quarter-mile cinder track, and then he walked back again with the same dignity, the servant rolling the wheel.

We had him in a course known as natural theology which we called "godology," in which he taught us by lecture, Genesis in the raw. He informed us that God made the earth and the firmament in six days, just like our days — 24 hours long, 60 minutes to the hour, 60 seconds to the minute, and God rested on the seventh day. To me the picture was God sitting on a rock all day long. Our class rustled a little and tapped with the feet slightly and the old man accepted our applause as our endorsement.

He went on with God's work after the serpent had gone into the garden, which pictured for us Eve unadorned standing there tempting Adam with an apple. That upset us. The class couldn't take that, we whistled and stamped and rose up and gave the College yell in the class, and the old man threw back his head and laughed with us, sitting there at the long table between two wood-burning stoves, his high hat on the table and his gold-headed cane across the top of his hat. . . .

President Bartlett resigned the Presidency in 1892 at the age of seventy-five but taught until his death six years later, in a mellow atmosphere that rather suffused the memory of past quarrels. Viewing the man in perspective his successor, William Jewett Tucker, wrote of Dr. Bartlett's zest and genius for work, his scholarly mind, his interest in the fine arts, his skill as a conversationalist, his personal warmth and optimism. Other contemporaries have said, however, that the College was never nearer dead than when Dr. Tucker took office; that while sister institutions were sharing with the empire builders the fruits of the industrial revolution, Dartmouth, with leadership less than inspired, had for four decades lived a life ingrown and parochial.

The Place

STEARNS MORSE

I

A more unpleasant spot on the Connecticut River . . . cannot be found than Hanover . . . a town if they had water to grind for the few poor Inhabitants who live there, they never did, and 'tis said by judicious men that for years to come they will not be able to raise their own bread.

Publicus to Governor John Wentworth, 1770

We have an austere climate. We are of a hyperborean race; vigorous, patient and happy. Our granite State, and her marble Sister on the other side of the river, are the cradle of a hardy and beneficent enterprise. Our institutions are nurses of a Caledonian independence. We are content with our position; proud of the northern Hive.

The Dartmouth. November, 1839

OF ALL the colleges established in the Colonies prior to the Revolution, Dartmouth alone was situated in the wilderness. This fact perhaps more than any other has given to the College its unique character: it is reflected in the somewhat grandiloquent, not to say a bit complacent, salutation with which *The Dartmouth* made its bow in 1839; in many subtle ways it is manifest in the middle of the twentieth century.

When Eleazar Wheelock made his memorable trek northward in 1770 he plunged into what was essentially a vast forest. Ten years before, the northernmost settlement was the famous Fort Number 4 at Charlestown. In the decade before that John Stark had penetrated as far as Baker's River in the Pemigewasset Valley; the Connecticut had been reached by various exploring parties at Piermont and Haverhill; Governor Benning Wentworth had made several grants of land and laid plans for taking possession of the "Rich Meadows of the Cohos"; but the hostility of the St. Francis Indians of Quebec and the vicissitudes of the French and Indian Wars had discouraged settlement.

In October, 1759, Rogers' Rangers, retreating precipitately from their raid on St. Francis, scattered down the valley of the Connecticut. Rogers and a ragged remnant finally reached Number 4. According to legend, ghosts of some of the Rangers haunted the slopes of the Presidential Range for years. The rigors and perils of this famous adventure give an inkling of the rigors and perils the intrepid Connecticut clergyman faced. The "choice white pine" of the valley were giant trees stretching two hundred feet or more into the sky, the first hundred feet without a branch, twenty to forty inches in diameter. Belknap, the historian of early New Hampshire, comments on the gloomy appearance of the forest of which the silences were broken only by the cries of the wild beasts.

If the gloomy forest was forbidding, what of the climate? Belknap described the air of New Hampshire as "generally pure and salubrious." What *The Dartmouth* called its austerity was due in Belknap's opinion to the immense wilderness and the snow-covered mountains, which give a "keenness to the air, as a cake of ice to a quantity of liquor in which it floats." Vermonters put it succinctly: we have two seasons, winter and August. Robert Frost sums it up:

> You know how it is with an April day
> When the sun is out and the wind is still,
> You're one month on in the middle of May.
> But if you so much as dare to speak,
> A cloud comes over the sunlit arch,
> A wind comes off a frozen peak,
> And you're two months back in the middle of March.

Undaunted as he was by the wilderness and the austere climate one suspects that Eleazar Wheelock wanted solitude. He was later to describe the solitude of this wilderness as "most favorable and friendly to the studies of the youth . . . free from a thousand snares, temptations, and divertisements which were and would have been unavoidable if this seminary had continued where it was, or been fixed in any populous town in the land." Indeed the nearest house in New Hampshire was two miles to the north of the Hanover Plain, "through one continued and dreary wood." Though there were as yet no populous towns in the valley, he could have found company if he had wanted it. By 1761 the French

[89]

and Indian Wars were over at last: Wolfe, dying on the Plains of Abraham, had conquered Canada for the British; Robert Rogers had removed the threat of raids by the St. Francis Indians. Governor Benning Wentworth had granted township after township in the name of George III in the Connecticut Valley, the "Garden of New England," always reserving lots for himself and mast pines for the Royal Navy. Orford along the river had been settled; Haverhill and Newbury, Vermont, at the Ox-Bow had become shopping centers for the towns north and south.

Nor was Wheelock the first settler in the town of Hanover. Edmund Freeman's log cabin on the river not far from the Lyme town line was the first house built in the township. He later moved to Lebanon, but not before he had built a house at Hanover Center. He and his brothers, settling there, may properly be called the first family of Hanover. Jonathan Freeman, notably, made the first survey of the town and planned the village with its Green, held a succession of town and state offices, and was at the turn of the century a member of the national House of Representatives. Some have regretted that the College was not located at Hanover Center, six hundred feet or so higher than the Hanover Plain, with its Parade Ground and Church facing Moose Mountain and its long view down the valley with hill after hill rising to Ascutney in the distance. Moreover, on the slopes of Moose Mountain rises Mink

Brook, flowing through the town for eight or ten miles, plunging in the last four miles of its course four hundred feet before its placid debouchment into the Connecticut river. This fall of water was the source of Hanover's early industries; as a recent historian has said, if Dartmouth College made Hanover, Mink Brook made Dartmouth College: it was Wheelock's first sawmill on its banks which sawed out the boards for the first college buildings.

In August, 1774, when Jeremy Belknap attended the fourth Commencement, he found that surprising improvements had been made in a few years. About a mile from the College, he recorded in his diary, were a sawmill and a grist mill with a one-room house in which six scholars lived and operated the mill "to the halves." "Several tradesmen and taverners are settled round the College in good buildings, — which gives the place the appearance of a village." He supped and lodged at the President's house, which had just been built on the rise where Reed Hall now stands.

Most of the buildings in the year of Belknap's visit were still of logs, with fireplaces six to eight feet wide for heat. Of the two taverns, one was good and one was bad. The good tavern had been built by Aaron Storrs on the southwest corner of Main and Wheelock Streets (adjacent to the place where in the twentieth century another Storrs was to run a bookstore and paper stand). This frame building, built in 1771, two years before the President's mansion, was moved in 1823 and dignified with columns nearly a hundred years later. As the oldest house in Hanover it now contains the Dekes. The bad tavern, on a College Street site between the Steele Chemistry building and Wheeler Hall (apparently as far as possible from the President's house and still near enough to the center of town for its custom), was operated by John Payne. Stumps of the great pines were still scattered on the Common and the lofty tops of the forest surrounding the little settlement were a constant reminder of the wilderness. Yet civilization was slowly getting the upper hand: already the townspeople were sensitive about the hogs running loose on the Common and were passing regulations to control them.

In 1796 Timothy Dwight recorded that the village contained perhaps forty houses, though several of them were "ragged and ruinous." The clearing of the lands in the vicinity had been largely accomplished so that no longer were the townspeople afflicted with clouds of smoke by day and by night with the awesome fires of burning wood on the high hills. Passable roads now led out of town, north, east, and south.

Norwich on the opposite side of the Connecticut could be reached by a ferry and in 1796 the first bridge was built, though it lasted only seven years.

Business as well as the College was humming: the hatters, potters, weavers, blacksmiths, tinsmiths, storekeepers, and carpenters found plenty to do. There were no architects, but though some of the houses may have seemed down at the heel, the yeoman carpenters who built them were not without an aesthetic sense. Dartmouth Hall, begun in 1784, had been completed — of wood, with the same Greek proportions though slightly narrower than its twentieth-century successor in painted brick. In addition to the Storrs Tavern and the President's House, a stately house had been built at the southeast corner of the Green, later the site of Wilson Hall. Sylvanus Ripley had built the handsome houses subsequently known as the Webster Cottage on Main Street and the Choate House on the north side of the Green. The names derived from their later occupancy by Daniel Webster and Rufus Choate as undergraduates. Adjoining Choate House on the northwest corner of the Green was the White Church, built in 1795 as the center of worship for a godly community. But by mid-twentieth century only one of the village's gracious eighteenth-century structures still survived on its original site.

Two decades after Wheelock's arrival Hanover had come of age. At his death in 1779 Hanover was temporarily Dresden. The Dresden Press, in its brief career near the southwest corner of the Green, had printed the first Dartmouth College catalogue and the *Dresden Mercury,* the first paper in the Upper Valley. Both College and town, like lusty young attaining their majority, were feeling their oats. Hanover was in the forefront of the movement for independence of the towns on both sides of the river. And in June, 1795, when the legislature met in Hanover, it was actually the temporary capital of New Hampshire. By this time, too, a weekly newspaper had been established: the first issue of the *Eagle* or *Dartmouth Centinel* was printed at Josiah Dunham's printing office "at the North-west Corner of College-Square," on July 22, 1793. The *Eagle* lasted six years, being succeeded by the *Dartmouth Gazette* (1799-1820) which printed in a black-bordered issue of December 30, 1799, the news of Washington's death two weeks earlier.

Hanover had by this time become what the first historian of New Hampshire called "a happy society": a town consisting of a due mixture of hills, valleys, and streams; the land well fenced and cultivated; the roads and bridges in good repair; a decent inn; the inhabitants mostly husbandmen; their wives and daughters domestic manufacturers; a suitable proportion of handicraft workmen and two or three traders; a physician and lawyer, each of whom should have a farm for his support; a clergyman of any denomination which should be agreeable to the majority; a schoolmaster, a social library, a club of sensible men; a musical society. "No intriguing politician, horse jockey, gambler or sot; but all such characters treated with contempt."

2

For the next hundred years Hanover remained a happy rural society, gradually growing in grace, the angularities of its Calvinistic origins softened by nature and time, its isolation slowly yielding to increasing communication with the outside world. Until after the Civil War, River Street (later West Wheelock) was an ugly scar leading to Ledyard bridge, built shortly before that conflict; its story-and-a-half houses and gaunt telegraph poles unrelieved by shade except for a scraggly elm tree half way down the hill. South Main Street leading to Mink Brook was little better, except for a few scattered pines and a few elms at the top of the hill. The majestic pines of the early years had disappeared leaving a few descendants in the College Park and the Cemetery, and a few stumps on the Green as late as 1830. Each class before 1820 had been expected to pull one stump. About 1830, Professor Charles J. Lyon has recorded, the citizens began to set out elms and some maples. In the next decade the Rev. John Richards, pastor of the College Church, planted elms on Main, Wentworth, and College Streets. In the eighteen sixties elms were set out on East Wheelock Street opposite the field where later the Alumni Gymnasium was erected; and in the early seventies forty elms were planted on West Wheelock Street. In later years the Village Improvement Society carried on the work of making the town what Professor Lyon has aptly called "The College of a Thousand Elms."

By mid-century, too, the Cohos Country had become less forbidding. In 1808 Alexander Wilson, the ornithologist, had come across country from Portland "among dreary savage glens, and mountains covered with pines and hemlocks, amid whose black and half-burnt trunks the everlasting rocks and stones, that cover this country, 'grinned horribly.'" By a generation later, however, the scenic and romantic aspects of the mountains had been discovered: in the July, 1840, issue of *The Dartmouth* a poet celebrated *The Old Man of the Mountains* —

> Among the hills of northern clime
> Where Alps on Alps contending rise,
> An aged sire, as old as time
> Stands looking eastward to the skies.

For stage routes had opened up the North Country.

In 1826 Lewis Downing established his coach factory in Concord, N. H., and in the next two decades Concord Coaches became famous all over the world. It was now possible to go comfortably by coach from Hanover to Concord and Boston, to Portsmouth, to Haverhill and Lancaster, to Burlington and other points in Vermont, as well as up and down the river. But the railroads sounded the death knell of the Concord Coach: by 1850 the Northern Railroad from Concord to White River Junction; the Concord and Montreal, from Concord to Woodsville; and the Connecticut and Passumpsic Rivers Railroad from White River Junction to Wells River were offering transportation to the citizens of the North Country. The coming of the railroads also dashed the hopes of Luther Wood for his Greek Revival hostelry, with its cut stone walls, its wooden columns and its third floor ballroom, which he had constructed in 1832 north of Hanover on the River Road, then the Boston-Montreal post road. By the late decades of the nineteenth century it had become the Haunted House; in the early years of the twentieth a favorite scene for fraternity initiations; in the 1920's and 1930's it succumbed to vandalism. Nor have the railroads withstood the ravages of time and the advance of progress: on December 1, 1959, the station at Lewiston across the river from Hanover was closed; the coaches and buggies in the service of the College community which in the middle of the nineteenth century clustered there at train time are one with Nineveh and Tyre.

As the College thrived and as the controversy with the University was resolved, Town began to disentangle itself from Gown. In 1820 Richard Lang moved his prosperous general store from the site of Webster Hall to a location north of his substantial house, built in 1795 on the later site of College Hall. The vacated store became a bookstore and a printing office and later a rooming house for students until it was moved away in 1865. Next to it, on Wentworth Street, Mrs. Julia Sherman kept a girls' school before the Civil War: the sight of the girls marching with their towels to a bath house south of the Green was cause for levity to the Dartmouth students. On the hill east of the Green President John Wheelock had owned a rambling house which he willed to "Dartmouth University" with a remainder to Princeton College. The house was called "Princeton House" for this reason and for a time "The Acropolis," by reason of its site. But the house burned in 1830 and the lot came into the possession of the College in 1847.

The archaeology of Hanover has to be horizontal rather than vertical; the movement of trade and craft from north of the Green had received great impetus from the building of the Dartmouth Hotel in 1813 at the southwest corner of the Green and later the four-story brick Tontine Building still farther south. But for some decades the various business activities of the Village were for the most part carried on in the wooden gabled buildings of various sizes that lined both sides of Main Street.

Though an act forbidding hogs and cattle to roam the streets was accepted by the town only in 1852, by 1836 the Green was finally plowed, leveled, and enclosed with a neat rail fence, and had begun to attain the simple dignity that was to be its characteristic for the rest of the century. Dartmouth Row presented approximately its present appearance. The Church and the row of white houses north of the Green greeted the visitor as he came up Main Street from the south; white houses likewise lined the west side of the Green. The town was still compact: to the south and west houses straggled to Mink Brook and the Connecticut; to the east beyond Dartmouth Row and to the north beyond the Medical School building, standing four-square on the hilltop, was farming country.

By mid-century Hanover had long ceased to be a frontier town and its politics had lost some of the fervor of the Revolutionary period. In the seventeen-seventies and early eighties its political temper was aptly indicated by the popularity of a pamphlet entitled, "The People the Best Governors." The constitution of New Hampshire, adopted in 1784, carried a provision that "no president, professor, or instructor in any college should have a seat in either House of the Legislature or in the Council" — a provision reflecting the distaste of the eastern section of the state for the agitation for independence of the Connecticut Valley towns and for the part the College was suspected of having played in this controversy.

But by 1800 Hanover had become an integral part of the state (though a suspicion of the College and its "radicalism" has lingered on in some quarters even to this day), and for the first quarter of the century Hanover, like the rest of the state, was predominantly Federalist.

In fact during the first half of the century it was more or less immune to both Jeffersonianism and Jacksonianism. It voted for John Quincy Adams and Henry Clay rather than for Jackson in the elections of 1828 and 1832; and though in the next decades it gave small majorities to the Democratic candidate for President in four elections, by 1856 it was safely Republican. During this period the abolition movement received strong support, but the generally tolerant attitude of the citizens in a time of heated controversy is indicated by the respect in which President Nathan Lord was held in spite of his pro-slavery beliefs. In religion, of course, though other denominations had churches in the town, the dominant church was the Congregational Church — the White Church at the head of the College Green.

> We can not get on with the man who trains himself to teach and not to search, or the man who spends his whole life in searching and none in teaching. – William Jewett Tucker, 1903.

3

After the Civil War a certain degree of sophistication entered the atmosphere of Hanover. *The Dartmouth* for November, 1867, contained an arraignment of the town's provincialism by a student contributor. Summer, he said, brought a few families to the hotel, "to mingle with the native aborigines." These visitors in turn brought new ideas and fashions for the ladies: their hair in rats, cats and mice, or a simple coil, their hats soupplates or turbans. One who had the misfortune to visit the town in winter, however, found that the citizens "trade, eat, sleep etc. for the benefit of the Institoot." There was never anything going on; everybody knew everybody else; the town was rife with rumor and gossip.

In the number for January, 1868, Kate Sanborn, Hanover's authoress, came to its defense. If the inhabitants *lived* for the College, she noted that they often found it difficult to sleep because of the noise made by three hundred young men. Perhaps the uncouthness she observed in these young men "from farm and workshop" might be softened, she thought, by the civilizing effect of the environment in which the professors' houses were always open.

When Edwin J. Bartlett (endeared to a later generation as "Bubby") arrived from Chicago as a freshman in 1868, he found the village still compact and primitive: West Wheelock Street, with its gully at the bottom, still without trees; no college buildings north of Wentworth Street; no houses on Park Street. In the spring the streets were seas of mud; rubber boots were the appropriate footwear. For their water the house-holders relied on cisterns to catch rain, and on springs and wells. A spring on a hill toward Lebanon supplied water through a mile-and-a-half lead pipe to several families, who were limited to forty gallons a day. One house boasted a force pump and a bathroom, which were dubious luxuries. Though some houses had furnaces, most of them were heated by stoves. In winter one saw ox teams with four-foot rock maple wood on sleds drawn up before the hotel.

Yet when Robert Fletcher arrived in town from West Point two years later to begin his fifty-year career in the Thayer School, he found much to entertain him. Residing in rooms, along with tutors Emerson and Lord, in the house of Professor John Proctor on the west side of the Green, he attended sociables and reading parties at Professor Charles Young's; played croquet; went on picnics to Enfield with Mr. Huntington, the banker and treasurer of the College, and his family; and in 1871 became engaged to the banker's daughter Ellen.

After their marriage they moved into a house on College Street where Professor Fletcher stoked six fires to keep warm: first the kitchen fire to be tended; then a fire to be started in the wood stove in the dining-room; coal fires to be tended in hall and sitting-room. Kindling to be cut; wood to be brought in from the shed, coal from the cellar. Methodical, as befitted an engineer, he arose at six and retired at nine-thirty. Before breakfast and prayers at seven, he attended to his toilet and the household chores, followed by half an hour of study; after breakfast, chapel and recitations till nine-thirty; then half an hour of exercise, "sanitary and recreative"; recitations, correspondence, and study till the twelve-thirty dinner; in the afternoon, the newspapers, more recitations and study, broken by a half hour of exercise; supper and recreation from six to seven, followed by another period of study, with three-quarters of an hour before bedtime devoted to relaxation and home duties. Though Professor Fletcher was doubtless a more systematic person than the average citizen, his day was probably not too unlike the normal Hanover routine during the eighteen seventies and eighties.

His diary also gives us a picture of the social life of the town. The Fletchers went on picnics and expeditions; there were mountain climbing, coaching, sugaring off in the spring. They gave evening parties at least once a year, with ice cream and cake for fifty to a hundred people. And there were the lecturers; the list from 1871 to 1900 is imposing: James T. Fields (thrice); Wendell Phillips (twice); John T. Gough; Whitelaw Reid; Matthew Arnold; C. D. Warner; Julian Hawthorne; Joaquin Miller; Josh Billings; Lew Wallace; T. W. Higginson; E. E. Hale; George Kennan (on his Siberian adventure) and numerous political figures.

For the less orthodox there were also theatrical entertainments at Kibling's Opera House, on the corner of College and Lebanon Streets. In 1879 Mrs. Fletcher went to a performance of *Pinafore* given there by the students, though her husband could not think it consistent with Christian profession to attend.

When Walt Whitman visited Hanover in June, 1872, he found the village a welcome change from Washington. If the seniors had hoped to shock faculty and townspeople by inviting so disreputable a figure to read a poem at the Commencement season, they were disappointed. With his long gray-white hair and tawny beard, his Byronic collar exposing his bare breast, he read *Like a Strong Bird on Pinions Free*, au-

[99]

dible only to those in the front pews. To an elderly alumnus it seemed: "Words, words, nothing but words." The poet was lodged in the house of the pastor next to the White Church, where the pastor's wife found him to be a considerate guest. Whitman looked out of his bedroom window and wrote to his friend Pete Doyle, the horse-car driver:

It is a curious scene, here, as I write, a beautiful old New England village, 150 years old, large houses and gardens, great elms, plenty of hills — every thing comfortable, but very Yankee — *not an African to be seen all day* — not a grain of dust — nor a car to be seen or heard — green grass everywhere — no smell of coal tar. . . . As I write a party are playing base ball on a large green in front of the house — the weather suits me first rate — cloudy but no rain.

Indeed the town was very colorful with its Yankee characters — one of them on its principal corner was Hod Frary, who became proprietor of the Dartmouth Hotel in 1857. By the sixties this hostelry had become a three-story brick edifice, with pitched roof and dormers above, and a handsome Greek portico fronting Main Street. Its lack of plumbing was succinctly emphasized by Mrs. Frary, a character in her own right, in her reply to a guest: "You want a bath? Didn't you see the river when you came up from the depot?" Frary had formerly been a shoemaker and had kept a copy of Shakespeare's plays before him on his bench; he used to discuss them with young Oliver Wendell Holmes of the Medical School. As an innkeeper he haggled for meat with the butcher at the door of the hotel, trimmed the oil lamps himself, carved the meats in the dining-room in full view of the guests, wiping the carving knife on the same trouser leg he used for lamp-black residue.

If the exclusive, or chief product of the colleges was the scholar, we should soon cease to have scholarship. We should have in its place pedantry. – William Jewett Tucker, 1905.

Two of the town's other characters were Ira Allen and Jason Dudley, both survivals of the stagecoach era. With the arrival of the railroads Allen, an expert driver on the turnpikes, established a livery business. In the year when the town was "redding up" for the College's Centennial he built a stable just off Main Street. He was the first to operate the stage from the Lewiston station to the village, stopping the coach on the hither side of the bridge to collect fares so that students would not jump off before it reached the hotel without paying. Rather podgy, with a baked-apple face, addicted to drink and peppery language, he was a fast driver, drunk or sober. Jason Dudley, his successor on the Hanover-Lewiston station route, had also been a stage driver before the railroad came. He delivered express about the village and achieved official status as driver of the town hearse. Mildred Crosby, belle of the village in the 1880's, recalled in later years with her inimitable twang Jason's lugubrious remarks to a Mrs. Edwards: "Well, Mis' Edwards, this ain't no sardine packin' factory and while I am head of this cemetery heads will match heads or the old woman won't be planted." To Mildred herself, who apparently was too tall to be buried in the family lot without her feet being in the cemetery path, he remarked ruefully: "We was lottin' on your being short like your mother, but you got one of those figgers that nothin' stops your waist but your heels." And once Mildred, riding with him in a buggy, protested at his flicking the horse with his whip: "Jason, if your horse acts like this, how can you trust him to draw the hearse?" Jason's reply: "Don't you suppose this old horse knows the difference between Mildred Crosby and a corpse?"

Aside from the dubious resource of occasional theatrical divertissements, faculty families relied upon themselves for entertainment in the 1860's and 1870's; supper parties in the spacious houses, simple games, the writing of impromptu verses, music, charades, but no card playing or dancing.

Despite its pious origins, however, the village was not without a degree of ill repute in the late nineteenth century. An edifice on the corner of College and Lebanon Streets had had a respectable enough beginning, first as a Methodist Chapel, later as a home for the Episcopalians. In 1872 it became Kibling's Opera House, and after the destruction by fire of the Dartmouth Hotel in 1887, Mr. Kibling appropriated the name and advertised his rates as $1.25 a day, 35 cents for supper. Often the object of investigation by the town authorities, the proprietor at one time illegally operated a bar which opened after twelve midnight and closed at dawn. The Law and Order League made raids, one of which at least was successful, for in the cellar was found what was identified as "a full-sized barrel of rum and potent alcohol of the kind that burns cheerfully, mixes well with gums to make varnish, preserves dead anatomies by abstraction of water and kills bugs." Nevertheless the bar still flourished and the Law and Order League imported a "spotter" from Boston feebly disguised as a special student in botany — with doubtful results.

The professions were well represented in the Hanover community. From 1801 till his death in 1845 Mills Olcott lived in the house next to the White Church, later known as the Choate House in honor of his famous son-in-law. A brilliant lawyer and a man of means, he developed the White River Falls Co.; was president of the Grafton County Bank; attorney for the College during its time of troubles; treasurer from 1816 to 1822 and Trustee until his death. Prominent in politics — as an old-line Federalist he attended the Hartford Convention in 1814 — he was presiding officer of the town on such public occasions as the visit of President Monroe; and general benefactor and supporter of community enterprises. Handsome, portly, immaculately dressed, he gave dignity and distinction to the community.

Hanover had other lawyers, of course, though the legal center of the North Country, for the first half of the century, at least, was in Bath. But perhaps no town in the whole state surpassed it in the eminence of its physicians, drawn there in part of course by the presence of the Medical School. Dr. John Crane, Hanover's first physician, came before the establishment of the Medical School, as Eleazar Wheelock's personal physician in 1770. Soon thereafter he set up his practice in a house on the south side of the Green, outliving Wheelock by seven years and dying destitute.

Two other physicians, not connected with the Medical School, were Dr. Joseph Lewis and Dr. Laban Gates. Dr. Lewis came to Norwich from Connecticut in 1767, accompanied Arnold on the expedition to Quebec, spent the winter in Hanover, and later settled at the west end of the river ferry, which he operated, as well as a mill on Blood Brook.

He was a rough character, habitually clad in a dirty buckskin suit. An episode indicates a keen interest in his profession, although it scarcely met with popular approval. He procured the body of Cato, a deceased Negro, and boiled it in a kettle to obtain the skeleton, after having removed the skin, which he had tanned in Hanover and used for an instrument case.

Dr. Gates seems to have been equally eccentric. Coming to Hanover in 1774, he built in 1785 a house at the southeast corner of the Green on the later site of Wilson Hall. Here he lived until his death at eighty-three in 1836. In 1801 his wife Huldah having left his bed but not his board, he tried to divorce her; public opinion, however, frustrated this attempt and Huldah remained in his house, at least, until her death three years before his. His domestic difficulties, his controversy with Wheelock about his inoculation of two students for smallpox, and his wooden leg, which gave him a shuffling gait, constitute his place in history.

The fame of Dr. Nathan Smith is based on firmer ground. His founding of the then fourth medical school in the country in 1797 has already been noted. Sir William Osler thought Dr. Smith's "Practical Essay on

Typhoid Fever," written in 1824, should be handed to every young physician. Dr. William Welch, a generation later, said of him:

Famous in his day and generation, he is still more famous today, for he was far ahead of his times, and his reputation, unlike so many medical worthies of the past, has steadily increased, as the medical profession has slowly caught up with him.

His skill, judgment, and coolness as a physician and as a surgeon operating without the aid of anesthetics early made Hanover the medical center for the region roundabout. His portrait by S. F. B. Morse reveals his distinction and suggests those qualities of intelligence, perceptiveness, and kindliness which made him so generally beloved in his day and his memory so inspiring to the professors and students who have followed him.

Smith's immediate successors were Dr. Reuben D. Mussey and Dr. Daniel Oliver, who had practiced medicine together in Salem, Massachusetts. Dr. Oliver preferred study and teaching to practice and added to his duties at the Medical School a professorship of Intellectual Philosophy in the College. A teacher and practitioner of medicine, a strict vegetarian and an advocate of temperance, Dr. Mussey was also a lover of music and served for many years as President of the Handel Society. It was his account of the blind and dumb eight-year-old Laura Bridgman in Etna which attracted the attention of Samuel Gridley Howe who took her to the Perkins Institution in Boston.

A noble career never starts out of other men's opinions or convictions. – William Jewett Tucker, 1906.

A narrative of both Town and College might easily be woven from the histories of fifteen or twenty Hanover families over the two hundred years of its existence. Of the College, apart from Wheelock and his descendants, there were among others the Lords, the Browns, the Youngs, the Chases; though many members of these families were also important in town affairs. In the Town and on Main Street were the Freemans, the Camps, the Deweys, the Bridgmans, the Storrs family, the Rands, and the Tanzis. None were more distinguished or more eminent in town affairs than three families of physicians who lived and practiced in Hanover from the period before the Civil War to the middle of the twentieth century: the Crosbys, the Frosts, the Giles.

The father of the first generation of "the gifted Crosbys" to make their mark in Hanover was Dr. Asa Crosby, an able physician and surgeon of Gilmanton, N. H. Of his seventeen children, four girls and seven boys (five of whom attended Dartmouth College) lived to maturity. Of these Dr. Dixi Crosby began his practice as an apprentice to his father in Gilmanton even before he received his M.D. from Dartmouth in 1824. His resourcefulness in grave-snatching brought his family into disrepute in the region around Gilmanton, possibly the reason his father retired to Hanover in 1833.

Dr. Dixi Crosby succeeded Dr. Mussey as Professor of Surgery and Surgical Anatomy in 1838. Long before this he had made a reputation as an outstanding surgeon and a pioneer in many operating procedures. By virtue of his professional eminence and of his personality he was looked upon as the head of the medical profession in the state until his death in 1873. "Dr. Dixi's Hospital," which he operated on College Street opposite the Medical School in connection with his instruction, was the first in town. His Main Street residence, considerably enlarged by the College in later years, and embellished with columns and a pediment in front, became Crosby Hall. Its quiet dignity, when occupied by the Crosbys, symbolized the importance of the family in Hanover; and also the personality of Dr. Dixi himself, a robust, imposing man with a large nose and full beard, exuding cheerfulness and confidence, as he lectured to his students, as he traveled the countryside in sulky and sleigh.

In 1853 Dixi Crosby played a significant part in the development of the oil industry. His nephew had brought him a sample of a liquid he had collected on his farm in western Pennsylvania. Up to this point little use had been discovered for this substance. To be sure, Samuel Kier, an enterprising Pittsburgh druggist, had bottled the petroleum which was contaminating his father's salt wells, and marketed it as Kier's Rock Oil. His circular described its properties in a jingle:

> The healthful balm, from Nature's secret spring,
> The bloom of health, and life, to man will bring;
> As from her depths the magic liquid flows,
> To calm our sufferings, and assuage our woes.

Dr. Crosby and his neighbor, Oliver Payson Hubbard, Professor of Chemistry, examined the nephew's sample and suspected its value for other than medicinal purposes. When George Bissell, 1845, revisited Hanover and called on his former professor, Dr. Crosby gave him a bottle of the oil and told him that he and Professor Hubbard thought it might be valuable. Bissell returned to New York and with his law part-

[105]

ner organized "The Pennsylvania Rock Oil Company," capitalized at
$500,000, and secured two hundred acres of Venango County oil lands.
They sent several barrels of the crude oil to Professor Benjamin Silli-
man, the distinguished Yale chemist, who reported that the distilled
product furnished an illuminating material superior to anything in use.
These activities culminated in 1859 in the drilling by Colonel E. L.
Drake of the first oil well in the country at Titusville, Pennsylvania.
And in 1867, Bissell Hall, the gift of George H. Bissell, was opened as
Dartmouth's first gymnasium, at the south end of the Green.

Upon Dr. Crosby's retirement from the Medical School in 1870 his son Alpheus Benning Crosby succeeded him. He had practiced with his father since his graduation from the Medical School in 1856, except for fifteen months of service as a surgeon in the Civil War. Affectionately known as "Dr. Ben," he was a gifted lecturer, whose humor, mimicry, and wealth of anecdote made him greatly in demand as an after-dinner speaker, to say nothing of their professional use to him as a regular lecturer at four other medical schools besides Dartmouth. In the five years before his death in 1877 he practiced in New York City, returning each year to Hanover for the summer term of the Medical School. In his twenty-one years of practice he was reputed to have operated more times than any other surgeon in New England.

With the two Frost doctors one looks ahead to the Hanover of the twentieth century. Carleton Pennington Frost received his M.D. from Dartmouth in 1857. After service in the Civil War and practice in St. Johnsbury and Brattleboro, Vermont, he returned to Hanover as professor of the theory and practice of medicine in 1870 and became the first dean of the Medical School, introducing much-needed newer methods of teaching medicine. The citizens of Hanover, however, knew him as a skilled and sympathetic practioner, though his abhorrence of shams and a brusqueness of manner "sometimes disturbed those who preferred bread pills to plain truth." His service to his patients was tireless. He was especially loved by children: his visit to an anxious mother between one and two in the morning to say that he had not been able to sleep until he had seen her child once more after a ten o'clock call was characteristic of his devotion to his profession.

Described as looking "like Michelangelo's painting of God in the Sistine Chapel, with his flowing white beard and great dignity," public-spirited and progressive, he was a member of the first board of precinct commissioners and an Alumni Trustee of the College. Before his death in 1896 he had seen the introduction of electric lighting on the Hanover streets and the formation of the Hanover Water Works Company to supply water to the village, two improvements he had vigorously promoted.

Dr. Dixi's Hospital had been closed in 1870 upon his retirement. In 1885 Dr. Frost led in the formation of the "Dartmouth Hospital Association," which secured a tract of land north of the village and started a small building fund. It was at Dr. Frost's suggestion that Hiram Hitchcock, a wealthy summer resident and a good friend of his, decided to give the village a hospital in memory of his wife. In 1890 the foundations were laid and in 1893 the Mary Hitchcock Memorial Hospital was dedicated. Dr. Frost was active in the planning of the hospital and, with his son Gilman Frost and Dr. William T. Smith, was a member of the first hospital staff.

At his father's death Dr. Gilman Frost was thirty-two; he had been teaching in the Medical School for three years and was to teach there forty-four years more until his retirement in 1937. As a teacher he made an unforgettable impression on his students. A stethoscope hooked in his vest armhole, with his black string tie askew, his thin sharply chiseled face often gray with pain and weariness from his migraine headaches, he grilled and tantalized them with masterly Socratic questions calculated to make them think behind the textbook facts, and enlivened the lecture hour with homely observations.

Like his father he looked ahead to the modern age rather than backward to the past. Excited by Roentgen's discovery on December 28, 1895, of X-rays, in the following January, his wife and brother standing by, he performed an X-ray of young Eddie McCarthy's broken wrist in the College physics laboratory in Reed Hall, an event recorded by Edwin Frost in *Science* under date of February 4, 1896, and thus established as the first *medical* X-ray on record in the United States.

As a practitioner he inherited his father's gruff brusqueness. His keen blue-gray eyes penetrated at once the shamming of a malingerer or hypochondriac. His views of child-bearing and child-rearing were Spartan, yet he operated a dairy route, his young sons driving the horse, to insure that his young patients should have a pure and wholesome milk supply. And his gruffness was merely the facade of a sensitive nature with sympathy for genuine suffering.

Though he lived into the fifth decade of the twentieth century, recording in his fine handwriting on thousands of three by five cards the genealogy of Hanover, he was for the younger generation a living reminder of the more austere days of nineteenth-century Hanover. Tall, gaunt, careless of dress he drove his buggy or rode his bicycle through its streets. And before his death in 1942 he could view with quiet Yankee satisfaction the progress, under the Gile family and their associates, attained by the institutions with which his family had been so intimately connected.

*   *   *   *   *

But we must return briefly to Victorian Hanover with its still unpaved streets; its hitching-stones in front of the stores; its sputtering gaslights which *The Dartmouth* derided; its water from the springs and wells of the Aqueduct Company; its open and often smelly drains; its neat houses with plumbing primitive or non-existent. The Choate House, as befitted its august position at the head of the campus, had perhaps the most elegant privy, a nine-holer, six holes on one side, three more at right angles.

Late General Grant architecture was coming into its own. Mansard roofs, verandas and ornate fences set the tone. Doyen of the new style

The personal culture which marks the gentleman is based on self-control.
– William Jewett Tucker, 1907.

was the "palatial residence" constructed for Adna Balch at the intersection of Main and Wheelock streets, catty-corner from the hotel. It boasted what is reputed to be the first genuine bathroom in Hanover and was named "The Golden Corner." The Balch house was matched by a similar mansion at the north end of town, on the later site of Rus-

sell Sage Hall, which had been built by Professor Henry Fairbanks and on his retirement sold to Hiram Hitchcock, donor of the Mary Hitchcock Hospital. Here Hitchcock lived in elegant seclusion until his death in 1900, taking an active part in college and town affairs, and financing largely the renovation of the White Church by his friend Stanford White. Except for the Kibbie farmhouse, open country lay beyond the Mary Hitchcock Hospital.

The year 1887 might be taken as a harbinger of the changes which were to take place in the town in the new century. On January 4th of that year, about two o'clock of a still, twenty-degree-below zero morning, a fire broke out in the wooden part of the Dartmouth Hotel. By mid-morning, with the help of an engine and fire company sent by special train from Lebanon, the fire had been stayed but not before it had destroyed an adjoining house, the hotel itself, and all the structures south of the hotel on the east side of Main Street up to and including the rambling Tontine office block. To this event and the advent of President Tucker in 1893 may be ascribed much of the town's improvement. The Tontine was replaced by an adequate brick block, the Dartmouth Hotel by a new edifice built by the College and named "The Wheelock" which with alterations became the Hanover Inn in 1902. The year 1893 saw the installation of electric street lights, the building of the reservoir back of Balch Hill, and the removal of the fence around the Green, the last reminder of the days when cows as well as students roamed the campus. Adna Balch having suffered reverses, The Golden Corner now housed a drugstore and a hardware store. But in February of 1900 this building burned, to be replaced the next year by College Hall, the first of the college buildings on the west side of the campus. The old Hanover was giving way to the new.

The ravages of nature have their compensations and until this decade the quiet village appears to have been relatively free from the ravages of sin. But one does not have to have read Faulkner or even *Peyton Place* to know that rural districts are not quite the idyllic regions of the pastoral poets. In 1891 the village was electrified by the brutal murder of a young women of twenty-eight who lived with her family on a farm just off the road to Lyme on the present Reservoir Road.

The story of Christie Warden's murder has been told many times. On the evening of July 17, 1891, Frank Almy, an escaped convict whom Christie's father had unwittingly hired in the haying season the year before and whose stormy courtship of the girl had been unsuccessful, had hidden himself on the Lyme Road at the edge of the Vale of Tempe to

await her return from a Grange meeting in the village. When she reached the hollow, accompanied by her mother, her sister Fanny, and another girl, Almy accosted the party. Threatening Fanny with his revolver he dragged Christie to a clump of willows where the light of the full moon could not penetrate. As she resisted his attack he shot her. When Fanny and a man who had responded to the cries for help entered the willow grove they discovered her dead body. But Almy had disappeared.

There followed the greatest manhunt on both sides of the river the North Country has ever seen. One afternoon a month later Mrs. Warden, Christie's mother, discovered that Almy was hiding in the Warden barn. The next day bells on Dartmouth Hall and the churches of Norwich and Lebanon sounded the alarm; twenty-five hundred people flocked to the barn; armed men with ladders and pitchforks began the search. The murderer was at last discovered, hiding in the hay; shots were exchanged; for two hours he held them at bay, though wounded in three places; at last he surrendered. He was taken to the hotel where his wounds were dressed; a crowd of fifteen hundred people in an ugly mood filed past the cot in his hotel room and were persuaded to disperse only when he fainted. He was tried and convicted of first degree murder at Plymouth and on May 16, 1893, he was executed at the Concord State Prison, a special train being run from Hanover to view the hanging.

4

One day in 1901 the first motor car in Hanover was observed by Ernest Martin Hopkins, President Tucker's secretary, as it stood in front of the C and G House. Mr. Hopkins remembers a rapid monologue by President Tucker inspired by this herald of the motor age: it portended a social revolution; it would bring in its train crime and highway problems, industrial and financial changes; many subsidiary enterprises would be called into being.

Dartmouth's revered president was a prophet not without honor. The extensive building program he himself had inaugurated belongs to the history of the College. Enough to say here that five years after his retirement all traces of the town were removed from the west side of the campus — the bank had moved to its new quarters at the corner of Main and Lebanon Streets, and been replaced by Robinson Hall in 1913. The nineteenth-century white houses which had given distinction to the west side of the Green gave way to substantial brick structures to serve the expanding needs of the College.

The town was slow in solving some of the highway problems President Tucker had foreseen. The central streets were paved, but in the spring the peripheral roads were seas of mud. Irate motorists, stuck hub deep in the clay of East Wheelock or South Park Street, muttered that Eleazar would have done well to start a brickyard instead of a college. And it was not until the third decade of the century when Henry B. Thayer, a senior Trustee, driving up from Connecticut, got stuck in the mud in front of the President's new house on Webster Avenue, that several of the outlying streets were paved.

> Judgment follows knowledge, and knowledge is slow, and hard, and late, the outcome of humility, and patience, and charity. – William Jewett Tucker, 1910.

By that time the village, which up to the 1890's had been compact and surrounded by fields, had sprawled lustily to the north and east. In the process the great barn off South Park Street, lingering remnant of the Agricultural College, had been torn down, scattering rats throughout the neighborhood. With the clearing of the ground for Baker Library in 1927 the last dwelling house disappeared from the edge of the Green.

Before Emily Howe became Hiram Hitchcock's second wife in 1900 she had given her birthplace, the old Wheelock mansion, to the town as a library. At her death in 1912 the Hitchcock mansion together with the forty-five acres lying between Main Street and the river came into the possession of the College, opening up new possibilities of development. The College later acquired a fine stretch of rolling country to the north of the town, with views from Moosilauke to Ascutney and with slopes for skiing in winter and golfing at other seasons.

At the turn of the century Professor T. W. D. Worthen, one of the first residents of Webster Avenue, at a time when Occom Ridge was largely a cow pasture and the land beneath a marsh, a haven for "snakes, frogs, turtles and dirty boys," took the initiative in building a dam at the north end of the marsh thus forming Occom Pond. On the eastern side of the town, the 15,000 seedling trees from Angers, France, presented to the College in the 1860's by Judge Joel Parker for Observatory Hill had become the College Park where, in 1882, the senior class built the Bema.

Meanwhile the Mary Hitchcock Hospital had grown to rival the College in bringing fame to the town. The Gile family had succeeded the Crosbys and Frosts. The reputation of Dr. John M. Gile, who began his medical service in 1896, the year of Dr. Carleton Frost's death, extended far beyond Hanover. Traveling in his automobile, often driving a hundred miles at night and returning to take up his work the next morning, operating in farm kitchens and lumber camps, the quiet, dignified surgeon with his trim Van Dyke beard was a welcome and familiar figure throughout the North Country. Dean of the Medical School from 1910 until his death in 1925, he was also a Trustee of the College and active in public service. His son, Dr. John F. Gile, who as a boy had accompanied his father on his journeys, carried on the family tradition as an equally capable surgeon and College Trustee, though ill health and a premature death cut short his career.

In 1927 Dick Hall's House was given to the College by Mr. and Mrs. E. K. Hall in memory of their son Richard, thus enlarging the capacity of the hospital facilities in Hanover by some forty beds. Served in the twenties by only a half dozen doctors the demands on the hospital and the need for specialists was increasing rapidly; ninety percent of the patients came from beyond Hanover. Under the imaginative leadership of Dr. John P. Bowler, by marriage another member of the Gile family and the son of Dr. John W. Bowler, long-time Physical Director of the College, the Hitchcock Clinic was organized, with offices in the hospital. By the 1960's it numbers some seventy doctors with multiple specialties.

In front of the old hospital, a model in its day, Faulkner House was built in the 1950's, a three-million-dollar addition made possible by the initial gift of a million dollars from Mrs. Marianne Faulkner of Woodstock, Vermont. Later the little X-ray machine set up in 1914 by Arthur Meservey, a young instructor in the Physics Department who was one of Dartmouth's early Rhodes Scholars, expanded into a building of its own, the Carter X-ray Unit. With this apparatus and the Cobalt-60 Tele-therapy Unit, together with the Billings-Lee Residence for nurses (also a Woodstock benefaction), with a department of physical medicine and rehabilitation, and with the Raven Convalescent Home and the Psychiatry Building, Hiram Hitchcock's initial gift grew to metropolitan proportions. The enlarged Medical School, the Hitchcock Clinic, and the Hitchcock Hospital (with as many employees as the College) have made Hanover an outstanding medical center, a far cry from the days of Dr. Nathan Smith but a monument to his vision.

5

Hanover and Dartmouth have come a long way, too, from the town and the College in the wilderness founded by the Freemans and the Wheelocks. If something has been lost in the process, the gains cannot be ignored. The distinction between the Freemans and the Wheelocks, between Hanover Center and the village on the Plain, between Town and Gown have at least become blurred. A twentieth-century Hanoverian may enter a polite demurrer to the nineteenth century observation of Rufus Choate's daughter that "in a country town you get a real aristocracy, in the city there's no time to be aristocratic." Perhaps it is because in Hanover too there is no longer time to be snobbish. John Bellows recalled an entertainment he attended in the late 1860's in which students and various Hanover ladies participated: Scenes from Dickens and Other Authors. There was considerable trepidation about its reception; one professor's wife did not care to take tickets; but the hall of the old Medical School was thronged with "the elite."

When the Nugget movie theater was built in 1916 next to the Howe Library, students thronged the three daily shows and when the townspeople and faculty attended there was no "elite." The Village Improvement Society took over the Nugget in 1922, and from its profits provided the town with many additions: Storrs Pond, new fire apparatus, school equipment, sidewalks, trees. The Nugget was burned in one of Hanover's most spectacular fires in January, 1944; performances were continued in Webster Hall; in September, 1951, the new Nugget opposite the Post Office was opened. There was again no question of an "elite."

Perhaps one evidence of the greater "democracy" of the town is the disappearance of domestic help. The wife of President Tucker once remarked that she had never made a bed in her life. Though few Hanover housewives in the nineteenth century could have made such a statement, most of them did have "maids." Even up to the time of the Second World War faculty families in relatively modest circumstances could afford a high-school girl who lived in, washed dishes, vacuum-cleaned, and took care of the children. But in the 1960's a regular "maid" had become in Hanover as rare a phenomenon as elsewhere in the land — a weekly cleaning woman, perhaps, or students to wash windows and baby-sit.

> The man of moral force is never absent. . . . He is at work when he is silent and when he is at rest. His better tastes gradually refine others, his larger desires quicken their interests, his judgments increase the weight of public opinion. – William Jewett Tucker, 1910.

In the 1870's Miss Sally Perry Smith, the daughter of President Smith, lived in an imposing house on West Wheelock Street and was considered the first lady of the town. Though she had "New York ideas," she was considered "democratic," yet she endeavored to enforce the rule that no one living south of the hotel was invited to a faculty dance. Even as late as 1911 the widow of a former College officer told a freshman nephew that one didn't associate with people south of Wheelock Street.

Perhaps the turning point toward a freer society was marked by the return of Mr. Hopkins and his wife to Hanover in 1916. Celia Stone Hopkins was the daughter of a local farmer. She attended the Hanover school, played with Hanover boys and girls, and, as Bishop Dallas said of her, "grew up into a woman of strength and charm and dignity." For ten years she was President Tucker's secretary until his retirement in 1909. At first she viewed the addition of young Ernest Martin Hopkins to the President's staff with some skepticism. But being a highly intelligent and perceptive young lady she soon came to appreciate his qualities. In spite of her charm when she and "Hop" returned to Hanover there was a certain lifting of eyebrows on the part of a few of the matrons who considered themselves arbiters of Hanover society. For some women this might have presented a difficult situation and doubtless Celia Hopkins was not insensitive to it. But she was a woman of considerable poise and independence, who would stand no nonsense: she and the President decided they would associate with whomever they wished to associate, regardless of social arbiters and regardless of protocol, except for those official occasions like Commencement when it seemed indicated. Moreover, her sister Mrs. Tibbetts, the widow of the College Registrar, was also a woman of dynamic, forthright personality. (After his retirement and Mrs. Hopkins's death, "Mrs. Tib" became Mr. Hopkins's second wife.) To the Hopkinses and to the Dickeys, more than to any other factor, may doubtless be ascribed the ease and informality of contemporary social atmosphere in Hanover.

Twentieth-century Hanover possesses many of the characteristics of an urban society; but, with the drawbacks of such a society, it possesses many of its advantages: comparative freedom from petty bickering, idle scandal, and gossip, the possibility for the individual to preserve "in the midst of a great crowd the independence of solitude."

Still, an elderly recluse occasionally hears rumors of the existence of strata and "sets," of wheels within wheels, in Hanover society: the younger set, the doctors' set, the wealthy retired alumni set. The fact seems to be, however, that if such sets exist they are continually intermixing. It is on the whole a young community. In addition to the lectures, plays, and other diversions an academic town provides, there are the various organizations to absorb a young father and mother in addition to whatever professional activities they may be engaged in — for many a mother has a part-time job. The PTA, schools to support — the League of Women Voters, the two Woman's Clubs, church activities.

The "official" Church of Christ, since the old building burned in 1931 and the new one — still white — was built on College Street, does not occupy quite the same status as the one Eleazar Wheelock gathered, flourishing though it is. And there is St. Denis, to prove that Protestantism is not the only way to heaven; St. Thomas, to prove that colonial New England sprang not only from Puritanism but also from the age of Elizabeth. Moreover, Catholic students have Aquinas House at the end of Webster Avenue and the Episcopalians Edgerton House on School Street for social life as well as worship. There are also the Lutherans, with a church of contemporary design, the Unitarians, the Christian Scientists, the Quakers.

Physically the town has acquired many of the unfortunate aspects of the "suburban sprawl." To be sure there are the houses with spacious grounds on the slopes of Velvet Rocks and Balch Hill; and many of the people who work in Hanover live in fine old houses in Norwich, Lyme, Etna, and Hanover Center. But Lyme Road, with the Cold Regions Research and Engineering Laboratory, built recently by the Army, with Rivercrest, a housing development built jointly by the Hospital and the College; and the West Lebanon Road with Sachem Village — back from the road, to be sure — and the houses springing up between the village and the Wilder dam present some of the aspects of "conurbia."

Main Street, however, presents much the same appearance it had in the nineteenth century. To be sure there are a few modern buildings: the Lang Block, south of the Inn; the recently enlarged Bank; the Post Office; the Nugget. Some years ago a far-sighted gentleman proposed that through traffic from north and south be diverted and Main Street converted into a mall with grass and trees for pedestrian shoppers. Trees have been planted but there is as yet no grass. Perhaps someday. At the south end of the street a new Super-Duper market has been built. The Hanover Consumers Cooperative (founded in 1936 with headquarters in Elliott White's garage and now doing a yearly business of close to a million dollars) has moved into modern quarters on South Park Street, the Corner Bookstore deserting its corner to take the Cooperative's place. But there is still Tanzi's where one meets everybody and gets the latest news. And if one is irritated by the new traffic lights and parking problems, there are always Moosilauke, the Franconia and Presidential Ranges, Moose, Smarts, Cube mountains, and the chain of Outing Club Cabins to flee to — for Hanover is still not too far from the wilderness.

> The question "What is there to do at Dartmouth in the winter?" gives rise to the thought that we might take better advantage of the splendid opportunities which the admirable situation of our College offers. – Fred H. Harris, 1909.

Despite its urbanization Hanover remains a town not too large to preserve a sense of community, its inhabitants sharing with each other their jokes, their joys, and their sorrows. When Julius Mason, a long-time postman, disappeared suddenly into a grassed-over cistern on West South Street, presenting to a startled housewife only his mailbag held high above his head, the news spread quickly from Tanzi's and the whole town chuckled. (And it was grateful to Julius Mason, too, for planting and tending on his own initiative flower borders near the travelled ways of public streets.) Likewise when, a few winters ago, Drs. Miller and Quinn, flying in Dr. Miller's plane from Whitefield, were lost in the Pemigewasset Wilderness and the wrecked plane with their bodies was not found for months, the entire town shared the anguish and suspense of their families in a community of sympathy not possible in a larger place.

*   *   *   *   *

At noon or at four o'clock long lines of cars back up on Main Street on each side of the red traffic light. One is conscious of the hum and bustle of a lively town. Yet just a few steps down Sanborn Lane one enters the quiet hush of the old Cemetery behind Massachusetts Row. Here under the towering pines, on the level plats and the slopes of the ravine lie the Hanover dead: the Wheelocks in their tombs; the Crosbys, the Youngs, the Storrs family, the Lords, the Frosts. . . . One can almost trace the chronology of the town in the monuments: the slate slabs of the remoter past, on many of which the inscriptions are barely legible, the marble slabs of a later day, the granite monuments of more recent times. In the deep shadow of these pines one can forget the fitful fever of our day.

Or one stands in front of Dartmouth Row late on a night of early June. The dormitories behind are quiet, for the students are studying for their examinations, but an occasional student passes on the sidewalk below, hand in hand with his girl, an occasional car glides by. Suddenly there is a shriek of sirens: a police car speeds around Inn Corner and rapidly disappears up College Street, followed by an ambulance. Perhaps there has been an accident up Lyme Road, the penalty of life in the motor age. Then the town subsides into quietness except for an infrequent car and the swooping of nighthawks about the lighted tower of Baker Library. Above the brick buildings across the Green, above the Cemetery, Venus shines in a clear sky. Again one's mind turns to the past. It is not too difficult to imagine the Green as it appeared after the first pioneers felled the giant pines. What, one wonders, would Jonathan Freeman of Hanover Center and Eleazar Wheelock of Hanover Plain think of the town and the College they founded in the wilderness?

The Faculty

STEARNS MORSE

I

Eleazar was the Faculty
And the whole curriculum
Was five hundred gallons of New England Rum.

THESE lines of Richard Hovey's are not altogether wild hyperbole: the first faculty of Dartmouth College consisted of Eleazar Wheelock and four tutors — Sylvanus Ripley, John Wheelock, Bezaleel Woodward, and John Smith, and of these tutors Wheelock, Ripley, and Woodward might legitimately be considered as extensions of the President since John Wheelock was his son and the other two became his sons-in-law shortly after assuming their tutorial duties. (Ralph, still another son, was forced to give up a tutorship after the first year because of his epilepsy.) But we cannot allow the poet's aspersion on the curriculum, which was far less intoxicating than whatever quantity of rum Wheelock brought to Hanover. The curriculum, indeed, reflected his chief interests — the classics and theology. It was by no means unique; it was simply the standard curriculum of all the Colonial colleges, such as Harvard and Yale, whose principal purpose was to provide the new country with an educated ministry.

As such it consisted of "the learned languages" through the first three years, the rudiments of speaking and writing in freshman year, geography and logic in sophomore year, English and Latin composition, metaphysics, and the elements of natural and physical law in senior year. This was substantially the curriculum till the third quarter of the nineteenth century, with changes in textbooks and the authors read.

Learning was pursued largely by rote and recitation; education in the sciences was meager. So narrow a curriculum may not seem to have been conducive either to an exciting quest for knowledge or to stimulating instruction, but when one considers the products of this "classical curriculum" — many of the Founding Fathers, for instance — one should not be too supercilious. After all, Homer, Thucydides, Euripides, Aristotle, and Locke on the Human Understanding, to say nothing of Holy Writ, are scarcely thin mental fare.

Wheelock's quartet of tutors faced in embryo many of the problems college faculties face today: the reconciliation of teaching with administration, scholarship, and the pursuit of civic and political activities. John Wheelock's activities seem mainly to have been assisting his father in handling the College's affairs; his career as his father's successor and his embroilment in the College versus University controversy has already been considered. Bezaleel Woodward also seems to have been principally an "administrator" and as such a man of considerably greater ability and sounder judgment than his brother-in-law — or his father-in-law for that matter.

A graduate of Yale in the class of 1764 Woodward was somewhat older than his colleagues, being twenty-seven when he married Wheelock's daughter Mary in 1772. This marriage, wholly apart from its familial aspect, seems to have been an indication of his general sagacity: a contemporary newspaper account describes "the amiable Polly Wheelock" as a lady "whose Virtue and Modesty require no Encomiums to recommend her" and their two souls as "mutually attuned and exactly fitted to each other."

> It is the institutional spirit which gives public value to an academic institution. – William Jewett Tucker, 1919.

He taught mathematics and served the College as Trustee, Treasurer, and Librarian. On Wheelock's death in 1779 he was for over a year virtually president, in the absence of John Wheelock. In 1784 the construction of Dartmouth Hall was entrusted to his practical business sense, though another man completed the building since other duties absorbed Woodward's time. A man of independent character, he did not hesitate to take issue with his rather awesome father-in-law, notably in the squabble over the smallpox outbreak. His versatility was particularly displayed in public affairs. In fact he was so active politically that in 1778 he resigned his tutorship to avoid compromising the College; the Trustees put his resignation "on file." For the next four years Wood-

ward figured prominently in the movement for independence of the Connecticut Valley towns. As a representative of the town of "Dresden" he went to Windsor and to Philadelphia to present their case to the Continental Congress. And so highly esteemed was he in Hanover that as late as 1794 he received twenty-three votes in the town for the governorship as an independent.

But in 1782 Woodward returned to his teaching; the Trustees removed his resignation from the file and made him Professor of Mathematics and Philosophy, a position he held until his death in 1804. His portrait reveals a man of frank, open countenance, of friendly but commanding presence. Samuel Swift, 1800, a prominent Vermont lawyer, recalled in 1872 his plain informal manners, his ability to mingle with men who had no connection with a college; he was more popular with the students, Swift said, than John Wheelock or Professor John Smith.

The best one can say of Professor Smith, on the other hand, is that he appears to have had a brilliant mind — of a sort. Master Samuel Moody, his teacher at Dummer Academy, brought him to the first Commencement in 1771 in Governor Wentworth's party; only nineteen he had already read Homer twice and the Greek minor poets. Entering Dartmouth in the junior class, he took his degree in 1773; in his senior year he read the Hebrew Bible through *nearly* twice. On graduation he remained for four years as tutor, resigning because his salary was both inadequate and too flexible. This won him a promotion: he and Wheelock agreed that he should "settle as Professor of English, Latin, Greek, Hebrew, Chaldee etc." or as much of these and other languages as the Trustees should judge necessary and practicable for one man. For all this he was to receive one hundred pounds annually, half in money and the other half in "wheat, Indian corn, rye, beef, pork, mutton, butter, cheese, hay, pasturing etc. . . ." It was eleven years before he received the full £100. And in 1805, though his salary was raised from $550 to $600, it was almost immediately put back again because of a disagreement over the pastorate of the College Church, which he had held since 1787. (His preaching was characterized as "ponderous and periodic.")

He was unquestionably industrious. He also had a considerable power of concentration: his devoted wife recorded that in his only study, a small room constantly occupied by his family and all the company they had to entertain, he sat at his desk, his attention immovably fixed upon his work, writing and re-writing. (To eke out his income he kept in his house the first "Hanover Bookstore.")

He did indeed publish: Latin, Greek, Hebrew grammars, an edition of Cicero's *De Oratore,* with notes and a life, though a Chaldee grammar never saw print. The students were awed by his scholastic attainments, which President John Wheelock eulogized as "attested by multitudes, scattered in the civilized world."

In his youth Smith was pale and slender, but in his later years he became the stoutest man in the village, weighing over two hundred pounds, though this did not prevent his dying of consumption in 1809. He was nearsighted, nervous, and timid: crossing the Green on a foggy morning, he mistook the blackened stumps for a she-bear and her cubs and rushed to the chapel, his gown streaming behind him, shouting, "A bear and three cubs! A bear and three cubs!" — a cry which was for many years a by-word among the students, whose attitude toward him was summed up by Judah Dana, 1795: "the best linguist in New England but did not know beans about anything else." No wonder that Richardson in his history in a moment of near-exasperation concludes that "both in the pulpit and in the classroom this singularly busy and conscientious pedagogue was a man of monumental dullness."

Sylvanus Ripley is a much more appealing figure. The fame of a

teacher quickly fades. Unless he is a Socrates to be immortalized by a
Xenophon, an Aristophanes, or a Plato; or a Jowett, interpreting
Plato's memory of Socrates, his personality is transitory, it vanishes
finally in the reminiscence in old age of the last of his pupils. So the
personality of Sylvanus Ripley, partly because of his premature death
and the meager facts available about him, seems at first to elude us. Yet
from bits of information here and there it is possible to gain an impression of the man as he appeared to his contemporaries and, more important, as an example of the liberal and humane tradition at Dartmouth.

> A young man who can acquire habits of extravagance at Hanover is
> possessed of rare creative genius. – Edwin Webster Sanborn, 1901.

Thus we know that when the thirty-four year old Governor Wentworth attended Dartmouth's first Commencement Ripley's *Salutatory
Oration upon the Virtues* attracted his notice. Was it the address itself?
More probably, says Wentworth's biographer, it was the engaging personality of this young man of twenty-two. The attraction was not merely
a passing fancy for two summers later Wentworth offered Ripley an
assistant rectorship at King's Chapel in Boston with the hope that this
might eventually lead to the rectorship. Thus opened out before him
the possibility of a brilliant career in the Church of England. What,
one wonders, was his attitude toward the prospect? We know only that
he did not accept the offer and that Wheelock replied that he could not
be spared. At this time he was pursuing his studies in divinity with the
President, to whom his loyalty is unquestioned. The proximity of Abi-
gail Wheelock, the President's daughter, whom he married in 1774,
may also have been a determining influence. But it seems unlikely that
the Governor would have made the offer if he had not felt in Ripley a
sympathetic temperament.

There still exist in Hanover two tangible monuments to Sylvanus
Ripley's memory: Webster Cottage, which he built for himself and his
wife in 1780 and the more spacious Choate House, which he built for
his growing family six years later. Do not these suggest, along with his
charm, a temperament somewhat more Hellenic than that of his Hebraic
father-in-law — this despite his undoubted orthodoxy as Professor of
Divinity, which he became in 1782, and his pastorate of the College
Church, which he held from 1779 until his death (after 1782, to be

sure, in association with his much duller colleague John Smith)?

Before becoming pastor of the Church he had been a missionary to the Indians and a chaplain in the Revolutionary Army. (And he was a Trustee of the College from 1775-87.) As a preacher he seems to have had a natural fluency: John Wheelock said that his sermons were seldom written; "his manner was pleasing and winning, his words flowed as promptly and readily in the pulpit as in the social circle." Though we know very little about his teaching, his popularity as a preacher and the affection for him of the Hanover children would seem to indicate that he was equally popular with his students.

Mr. Ripley was called in December of 1786 to fill the pastorate of the Hanover Center Church. He named the first Sunday in February, 1787, as the time he would announce his decision, but at the end of the services he told his congregation that he would defer the announcement because of the extreme cold. On the way back to Hanover with three others in a blinding snowstorm he was thrown from the sleigh and his neck was broken. Thus died at thirty-eight perhaps the most attractive of the young faculty Eleazar Wheelock had gathered about him.

2

. . . not excluding any Person of any religious denomination whatsoever from free and equal liberty and advantage of Education or from any of the liberties and privileges or immunities of the said College on account of his or their speculative sentiments in Religion and of his or their being of a religious profession different from the said Trustees of the said Dartmouth College.

Charter of Dartmouth College

The genial and witty Roswell Shurtleff, who in 1804 succeeded to the chair of divinity seventeen years after Ripley's death (it had been vacant ever since), seems to have been akin to him in spirit and temperament. The day he entered Dartmouth in 1797 he met Daniel Webster in the washroom of the hotel; he lived to see the election of Lincoln, dying in February, 1861; thirty-eight of his eighty-seven years were spent on the faculty of the College, the last eleven as Professor of Moral and Intellectual Philosophy and Political Economy. In his zeal for reading he had weakened his eyes after recovering from the measles before he entered college; nevertheless he persisted in his education and became an accomplished classicist and a popular teacher.

His theology was of course orthodox. Though he took delight in the religious revivals which occurred during his pastorate of the College Church, his orthodoxy was not of the fire and brimstone variety — "he took pleasure in saying pleasant things." He took pleasure, too, in

modern agnostics as well as in the pagan classics. There is a happy glimpse of him in his old age sitting before a snug wood fire, smoking a cigar, his writing table piled high with books and papers. Looking up from his book to the former student who had come to call he said: "I am just finishing Gibbon for the seventh time and he grows richer with every reading."

Dr. Nathan Smith in a moment of impatience referred to the early professors as "a pack of literary drones." Possibly this expression sprang from irritation at the scanty attention paid to science in the early curriculum. Dr. Smith left Hanover to go to Yale, but the Medical School he had founded flourished and drew to its faculty men of scientific bent who generally taught in the College. Thus Dr. Daniel Oliver of the Harvard class of 1806 became in 1823 both a professor in the Medical School and a Professor of Intellectual Philosophy in the College. He was considered by John Willard, 1819, a tutor in that year (he later founded the Willard Professorship), "the finest scholar connected with the college."

In 1816 another young Harvard scientist arrived in Hanover. Dr. James Freeman Dana was Lecturer in Chemistry in the Medical School from 1816 to 1820, Professor of Chemistry and Mineralogy from 1820 to 1826, being also professor of these latter subjects in the College. Dr. Dana's primary interest was research and for the first time perhaps Dartmouth was faced with a dilemma which has lasted to the present: how to attract and hold scholars whose primary interest is in the pursuit of knowledge and yet who are at the same time stimulating teachers of undergraduates. The problem was not solved in Dana's case: he did not find the atmosphere of a provincial college favorable to investigation and accepted a call to the College of Physicians and Surgeons in New York in 1826, to continue his researches in chemistry and the new science of electromagnetism and the publication of his results in the scientific journals. Among his listeners at the series of popular lectures he delivered on electromagnetism in 1827 before the New York Lyceum was the portrait painter, Samuel F. B. Morse, whose interest was aroused in the subject by the lectures and subsequent conversations with Dana, an interest which resulted ultimately in the invention of the telegraph. But Dana did not live to see this, dying prematurely at the age of thirty-four in 1827.

Another Harvard alumnus arrived in Hanover on July 24, 1838, with his friend Ralph Waldo Emerson, who delivered an oration on *Literary Ethics,* as a guest of the Dartmouth Literary Societies. Dr. Oliver

Wendell Holmes, Emerson's companion, later recorded, however, that the silver shower of his eloquence appeared to have "left the sturdy old dogmatists as dry as ever." Perhaps it was because, as a student reported, the address was too deep or too dark to comprehend. Nine days before this Emerson had delivered before the Harvard Divinity School an address which startled that supposedly liberal institution to such an extent that he was not officially welcomed at Harvard for thirty years.

Holmes remained for three years as Professor of Anatomy and Physiology and, though hardly a Calvinist, seems to have been happy in Hanover where he lived at the hotel. Far down the valley one caught blue glimpses of Mt. Ascutney. In *Elsie Venner,* which Holmes wrote years later, one may find an echo of his Hanover experience: Elsie Venner, victim of pre-natal influences, lived in a cottage at the foot of that mountain.

If the good doctor's Unitarianism left Hanover as unruffled as had his distinguished friend's oration, it was not because the Calvinism of the community had appreciably softened. In 1835, three years before Holmes came to Dartmouth, Professor Benjamin Hale had become a victim of one of the two violations in Dartmouth history of the principle of religious tolerance which Eleazar Wheelock (or more probably Governor John Wentworth) had inserted in its charter.

Hale, a native of Newbury, Massachusetts, had entered Dartmouth in 1814, but had left at the end of his freshman year because of ill-health and, after pursuing his studies at Dummer Academy, entered Bowdoin, from which he was graduated in 1818. In 1819 he attended the Theological Seminary at Andover, Massachusetts, where he became especially interested in ecclesiastical history. He came to Dartmouth at a time when, in the words of his predecessor, physical science at the College "was like a log anchored in the stream which served only to show its velocity." Engaged to give lectures in chemistry to the medical class, to which members of the senior and junior classes were admitted, and instruction to the junior class in a chemical textbook by daily recitations, he added to this assignment another course of lectures in the College, together with lectures in geology and mineralogy and physics; and for two years assisted also in the instruction in Hebrew. Moreover, he added five hundred specimens to the meager collection of minerals.

If Benjamin Hale had confined his zeal to his scientific activities all would have been well, for he was unquestionably popular with the students. In September, 1828, he was ordained a Deacon in the Episcopal Church by the Rt. Rev. Bishop Griswold at Woodstock, Vermont, and in January, 1831, ordained a priest by the same prelate at St. Paul's Church in Newburyport. In spite of his teaching he found enough leisure to conduct Episcopal services, wearing a gown, at Windsor, Woodstock, Lyme, and other places in the vicinity, not infrequently in Congregational Meeting Houses, as well as to conduct services in his own house. These services were generally held in the evening; in the morning he was a regular attendant at the College Church.

When, however, he transferred the services in his house to the Medical Building, the faculty voted to ask President Lord to have them discontinued. At the President's request he abandoned the Medical School services, returning them to his house. The services were popular; moreover, he began to make converts, especially in Norwich, and showed a somewhat tactless satisfaction in this endeavor. By this time the Congregational divines of New Hampshire were aroused and made representations to the Trustees. At the annual meeting in 1835, since it was evident that Hale was unlikely to give up his chair, the Trustees voted to take it out from under him by abolishing the professorship in chemistry and voting to add a professor to the department of mathematics and natural philosophy who should devote a portion of his time to chemistry.

I am a Yale man. I am endeavoring to bestow upon you a great compliment when I say that Dartmouth is more like Yale than any other American college. – William Howard Taft, Hanover, 1912.

This high-handed action created a considerable stir. Hale himself wrote a *Valedictory Letter to the Trustees of Dartmouth College* reviewing the controversy and charging that his removal could only be ascribed to sectarian prejudice. In a pamphlet signed "Alumnus" the Trustees presented their side of the case which called forth a spirited rejoinder by "Investigator," who was Professor Daniel Oliver, also an Episcopalian. "Alumnus" gave away the show, in spite of his denial of sectarian prejudice, by adducing as a final reason for Hale's dismissal the fact that the course of events was giving to the College "the reputation of exerting undue influence upon young men, in circumstances, in which they were ill enabled to investigate the matter thoroughly, to divert them from forms of worship to which they had been bred, and to which the many supporters of the institution are attached" — a line of thought employed in such cases from the time of Socrates.

The episode was unfortunate for the College. Though the Trustees were defended in the ensuing discussion in the press, one journal, as Richardson puts it, "pertinently asked whether it was henceforth to be illegal in Dartmouth to advocate the creed of him to whom she owed more than to any other man save Wheelock himself, John Wentworth." And the controversy stamped the institution in the popular mind as narrowly and illiberally orthodox. Hale himself went on to the presidency of Geneva (later Hobart) College in New York, a position he held with distinction until his resignation in 1858.

The other victim of religious intolerance could perhaps hardly be called a victim: his controversy with the trustees ended in a draw, if not indeed in a victory. Alpheus Crosby has been overshadowed in Dartmouth College history by the prominence of his brother, Dr. Dixi, and his nephew, Dr. Alpheus Benning Crosby (Dr. Ben.). But he was probably the most gifted of the "gifted Crosbys": genius is more than once the word used for him.

Alpheus Crosby picked up a desire for learning from the academy scholars and medical students boarding with his father's large family at Gilmanton. He learned to read at three from scraps of paper; in a letter to one of his brothers written when he was eight and a half he requested Cicero's orations and wrote that he expected to get through Virgil's Georgics that week. At nine and a half he finished the Greek Testament. Yet he was no bookworm: "a playful little rogue," one of his brothers called him. In his tenth year his brother Nathan took him to Hanover where he was examined by various members of the faculty including Rufus Choate, the young tutor in Greek, who had just graduated, and pronounced fitted for college. Not unnaturally his family thought he was too young so he spent the next three years studying Hebrew under the Rev. John L. Parkhurst and then going to Exeter. In 1823 he entered college, "in a boy's jacket with ruffled collar turned back over it," at the age of thirteen — the parallel with George Ticknor comes to mind — and graduated in 1827, far and away at the head of his class.

For three years he tutored in the Moor's School and at Dartmouth, then attended the Andover Theological Seminary. In 1833, not yet twenty-three, he was called back to Dartmouth as Professor of Latin and Greek. His reputation as a scholar was already established — he was held up to the faculty as an example they might well emulate. He produced nearly a score of volumes on the Greek language and literature — grammars, editions, commentaries. His fame as a classicist, both

[129]

in this country and Europe, was probably equaled only by that of Professor Cornelius Felton, later President Felton, of Harvard.

If it may have been fanciful to characterize Sylvanus Ripley as a Hellenist, there can be no doubt about Alpheus Crosby's Hellenism. To him "the stern old Roman was less attractive than the more polished Greek" and in 1837 he relinquished the chair of Latin to devote himself solely to Greek. An amusing letter from Theodore French, Jr., 1852, to his "Friend Tom" (who appears to be absent from College, for some reason) gives us a glimpse of him:

If Crosby is here next spring he will probably screw you like vengeance on the subject of Greek roots and the history of Greek declensions. . . . This aforementioned professor Crosby is one of the strangest specimens of human depravity extant. I suppose that without doubt he is the best Greek scholar in this part of the world. He is a perfect gentleman and shows it too in his intercourse with his classes and he is very much liked by the students.

His translations were likened to "celestial music"; he "entered into the secret chambers of Greek thought, and became himself a Greek."

In 1849 he published anonymously two pamphlets dealing with religious matters which did not meet with the favor of those influential members of the Dartmouth constituency who still cherished orthodox Calvinist notions of eternal damnation. The first, entitled *A Letter of the Celebrated John Foster to a Young Minister on the Duration of Future Punishment,* was a defense of the Universalist position by a noted unorthodox Baptist clergyman and essayist in England. In his comment on the *Letter* Crosby raised searching questions as to the publishing activities of the American Tract Society, a subsidiary of the Congregational Church. The other pamphlet, prompted by the Millerite movement of the period, dealt with the scriptural teachings as to the Second Coming of Christ, the End of the World, the resurrection of the dead, and the General Judgment.

The student has nerves; and he sometimes bays at the moon. He is subject to lunar rages which arise from dead calm, swell almost to mob violence and subside without a trace. – Edwin J. Bartlett, 1922.

These publications were promptly brought to the attention of the Trustees who at their Commencement meeting decided on his removal and requested him to appear before them to show cause why this action should not be taken. Professor Crosby had become wearied of teaching, doubtless finding the callow undergraduates of his day more and more immune to his enthusiasm for the Greeks, and had decided to retire, though he hoped to retain a connection with the College without salary. When, however, at nine o'clock one evening he received the summons to appear before the Trustees at eight-thirty the next morning, he gave up thought of resignation and stated defiantly that his theological views and activities were matters with which the Board had no concern whatsoever. The Trustees, recalling the unfavorable publicity attending the removal of his position from Professor Hale, retreated. Through the diplomacy of President Lord the controversy was amicably settled: the Trustees agreed to expunge their charges and votes from the record; Professor Crosby promised to resign provided that he was still kept on the roll of the faculty as professor emeritus. This honorary position he held until his death in 1874.

The Hale and Crosby episodes seem to have had a salutary effect on the future of freedom of thought in the College. Some years afterward Daniel J. Noyes, 1832, who became Professor of Divinity in 1849 and Professor of Philosophy twenty years later, could say to a student who queried him about the divinity of Christ: "Believe what you can, be true to what you believe and God will not condemn you." In the latter half of the century as Professor C. D. Adams was to point out, the influence of Darwin, of the scientific movement, and of the graduate schools had a profound effect on the old theology. In 1893 William Jewett Tucker, after his trial for heresy and acquittal, became President and the reputation of Dartmouth as a liberal institution was firmly established. Dr. Tucker, as a young clergyman in Manchester, New Hampshire, had lived in the family of Alpheus Crosby's brother. On October 13, 1910, on the one hundredth anniversary of Crosby's birth, there was a memorial service in Salem to the "Renowned Greek Teacher." Among the tributes read was one by William Jewett Tucker.

3

I went to Dartmouth College, and found the same old Granny system which I met there twenty-five years ago.

Emerson's Journal. Entry for July 24, 1863

. . . earnest hard-working men feeling strongly the necessity of setting a good example. But they were deep in the mud of precedent and of college poverty.

Edwin J. Bartlett

Emerson's comment was directed at the "system" of choosing the Commencement orator by lot instead of by merit. If it seems to indicate that he had no very high opinion of the intellectual sprightliness of the College it should be said that Dartmouth's intellectual status in general could not be considered much worse than that of other New England colleges. "I think the College struck bottom in 1853," President Eliot once said of Emerson's Alma Mater. There, as at Dartmouth, the system of rote and recitation, of wading through Homer "as though the Iliad were a bog," still reigned; and the faculty were scarcely better off than the Dartmouth faculty in the 1870's, as Professor Bartlett described their plight. It is true that Harvard in the sixties numbered such names as Wolcott Gibbs, Benjamin Peirce, Louis Agassiz, Francis J. Child, Longfellow and Lowell.

Dartmouth was still remote, its faculty was isolated, unable to meet frequently with men of similar interests. The curriculum was still fixed and narrow: as late as the 1870's only one elective, either French or calculus, was allowed. For over a century after the founding of the College religious orthodoxy was an indispensable prerequisite for a member of the faculty and it was customary long after mid-century to open the faculty meetings with prayer; not much inspiration, Professor Bartlett remembered, deriving from this venerable custom. Altogether, he recalled, it was "a college of pinched and grinding frugality almost without aesthetic adornment." The faculty were almost exclusively Dartmouth men to whom there were few graduate courses available in the country, and study abroad was beyond the means of most of them. Finally, though Dartmouth's presidents were men of high character and some of them of considerable ability, none until Dr. Tucker approached the stature of President Eliot, under whose leadership Harvard had developed before the end of the century into one of the great universities of the western world.

Yet it is possible to exaggerate the gloomy pigments. A classical education was not without merit as its products frequently demonstrated. Take Dr. John Ordronaux of the Class of 1850, for instance. After graduation he studied law at Harvard and practiced it a few years until he decided to become a doctor. Nine years after his graduation he became Professor of Medical Jurisprudence at Columbia and in 1864 lecturer in that subject at his Alma Mater; before his career was over he was holding lectureships or professorships in several other institutions. Whatever the value of his classical education may have been to him professionally he evidently derived enjoyment from it. In *The Dartmouth* of the late seventies and early eighties one finds many translations by him — of Horace's *Odes* into English and of English hymns

Commencement at Dartmouth College.

AUGUST 26th, M DCC XCV.

THE ORDER OF THE PUBLIC EXERCISES.

FORENOON.

1. A Salutatory Oration in Latin. By SAMUEL FOWLER DICKINSON.

2. A Greek Oration. By ELI EMMONS.

3. A Forenfic Difputation. The Queftion—" *Is the Political Eftablifhment of a uniform Syftem of Education advantageous to a Community ?*" By SAMUEL ALDEN, JOSHUA HEYWOOD, DUDLEY [TODD, and GEORGE WASHINGTON PRESCOTT.

4. A Dialogue, on " Conftitutional Freedom." By HEMAN ALLEN, ROHAN PRENTICE FIELD, and BENJAMIN RUGGLES WOODBRIDGE.

5. A Syllogiftic Difpute, in Latin. The Queftion—" *Is there an original difference in the mental faculties of mankind ?*" By JOSIAH PRENTICE refpondent. JOHN HASKELL and BENJAMIN [FRANKLIN PIERCE opponents.

6. A Dialogue in Englifh, on " *The State of Poland.*" By JUDAH DANA, ABIJAH BIGELOW, and JOSEPH BRIDGMAN.

7. A Poem in Englifh. By HOLLAND WEEKS.

8. An Oration in Hebrew. By ASA CARPENTER.

9. Differtations on Various Subjects. By ALPHEUS CHENEY, GEORGE GROUT, NATHAN MOODY, and NATHAN PARKS.

AFTERNOON.

1. An Oration in Englifh, on " *Thunder Storms.*" By JOHN VOSE.

2. A Forenfic Difputation—" *Have Savage Nations an exclufive right to the territory which they occupy as hunting ground ?*" By SAMUEL BURNHAM, JOHN EASTMAN, DAVID STORRS, and NICHOLAS EMERY.

3. An Oration in Englifh, on " *The connexion of Morals with Political Society.*" By THOMAS SNELL.

4. A Poem in Englifh. By DAVID EVERETT.

5. A Dialogue in Englifh, on " *The caufes of Vegetation.*" By NATHANIEL WELLS and LUTHER JEWETT.

6. An Oration in Chaldaic, on " *The importance of Piety to Sovereigns.*" By JOHN NOYES.

7. A Valedictory Oration. SAMUEL WORCESTER.

FROM THE PRESS OF DUNHAM & TRUE.

into Latin, among them *Nearer My God to Thee* into "isometrical Latin rhyme," "an entirely unique performance of its kind, so far as we know." The intellectual and cultural climate during this period was doubtless bleak. Yet Amos N. Currier, 1856, looking back fifty years, thought that the faculty of his time gave the College "an atmosphere of culture, refinement, mental alertness."

In 1860 Smith, Mason & Co. of New York published a large topographical map of Grafton County, "from actual surveys" by H. F. Walling (the surveys were made by Walling and his assistants pushing an odometer along the highways and noting the names of the householders). On insets around the edges are plans of towns and villages and occasional pictures. Next to an engraving of Dartmouth Row and the green, with its rail fence, is the Directory of the Faculty. Roswell Shurtleff and Alpheus Crosby are still listed as Professors Emeriti; Dr. Dixi Crosby is one of the six professors of the Medical School; Rev. John Newton Putnam, A.M., is listed as Professor of the Greek Language and Literature. The latter, Professor Crosby's successor, may well have been a man Amos Currier had in mind as giving the College an atmosphere of culture. He is described by an undergraduate of the sixties as a man of perfect character, with a face of rare beauty, wavy black hair, large dark eyes; what he had to say never perfunctory, never dull. Another popular professor was James Willis Patterson, who held two chairs, as acting Professor of Mathematics and Professor of Astronomy. "Patt" was described by the same undergraduate as in the prime of life, tall, well-proportioned, florid; he was often called upon by students for speeches during the Civil War. (His gift for oratory was to take him to the United States Senate in the same decade.)

> In the progress of time nothing has developed in college government so wholesome and genuine as self-control through a representative group.
> – Edwin J. Bartlett, 1922.

Two other names in the Directory of 1860 are worthy of notice: those of the President, Nathan Lord, and of the Rev. Samuel Gilman Brown, Evans Professor of Oratory and Belles Lettres, the son of President Brown and himself soon to become President of Hamilton College. Lords, Browns, and Bartletts have played almost if not quite as prominent a part in the history of the College as Crosbys, Frosts, and Giles have played in Hanover's medical life.

Of the other names on the 1860 roster most if not all of them have

[134]

been long forgotten. Ira Young, Professor of Mathematics, had died in 1858 and so a family which is unique in the college chronicles for having served on the faculty for four generations is not represented in the Directory for 1860. Ebenezer Adams, of the Class of 1791, the progenitor of the Young and Proctor dynasties, was succeeded on his retirement as Professor of Mathematics in 1833 by Ira Young, who in the same year married Eliza Adams. Ira Young's son Charles became Professor of Astronomy, and his daughter married John C. Proctor, Professor of Greek from 1870 to 1879. Their son Charles Proctor, 1900, returned to Dartmouth in 1907 to follow in his grandfather Young's footsteps as Assistant Professor of Mathematics and after two years to transfer to physics. (One of his by no means incidental achievements had been to persuade Ernest Martin Hopkins, who had left college in his freshman year for financial reasons, to return and room with him.) Charles Proctor's sister was the wife of Sidney Fay, who left the Dartmouth history department in 1914 for Smith and some years later Harvard to make a reputation as one of the leading "revisionist" historians of the outbreak of the war of 1914. Thus this family served the College with distinction for a period of one hundred and thirty-five years, from 1810, the date when Ebenezer Adams "of the roaring voice" joined the faculty, to 1945 when Charles Proctor, whose voice was singularly gentle, retired.

The most famous member of this family was Charles Augustus Young, of the Class of 1853. Entering college at the age of fourteen, he graduated at the head of his class of fifty. Edwin Sanborn, one of his teachers, described him as uncommonly quick, learning anything with great facility, excitable and playful in recitation, always better prepared than anyone else, in character faultless, in piety commendable. As a senior he had accompanied his father Ira to Europe to purchase apparatus for the observatory made possible by Dr. George C. Shattuck, 1803, of Boston. On graduation he taught the classics at Andover and studied at the Theological Seminary. His passion for science, however, got the better of his "commendable piety" and in 1857 he went to Western Reserve as Professor of Mathematics, Natural Philosophy and Astronomy. On his father's death President Lord wished to recall him to Dartmouth, but certain members of the faculty, apparently considering him too big for his breeches, objected and Professor Patterson retained the chair of astronomy he had temporarily taken over at Ira Young's death.

In 1865, however, the views of President Lord and Professor Sanborn prevailed, and Charles Augustus Young returned to Dartmouth as Professor of Astronomy and Natural Philosophy, a position he retained until 1877 when he was called to Princeton. The "college poverty" Edwin Bartlett referred to prevented the Trustees from meeting the conditions under which he would have consented to remain and he accepted the Princeton offer. Already he had made distinguished contributions to the study of the physics of the sun with a spectroscope of his own design and had led various expeditions to study eclipses of the sun. The rest of his career belongs to the history of American science, in which he made a name as one of the most eminent of American astrophysicists, and to the history of Princeton University where he became known to the undergraduates as "Twinkle" Young. His Dartmouth students, too, considered him the most distinguished member of the faculty of his time. The Princeton nickname, says Edwin Bartlett, was most appropriate: his black "eyes twinkled and so did the stars." Not that they were always able to follow him, for he was "quick as a toad's tongue"; he would cover the blackboard with formulae which might refer to the functions of x, the digamma, or the Morse alphabet and say: "You see how simple the process is!" Not all of them saw. Yet he was genuinely humble.

Though Edwin D. Sanborn was not always as percipient in his judgment of his students as he was of Charles A. Young, he was one of Dartmouth's great teachers in the nineteenth century. Perhaps this was partly because he recognized the limitations of the teacher: a favorite quotation of his was from Gibbon — "The power of instruction is seldom of much efficacy except in those happy dispensations where it is almost superfluous." "Almost" — herein lies the justification for the teacher of men like Charles A. Young. And for men less brilliant there is ampler justification, as Sanborn's students would testify.

New Hampshire born he graduated from Dartmouth in 1832, studied theology for a year at the Andover Theological Seminary while teaching at the Academy, flirted for a time with the law but was called back to his Alma Mater as a tutor in 1835, and become Professor of Latin in 1837 when Alpheus Crosby wearied of that subject. He was not in the 1860 Directory because the year before he had gone to teach at Washington University in St. Louis, returning to Dartmouth in 1863 as Professor of Oratory and Belles Lettres, a position he held until 1880 when he became the first Winkley Professor of Anglo Saxon and English Language and Literature. He resigned in 1882 and died three years later.

During this latter period Sanborn was considered the strongest personality on the faculty. He had early acquired the nickname "Bully": his only qualities for a bully, Edwin Bartlett wrote, were vocal and physical, but he was a bully professor. And a man of great energy: as inspector of buildings in the 1840's he visited the recitation rooms before morning prayers at six o'clock to be sure the blackboards were cleaned and the rooms in order. Stout in physique he had a large head, a broad open face, adorned in his younger days with side whiskers, in his old age with a full beard. Body and soul bespoke vigor, health, robustiousness.

> . . . I have come to realize that among 600 angels selected at the age of adolescence a considerable percentage would start to moult after a few months of, shall we say, academic freedom. – E. Gordon Bill, 1924.

He brought to the classroom an extraordinary range of interests, based on encyclopedic reading, and a phenomenal memory: he could recite in his classroom, his daughter wrote, pages of Scott's novels, which he had not read since early youth — he could and did, "Bubby" Bartlett adds. Yet these bluff masculine qualities were matched by penetration, insight, and a warm personal relationship with individual students, a marvelous accuracy in analyzing their strong and weak points, so that a student went away from an interview buoyed up by wise and wholesome advice.

He lived in a large two-and-a-half-story house on the west side of the Green through whose hospitable door entered not only students and colleagues but eminent guests: Rufus Choate, Edward Everett, Salmon P. Chase, Wendell Phillips, Oliver Wendell Holmes, Edward Everett Hale, President Eliot. Its cellar, Kate Sanborn wrote, was redolent of Baldwins, Pearmains, Russets; the house contained few *objets d'art* other than whale oil lamps on the mantel and two chromos, Wide Awake and Fast Asleep, given to every subscriber of the *Christian Union,* in the drawing-room. But the walls of her father's domed study in the wing were papered with a panorama of the Bay of Naples. This room is appropriately preserved intact in the Sanborn English House, erected to his memory by his son, who stipulated in his will that the building should preserve in perpetuity that intimate relationship between teacher and student which had characterized his father's career.

If "Bully" Sanborn was distinctly in the native grain, Arthur Sherburn Hardy, Professor of Mathematics, brought to Hanover its first genuinely cosmopolitan personality. His father, Alpheus Hardy, was a wealthy merchant and philanthropist, a man of culture, trustee of Amherst and Phillips Andover, a supporter of foreign missions. At the age of twelve young Hardy was put to school in Neuchâtel in Switzerland, where he learned to speak French fluently. After a voyage to Spain on one of his father's ships he prepared for Amherst at the Boston Latin School and Andover. After a year at Amherst he entered West Point from which he graduated in 1869. He taught at West Point for a time and served as a second lieutenant in the Third Artillery on the Dry Tortugas. But eighteen months in the Army was enough and he resigned to become a professor of mathematics and civil engineering at Grinnell College in Iowa. In 1872 he was invited to teach in the Chandler School at Dartmouth but was unwilling to accept without further study. After a year as *élève externe* at the École des Ponts et Chaussies and the Conservatoire des Arts et Métiers — he deliberately chose Paris rather than Berlin because of his affinity with the French — he assumed in 1874 the professorship of civil engineering at the Chandler School, transferring to the chair of mathematics in the College in 1878.

Our running game was undoubtedly superior but our defensive playing against your forward passes was dumb. – Alonzo Stagg, 1925.

His students later remembered him as one of the most brilliant and versatile men they had ever known. His interests were by no means confined to the European orbit: one of his books, published in 1891, was the *Life and Letters of Joseph Hardy Neesima,* a cultured Japanese who had followed him at Andover and Amherst as a protégé of his father's. He was a notable lecturer, whether the subject was mathematics, art, architecture, or Spain. And an accomplished musician: in his library hung a sheet of music, *À la Nuit* by Gounod, a souvenir of a precious hour at the composer's house in the Paris suburbs where they had sung the song. He was a perfect horseman, excelled at tennis, chess, and cards; was a connoisseur of food and wine at a time when card-playing and wine-bibbing were still generally frowned on in Hanover. For Hanover was still a rural village where Hardy, as Philip Marden remembered him, was "always a distinguished figure by dress and carriage," a debonair man-of-the-world where there was at the moment none other.

To cap it all he was not only the author of competent textbooks in mathematics — Professor Bancroft Brown has called him the one

example of mathematical competency in nineteenth-century Dartmouth — but a successful novelist as well. Though his novels are now forgotten they were closer to those of Henry James than to the run-of-the-mill romances of the period. And if the phrase, "Mr. Hardy, the novelist," was mentioned in polite society the question was raised: "*Which* Mr. Hardy?"

The spectacle of the contrast between the formidable Samuel Colcord Bartlett in topper and frock coat on a bicycle and the urbane Professor Hardy on his handsome gray charger doubtless gave great delight to the undergraduates. Indeed there could scarcely have been two men of more incompatible temperaments in town. Yet they seem to have collaborated amicably in the landscaping of the College Park in the early 1880's. The President suggested the idea and Hardy, with the help of Bobby Fletcher, superintended the work, procured the iron gazebo which crowned the ledge on the western summit, an edifice that has vanished. But Hardy became one of the leaders of the movement to force the President's resignation — the "chief conspirator" President Bartlett called him. When that event occurred in 1892, *The Dartmouth* gave voice to general undergraduate opinion — there was one man above all others: "He is a man of great intelligence, of progressive ideas and of broad education . . . young, active and abreast of the times, Professor Hardy would make an ideal college president."

The next year Hardy resigned, whether from disappointment or a desire for wider fields of activity. For two years he served as editor of the *Cosmopolitan,* succeeding William Dean Howells. In 1897 McKinley appointed him minister to Persia. He continued in the diplomatic service for some years, as envoy to Greece, Roumania, Servia, Switzerland, and — finally — to Spain, having in 1902 been also offered the position of Assistant Secretary of State by John Hay. In 1905 he was abruptly displaced at Madrid by President Roosevelt as the result of a misunderstanding which was cleared up between him and Roosevelt some two years later, to their mutual satisfaction.

But by that time he had retired to Woodstock, Connecticut. He continued to write, notably a series of short stories in *Harpers* about Inspector Joly, a delightfully humane Parisian detective, a sort of forerunner of Simenon's Inspector Maigret. But literary fashions change. Though he lived to be eighty-three, dying at Woodstock in 1930, his reputation had faded.

*   *   *   *   *

By this time the classical curriculum was beginning to crumble. With the establishment of the Chandler School in the early 1850's the sciences had breeched the Greek and Roman wall. Edwin Sanborn as early as 1854 was grumbling about the inferior position of the "literary departments." By the 1870's graduate schools were in existence at Yale, Harvard, and Johns Hopkins. Prospective teachers and scholars no longer had to go to theological seminaries — or in rare cases to Europe — for advanced study. President Bartlett's scholarship, says Richardson, was both profound and productive, but it was limited to researches in Old Testament literature and this was not enough for the modern age.

Moreover by mid-century the educational ideas which had been gently simmering began to come to a boil. Up to that point the New England colleges had been about on a par as regards size and educational purpose; there were years when Dartmouth's enrollment was larger than Harvard's. Harvard and Yale were now forging ahead: in 1869 Harvard had an enrollment of over a thousand, Yale of over seven hundred — nearly twice that of Dartmouth's, the next highest of six other eastern colleges, including Princeton. And at Harvard the new president, who was not a clergyman but a chemist, was stirring up a hornet's nest of radical educational notions.

At Dartmouth the undergraduates had found a voice in the college newspaper, still a monthly. In July, 1870, the editor complained that young tutors were the failure and sham of American colleges, a disappointment to freshmen eager for college. (This was not a new complaint; nearly a hundred years before a Harvard student had described his tutors as "low born despicable rustics"; and at Oxford early in the seventeenth century the Head of a college had said the same thing, though more politely.) By 1882 *The Dartmouth* was saying that the College wisely had few inexperienced tutors, who gave a *less* satisfactory education than that obtainable in preparatory schools.

In 1870 the paper noted the rumors that Yale was about to introduce the elective or "restaurant" system; President Eliot had called the regular curriculum a "Procrustes bed," but Dartmouth would adhere to it, though the faculty had been authorized by the Trustees "to make limited and cautious use of the elective principle." A year later the editor was outspoken. The "disciplinary" subjects occupied more than half the college course. Too much time was spent on the ancient languages, too little on the modern; there was hardly an American college whose best students could employ French in conversation. In 1876 the editor lamented the lack of provision in the curriculum for a study of history; there should be a Chair of History, other colleges had it: "Why can't we do something *first?* Must conservative Dartmouth always *follow?*"

In 1881 the faculty and Trustees bestirred themselves slightly. Though the revised curriculum of that year was by no means revolutionary, required work in the classics and mathematics was considerably reduced and a polite bow was made to the elective principle. And in 1893 Dartmouth, like Harvard in 1869, had a new President — with similar results. In the issue for April 24, 1893, the College paper greeted with approval President Tucker's announcement that a professor of history and a professor of sociology were to be appointed at last: Herbert D. Foster of the class of 1885 and David Collin Wells, Yale, 1880. "A little more young blood is by no means unfortunate for the college." The "new" Dartmouth had arrived.

4

Dartmouth was never new until William Jewett Tucker assumed the presidency in 1893.

Bancroft H. Brown. Dartmouth *Alumni Magazine,* February, 1958

Though Bancroft Brown's statement is essentially true, I cannot take leave of the nineteenth century without saying a word about three stalwarts of the old Dartmouth who lived well on into the new: "Type" Hitchcock, "Clothespins" Richardson, and "Bubby" Bartlett.

Charles F. Hitchcock was the member of Dartmouth's nineteenth-century faculty whose reputation as a scientist was second only to Charles A. Young's. If the Hanover Plain may be thought a natural point of vantage from which to view the sidereal universe, it is likewise fitting that Hitchcock as a geologist should have been drawn to Hanover by the granite of New Hampshire. His father was President of Amherst and also a professor of geology there whose expressed object, he said, was "to illustrate, by the scientific facts which I taught, the principles of natural theology." Allan Macdonald used to say that teachers were "reformed parsons"; the younger Hitchcock seems to have been one of them. For though after his graduation from Amherst in 1856 (before he was twenty), he assisted his father in a geological survey of Vermont, he also pursued theological studies at Yale and — like Edwin Sanborn and Charles A. Young — at the Andover Theological Seminary. The defection of these three men from theology to teaching is an illustration of what Robert Le Duc has felicitously called, in his little book about Amherst College, the progress of American education from piety to intellect. Hitchcock came to Dartmouth in 1868, being appointed that year as the State Geologist of New Hampshire. His three-volume work on the Geology of New Hampshire (1874-78) was his principal work, though after his retirement in 1908 he studied the volcanic craters of Hawaii, where he died in 1919 at eighty-three.

> Dartmouth is at the edge of a forest. In the evening the students carry their dinner and their books into the depths of the woods. During the fine weather they pass the night there and the farther away the better they like it. – André Maurois, 1928.

With Charles A. Young he was one of the founders of the Dartmouth Scientific Association: his telegram to this society at a meeting on September 28, 1870 — "No longer call New Hampshire azoic, Silurian fossils just discovered" — excited the society and created a stir in the scientific world. He is also memorable for his winters spent with J. C. Huntington on the summits of Moosilauke and Mt. Washington to conduct studies of the weather. Able teacher and sound scholar, he founded at Dartmouth a distinguished department of geology whose reputation was further enhanced by his twentieth-century associate Professor James Walter Goldthwaite and has been maintained by their successors of today. He has been immortalized, among geologists at least, by Lake Hitchcock, a body of invisible water stretching from East Haddam, Connecticut, nearly to Lyme, from which the Hanover Plain emerged after the glacial period to become the seat of Dartmouth College, thus demonstrating that New Hampshire is not indeed azoic.

Charles F. Richardson illustrates the erosion of piety by belles lettres as well as by science. He was editor of *The Dartmouth* in 1871 and the year before that wrote an unfavorable review of Elizabeth Stuart Phelps's *Gates Ajar,* preferring his own highly fanciful theory of heaven to her golden streets and pearly gates. Nevertheless in his history of American literature he devoted a page to Miss Phelps's novels and stories, though barely mentioning Mark Twain. He was editor of the *Sunday School Times* as well as other journals before coming to Dartmouth in 1882 to succeed Edwin Sanborn as Winkley Professor and to be the sole English teacher until Fred P. Emery, 1887, came from M.I.T. to assist him in 1894. In his second year at Dartmouth he gave a course in American literature, the second in the country, Moses Coit Tyler's at the University of Michigan in 1775 having been the first. He continued as Winkley Professor until his retirement in 1911, dying two years later.

A library at Sugar Hill, given to the town by his widow, and his history of American literature published in two volumes in 1886-88 are tangible monuments to his memory. This history was the first comprehensive account (Tyler's three volumes, perhaps more scholarly, stopped with the Revolution). Barrett Wendell's *Literary History of America* did not appear until 1900. Though Richardson's style may not be as impeccable as Wendell's his history is eminently readable and the Dartmouth don in a cursory comparison holds his own with the Boston Brahmin in matters of literary judgment and taste. Both men, of course, belong to the genteel tradition, though Wendell's gentility was rather more glacial for he disdained to discuss figures which the more catholic Richardson included in his book. (But, though Wendell also dismissed Mark Twain in a word, he did at least concede that *Huckleberry Finn* was a masterpiece.)

Richardson obviously preferred the "romantic" writers to the "realists" who were coming to the fore. If to a more sophisticated generation his judgments may thus seem curiously limited and askew, it should be said that he at least took the risk of discussing living writers and in this was more daring than the parochial and cautious Bostonian. But they both recognized before most of their academic contemporaries that American literature was worthy of study. And they both loved literature, communicating their love to thousands of students.

The undergraduates chose not literature but Professor Richardson, Edwin Bartlett wrote, as Dartmouth emerged from the rather stern and unadorned life of its first century. In his very first year he won the enduring nickname awarded him in a jingle written by Arthur Whipple Jenks, 1884:

> Thy head is large, thy lower limbs are slim,
> In clothes and figure thou appearest trim;
> So may this appellation to thee stick:
> Thy name henceforward shall be *Clothespin Dick*.

Indeed the tall figure in the gray sack suit (an innovation in the days of the frock coat) with the genial face and whimsical smile brought a note of informality to the campus. He was a modest gentleman — "so large an element of imperfection," he wrote in his letter of resignation to President Nichols, "has mingled with my toil." He made his students feel, one of them wrote, that they knew English literature as well as he, but that he simply happened to have made a more careful study than they.

Another alumnus of some years later remembered a line of Shelley's — "Where music and moonlight and feeling are one" — quoted by him in a swift talk on reading, thus shining as one of the "few bright star points set in darkness" of Robert Frost's months as a freshman in 1892.

How is one already deeply in debt to "Bubby" Bartlett for many a sparkling reminiscence and vivid phrase with which to enliven this chronicle to do further justice to him? Though I lived in the same village with him for nine years I never set eyes on him; from his retirement in 1920 to his death at eighty-one in 1932 he was, because of ill health, largely confined to his little Wheelock Street house crouched between the towering Dekes and Phi Gams. Yet his slight wiry body, physically vigorous until old age, his thin expressive face, are as vivid to me as if I had known him for years and if this is so it is because his power to convey his personality through the written word was extraordinary.

The Bartlett family has served Dartmouth College for over a century if one follows it from the days when Samuel Colcord Bartlett, 1836, became tutor for a year in 1838, and President from 1877 to 1892; records Edwin ("Bubby") Bartlett's term of service in the chemistry

A Study in Curves : by
Botticelli R. Bugg

department from 1879 to 1920; and adds to the roster the name of Professor Bartlett's nephew Donald now in 1964, Professor of Biography. The contentious period of President Bartlett's administration and the many-faceted qualities of his diamond-sharp personality have been described. Many of the father's qualities were passed on to the son, not least of them the keen wit. (One instance of Samuel Colcord Bartlett's repartee merits preservation. In 1887 one of the students in the President's senior Bible class was a brash young man named Goddard — he later achieved eminence as a journalist. One day this dialogue occurred in class: Goddard: "President Bartlett, is anything impossible with God?" The President: "Goddard, only one thing is impossible with God. He could not have made your mouth any larger without making your head an island.")

Though "Bubby" Bartlett's wit was keen he must have been somewhat mellower than his father; at any rate during his long career of teaching he conveyed the impression of a personal interest in his thousands of students. Not a great scientist, as Charles E. Bolser, his colleague for many years, recorded, he was a great teacher of science. Accuracy for him was the first essential and a reverence for facts — "yet he knew how to make the bending of theories around them fascinating." He was at his best, Professor Bolser wrote, as an expert witness. His quick logical mind, his mastery of Anglo-Saxon English won for him an enviable reputation in the courts of New Hampshire and the adjacent states. A stalwart Republican, a man of strong convictions, opinionated, sometimes stubborn, he was never unreasonably prejudiced. His friendship for John King Lord, one of his father's chief opponents, is the mark of a magnanimous spirit.

His love and concern for the College are illustrated in many ways. His address at the laying of the cornerstone of the Alumni Gymnasium points up his interest in athletics — he played baseball, tennis, golf as well as excelling at chess and whist. An article he wrote on football at seventy-five shows a detailed knowledge of the game; for though his various reminiscences breathe affection for the past he lived always in the present and never bemoaned "the good old days." For years he presented the candidates for degrees at Commencement: "Bubby has a perfect genius for brief epigraphy. He can describe a man and his works in two lines with the vividness of a chemical reaction," Philip Marden wrote. As for instance, in presenting the Rev. James L. Barton for the degree of D.D.: "The honored ambassador of the one great power which gives us hope of lasting peace on earth and good will toward men."

[146]

The vivid quality of his writing and the purity of his sentiment is revealed in an article he wrote for the *Alumni Magazine* on the SATC in February, 1919. He had a bad dream: a wild beast was loose in the world; those who opposed the beast grew very tired.

Sadly late, for very shame and because the beast might catch them too, the neutral bystander had to help. And it seemed that the ones to meet the onslaught of the beast were the little boys who had grown up in our homes, or who had played the games and sometimes done the tasks of college life.

But, as in a true fairy tale or imaginary dream, some object — a winged slipper, a cloak of invisibility, a drop of blood — remains to testify to the reality of the tale or the dream, so of this horrible dream the tangible evidences remained: in Rollins Chapel the flag of 72 gold stars — and "at least ten more will take the vacant places."

One is tempted to go on quoting. Better to close with his qualifications for the college teacher (which might be an unconscious self-portrait). "No man, not even a starry genius, should get by into college work who did not add a minor to his profound major learning, to make him human. But I should be so liberal in accepting the minor that old conservatives would view me with alarm." The minor might be true excellence in billiards, or any game of skill; any cultivated talent as for music, for cooking, for preaching; a lively hobby like photography or wood life; a gift for languages, wide travel, long residence in foreign lands; public service from page to legislature to President. "Possibly under some circumstances marriage." There it is, from an "old conservative" of seventy-four, with the fillip of humor at the end. *Ave atque vale*, Bubby Bartlett, alas that your memory like that of all temporal things should ever fade.

5

Many members of faculties are interested in administration to the degree of criticism; few, very few to the degree of responsibility.

William Jewett Tucker

We have now arrived in our survey of the faculty full into the twentieth century and we must accelerate our pace. For this is the century when Clio, a flustered and harassed maiden, has lost her dignity if not her maidenhood. Even before the Second World War higher education had become a big business; after the war with the cascading of grants from the foundations and from government, with the perfection of the science of public relations, and with the great influx of students, it became even bigger and administrative officers proliferated. (Parkinson's Law was discovered.) Not only at Dartmouth but at other colleges and universities the century spawned chancellors, presidents, vice-presidents, provosts, deans, associate deans, assistant deans, directors of personnel, and, perhaps as a logical conclusion — psychiatrists. This was a· development unknown to English universities, which muddle through with committees manned by professors in rotation (generally without secretaries), or to continental institutions like the Sorbonne — if we are to credit the admonition: *Si vous cherchez l'administration, addressez-vous au concierge.*

A curious outgrowth of this situation is the development of antagonism and in some cases outright hostilities between faculties and administrations. It is tempting to speculate whether this phenomenon may not be in part a reflection of our federal system with its balance of powers and the mutual jealousies and suspicions of the executive and legislative branches. If so it is unfortunate that in the academic world there is no third organ like the Supreme Court to adjudicate differences. Not the trustees — they are too closely bound to the administration. Not the alumni — except as they operate as Alumni Councils and Boards of Overseers — they are too busy watching the athletic teams and raising funds for the support of their Alma Maters.

It is also a curious fact that in general the administrators come from the faculty. Yet it also seems to be true that once a professor becomes an administrator he loses caste with his colleagues: lost to them in administrative depths he seems to suffer a sea change into something strange, if not rich. Yet, despite what I have said, it is only fair to say that at Dartmouth, in the twentieth century, relations between administration and faculty have been marked on the whole by cooperation rather than by contention; and this is as it should be since they are both engaged in the common enterprise of education.

The careers of John King Lord and Richard Husband as teacher-administrators show that the classics could still make a vital contribution to Dartmouth. Lord was the grandson of the President — and he was also the father of Dr. Frederic Pomeroy Lord, who was for thirty-five years Professor of Anatomy in the Medical School. John K. Lord, beginning as tutor in 1869, taught Latin for forty-seven years; in 1909 he was nearly elected President. In 1916, the year after his retirement, he was elected a Trustee and served on the Board until his death in 1926 rounded out fifty-seven years of dedication to the College. He was also active in church, town, school, and hospital affairs; and completed the history of the town and College begun by Frederick Chase. Samuel L. Powers, 1874, gives a thumbnail sketch of him as a tutor of twenty-two: dark eyes, jet black hair, a clear complexion; his manner of conducting a recitation, his rapid questions during the sixty-minute period calling to their feet every member of the class, not unlike that of a West Point martinet. Yet he was popular. He had time, too, for scholarly editions of Cicero and Livy and for study in Germany and Italy in the 'eighties.

Richard W. Husband was born in the year Lord began to teach and came to Dartmouth in 1900 as an instructor in Greek, later turning his attention to Latin. That his interests were not narrow is indicated by his book, published in 1916 by the Princeton University Press, *The Trial of Jesus before Pilate,* which reflected his studies of Roman legal procedure. He was a stimulating teacher as well: groups of students read Latin and Greek with him voluntarily in the evenings. In 1910 he directed a memorable performance of *Oedipus Tyrannus* in Greek, with a set designed by George D. Lord and Homer Eaton Keyes.

When President Hopkins, returning from his personnel work in the War Department, appointed Husband in 1920 as perhaps the first college director of personnel in the country, he brought to this position not only his sound classical training but his experience in war work on the state Committee of Public Safety. For he possessed an ability to make contact between academic and business and professional circles and a sympathetic understanding of the young. In his new position he pioneered in the introduction of psychological tests, faculty reports, vocational guidance, and psychotherapy for men under nervous strain. Thus the scholarly classicist became nationally known as an expert in this new field. But this career was cut short by his death at fifty-five in 1924.

The term of another teacher-administrator, Craven Laycock, 1896, as Dean of the College from 1911 to 1933 is the longest in this office to date in Dartmouth's history. Thousands of alumni remember the tall imposing figure, the granitic face, with the humorous twinkle in the eyes which belied its sternness, the deliberate sonorous voice, with its Yorkshire burr (for he was born in Bradford, England in 1866), a voice which was inimitable — except by Professor Allen R. Foley. As a teacher of public speaking he was notable for his efforts to clear students' minds of muddle, to make their writing and speaking concise and

definite, stripped of bombast. (These qualities of clarity and concision he brought to those occasions when he presided over faculty meetings — one can still hear him saying: "The chair is in doubt.") He could be stern and peremptory: this the student who faked a telegram and lied about it quickly discovered: "Young man, you're out of college." But his essential kindliness was more characteristic, as that student discovered who also lied to him about a request for a cut but came in to confess the lie, ready to take punishment: "Young man, you haven't lied. You haven't come into the office. If you'll forget the whole thing, so will I." Or as Courtney Anderson, 1931, discovered when summoned to explain why he had cut classes for nine consecutive days. "I've been writing a novel, sir — sixty thousand words." "Young man, you're the sort of man we want at Dartmouth." Anderson remained to become one of the early Senior Fellows. And Craven Laycock remains at Dartmouth: his bronze bust stands on the top floor of Baker Library, the brightly polished nose a testimony of his power to give moral support to superstitious undergraduates before their examinations.

E. Gordon Bill was equally awesome to a timid freshman or a timid faculty instructor. Tall and robust he possessed, like Ebenezer Adams, his long-ago predecessor in the mathematics department, a roaring voice — it was said that you could tell not only whether he was in his office in Parkhurst but even whether he was in town. Bill came to the United States from Nova Scotia: a one-room schoolhouse, an A.B. from Acadia, a Ph.D. from Yale, in 1908, and study at Bonn accounted for his formal education; working in a lumberyard and as surveyor for the Canadian Pacific Railroad filled the gaps.

He came to Dartmouth in 1912 as an Assistant Professor of Mathematics. During the War he was on leave to serve as a statistician and later Director for the Canadian Service Draft. He was, therefore, a natural choice of President Hopkins to implement the Selective Process of Admissions, adopted by Dartmouth in 1921, thereby creating considerable stir, and much severe criticism by some colleges which later imitated many of its features. "I have a hunch" — after he became Dean of the Faculty in 1933 his hunches became a byword. He was blunt, erratic, unconventional; Owen D. Young once said in a speech at a Dartmouth dinner in New York: "I like this Dean who pretends to be hard-boiled but who is at heart a poet." Appropriate, then, to round out his portrait with two poetic tributes: Kenneth Robinson's toast at the unveiling of Paul Sample's portrait of him:

Oh Gordon Bill
Long may you fill
These academic cloisters
With hearty wit
And lots of it,
And fresh ideas — and oysters.

Now Sample (Paul)
Enshrines them all
— The splendid things our Dean is —
Wherefore we toast
Our pictured host
In champagne or Martinis.

Two men of parts
Combine their arts
To earn this toast we're giving
— The painter of the American scene,
And he whose art — I mean the Dean —
Is his by American living.

And Franklin McDuffee's "Dartmouth Undying" — "Belatedly but whole-heartedly dedicated to E. G. B. who has done so much to keep Dartmouth alive."

6

I cannot praise a fugitive and cloister'd vertue, unexercis'd and unbreath'd, that never sallies out and sees her adversary, but slinks out of the race, where that immortall garland is to be run for, not without dust & heat.

Milton: Areopagitica

The Anglo-Saxon tradition of education is that, though never attaining ideal perfection, we approach it nearer and nearer by ever increasing our store of knowledge, that by inquiry, discussion, and investigation we progressively acquire ability to distinguish truth from error; and that freedom to inquire, to speak, and to investigate is the essence of the liberty we prize.

Ernest Martin Hopkins: Fragments of Truth

As Dr. Tucker put it, Eleazar Wheelock gave to the College the stamp of religious adventurousness; he and John Wentworth especially wrote the principle of religious tolerance into the charter. Dr. Tucker brought to the Dartmouth of the twentieth century intellectual adventurousness and affirmed the principle of intellectual tolerance. These principles were, no doubt, reinforced by the nineteenth-century *Lern-*

Dartmouth Undying

(Belately but whole-heartedly dedicated to E.G.B.,
who has done so much to keep Dartmouth alive.)

Dartmouth! — There is no music for our singing,
no words to bear the burden of our praise,
yet how can we be silent and remember
The splendor and the fullness of her days!

Who can forget her soft September sunsets,
who can forget those hours that passed like dreams—
The long cold shadows floating on the campus,
The drifting beauty where the twilight streams?

Who can forget her sharp and misty mornings,
The clanging bells, the crunch of feet on snow,
Her sparkling noons, the crowding into Commons,
Her long white afternoons, her twilight glow?

See! By the light of many thousand sunsets
Dartmouth Undying like a vision starts:
Dartmouth — the gleaming, dreaming walls of Dartmouth
miraculously builded in our hearts.

Franklin McDuffie

[153]

freiheit which men like George Ticknor brought back from Germany; that freedom from the vassalage, as President Quincy of Harvard put it in 1840, in which the mind was held "by sects in the church, and by parties in the state." But the tradition of "academic freedom" had its roots in the Promethean daring of the Renaissance, and back beyond that in ancient Greece. For Anglo-Saxons it has its springs in the Elizabethan age, in the voyages of the explorers; in the science of Bacon; in the humanity of Shakespeare; in the voice of Milton.

At Dartmouth intellectual adventurousness has been mirrored in the curriculum: in the courses in evolution and citizenship for freshmen initiated after the First World War; in the Great Issues course for seniors inaugurated after World War II. But it is something less tangible than policies and courses; it is an atmosphere in which men's minds, not tacked down like carpets, are left free to soar and be blown about by various winds of doctrine like autumn leaves. This has its dangers, of course, as is illustrated by the postwar disillusionment, skepticism, rebellion, and hedonistic license of the 'twenties. It may lead to an indecisive liberalism: too much learning, too much arguing about it and about. Though this, too, is important: one of Dartmouth's most stimulating teachers was Rees Bowen who brought to the College his experience in Welsh mines, his training at Oxford, Yale, and the London School of Economics, and his voluminous reading (it was said he read at least one book a day). And it was doubtless salutary that his characteristic "on ze one hand — but on ze other hand" often left the bewildered student like the donkey halfway between two bales of hay. It may lead — "on the other hand" — to the too hasty adoption by immature minds of a rigid dogmatism, as Mr. Hopkins realized in the 'thirties when he acknowledged the risks of extending freedom "to the proponents of systems which stand for suppression of all freedoms except their own."

But in spite of the dangers, the freedom to think, write, speak, and teach has provided a heady and stimulating atmosphere at Dartmouth — for those who wish to breathe it. On the lighter side it gave scope to the airy sophistication of a William McCarter ("The Scarlet Letter is the Red Badge of Courage"); or to the wit of a George Frost with his reference to Sidney Cox's "jarring of false bottoms" and the worship of Rosenstock-Huessy's students for the "very air he walks on." More important it drew to Dartmouth men whose strong and stimulating personalities attracted a following of loyal, devoted, and intelligent students: men like John Mecklin; like James MacKaye in philosophy, with his relentless logic; men, indeed, like Sidney Cox in English, and Rosenstock-Huessy, whose dynamic thought led in 1940 to dynamic action in the establishment in Vermont of the William James Camp community service experiment, since acknowledged as the forerunner of the Peace Corps.

The figure of autumn leaves blown about by the winds of doctrine suggests aimlessness. But anyone knows that a ship, however much it may tack, must follow a course if it is to reach its goal. As Don Juan pointed out in *Man and Superman,* "to be in hell is to drift: to be in heaven is to steer." (Here we come to the moral, Puritan overtone.) Thus, with all his emphasis on freedom, President Hopkins emphasized also a sense of purpose; and President Dickey has constantly pointed out the necessity, not only for exploring all the facets of a problem, but for making choices.

Thus tradition and continuity are essential to an institution's influence. It is fortunate (and not merely fortuitous) for American education that President Eliot in 1869 set the course for Harvard which was followed, not only by himself but by his two successors for over eighty years — and continued indeed by Mr. Pusey in his firm resistance to McCarthyism. So at Dartmouth the tradition of academic adventurousness has been upheld by three strong helmsmen for seventy years from 1893 to the present (including the Nichols interregnum). The influence of many excellent institutions has been weakened by vacillating courses and too brief, if often brilliant, successions of leadership. Thus it is not accidental that in the reaction and hysteria of the 1920's Mr. Lowell at Harvard and Mr. Hopkins brought to the valiant defense of academic freedom not only the force of their personalities but the authority of two institutions older than the Republic. It should also be added that, despite Upton Sinclair and *The Goose Step,* this defense owes perhaps as much to the governing boards of these institutions as to their faculties. But now to cite a few concrete instances.

George Ray Wicker, who had just received his doctorate at the University of Wisconsin and been brought to Dartmouth in 1900 by Dr. Tucker, was at the beginning of the Hopkins administration Professor of Economics, an able scholar whose brilliant and incisive teaching made him extremely popular with students. He looked like Woodrow Wilson — indeed, when teaching at the University of California in the summer of 1914 he was sometimes taken for the President. Though an admirer of Wilson, he had in 1912 actively participated in the Progressive Party in New Hampshire and was an intimate friend of the progressive Governor Bass and of Winston Churchill whose novels, *Coniston* and *Mr. Crewe's Career,* dealt with the domination of state politics by the Boston and Maine Railroad. Wicker fully shared Churchill's views and was outspoken in his attacks on the corporation and its officials, two of whom, Benjamin Kimball, President of the Concord and Montreal, the B. and M.'s New Hampshire subsidiary, and Frank S. Streeter, for years general counsel of the railroad, were perhaps the most influential members of Dartmouth's Board of Trustees.

Wicker's attacks inevitably aroused opposition to him in the state. One day President Hopkins received a letter from a prominent member of the legislature with a petition signed by one hundred members of that body requesting that Wicker be fired and threatening the withdrawal of the state's yearly contribution of $5,000 to the College if he were not. Mr. Hopkins replied that he would present the letter to the Trustees, though he thought he knew what they would do with it. At the next meeting of the Board he read the letter. Mr. Kimball, an imposing bearded gentleman, familiarly known as "Uncle Ben," asked, "Who wrote that?" Mr. Hopkins handed him the letter. "Uncle Ben" read it and looked up. "I don't think we've got to the point where the legislature can admonish Dartmouth College as to what it should do. I move its rejection." Wicker continued with his teaching and his outspoken views until his sudden death in 1917.

That same year Mr. Hopkins, in pursuit of his conviction that the academic world should occasionally be given a tonic from the world of affairs, appointed — in spite of strong faculty opposition — James Parmelee Richardson, 1878, as Parker Professor of Law and Politics. Richardson was by no means a radical; he was a Boston lawyer, a stalwart Republican, and a conservative in the best sense of the word. An imposing, not to say ponderous man, six feet, five inches in height, he possessed a dominating personality; in faculty meetings he disposed of what seemed to him erratic and unsound ideas in a deliberate voice to which a slight nasal twang gave an accent of scorn. Yet "Big Jim" was not to be pigeonholed. He confounded those who considered him humorless and pompous by the gusto with which he sang *A Policeman's Lot Is Not a Happy One* on the stage of Webster and performed in other Gilbert and Sullivan operas. And in 1927, at the height of the Sacco-Vanzetti agitation, he astounded his conservative friends by reporting to the Governor of Massachusetts the prejudicial remark — the reference to Sacco and Vanzetti as those "anarchistic bastards" — made to him at a football game by the trial judge, a friend and fellow-alumnus. This was given wide publicity. He received the ecstatic plaudits of the proponents of Sacco and Vanzetti, plaudits which he scarcely relished; and of course the equally pronounced objurgations of those on the other side. These reached their climax when an irate gentleman wrote offering $50,000 to the College if Richardson were fired. Mr. Hopkins passed on this offer, suggesting facetiously that it be accepted and that they split the amount between them. "Big Jim" was not amused. Neither was he fired.

John Moffatt Mecklin's quest for freedom, as he called his auto-biography, began with his birth in Mississippi in 1871 and ended only with his death in Hanover eighty-five years later. It is the story of a ranging, restless, and probing mind, of a man with a subcutaneous indignation at intolerance, as Malcolm Keir put it, with an intensely passionate moral fervor, pursued by and pursuing the Hound of Heaven, though in his case the Hound was not God but the search for truth and freedom. Son and descendant of Presbyterian ministers, he studied under Woodrow Wilson's father at the Southwestern Presbyterian University in Tennessee; got his Ph.D. at the Princeton Theological Seminary in 1896 and entered on a pastorate at Dalton, Georgia, the same year. There he married a woman of great tact and sympathy whose insight persuaded him that teaching rather than the ministry was his natural bent.

In 1897 the Mecklins went to Germany where, two years later, he received his Ph.D. from the University of Leipzic. He traveled in Italy and in 1900 he went to Greece. There the Calvinist became a Hellenist, though he later confessed that the Greek ideal of nothing too much was not for him.

For three years he taught Greek at Washington and Jefferson and in 1905 was called by the President to teach philosophy at Lafayette. Here the students responded eagerly to the stimulus of his ideas; but his teaching became increasingly harassed by the Calvinist President, who accused him of disturbing young men's minds, being a President-baiter, and raising sinful questions of evolution. After eight years the harassment reached a climax: he was summoned from the bedside of his wife, dying of cancer, to defend himself before a board of trustees almost equally divided between his partisans and his opponents. Weary and distressed he refused and offered to resign — an offer which was eagerly accepted. On the announcement of his resignation the entire senior class rebelled and passed resolutions demanding the President's resignation. The affair became a *cause célèbre:* during the next year an investigating committee of the American Philosophical and the American Psychological Associations rendered a report which resulted in the formation of the American Association of University Professors and a demand from the Lafayette trustees for the President's resignation.

Meanwhile Mecklin had been immediately invited by the Chancellor to take charge of the University of Pittsburgh's department of philosophy. Exhausted, disillusioned, cynical, suffering somewhat from a martyr complex, he found the university a haven where his teaching was unquestioned; in 1915 he met and married his second wife. But he became increasingly disturbed by the chasm existing between the Scotch-Irish Presbyterian pillars of society and the hunkies, wops, Polacks, and Negroes of the mills. And the outbreak of the great strike of 1919 made him rudely aware of the conflict between the ideals of Christianity and Jeffersonian democracy and the brutal realities of the industrial feudalism of the steel city.

Appalled at the suppression of the strikers, he and others arranged a meeting in Duquesne whose mayor had boasted that "Jesus Christ himself could not hold a meeting in Duquesne." The speakers were arrested and the mayor was upheld by the courts. At a crowded meeting held later in Pittsburgh he made the headlines with his statement that Duquesne had witnessed the "lynching of the Constitution of the United States"; for this the university authorities called him on the carpet.

Fortunately at this point President Hopkins, though forewarned that he was dangerous and a rabble-rouser, offered him a position at Dartmouth. Soon after his arrival at Dartmouth in 1920 he was asked to speak to the freshmen on the steel strike. At the close of his talk a dozen freshmen excitedly insisted that he had been talking "socialism"; one boy, white and tense, whose father was in the steel business, declared that what he had said was false. Mecklin told his objectors to have it out with their instructors — that was the Dartmouth way. It was the Dartmouth way: the famous Hopkins liberalism had met the test.

At this time Dr. Tucker had withdrawn from Hanover life, being seen more and more infrequently driving out in his victoria. But Mecklin became increasingly fascinated by his writings — his speeches and chapel talks. He found the great President's heritage of freedom Dartmouth's most precious possession. Had he reached the end of his quest? Not really. He had at last found peace in cloistered Hanover, but he was bothered by its remoteness from the harsh realities of a Pittsburgh. He pondered these matters as he fished for bass in the Connecticut with "Dad" Bowman of the Hanover Inn barbershop, or

[158]

for lake trout with his fellow-members of a Laurentian Mountains fish-and-game club. The celestial trout still eluded him. What were the stereotypes, the historical fictions, the social myths which made his fellow-club members Vermont Republicans, his native Mississippians members of the Ku Klux Klan? What had happened to Dr. Tucker's religious humanism which had been the bulwark of his devotion to free-dom? Was *laissez-faire* freedom enough, either for a vigorous economic or a vital intellectual society? Was not a creative and purposeful free-dom possible? These were the questions he pondered in his books and raised with the students in his classes.

At first he had been taken a little aback by the easy complacency of his Dartmouth students, most of them from well-to-do suburban fam-ilies. At one of his early classes he noticed two students in the front row who seemed to be absorbed by the lecture. What had most inter-ested them? They replied with embarrassment that they had made a wager as to how far he would go in his ambulations before he knocked the hat on his desk off onto the floor. Were these handsome and charm-ing youths impervious to the teaching he had gained through tears and sweat?

He need not have worried. Long before he had run his Dartmouth course he had become a legendary figure on the campus. With his mellifluous Mississippi drawl, his histrionic mastery of all the rhetorical devices of old-fashioned southern oratory, with his white hair, erect carriage, his expressive face, which twisted itself "into a thousand con-tortions," he held his listeners spellbound. His courses were jammed. Thomas W. Braden, 1940, spoke for them all: John Moffatt Mecklin at his retirement was "the most important single influence on student thinking."

In 1925 students at Montana State University published a magazine which brought down upon them the wrath of the citizenry. A character in one of the stories published was a harlot; in another sketch the phrase "son-of-a-bitch" was used three times to illustrate the subtle intonations with which it might be said. The legislature was in a turmoil; headlines screamed; resolutions were passed demanding the head of Sidney Cox, the English instructor who was the faculty sponsor of the magazine. Though the administration stuck to its guns in de-fense of Cox, Montana State had become so unpleasant for him that he decided to look elsewhere for a job.

In 1911 he had come from Bates to the Plymouth, New Hampshire, High School to teach. Young, enthusiastic, still somewhat Puritanical (he did not approve of Whitman), he met at a dance one night an older man who was teaching psychology in the Plymouth Normal School. He did not quite approve of the older man, either; let the latter tell it: "By saying something flippant about the theme papers he had to hurry away to correct I angered him to the point of his inquiring behind my back if it was because of alcohol I had got no further up in the world at my age." In spite of this the two (the other was Robert Frost) became fast friends.

So, when Sidney Cox got involved in the uproar in Montana (Mencken later asked him to tell his story for the *American Mercury,* but he refused), Robert Frost came to Mr. Hopkins with the tale and told him that Sidney Cox, a great teacher, was looking for a job. Mr. Hopkins listened sympathetically and in spite of the lack of enthusiasm of the English Department he recommended Cox's appointment to the Trustees. He told the tale in full. There was a moment's silence. Then Fred Howland — in his great bulk as magisterial a personality as "Uncle Ben" Kimball — spoke up: "The question is, Mr. President, is Mr. Cox going to call *us* sons-of-bitches if he comes. I move his appointment."

It was to be nearly twenty years before Sidney Cox won the full approval of his department. They thought he wore his heart too much upon his sleeve. Of his book, *The Teaching of English,* one of them said: "It's what we all do, but we don't *talk* about it." Sensitive and defiantly independent, he held to his course. He won, as I have said, the enthusiastic devotion of a host of students. And at his death in 1954 both students and colleagues would agree that Sidney Cox would go down in Dartmouth's annals as one of its great teachers.

In the depression of the thirties intellectual adventurousness met its severest test at Dartmouth. Students who were sons of bankrupt brokers became Marxists, if not actual Communists. There were mass meetings and "peace strikes," letters to *The Dartmouth:* one member of the faculty offered to lead a detachment of fellow ex-Marines to Washington to assassinate any member of Congress who voted for war. The League Against War and Fascism was active; many members of the faculty belonged. It was suspected of being a Communist-front organization and indeed it was. Though there was not to my knowledge a Communist member of the faculty in the organization, there were some fellow-travelers, who were in fact really Jeffersonian individualists or philosophical anarchists: in the unlikely event of a revolution, Bolshevik style, they would have been shot in the early stages. One member of the faculty ran for the United States Senate on a Farmer-Labor ticket and received a hundred votes in Hanover, though he ran far behind Senator Bridges and his Democratic opponent in the state. Parents and alumni were alarmed. But the President held the fort: though his knees may have trembled when he addressed alumni meetings, no one would have guessed it. Though he may occasionally have used the Jeffersonian tactics of reason and persuasion, never was the slightest pressure brought upon any teacher in the institution — as Sir Osbert Sitwell's father was fond of saying, "We happen to know." And although once or twice the student straw vote, contrary to general custom, may have gone Democratic, the College like the country weathered the storm. Even before the Stalin purges and the Nazi-Soviet pact the fellow-travelers, like the ideal Communist state, had begun to wither away. It was at the beginning of this turbulent period that Jose Clemente Orozco, the revolutionary, though not Communist artist, came to Hanover.

Artemas Packard, eloquent champion of Orozco, was scarcely a fellow-traveller. As chairman of the Art Department he had superintended in 1928 its transfer from Victorian Culver, the home of the "Dungies" before they were removed to Durham, to its new home in Carpenter and had also begun the process of bringing able young men to Hanover to revitalize the department. Urbane and debonair, he was a man of manifold interests — cooking, collecting junk, fishing, mycology, tele-

phoning by the hour, needling colleagues and students — in addition to his professional concerns; so many in fact that the unthinking considered him a mere dilettante. But he was devoted to teaching in its broadest sense, willing to give an unconscionable amount of time to individual students. He was a man of creative ideas, violently opposed to the departmentalization of knowledge and teaching. He would have heartily endorsed — if he had lived to hear it — William Schuman's statement at the inaugural of the Hopkins Center that too much "of academic pursuit of the arts is concerned with talk or writing about art . . . but not with art in direct experience." Indeed, this was an essential part of his creed, as expressed in his own words, in discussing the importance of the Orozco frescoes: to bring out into the open "matters which have been hitherto confined to the rarefied atmosphere of the classroom and to the polite mumbo-jumbo of the salon and the tea table." In pursuit of this purpose he had brought Lewis Mumford to Hanover, first for a series of lectures on the Brown Decades, later during several years for lectures and seminars. It was he also who urged Dean Bill to find a place for Walter Curt Behrendt, engineer, architect, Finanzrat who, under the Weimar Republic, had been responsible for the planning of Berlin (and who, in the all too few years before his death in 1945, acquired a following of devoted students comparable to that of the men I have mentioned above).

It is still, however, not to be forgotten that our colleges were founded and sustained through years of drastic toil by men of religious fervor, who, in self-sacrifice, literally gave their lives for the perpetuation of institutions designed no less for spiritual inspiration than for intellectual command. – Ernest Martin Hopkins, 1916.

With the beguiling diplomacy Artemas Packard liked to employ — he was also a politician *manqué* — and on the assumption that the benign influences of the Art Department should penetrate everywhere he invited the Librarian of the College to reflect upon the small Orozco fresco in the Baker-Carpenter passageway which was the extent of the painter's initial undertaking. After Mr. Goodrich had duly admired it, Artemas Packard said: "Nat, what do you intend to do with all that blank space in the reserve room of Baker?" Mr. Goodrich was not taken in: "What do *you* want to do with it?" They both went to the President.

Thus Orozco was commissioned in June, 1932, with the title of visiting professor of art, "to teach by doing," without any restrictions; thus

[162]

was extended the principle of academic freedom to the field of public art. For the next two years students, walking through the reserve room or studying there, watched Gobin Stair, 1933, preparing the wet plaster; saw the little Mexican with the mustache, the thick glasses, and the crippled left arm on his staging, drawing the patterns, painting in the colors. While the process went on and when it was done there was violent discussion pro and con. Many agreed and would still agree with Mrs. Roosevelt that the frescoes were propaganda. Perhaps the artist thought so, too, though the admirer of Michelangelo could scarcely help being an artist first. If he feared that the walls might be disfigured as some of his frescoes in Mexico had been disfigured by irate observers he need not have been alarmed.

> If the only options available to this college were to graduate men of the highest brilliancy intellectually, without interest in the welfare of mankind at large, or to graduate men of less mental competence, possessed of aspirations which we call spiritual and motives which we call good, I would choose for Dartmouth College the latter alternative. – Ernest Martin Hopkins, 1927.

One day Victor Cutter, a Trustee, and for years President of the United Fruit Company, anathema in many quarters in Latin America, stood before the panel which depicts an erect Zapata, with rifle, and cartridge belt crossed over breast, while fat capitalists sprawl below over the gold pieces spilling out from their moneybags. Cutter turned to Artemas Packard: "Who knows but that in fifty years we may be saying that there's a lot of truth in that?" And one day the Rev. Ambrose Vernon brought two other clergymen to view the almost completed work. Dr. Vernon had recently retired as Professor of Biography, having returned to Hanover in 1924 — he had been pastor of the White Church from 1904 to 1907. Dr. Vernon himself, because of his solicitude for interned Germans in the War, had not escaped the intolerance of the war period, becoming, as a friend put it, "another instance of a heresy trial with one Christian present." The three clergymen looked at the panel on which a flaming el Greco Christ against a background of guns and broken columns towers above the cross which he has just cut down. They nodded their admiration and approval. Art or propaganda — what matters? Dynamic in their splashed patterns of color the frescoes are a testimonial — along with Hopkins Center in this current year of grace — to aesthetic adventurousness.

[163]

He settled *Hoti's* business — let it be! —
Properly based *Oun* —
Gave us the doctrine of the enclitic *De,*
Dead from the waist down.

Browning: "A Grammarian's Funeral"

The aim is the 'teacher-scholar' and every college has had enough of these 'great teachers' in the past to know that the aim is not an impossible one.

John Sloan Dickey

The controversy between the College and the University in the early nineteenth century is symbolic of a quandary which has confronted Dartmouth ever since and has perhaps at no time been more perplexing than today. It was a problem which did not bother Eleazar Wheelock, who started out at least with the simple purpose of bringing the blessings of Christianity to the heathen. It arose only when the question came up of bringing the blessings of science to white Christians as well as Indians, that is with the establishment of the Medical School. The establishment of the Chandler School complicated things: I have noted how Edwin Sanborn resented its intrusion upon the humanities. Then the Agricultural College came along. These complications seemed to be solved by the merging of the Chandler School with the College in 1892 and the removal of the "Dungies" to Durham in 1893. But meanwhile in 1871 the Thayer School had been founded; and in 1900 the Tuck School was established. And on the national scene the proliferation of graduate schools and the reverence of German scholarship occurred.

Consequently questions begin to swarm. When does a college become a university? How many graduate schools does it take to accomplish this transformation? And especially for Dartmouth, what are the advantages and the disadvantages of a cluster of graduate schools about its undergraduate campus? What effect, good or ill, does this have on undergraduate instruction? What is the effect of Dartmouth's isolation from metropolitan centers upon the scholarship of its teachers? To what extent would its development into a full-fledged university enhance or conflict with its fundamental purpose as an undergraduate liberal college? It is not, of course, my intention to try to answer these questions; merely to reflect their impingement on Dartmouth's growing faculty in the twentieth century.

It is a truism that curiosity and a love of learning, unless inborn in a

student, cannot be stimulated in him by a teacher who has not himself a curious and inquiring mind. It also seems to be true that a teacher, unless he is a genius, loses his creative fire if he has no contact with colleagues who are also explorers, concerned with productive scholarship or creative activity. (The question as to how these are to be defined I may be allowed to dodge.) Herein lies the advantage of a university; and it has to be confessed that Dartmouth's isolation partly accounts for the fact that the majority of its faculty through the nineteenth century were neither productive scholars nor stimulating teachers — despite men like Alpheus Crosby, Charles Young, Hitchcock, Sanborn, Arthur Sherburn Hardy. But let us have done with bleak generalizations and consider what this means in terms of the flesh and blood of the Tucker and succeeding administrations.

The classics were not lacking in scholars who were also teachers: John K. Lord and Richard Husband have already been cited. Charles Darwin Adams, Professor of Greek from 1893 to 1927, is another example. But his very name, happily or unhappily, depending on one's point of view, illustrates the fact that the classics were being pushed out of the front pew by the sciences (not to mention the social sciences) just as in theology, under the influence of the evolutionary hypothesis, liberal clergymen were supplanting the orthodox in the pulpit. To put it in another way the classical influence at Dartmouth was becoming more certainly a blend of Hebraism and Hellenism: Adams was a liberal Christian, finding, to quote Royal Nemiah, "as much revealed truth in the dialogues of Plato as in the prophetic books of the Old Testament." His scholarship was exacting and he was exacting in the standards he set for his classes. And he still held to old-fashioned notions about the role of the teacher in molding the character and manners of his students. He tended to disapprove mildly of the cigarette-smoking habits of the young Ernest Martin Hopkins though as time went on he admitted that perhaps there was not too much difference between cigarettes and a pipe. Nevertheless he was essentially kindly and tolerant. With his erect carriage, his fleeting perhaps a little nervous smile, with his clipped rather high-pitched voice, he was listened to as respectfully by his colleagues in faculty meetings as by his students in the classroom. An era passed, perhaps, when at his retirement the last dinner given by the faculty as a whole was given to this gentleman of the old school.

To him and to Harry Burton, Professor of Latin, a new generation of classicists succeeded: W. Stuart Messer, whose ability as an administrator was also notable; John Barker Stearns, whose passion for archaeology led to a division of his time between the classics and the art department and whose Yankee individualism delighted in startling the conventional by such antics as delivering Fourth of July orations in silk hat and frock coat; and Royal Case Nemiah whose quiet irony appealed especially to the undergraduate mood of the 'twenties and concealed a romantic devotion to the classical heritage. When enrollment in Greek and Latin began to dwindle these men kept the torch of classical studies alight in courses in classical civilization given in English.

The question arises whether the existence of a graduate school of arts and sciences might not have made for better instruction in the modern languages at Dartmouth. As Richardson has pointed out, the introduction of modern-language study was an uphill business — it was only in 1859 that President Lord was able to finance a professorship and appoint a teacher of modern languages of full academic standing. And even then they had difficulty in competing for time with other subjects like the classics, long intrenched in the curriculum, or the sciences aggressively pushing their way.

It was doubtless in an attempt to remedy this situation that Dr. Tucker brought in two brilliant young men from Harvard, Louis H. Dow in 1899 and Prescott Orde Skinner in 1900, both of whom had also studied in Paris. (Dow at first was an instructor in Greek.) These two members of the "kid faculty" were men of great promise. Dow was tall and handsome — Bernard Berenson once recalled him as the most charming of his contemporaries at Harvard. One sees them now in memory setting out or returning from their five- and ten-mile walks: Dow with a cane striding majestically along, Skinner, shorter and more agile, ambling with twisting shoulders beside him. Dow was a lover of Molière, Montaigne, Shakespeare; Skinner read easily Latin, Greek, and German as well as the Romance languages. He was insatiably curious on matters ranging from vintage wines to Kraft-Ebing. Both of them were members of a small group of men, dubbed by an outsider who suspected them of being subversive, the Anarchists, who met to discuss the latest figures in the world of ideas: Nietzsche, Bergson, Einstein, Freud — on whom Dow read a paper. (Some of the other members were the elder Dr. Gile, Mr. Hopkins, Wicker, W. K. Stewart, Wilmon Sheldon, "Cy" Young — of the mathematics department — John Poor.)

> Scholarship as a product of the college is incomplete except as it be established on the foundation of character which is not only passively good, but which is of moral fiber definite enough to influence those with whom it is brought into contact. – Ernest Martin Hopkins, 1916.

If Louis Dow and Orde Skinner lost much of their youthful fire (which a few brilliant graduate students might have kept burning), it was because most of their time and effort had to be given to elementary language instruction. The College has made valiant attempts to improve matters. It has brought in men whose native language is French: the Belgian Leon Verriest, for instance, in 1922, the lively Francois Denoeu in 1929. In 1930 came Ramon Guthrie, poet, novelist, and painter, as well as stimulating teacher of French literature. In the same year Charles R. Bagley, with training at Duke and Oxford, with intimate knowledge of French life gained at first hand as a captain in the AEF and from later life in France, came from Swarthmore to take charge of the Honors program in French, a man of lively scholarly interests, broad culture, and North Carolinian charm. The addition of these two men rejuvenated an aging department and attracted other able scholars and enthusiastic teachers. This, with the more intensive methods of language instruction resulting from the War, the introduction of the language laboratory, a greater flexibility in the language requirement with the adoption of the three term, three course curriculum, and, belatedly, a provision for study abroad (in other languages as well as French) have made the study of the French language and literature come alive for an increasing number of undergraduates.

If Dartmouth had possessed laboratories such as a university would supposedly have provided it is quite likely that its scientific advancement would have been hastened. Charles A. Young and Edwin Frost, at least, possessed the Shattuck observatory to play with; and Charles Hitchcock had all New Hampshire for his laboratory. Edwin Bartlett pointed out in 1913 that the facilities of the chemistry laboratory in Culver were reasonably good for half the numbers who thronged it; it was not until 1921 that the opening of Steele Hall relieved the pressure. And it seems unlikely that Nichols and Hull would have been able to conduct their famous experiment if Wilder Hall had not been built in 1897: their epoch-making measurement of the infinitesimal pressure exerted by a beam of light which, as another Dartmouth physicist, Willis M. Rayton, later said was the first experimental proof of the detailed validity of Clerk-Maxwell's electromagnetic theory of light and was to have importance for the quantum theory. This experiment conducted in the years 1900-03 earned for Dartmouth in the scientific world, Robert Davis, a senior in 1903, said years later, a respect "how much more valuable than the opinion of platinum blondes of Brooklyn as to our team."

Nichols departed in 1903 to accept a chair at Columbia, but his as-

sociate continued to teach at Dartmouth until his retirement in 1940. A Canadian, Hull had been associated with Michelson and Millikan — who were later to receive Nobel prizes — at the University of Chicago, had worked at the famous Cavendish Laboratory at Cambridge, and had come to Dartmouth in 1899 through the efforts of Nichols and Edwin Frost. After Nichols left Hull continued his researches and instituted a weekly seminar to encourage his younger associates to keep abreast of expanding physics in an expanding universe. He is today remembered by thousands of students (whose names it was his boast *he* also remembered!) as a brilliant teacher, delighting in such gadgets, for instance, as a photoelectric cell rigged up to ring a bell and startle latecomers out of their wits. He was a striking refutation of the notion that scientists are cool, rational, and perhaps a little arid. Though Hull possessed the tolerance and skepticism of the scientist he was yet passionately opinionated and dogmatic; no one on the faculty was more capable of stirring up a hornet's nest of controversy by letters to *The Dartmouth* and pronouncements — defending prohibition, for instance — on matters outside his field. One recalls him at faculty meetings: there rises slowly from the front bench a man with white hair, bushy eyebrows, twinkling eyes behind glasses and, with a bird-like toss of his head, begins an ambulatory speech in which he registers with sarcasm and devious wit his objections to some action being debated — to the obvious irritation of Craven Laycock, if he is presiding. Perhaps it was partly the Irish in him. At any rate he was unpredictable; a beautiful illustration of Heisenberg's Principle of Indeterminacy: you thought you had your finger on him, but the next moment his velocity had whisked him away.

The career of another brilliant physicist brought to Dartmouth in Dr. Tucker's administration is an illustration of the capriciousness of fate. In September, 1893, *The Dartmouth* welcomed among other able newcomers to the faculty Albert C. Crehore, who had just received his Ph.D. in physics from Cornell and was joint author of a book on alternating currents. Five years later in commenting on the prestige brought to Dartmouth by such men as Arthur Sherburn Hardy, for instance, *The Dartmouth* recorded its pleasure at the recognition shown the work of Professor Crehore by the most eminent scientists. But a year later it was lamenting his departure: the loss of so highly esteemed a scholar and so popular a teacher was a distinct blow to the College.

Crehore left Hanover for Cleveland to oversee the construction of apparatus for use in connection with his invention, the Synchronograph, for the rapid transmission of intelligence by alternating current. (At Dartmouth also he had built an apparatus for measuring the speed of projectiles.) The money obtained from the sale of his inventions in communications to the A.T.&T. went into his company which failed, and he sank into obscurity, penniless and forlorn. Forty years after leaving Dartmouth he was discovered by a Cleveland newspaper reporter — rescued from oblivion only to be returned to the obscurity of secret work for the Pentagon on an intercontinental ballistic project on which he was at work at the time of his death — a neglected genius who once taught at Dartmouth.

> As the north country weaves into the souls and minds of its men those patterns of ruggedness, of sturdiness and individuality and self-expressive independence, so these men in turn weave it back into the fabric of the life of the society and the groups and the environment within which they live. – Ernest Martin Hopkins, 1923.

Fortunately for the College (as well as for himself) a similar fate did not attend another addition to the faculty whom *The Dartmouth* welcomed in the same year of 1893. William Patten received his B.S. from the Lawrence Scientific School in 1883, spent three years at the Naples Zoological Station, Trieste, and Leipzic (where he obtained his Ph.D. in one year) and came to Dartmouth as Professor of Zoology. He taught here thirty-seven years, retiring in 1930. His search for "the missing link," in more technical terms for the ostracoderms, took him through these years out of museums on expeditions to Canada, Newfoundland, Scotland, Spitzbergen, Russia, Australia, Java, Central America. Indefatigable in research, he was no less distinguished as a teacher. He made such an impression on Ernest Martin Hopkins as a student that when, as President, he sought a man to take charge of the orientation course in Evolution, Patten was the logical choice. He deliberately curtailed his research for this purpose, with the understanding that he be released to return to it after two or three years but at the end of that period asked that the agreement be torn up: for, he said, he knew of no satisfaction in working with advanced students comparable to the satisfaction of teaching freshmen. The Patten influence lives on today in the Department of Biological Sciences, distinguished alike by the high quality of its research and by the popularity of its lectures in its elementary courses.

In 1909 Ernest Fox Nichols returned from Columbia to Dartmouth as President of the College. Though he soon found himself miscast as an administrator, he naturally continued Dr. Tucker's policy of adding competent scholars to the faculty. That year Charles N. Haskins was brought into the Mathematics Department. His undergraduate training had been at M.I.T.; he had won his doctorate at Harvard — the first mathematician to come to Dartmouth with an earned Ph.D. He built up the mathematics library; brought in, as the years went on, brilliant young instructors and, as a master of twelve languages, could qualify as a humanist. A man who could and did install a complete plumbing system in an old house, he won the respect of the "townies." A bulky, rather ungainly man he won the nickname of "Hippo." As the years went by he was listened to by the faculty with respect — at least by those who could hear him, for his voice hardly reached beyond the front benches. Though a brilliant mathematician he seems to have been no better a teacher than Sir Isaac Newton. Two years later he was joined by John Wesley Young, an associate of Oswald Veblen at Princeton. He was not only a brilliant mathematician but a good teacher; and as Head of the Department more adventurous than Haskins, going farther afield for new instructors than Cambridge.

During the Tucker and Nichols administrations the recruitment of scholars was not confined to mathematics and the sciences. In 1898 a chair in economics was established and Frank H. Dixon was appointed to it; in 1900 with the establishment of the Tuck School he acted as its director. He became nationally known as an authority on railroads and in 1919 left Dartmouth to become chairman of the Department of Economics at Princeton.

I have already noted the appointment of Herbert Darling Foster as the first Professor of History in 1893. His graduate work had been done at Harvard and after his appointment he pursued his studies further at the Universities of Berlin, Leipzic, and Geneva. Known to a later generation as Eric the Red because of his full red beard, he was an accomplished scholar, though his Dartmouth and Geneva associations led him to become perhaps unduly preoccupied with Daniel Webster and Calvinism. And although some of his colleagues thought that his temperament or his German training may have made him somewhat dictatorial, he built up his department, bringing in Sidney Fay, for example, and in 1914, when Fay left for Smith, Frank Maloy Anderson from Minnesota, with graduate work at Harvard and the Sorbonne. Anderson — he had become fatherless when ten years old and had had to work for his education — was indefatigable in research, continuing at it after his retirement in 1939, indeed until his death at ninety. At Versailles in

1918-19 he framed the statute for the International Labor Organization. His subsequent lectures at Dartmouth on the First World War and its origins were popular — their lively substance making his students forget "that definition-defying mannerism that is neither drawl nor stammer nor yet wholly deliberation" as Francis Brown, 1925, has recalled it. A Democrat in a Republican community, he was a man of strong convictions: of the Orozco frescoes he said that the American Baedeker for the year 2000 would triple star them as examples of the degradation of American art in the early twentieth century; still, they proved that at Dartmouth thought was free. With his tall, spare, stooped figure, his lean face with its pince-nez, and his white hair parted in the middle he was in his later years a striking figure on the Dartmouth scene.

The departure of Nichols to Columbia, Dixon to Princeton, and Fay to Smith (later to Harvard) points up the difficulty an undergraduate faculty faces in defending itself against raids by the universities. This situation arises, of course, from the general assumption that the undergraduate college emphasizes teaching whereas the emphasis in the university is on scholarship. In February, 1906, an editorial in the *Dartmouth Alumni Magazine* on the preceptorial system initiated at Princeton by Woodrow Wilson addressed itself to this matter, hailing the innovation as evidence of a reaction in American education against Germanic methods and the Ph.D. fetish. The editor concluded with the statement that the effect of emphasis upon the Ph.D. degree was to make prospective teachers "largely interested in the acquisition of knowledge rather than its dissemination."

The glove was picked up in the April issue by Sidney Fay, who pointed out that of the forty-eight Princeton preceptors, thirty-five were Ph.D.'s and that though he would by no means contend that every member of a college faculty should hold that degree, teaching should be regarded as a profession like the law or medicine and that there was no better evidence of careful and exact training than the doctorate. The editor stuck to his guns and three years later returned to the charge with the statement that "the increase of intellectual acumen in modern training ought not to be so often accompanied by atrophy of the bowels of compassion," and the expression of the hope that in time requirements for the degree would be broadened or a "new degree devised requiring a like amount of work but of different scope."

The significance of these editorials is that the editor, then a young man in his late twenties, became in 1916 President of Dartmouth College. As President he continued the attack: in the undergraduate college emphasis on teaching ability, rather than on research, was essential. Such utterances brought down on his head, of course, as L. B. Richardson said, "heated rejoinders . . . in which the strictly objective attitude, which the training for the degree is supposed to inculcate, was not always clearly in evidence": this was what happened when a businessman became president of a college; he was undermining the very foundations of scholarship in America; and so forth.

> A man who has once lived in a society where the moral and intellectual tone was high, has by that very fact had his courage raised to attempt things of which he otherwise would never have dreamed. – Ernest Martin Hopkins, 1924.

Mr. Hopkins was in the minority, but he was in good company. In 1903 no less a person than William James, writing indeed as a university teacher, had attacked "the Doctor-Monopoly in teaching" as in reality "but a sham, a bauble, a dodge, whereby to decorate the catalogues of schools and colleges." And at Amherst during these postwar years the brilliant Alexander Meiklejohn, with a strictly academic background, was pursuing the Socratic goal of making men think before attempting to add to the accumulation of knowledge. At a time when more than half of American undergraduates ended their education at college Mr. Hopkins conceived that the purpose of the undergraduate college was to prepare men for intelligent leadership in a democratic society: the courses in evolution and citizenship in his administration, the Great Issues course in the next were geared to this purpose. The purpose of the American liberal college, with its millions of students, he conceived, was something quite different from that of the European — at least, the Continental — university, with its specialized training offered to a limited elite. This conviction that learning should never be apart from life was at the root of Mr. Hopkins's conception of American education and of his skepticism of too much emphasis upon the Ph.D.

That Mr. Hopkins had no prejudice against thhe Ph.D. degree when kept in perspective is indicated by the fact that many, perhaps the majority, of the teachers who came to Dartmouth during his administration possessed this degree. I may cite in illustration four members of the English Department who came to Hanover in the twenties. James Dow McCallum joined the department in 1922 by way of Columbia and Princeton, where he had written his thesis on John Morley, the

English liberal. His lectures, particularly on the great Victorian figures, were colorful and popular. He himself was a colorful figure, tall, long of face, red-haired and red-mustached, quite the reverse of the languid aesthete Bunthorne whom he once impersonated on the boards of Webster Hall. A year later Henry McCune Dargan appeared on the scene — perhaps the most brilliant man, President Neilson of Smith once said, who had received the doctorate in English at Harvard during the period when Neilson taught there. Dargan's field was the eighteenth century. Stout, not to say bulky, downright in his opinions and in his expression of them, he might have been, but for the slightly southern voice, the Grand Panjandrum of English letters in that century himself as his long eloquent periods, not to say paragraphs, issued forth without his scarcely pausing to take breath.

> The emotional alumnus whose knowledge of his university is solely a sentimental harking back to his undergraduate days is an incomplete alumnus of minimum value to his alma mater at his best and a positive detriment at his worst. – Ernest Martin Hopkins, 1924.

In 1928 William A. Eddy arrived, with a doctor's degree from Princeton in 1922 and five years of teaching at the American University in Cairo. The son of American missionaries in Syria, Eddy mastered the Arabic tongue, later writing textbooks and the only rule book for basketball in that language. A dramatic personality he — or his image — had a habit of appearing under startling circumstances. A nurse, for instance, in the First World War, thought she had said a final farewell to him as he was about to be shipped home to die from severe wounds received as a captain of Marines in battle (for which he won his first Distinguished Service Cross); and then some ten years later there he was, or his ghost, with a limp and a cane, across the room at a Hanover cocktail party. This instinct for the dramatic he brought to his course in satire — he had done his graduate work on Swift. He was at Dartmouth only eight years, leaving to become President of Hobart and William Smith at Geneva, but he returned again and again to Hanover until his death in Beirut, Lebanon, in 1962.

He found more excitement in teaching and in military activity than in a college presidency, a profession, he said upon his resignation in 1941 to rejoin his beloved Marine Corps, with which he was definitely out of love. During the war Colonel Eddy reached the climax of a spectacular career: as a naval attaché at Tangier, operating under the command of General Donovan of the OSS and the direction of General Mark Clark, he performed a series of daring exploits — one of them was the kidnaping of General Giraud and bringing him to North Africa — which prepared the way for the North African invasion. (These achievements won him a second DSC.) Following the War he served as American Ambassador to Saudi Arabia. The warmth of his outgoing personality makes him still a vivid figure to his old friends in Hanover; and his adventurous career is quite in key with the adventurousness of the institution where he taught for eight years.

E. Bradlee Watson (A.B. Dartmouth, 1902, Ph.D. Harvard, 1913) is another figure from the Middle East. He returned to Hanover in 1923 from years of teaching at Robert College in Constantinople. Rather stout and pudgy he looked, especially in his later years, like nothing so much as the dormouse in *Alice in Wonderland*. And it has to be admitted that, according to some of his students, it was the dormouse's drowsiness that was uppermost in many of his lectures. But the drowsiness came startlingly awake in his associations with individual students and with his friends, or in his impersonation of Falstaff on the stage of Webster. The drama was his great enthusiasm. It was he who organized the Experimental Theatre in 1927 which has played so great a part in the drama at Dartmouth. With Warner Bentley, Bradlee Watson conducted for years the course in playwrighting: many of the men who took it have, either in the drama or in other fields, achieved distinction and hold their mentor in affectionate remembrance. After his retirement he remained at Dartmouth for several years bringing his linguistic talents to the teaching of English to foreign students — sixty students from thirty different countries. And at eighty, the year before his death, he was still active, still bubbling with wit and humorous anecdote, the only white teacher at St. Paul's College for Negroes in Virginia.

These four men considerably blur the image of the college professor as a pedant doddering in dusty libraries or peering with rheumy eyes at test tubes in laboratories. Speaking of eyes it is pertinent at this point to cite the career of a man who spent the better part of his life in trying "to discover how we see things" — in more than the visual sense, for as a friend described him he was also a "frontiersman of the mind." And somewhat of a Leonardo da Vinci, too. President Dickey in his citation awarding him an LL.D. in 1954 ticked off Adelbert Ames, Jr.'s achievements: polo player, lawyer, painter, sculptor, soldier, sailor, inventor, scientist. After graduation from Harvard in 1903 and the Harvard Law

School in 1906, he gave up law practice in 1910 and turned his attention to sculpture — the Shawmut Bank Indian was one product of this talent — and to painting. The problem of perspective led him to become a Research Fellow at Clark in 1914; and after his service as an aerial observer in the War to ask the help of Charles Proctor, whom he had met at Cambridge in 1912, to work on the problem of "measuring the optical characteristics of the eye as a camera." From 1919 to 1923 the two men worked together on the top floor of Wilder.

His friend and classmate Horace Kallen — they had both studied philosophy under William James — has summed up what happened in the search for answers:

the devising of camera lenses patterned like the lenses of the human eye; the discovery of the perceptual defect called "aniseikonia" and of aniseikonic glasses which correct it; the establishment of the Dartmouth Eye Clinic; the unyielding struggle to say in words what he had come to understand regarding the interplay of vision and action in the human being's self-altering up-keep of his being human.

And the invention of ingenious devices to demonstrate this interplay, now housed in the Perception Demonstration Center at Princeton University through the instrumentality of Professor Hadley Cantril, 1928, one of Ames's recent collaborators. And the pursuit of these questions into the realm of psychology and philosophy which led John Dewey to consider Ames's work "the most important work done in the psychological-philosophical field during this century."

It is true that this opinion was not always shared by fellow-workers in these fields. But when Hadley Cantril mentioned their objections once to Einstein he replied, smiling broadly, "I learned many years ago never to waste time trying to convince my colleagues." It is true also that Ames was not a teacher and had little connection with undergraduate life. But this did not at all bother his good friend Ernest Martin Hopkins, who recognized the value of the presence in Hanover of a man who cut across all the artificial boundaries of knowledge. And indeed who is to say that his influence was wasted on the desert air? At least one former student at Dartmouth testified years after his graduation that a walk with Ames had changed his life at a crucial period: in reply to his probings into the age-old problem of good and evil Ames said, "Before you say that a thing is good or bad, say that *it is*." As President Dickey has also recently pointed out, many of his suggestions have come to practical realization in the Hopkins Center. In Adelbert

Ames the "two cultures" met and fused. Lucien Price once asked Alfred North Whitehead whether a scientific age was hostile to poetry. Not necessarily, the philosopher thought; if some of the great poets had lived in our time they might have been scientists; Shelley, for instance, might have been a chemist or a physicist. "Take Professor Ames of Dartmouth," he went on, "a man whose discoveries in the field of psychology and optics have made him eminent in Europe and America. If you were to talk with him you would at once discover that you were speaking with a poet and a mystic."

If the influence of the college leads away from the world's back yard, it has not existed in vain. – Ernest Martin Hopkins, 1925.

William K. Stewart was neither a poet nor a mystic, but during his forty-four years at Dartmouth — he came in 1899 as an instructor in German and retired in 1943 as Professor of Comparative Literature, a department he initiated in 1919 — he made a profound impression on his students. A native of Canada, he graduated from the University of Toronto in 1897 and continued his studies at Harvard and, after coming to Dartmouth, at the Universities of Berlin, Leipzig, and Paris — to say nothing of countless hours spent in the British Museum. He was fluent in French, German, Italian, Spanish, and Scandinavian; made fifteen trips to Europe, to say nothing of travel in the United States; loved Beethoven and Wagner: in short he was a man of wide culture as well as of great erudition — a "good European," to use Nietzsche's phrase. According to Professor Herbert F. West, who succeeded him in Comparative Literature, he was most influenced by the tolerance of Montaigne and the English and French rationalists, but he had a genius also for expounding the most abstruse writers, whether in philosophy, economics, politics — he was one of the first, for instance, to expound the ideas of the Italian sociologist Pareto. Though he wrote two books and many articles he considered teaching paramount and was held in great respect by students and colleagues alike for the brilliant lucidity of his mind and his complete intellectual integrity.

A similar power of impassioned objectivity — to use a paradox which most nearly states the case — characterized the teaching of Malcolm Keir in economics. Keir had studied at Wesleyan and the University of Pennsylvania, from which he received his doctorate in 1916. He came to Dartmouth from the War Department in 1919 and throughout his active teaching years he was in demand because of his knowledge and

[178]

his fairness as a mediator in labor disputes. Like Stewart he had a passion for facts and a dispassionate interpretation of them. His travels into every state in the Union were embodied in *The Epic of Industry* (1926) and *The March of Commerce* (1927), two volumes in the Yale Pageant of America series. Pragmatic in his approach he never allowed the preconceptions of economic theory to govern the presentation of his facts; thus it was that for the students who flocked to his lectures on manufacturing, commerce, and labor economics was never a dismal science. It is no wonder that the head of one of the largest corporations in the country told his son that whatever other course he took at Dartmouth he must take Keir's course in labor relations.

None of these men was an actor unless playing their parts straight in a lively fashion may be called acting. But teachers are often actors *manqués* as well as parsons *manqués*. Professor Lewis Stilwell, for example. Stilwell came to Dartmouth in 1916 as an instructor in history. His *Migration from Vermont* is a minor classic of scholarship as Stilwell himself is a classic example of the scholar who found his greatest satisfaction in teaching. As Director of the course in Citizenship and as Professor of History he became one of Dartmouth's greatest teachers. Hatless even in the coldest weather, his slouch, his ambling gait, his quizzical smile, his infectious guffaw became affectionately known to generations of students who looked on him as a contemporary and friend. On the night of Lew Stilwell's death in an automobile accident, April 12, 1963, John Gazley, like himself one of Alexander Meiklejohn's young men at Amherst and an associate and friend for fifty years, speaking over WDCR, emphasized Stilwell's concern with his students' personal problems, his willingness to give them time far beyond the call of duty. As much of an individualist as Thoreau, he built a cabin for himself on an island in the Connecticut. His experience in the First World War, his reading of history, his sensitive but tough-minded temperament had burned into him a hatred of war. But this did not prevent him from being a military historian of the first order, giving even in his retirement his "Battle Nights" to which students flocked by the hundreds and a wider audience listened by radio. In these lectures he was a consummate actor: it was not merely the impressive marshaling of facts (without a note); his facial play, his modulations of voice, the deliberately low key, the rapport established between him and his auditors are qualities which defy reproduction or preservation by radio, movies, TV, or the printed word. It is this in the last analysis which makes the teacher's, like the actor's, an evanescent art.

[179]

How to convey, for instance, to one who did not know him the baroque expanse and the guttural Bavarian enthusiasm of Stephan Johann Schlossmacher, with his broad-brimmed hat, cane, and swinging gait? He came to Dartmouth in 1930 and at once organized the Deutsche-Studenten Verein, whose name was later changed to Studenten-Verbindung Germania. Thenceforth Germania and Schlossmacher were synonymous. Germania transcended mere Gemütlichkeit, though there was plenty of that, with its talks on German culture, its singing and its pageantry; its presentation of German plays from the farces of Hans Sachs, the classic writers, and contemporary playwrights, its sponsor, in more than one summer, taking his strolling troupe to the Fatherland. Herr Schlossmacher was a reminder, as his colleagues wrote, of an older gracious German tradition, with the "innocence and transparency of a child, the unpredictable and explosive energy of youth." Germania celebrated its Stiftungsfest on its twenty-eighth anniversary on May 17, 1958. Not quite one year later, at the very end of a meeting, Stephan Schlossmacher died suddenly of a heart attack.

Or how to convey the romantic quality of Allan H. Macdonald, with his bronzed face and neatly trimmed mustache, his broad shoulders, his vigorous walk? Though his life of Richard Hovey was published posthumously, he was primarily a teacher. He possessed insights men of greater 'scholarship' often lack; his lectures on D. H. Lawrence, for instance, came closer to an understanding of that tortured genius than almost anything I have read about him. For he passionately believed that education does not come through books alone: "axioms of philosophy are not axioms until they are proved on our pulses" was one of his favorite quotations from Keats. His essential earthiness was expressed in his love of gardening; his love of painting is memorialized in the Allan Macdonald studio in Hopkins Center.

It is fortunate that Kenneth Robinson, before his death in December, 1961, had recorded some of the lectures which made his course in contemporary American literature the most popular course at Dartmouth in the years before his retirement in 1959. But though the recordings may reproduce the voice, even to his "incessant use of the syllable 'ah', to the point not far short of a stutter," though they may reproduce the facts, anecdotes, quotations, illuminations that came forth in a spate, they cannot reproduce the ruddy face, the humorous twinkle, the involuntary wink as he looked up from the bright yellow pages of his manuscript, the autumnal colors of his coats and suits, or

[180]

the natural friendliness and sympathy, despite the reserve, which endeared him to student and colleague alike.

It is pleasant to record that the Shakespeare course for the past half century has been in the hands of poets as well as scholars. Fred P. Emery succeeded to Professor Charles F. Richardson. Emery was a slim dapper gentleman, even in his sixties, always impeccably dressed, even at a time of some sartorial slackness. He was noted for a faultless memory, a mastery of the perfect phrase, the apt quotation: once when students asked him to plead their cause with Dean Charles Emerson he declined, saying that Shakespeare had written a better prayer for their needs — "Use lenity, sweet Chuck." He had collected a "Shakespeare library," that is, the books which Shakespeare, on the evidence of his plays, must have read. It filled only a shelf or two and was a graphic illustration of his small Latin and less Greek.

> . . . it is the spirit of the aspiration and not the letter of the particular method which counts. It is the spirit which is important. Better the wrong method with the right spirit than the right method uninspired. – Ernest Martin Hopkins, 1928.

Professor Emery was succeeded at his death by Professor Henderson, who held the course for twelve years until his own sudden death in the summer of 1939, upon which it was divided briefly between Anton Raven and Franklin McDuffee. Raven's *Hamlet Bibliography and Reference Guide* (1936), a compilation of over two-thousand references in several languages to the play, was, as Henderson called it, "a monumental labor" of scholarship.

Franklin McDuffee, like Henderson, was a poet. Graduating from Dartmouth in 1921 he went to Balliol where he won the Newdigate Prize for his poem on Michelangelo, a prize won before him by such diverse men as Matthew Arnold and Oscar Wilde. Franklin McDuffee was a sweet and gentle person, a stimulating and sympathetic teacher. Goethe's famous simile in which he likened Hamlet to a fragile vase shattered by an oak tree was more applicable to Franklin McDuffee than to Hamlet: suffering from ill health in body and soul he committed suicide in January, 1940, when only forty-one. But in *Dartmouth Undying* he won his own immortality.

After McDuffee's death the course was taught briefly by a committee of the department, no way to teach Shakespeare. Fortunately this was soon discovered and Francis L. Childs took over, bringing to it not only his scholarship but his flair for the dramatic, his great gusto, his *joie de vivre,* which made it "the best course" they took in college even for men not majoring in English.

It is no disparagement of any of these men to say that under Henderson the Shakespeare was unique, not only on Dartmouth's but on any campus. Some might have thought that Goethe's misleading simile of the fragile vase would also apply to him, but this would be a superficial judgment. He was educated at Kimball Union Academy in Meriden, at Brown, and at Princeton, where he received his Ph.D. in 1915. He served as an editor for Macmillan and in 1917 enlisted as a private in the British Army, being gazetted second lieutenant in the Royal Artillery just before the Armistice. Returning to America he served as a literary assistant to Winston Churchill at Cornish and briefly as secretary to Tagore during the Indian poet's American visit. Then he taught at Yale and came to Dartmouth in 1925.

Though he was to spend the better part of his life in New England his roots were in the old: he was born in Jamaica of a family who had been missionaries there for two generations. Thus when he came to Hanover at thirty-eight with his English heritage and his soft English voice one might fancifully have thought him a ghost of Rupert Brooke translated from "some corner of a foreign field / That is forever England." He looked, indeed, like a somewhat younger Prince of Wales, though there the resemblance ended: he did not accept Edward VIII's desertion of the realm for the woman he loved as consonant with a Shakespearean conception of kingship. There was in Brooks Henderson also a strong strain of Miltonic Puritanism.

He quickly became a marked figure, strutting with his broad-brimmed hat and his cane about the campus — a cane which he did not hesitate to use on the legs of any hapless student whom he caught reading in the Tower Room with his feet up on an upholstered chair. His eloquence was phenomenal; he lectured and spoke with a fluency unmatched even by Dargan's Johnsonian periods, the effortless torrent of his words flecked with passage after passage from the poets, for his memory was also phenomenal. And if Hamlet and Mercutio colored his image of Shakespeare more strongly than Falstaff and Juliet's nurse, it was not because he was averse to Rabelais. For he was a full flower of the Renaissance: most appropriate that with grace and courtesy he should have written an introduction to Castiglione's *Courtier.*

It was Franklin McDuffie who most sensitively caught the lonely, elusive qualities of Brooks Henderson, his underlying sweetness and

[182]

generosity, yet his quick temper, his intellectual arrogance; and of Brooks Henderson's world — "the world of a great and imperious idealism, its senate peopled by those images of Shakespeare, Homer, Virgil, Dante, and Milton which Brooks had made in his own image, though surely he had endowed them with nobility, beauty, and light."

David Lambuth came to Hanover in 1913. In his heritage was blended the adventurousness of the frontier and the cosmopolitanism of the wide world: a pioneer ancestor, who was a friend of Daniel Boone's; a maternal grandfather, who fought with Bedford Forrest; his father's father, who was a missionary in China where both his father and he were born. Coming to America in 1891 when he was twelve years old, he graduated from Vanderbilt in 1900 and studied further at Columbia and in Europe. In 1919 President Hopkins abolished the archaic Head of Department and substituted the more democratic rotating chairmanship. As chairman, David Lambuth increased the offerings in contemporary literature and emphasized courses in creative writing. For the whole of education, he thought, lay in self-expression with the analysis and logical thought necessary to it: he was a great admirer of the Italian philosopher Benedetto Croce, of whom he made an intensive study. Ideas excited him and he believed that students should be similarly excited.

Prosaic people — and some not so prosaic — mistook for pose what was a lively flair for the dramatic and the picturesque. In 1923 he built a house which he had himself designed: Badgery — the name was from Barrie — became a center of gay talk at afternoon tea or dinner for students, colleagues, and visiting lecturers. The Lambuths dressed for dinner — though those who did not dress were equally welcome. He himself often appeared in a cream-colored dinner jacket, lined with scarlet or in black with a gay cummerbund. He was a *bon vivant,* a lover of good food and fine wines. (When he gave a talk once in the Tower Room on wine, its history and uses, a student exclaimed: "What the hell does he know about wines? I've never seen him drunk in his life.") His wife, Myrtle Lambuth, from the Shenandoah Valley, was a memorable figure as she skittered in and out of the Main Street stores, with a black-velvet beret poised carelessly on her head, with her long coat, long skirts, and high-buttoned boots, or as she looked for the Lambuth Packard, the color of the best dairy cream, so chosen that she would always find the right vehicle. She helped to keep the conversational ball tossing in the air at Badgery. "Lightly, lightly!" she

would say when the talk threatened to go solemn. Or: "He twinkles!" when a young instructor capped her quotation from Shakespeare. Brooks Henderson, she said, kept her in hand: "He pokes me gently with his toe, if I go too far astray."

To Badgery came the literary figures visiting Hanover: Curtis Hidden Page (who had recently taught in the English Department) with his translations of Japanese hokku; Robert Frost — often; Rebecca West; Frank Swinnerton ("Swinnie"); James Stephens, with his lilting Irish brogue. For two years in the early twenties a student in tails served as butler, playing his violin between courses outside the dining-room door. The student was Bravig Imbs, a bright and brash youth from Chicago, coming to college on a shoestring. In return for his domestic services the Lambuths gave him bed and board and other financial assistance; moreover, David Lambuth listened to his poems and stories. At the end of his sophomore year he betook himself and his violin to Paris. Possessing a talent for more than total recall he embodied his experience at Badgery in a novel at the suggestion of Gertrude Stein: from the perspective of nearly forty years *The Professor's Wife* does not seem quite so unkind and distorted as it did when he sent a copy inscribed to David and Myrtle Lambuth, "to whom" — and indeed he did — "I owe so much."

In the garden room at Badgery, David Lambuth during the twenties conducted his English 51 with "delicacy of judgment," Benfield Pressey wrote, "instinctive tact, a keen discernment of the capacity of the student." Out of this course came several writers and at least three poets of distinction: Richmond Lattimore, who has written distinguished translations from the Greek, as well; Richard Eberhart and Alexander Laing — the two latter, with Arthur Dewing, the editor of *This Our Purpose,* carry on today the tradition of English 51.

The Lambuths brought color and gaiety to Hanover — and some said the custom of afternoon tea (though this statement was in error). David Lambuth had a rococo quality (not in the pejorative sense) with his slim erect carriage, alert and expressive face, with its neatly trimmed beard and mustache (later he became stouter and the beard whiter and thicker), with his jaunty beret and Alpine cape — which one may still see in the portrait in Sanborn House by Peter Gish:

> With news of nations in his talk
> And something royal in his walk,

[185]

as Elizabeth Marsh, an intimate friend of the Lambuths, quoted from Edwin Arlington Robinson. With his death at sixty-nine in 1948 vanished one of the "characters" whose passing from the Hanover scene the *laudatores temporis acti* mournfully lament.

I must draw this chronicle to a close with at least a brief account of three other "characters" and, finally, of a man rather to be described as a personality.

> The influence of a college education ought to be such that men should desire as complete knowledge of the merits of what they do not believe as of opinions which they hold as convictions. – Ernest Martin Hopkins, 1927.

"Doc" Griggs, tall, round-shouldered, could be seen, until his death in 1964 at the age of 85, shuffling up Main Street for his morning paper, the drooping corners of his mouth suggesting a sardonic outlook which may be more accurately described as a skeptical amusement at the human show. The "Doc" was real: Leland Griggs held one of the few — to date — Dartmouth Ph.D.'s, a degree which, after graduating in 1902, he received in 1907 for work done under William Patten. The citation prophesied in a capsule his forty years in the Zoology Department. "A calm clear-eyed student of Nature, with the discriminating vision of the Naturalist for the near at hand and the long-range vision of the Poet for the distant scene." This sums up: his service for years as adviser to the Outing Club, the Canoe Club, Bait and Bullet; his cabin parties, famous for young roast pig in the winter, strawberry shortcake in the spring; his course in photography and his hundred lantern slides of spiders' webs, best photographed in the early morning when the dew was on them; his humorous talks to students and on the alumni circuit in which, as he said, he played the fool and supplied the fun, Laycock the sentiment; the cage behind his house with its bear, timber wolf, coyotes, coons, porcupines, hawks, owls; finally his course, Zoology 17, in which the students read Hudson's *Green Mansions* and *Far Away and Long Ago* and met in groups of two and three to eat supper and read book reviews before the stone fireplace in his cabin on Clark's Pond, returning to Hanover at midnight. His aim was not merely to teach zoology but to open the eyes and minds of his students to the whole picture of nature. He was famous for his taciturnity, but when he did speak it was with a humorous twinkle and in an absolute monotone.

One of Griggs's cronies was John Poor — they met often on Sunday nights when Poor entertained a few friends, Town and Gown, with oyster stew and coffee — coffee, Griggs said, which would take the varnish off the chair you were sitting on. He graduated from Dartmouth in 1897, and after serving for one year as principal of the Hanover High School, went to Princeton to study astronomy under Charles A. Young, receiving his doctorate in 1904. He returned to Dartmouth in the Department of Astronomy and Mathematics, taking a year's leave in 1911 to study at Lund University in Sweden.

By the twenties John Poor had become a legendary figure in Hanover. Careless about dress, haircuts, and his straggly mustache, he once replied to a young instructor who told him how flattered he was to have just been taken for the professor: "Like hell you were, you went home and shaved." Andrew Foster, 1925, remembered "the half melancholy, half sardonic quality of his personality." Sardonic he often was: as when he soaked some kernels of corn in alcohol and surreptitiously dropped them into John K. Lord's chicken yard on the way home from the observatory and speculated the next morning with Johnny K, on what could have caused the peculiar behavior of his poultry. Or when a student insisted that he deserved a B, he said, "O.K. I've erased the mark," and when the boy had left, turned to Griggs and said: "Too bad that boy wanted a B so badly. I had to change it from an A."

An agnostic, he suggested to his young daughter that she confine a budding tendency to profanity to her conversations with him — he could appreciate it, others might not. And when he learned of a tentative proposal to build a Gothic cathedral on the site of his observatory with a spire which could be viewed for miles up and down the valley, he vowed they would build it over his prostate gland.

But he was also kind and understanding, on Thanksgiving and Christmas trudging about to deliver baskets of food to the Hanover needy. A classics major, wishing to read in Greek the astronomical writings of Aristarchus, once sought his help. They worked regularly together at the observatory, the student translating, Poor explaining the mathematics. His interests were not confined to astronomy; he read widely in English literature, the classics, ancient history, political science. And if he was known primarily in Hanover for his many quips he was known in the world of astronomy for his researches in the orbits of comets and asteroids and his mathematical prowess, being a fellow of the Royal Astronomical Society of Sweden and a member of the British Royal Academy. When his colleague Louis Lazare Silverman of the Mathematics Department spent a winter in Moscow in 1923-24, the Soviet scientists he met always inquired about John Poor.

He shared with Louis Silverman, who played the viola, a passion for music. They both played in the Handel Society Symphony Orchestra, of which for many years Poor, who played the clarinet, was President. He tied the striking device of the Dartmouth Hall clock before the concerts — this was before Baker Library was built. With the building of Baker he set to work on a study of the theory of "change" ringing and when he had mastered it prepared the copy from which the playing records of the changes were made; if occasionally they may miss a note — as they sometimes do — let it be a reminder of John Poor's whimsicality and wry humor — which he could turn against himself. Of a road sign, Passable but Unsafe, he remarked, "That ought to be over my classroom door." Another time: "When I walk across the campus for my paper I always look at the flag. If it isn't at half-mast I know I'm alive." On December 11, 1933, the flag was at half-mast.

One day in June, 1945, the flag was at half-mast for George Dana Lord, dead at eighty-two, twelve years after his retirement from forty-six years of teaching Greek and Archaeology. By some trick of memory I see the fused image of George Lord and the Harvard philosopher Josiah Royce standing at the foot of a stairway while students flock past unheeding. Perhaps it is because both men were short and had large heads, Royce's being the larger. More likely it is because both men conveyed an air of calm benignity in the midst of the passing throng. George Lord, with his florid face, white hair, and bright blue eyes under shaggy brows, conveyed intensity as well as benignity. This quality was evident in his speech, delivered deliberately in a resonant well-modulated voice which had the power of ranging from a quiet rambling preamble to end in a burst of explosive energy.

The impression he gave of an Olympian remoteness doubtless stemmed from the fact that though in his earlier days he must have had many students in his Greek classes, by the twenties they had fallen off to the few students who attended his classes in archaeology (conducted as William McCarter recollected from Burpee's seed catalogue). Thus it was that in his later years he gave the impression of a Chinese mandarin suddenly arrived upon the hurrying Hanover scene. Thus he liked to come upon some anonymous student suddenly, fire a penetrating observation and depart.

Leon Burr Richardson, Dartmouth's historian, lived in the present as well as the past, and was also concerned about Dartmouth's future. If

I have suggested that he was a personality rather than a "character" it is not that he did not possess salient qualities, but that his distinguishing characteristic was centrality rather than eccentricity. This was apparent in his solid frame, his purposeful walk with feet firmly planted on the ground, his massive saturnine face which won him the nickname "Cheerless," though this was originally bestowed upon him to distinguish him from another Richardson, known as the "cheerful idiot" because of his ebullience.

He considered himself miscast as a teacher of chemistry and he was not the only one to think so. Upon graduation in 1900 he was offered appointments in three different departments, English and History as well as Chemistry. He would have preferred to be a teacher of history, as his avocation shows, but is said to have been put off from this career by the arbitrary temperament of Herbert Darling Foster. Nevertheless, his thousands of students, and his textbooks, which went into several editions, are witnesses to the effectiveness of his teaching.

> It is comparatively simple for a person to develop brain power, but it is difficult to develop the essential blend of knowledge, purpose, and the sense of proportion which constitutes intelligence. – Ernest Martin Hopkins, 1931.

His breadth of interests and his strong convictions led Mr. Hopkins to give him a semester's leave in 1924 to study the educational institutions of the United States, Canada, and Great Britain. From his investigation of the English and Scottish universities he came back impressed with the fact that graduates of these universities were expected to know at least one subject well; that the undergraduates were expected to work on their own; and that under no circumstances was the brilliant man to be sacrificed to the dunce. These conclusions he embodied in his famous Report on the Liberal College, published in 1924; together with three recommendations: first, that the freshman year be largely prescribed; secondly that thereafter freedom of election be limited only by a requirement of distribution in various fields; thirdly that the last two years be devoted to a major more extensive in scope and different in kind from that ordinarily given in American colleges. This report, together with an able undergraduate study, formed the basis of the new curriculum, embodying comprehensive examinations in the major subject and a provision for Honors work, which was adopted by the faculty and Trustees in 1925. Richardson, as Chairman of the Committee on Educational Policy, advocated the changes in a series of faculty meetings, with customary clearness and concision. Also with barbs of dead-pan wit, not to say level blasts of withering scorn for remarks he considered particularly inane — for "Cheerless" did not suffer fools gladly. Nor did he at any time in his long career of participation in faculty debates spare either friend or foe. "After the President's preposterous statement I move we adjourn." Perhaps it was after some such remark that Mr. Hopkins said to him as they were leaving the faculty room in Parkhurst: "I'm going to change your seat from the front row. If I don't I'll throw the lamp at you sometime."

Needless to say, however, EMH and LB held each other in the utmost respect and affection. Leon Burr Richardson was noted for his undemonstrativeness. But no one who knew him well could have any doubt of the depth of his devotion to his old college contemporary or of his loyalty to the institution to which they had both devoted a lifetime of service.

*   *   *   *   *

The Faculty Room in Parkhurst. Modeled on the House of Commons, with its oak paneling, its sloping benches on both sides of the raised platform where the President presided, and its three rows of seats at the end for the novitiates, it was the scene for years of droning discussion as well as for redeeming moments of scintillating wit. When LB took his seat on the faculty in 1902 (Parkhurst was not built till eight years later), it seemed to him in his unsophisticated innocence that his seniors were a race of intellectual giants which, alas, he said, writing forty-two years later, did not seem to have a current counterpart.

A newcomer in the 1920's had a similar experience. On the platform sat the President in his high-backed chair, flanked by Dean Laycock and Dean Bill, facing the large posthumous portrait of the Founder across the room. From the back benches he looked in awe at the men on the front benches: C. D. Adams, the two Richardsons, Gordon Ferrie Hull, George D. Lord with his white thatch, Haskins, John H. Gerould, John Poor. . . . And he was equally impressed by the youth of the men on the benches behind them, most of them seemingly as young as he.

In the mid-forties the scene had changed. If he himself had not yet reached the front benches he was creeping up to them and Robert Conant, the Registrar, had abandoned the system of assigning seats, except to a few senior members. Where were the young men? They were not yet back from the War, but when they came back would they not be far outnumbered by men now, many of them, old and tired?

Nature takes care of these things: the young men came back; still younger men came to take the place of those who were retiring; and the men who had grown war-weary of teaching in the elementary courses for the V-12 unit found themselves revivified to meet the challenge of mature veterans who were now surer of what they wanted in the way of an education. The College grew, the faculty grew. In the 1770's four or five men composed the faculty; in 1860 there were sixteen active members; in 1916 around 140; in 1945, 275, more than nine-tenths of whom had known Mr. Hopkins as President. The faculty room in Parkhurst was too small for faculty meetings; in the simple, impressive ceremony in which Ernest Martin Hopkins turned over the governance of Dartmouth College to John Sloan Dickey on November 1, 1945, it was used for a faculty meeting for almost the last time. An era had ended.

> . . . I have been calling particular attention to what should be the central aim of the liberal arts college, such as Dartmouth is, to develop a habit of mind rather than to impart a given content of knowledge. – Ernest Martin Hopkins, 1931.

Once again a "new" Dartmouth had arrived. Already the faculty had delegated most of its responsibility to a Faculty Council of some forty members; in 1953 this was replaced by an Executive Committee of about half that number. This Committee wandered about the campus during the ensuing years in search of an appropriate meeting place — it has apparently come to rest in the Drake Room of the Hopkins Center. The full faculty, for its three meetings or so a year, met in the 1902 Room in Baker, in this year of grace in the Filene Auditorium. But the old intimacy has gone, and with it something else perhaps.

In 1946 the Trustees affirmed the principle of securing a faculty second to that of no other undergraduate liberal arts college, announced the initiation of an active recruiting program to assure fresh vigor in the blood stream, and a more rigorous promotion policy to insure that deadwood did not accumulate. In 1954 Donald Morrison, the youthful Dean of the Faculty, could announce that more than thirty new young teachers had been attracted to Dartmouth.

In 1957 the new three-term, three-course curriculum was adopted.

[191]

(A quarter system had been briefly considered in 1917 but abandoned.) Since 1925 there had been no major change in the curriculum, only minor adjustments necessitated by the ROTC units and the introduction of Great Issues. The purpose of the new curriculum was not to save time or to permit acceleration (though the introduction of a fourth, summer, term in 1963 might have to some extent this effect) but to improve the quality of the work and to emphasize the importance of giving the student greater responsibility for educating himself.

All this has had its effect upon the faculty. The present scale of faculty salaries and the introduction of many "fringe benefits" have given Dartmouth a strong position in the Ivy League; the flow of grants for research, especially in the sciences; and the institution of a generous Faculty Fellowship Program for research or creative activities are attracting young and able teachers to Dartmouth. Moreover, the three-term system allows for a leave every fifth year instead of every seventh, as under the old system of Sabbatical leaves, which, incidentally, Dartmouth was one of the first to initiate. Already these developments have resulted in giving Dartmouth undergraduate instruction a group of brilliant young teacher-scholars. The expanded Medical School has also brought to Dartmouth several extraordinary medical scientists.

With all this the old problem of whether Dartmouth should be primarily a liberal undergraduate college is again acute. New times, new needs. Whereas a decade or so ago less than half of the senior class went on to graduate study, in 1963 the figure approached 80 per cent. Already a Ph.D. program in mathematics and molecular biology has been instituted. At Dartmouth, as at other institutions, the loyalty of the younger men has tended to shift from the institution to their disciplines. For young men on the make the prospect of larger salaries at state institutions and the greater prestige of teaching at a university, to say nothing of the stimulation of advanced students and learned colleagues have exercised a strong pull, resulting in a more rapid turnover, perhaps, than was the case in more tranquil days. But on the other hand the advantages of living in a quiet rural community (though those who knew the older Hanover might not call it that) have brought to Hanover a number of somewhat older men whose reputation in their fields is firmly established. At any rate the present administration is aware of the risks as well as of the exciting possibilities. So let those who are concerned about the passing of the "old" Dartmouth rest assured. If over 60 per cent of the present Dartmouth faculty is new since 1952, it will not always, let us hope, be new.

The reader has doubtless noticed the infrequency of reference to the Associated Schools, since I have meant to concentrate on the faculty of the undergraduate college. Even so, on this basis alone the roster must contain men like Harry Wellman, long Professor of Marketing at Tuck and the composer of the music of *Men of Dartmouth,* who was the mentor of many thousands of Dartmouth students who never looked inside the walls of Tuck; and Herman Feldman, Professor of Industrial Relations at Tuck until his premature death in 1947 who, with the Rev. Roy B. Chamberlin, for many years Chapel Director and Fellow in Religion, compiled *The Dartmouth Bible.* But I must stop.

In all colleges there have been strong departments and weak departments and at different periods departments have been now up, now down. I should have made no attempt, had I been able, to engage in comparisons or to plot fever charts in the course of this informal chronicle of the Dartmouth faculty; only to select here and there through the College's long history individuals who have given it its color or affected, however slightly, its intellectual climate. I have not intended to include in this account anyone who was dull or mediocre, though perhaps John Smith is an exception. On the other hand the omission of a person is by no means an indication that he was mediocre or dull. The choice has frankly been governed by my personal bias of interest, recollection, or affection. Let me borrow from Sir Thomas Browne: "Who knows whether the best of men be known? or whether there be not more remarkable persons forgot, than any that stand remembered in the known account of time?"

Yet the reader has doubtless wondered at the omission of two names. Vilhjalmur Stefansson first came to Hanover as a lecturer, brought here by Dean Bill. In 1947 he became Arctic Consultant to the College, and in 1951 came with his wife to Hanover to live, at the time his famous library was lodged permanently in Baker. Robert Frost's association with Dartmouth was even longer — from the few months he spent here in 1892 until his death, a span of over seventy years. In 1916 he was brought back to visit the first college he ran away from by Harold Rugg and continued to return from 1943 to 1946 as a Ticknor Fellow, conducting seminars in Baker, and once or twice yearly thereafter. But now, alas, the visits have ended; in the words of the late

President Kennedy: "He had promises to keep and miles to go, and now he sleeps." Frost and Stefansson were, in Frost's words, "loose-enders." But this does not mean that they were not two of Dartmouth's greatest teachers. The impress, however, which they have made on the arts and sciences of our time belongs to the world far beyond the walls of Dartmouth College. It is fitting that their names should close this chronicle: two names which not only symbolize the possibility of the fusing of the two cultures in our modern world but symbolize also the life of intellectual and spiritual daring to which this College, almost two hundred years ago, was consecrated. Vilhjalmur Stefansson and Robert Frost — two poets, two explorers.

The Students

RALPH NADING HILL

I

Having made the best preparation I could, under my circumstances, I set out with three others for Dartmouth College, September 28, 1772. I took my axe and such articles of clothing and a few books as were most necessary. We took with us one small horse, on which the youngest and feeblest of our company rode most of the way. Three of us traveled on foot, and for a part of two days each footman swung his pack soldier-like, when at length we contrived to place our packs on our horse. This distance was computed to be one hundred and eighty miles. I had only about fifteen shillings in money to bear my expenses on the journey; and as this proved insufficient, I received some more from one of our company. We traveled on an average of about thirty miles a day. I had never before been twenty miles from home, nor gone on foot a whole day at a time. I became excessively weary and at times almost ready to lie down in the street. On the third day, as we went from Hartford, on the east side of the Connecticut River, we reached Chickopee River, in Massachusetts, and finding the bridge gone, three of us forded the river. One rode the horse over, and ascertained that it was not dangerous on account of its depth. We pulled off our stockings and shoes, and waded across about ten rods; the water was cold, the stream rapid, and the bottom covered with slippery stones. . . .

THUS did Joseph Vaill and three Osborn brothers, all of Litchfield, Connecticut, bent upon an education at Dartmouth regardless of the physical and mental travail necessary to achieve it, thread their way north to the infant settlement of Hanover, which they reached on October 5. By sawing logs at the College mills at Mink Brook they exchanged the daytime sweat of their backs for board and keep and whatever learning the light of burning pine knots in their primitive cabin afforded them at night. Jeremy Belknap reported their "philosophic, laborious life" when he walked to the mills during the Commencement of 1774. The crude dwelling students had built there was a curiosity consisting

of one room and one chamber; the stairs outside. The chamber is arched with boards for the better sound of the voice in singing. The chairs and tables are contrived in an odd manner, and they have a wooden clock. At the door is an upright pipe with a spout like a pump, which is continually running with brook water conveyed down a covered descent; so that they have only to hold a vessel under it and it is immediately filled. They have a neat poultry house built of sawed strips of wood in the form of a cobb house with four apartments. . . .

Vaill reported that a "more solitary and romantic situation" could scarcely be found and that the "howling of wild beasts and the plaintive notes of the owl greatly added to the gloominess of the night season." During their first week in Hanover he and the Osborn brothers slept on the floor with narrow Indian blankets as coverings, but soon furnished themselves with wooden bunks and straw ticks, with crude culinary implements and with enough firewood to fend off the crisp night chill.

Throughout the fall they diligently fed logs to the up-and-down saw until winter robbed it of its power, and during the spring freshet managed to cut 60,000 feet of pine. They also tended the grist mill, cleared and burned several acres, sowed them with clover and planted an acre of corn and a garden. One of the Osborns died in an epidemic of measles, and in the fall of 1773 Vaill suffered an enfeebling attack of fever and dysentery. In order to cut 70,000 feet of boards during the following spring they had to saw every evening except Saturday and Sunday. They did not immediately enter College, for they had neither preparation, money nor credit. Upon acquiring these they traveled four miles a day, often through deep snow, to recite to their tutors.

Prior to the Revolution and for many years thereafter the survival of the fittest was not mere doctrine in Hanover. Richardson has observed that by "the mere force of circumstances a selective process was in operation which probably has never been equalled in efficiency in the history of the College." Driving a cow to Hanover and milking it on the way for subsistence at the beginning of his sophomore year, Samuel Hidden of the Class of 1791 plied his trade as a shoemaker in his room secretly, for he thought this beneath the dignity of a college student, until one day the President entered and deposited all of the family shoes for repair.

[197]

Since many students would have gone hungry without some avocation to pay their board and tuition, the calendar was expressly designed to provide an interval of teaching. The fall term began in October and continued until the end of December, when nearly all the students departed for eight or more weeks of teaching in Vermont and New Hampshire. In late February they returned for the second term, which ended with a two-week vacation the first of May. The summer term ran until Commencement in August. Despite efforts guaranteed as wholehearted by their struggle for survival, most students at graduation were still indebted to the College, thus aggravating its chronic poverty.

[198]

The attitude of the administration was that of a benevolent dictatorship; the student exchanged the grindstone existence of the family farm for a life perhaps even more circumscribed under the paternal eyes of the Wheelocks. Eleazar Wheelock appeared at chapel at five o'clock in the morning, or in winter "as early as the President could see to read the Bible." The first recitation followed in a room whose pine benches, firewood, blackboard, instructor's chair and table the students had furnished. Breakfast was next, then study, another recitation, midday meal, study, and more classes in the afternoon. The day ended with prayers at six, or "as late as the President was able to see." Rhetorical exercises occupied Wednesday afternoons. Saturday was free except for evening prayers. On Sunday students were forbidden to leave their rooms except to attend church twice (in addition to morning or evening prayers) and for meals. At all unspecified hours they were expected to remain in their bare and drafty rooms, where they were visited at least once a week by a member of the faculty.

Even the building of Dartmouth Hall seems to have afforded little improvement in their accommodations. Upon his arrival in Hanover in the winter of 1796 Samuel Swift was assigned to a cold chamber on the lower floor of "the great wooden air castle in which most of the students had their rooms." The green pine that he lugged in would not burn in his fireplace. There were the cheerless journeys to the privy at the rear on the subsequent site of Fayerweather Hall. This primitive structure was known as "the Little College," and later to the classically-minded young gentlemen of the mid-nineteenth century as "the Temple of Cloacina," and finally to the youths of later years simply as "Number Ten."

It is curious that among all the volunteers for this drudging regimen a renegade was destined to become the patron saint of eighteenth-century Dartmouth. The sulky that brought John Ledyard from Connecticut to Hanover in 1772 was the first ever seen on the Dartmouth Plain.

According to Jared Sparks, who interviewed a classmate of Ledyard's over half a century later, the horse and sulky

gave evident tokens of having known better days, and the dress of their owner was peculiar, bidding equal defiance to symmetry of proportion and to the fashion of the times. In addition to the traveller himself, this ancient vehicle was burdened with a quantity of calico for curtains, and other articles to assist in theatrical exhibitions, of which he was very fond. . . . The stage was fitted up, and plays were acted, in which Ledyard personated the chief characters. "Cato" was among the tragedies brought out upon his boards, and Ledyard acted the part of old Syphax, wearing a long gray beard and a dress suited to his notion of the costume of a Numidian Prince. . . .

During his brief career as a freshman Ledyard and some companions astonished their superiors with a petition to spend part of their leisure hours "stepping the minuet and learning the sword"; and with a request to sleep in snow three feet deep at Velvet Rocks, two miles east of the College. By scraping the ground bare, by laying down evergreen boughs and adding to their blankets a covering of snow, they passed a comfortable night and reappeared the next day.

Ledyard's next escapade, only four months after his arrival in Hanover, was a fourteen-week safari among the Iroquois of the Six Nations. His final exit (it was voluntary but must soon have become compulsory) was by water. During the absence of the President in the spring of 1773 he felled a large pine on the Connecticut River bank and hewed a dugout in which he fashioned a shelter of willow twigs. With a blanket of bearskin, a supply of dried venison and with Ovid and the Greek Testament as intellectual nutriment, he set sail near the future site of the covered bridge that was to bear his name. Floating south with the current he nearly capsized at Bellows Falls. From there the Connecticut bore him safely to Hartford, one hundred miles downstream, and into a life of variety and excitement paralleled by few of history's vagabonds.

Eleazar Wheelock's claim that "Peace, Love, Satisfaction, Cheerfulness, and Contentment are our daily repast" may have served the purposes of propaganda better than truth, although it seems clear that most students were reasonably content under his zealous leadership. "No father," wrote David McClure of the Class of 1773 "watches over his rising offspring with more tenderness, than he manifested to the School and College. Neither unfeeling authority nor mercenary fines, ever alienated the affections, or hardened the hearts of his pupils. His temper and manners were mild and pleasant, and those under his care obeyed from affection and respect."

With an easy and familiar style of preaching he made palatable even the long hours in chapel, McClure recalled. "When he proclaimed the curses of the law, . . . the pulpit was clothed in thunder, the coruscations of truth were as forked lightning. . . . When he addressed the humble saint, his voice was that of angels who welcome the spirits of the just to mansions not made with hands. . . ." His successor, brusque John Wheelock, was constitutionally unable to make the students his friends. He was accustomed to end a conference with: "Will you sit longer or will you go now?" No student, in the memory of the erudite George Ticknor, was ever known to sit longer. The younger Wheelock insisted that students uncover their heads when within six yards of him, that they speak with deference, and never contradict him. In a diminishing scale of courtesy they were expected to lift their hats when within half as many yards of a professor as of the President, and so on down through the tutors and upperclassmen. Expulsion from College was the lot of those guilty of blasphemy and the traditional legal crimes. Gambling, drunkenness, lingering at a tavern after nine p.m., keeping firearms, "indecent clamor" and "disorderly night walking" brought lesser punishments. Students were required to pay in advance for their board in Commons and to provide their own plates, knives, forks, teacups, and tea. But no directive ever succeeded in preventing hideous outcries in Commons through the years. When the students would not eat out of the College trough they were put out to pasture to forage for themselves.

The sad deterioration of student decorum during the regime of John Wheelock appears to have been owing as much to the state of society and religion after the Revolutionary War as to the President's inadequacies. A majority of the students had in the beginning come to Hanover from Connecticut as a young color guard of the revivalist movement. The elder Wheelock had indeed recruited many of them from the very hearthstone of Yale, which was not in sympathy with his New Light brethren. (Since 121 of the 284 graduates of the first twenty classes came from Connecticut it is clear that the trek from that state continued well into the presidency of John Wheelock.) The revivalist movement of the Great Awakening seems to have reached its peak in Hanover at the outset of the Revolution when, according to Eleazar Wheelock, all vice was driven "into corners." Asserting that the carnival sidelights of Commencement were improper facets of a worthy

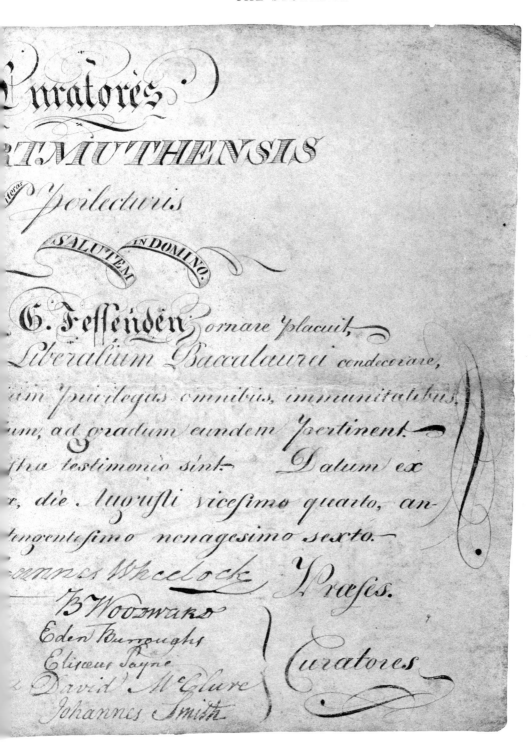

ceremony, the Class of 1775 went so far as to petition against public attendance.

The descent, following the war, from this plateau of propriety was documented by a student of Moor's School, who wrote that the

stage at that time exhibited scenes wounding to Christian piety, and to which modesty was indignant. In a quarrel on the stage one would stab the other, and he would fall as dead, wallowing in blood from a concealed bladder, which was wittingly punctured by the point of a sword. A student would take the stage, assuming to be a preacher, and with a pious tone would *barbecue* Scripture, with a view to shower contempt upon unlearned ministers. One of these young preachers . . . said that "Nebuchadnezzar's fundament was het seven times hotter than ever it was before. . . ."

In his *Reminiscences of Professor Shurtleff,* Josiah W. Barstow tells of a saturnale which ended only when President John Wheelock broke down the door to the student's room. "Bacchus," he announced in the midst of a scene of great disarray, "was ever wont to reckon himself as the noblest of the gods!"

The problems that the elder Wheelock faced in collecting tuition (one backslider told him he regarded his education as "a gift from Jesus Christ," and another, that he was as worthy of charity as any Indian) became aggravated during John Wheelock's presidency. Many students refused to honor bonds they had provided to protect the College from loss of revenue. Religion was so far in decline that only one member of the Class of 1799 was known publicly to have been a professing Christian. The backwash of the war spared no city, town, or institution from flotsam, yet episodes of rebellion and disorder had their antidote in such testimony of serious intent and accomplishment as that of the President of Yale, Timothy Dwight. Following a visit to the campus in 1803 he wrote that he "attended divine service in this place, and never, unless in a few instances at Wethersfield many years since, heard sacred music which exhibited so much taste and skill as were displayed there."

At the same time that one senior of the Class of 1811 was complaining that "tumultuous whirlpools of dissipation are now surging over this plain, and far too many are already immersed in its destructive commotions," a proper and fastidious classmate, John Blanchard, was writing to his sister, Phoebe:

I have just returned from Concord . . . where I went to purchase garments suitable for my graduation.

They are very handsome, but the cost was more than I had anticipated. While there I met with several of the young ladies of Concord. I found them much more attractive than those of Peacham. They are gay, but not forward; handsome but not frivolous. They dance, oh yes, but in an attractively demure style.

Now Phoebe, will you please hurry up and finish weaving the cloth for my trousers . . . ? I wish to have them made by the tailor here before the RUSH of orders that might cause delay. . . .

If such a letter gives no hint of a threadbare College, still less does one written sixteen years previously by Judah Dana about the Commencement of 1795:

I dressed myself in my black Commencement Suit; Black coat, waistcoat, and small clothes, large silver shoe buckles, black silk gloves, and a black Cocked Hat, with my hair cued down with a black ribbon, and my head and hair powdered as white as the driven snow. Thus dressed, at the sound of the Bell, I repaired to the front of the President's House, where a Procession was formed, and proceeded to the Meeting House. . . .

The truth undoubtedly was that on Commencement or other special occasions poverty yielded temporarily to grandeur by way of the borrowed or rented outfit, or a special dispensation from the family till. As for reducing the student body to a common denominator of frivolous dissipation during a period of unrest or moral decline, or to pervading seriousness during a revival — such deductions were probably no more conclusive (or inclusive) then than now. Certainly the straight and narrow path was much more easily found and followed in the early days with Congregational ministers in the president's office and visiting revivalists lighting the way.

Hanover was the scene of the repentance and lifelong conversion of more than one errant undergraduate. During an early nineteenth-century revival one student became completely exhausted by attempting to outrun his wicked thoughts. The rescue of Levi Spaulding, who graduated to an important life as a missionary abroad, had, according to a classmate, taken place in a pine grove on the Connecticut.

I well recollect the morning — I can never forget it, when, having been oppressed with a load of his guilt for many days, his countenance cast down, and his flesh wasted by the agony of his spirit, this interesting youth invited me to a solitary walk for the purpose of conversation. We wandered the distance of a mile until we reached the bank of the Connecticut river. Every moment had been occupied in the great subject of the soul's salvation. S—— was agitated beyond expression. He knew he was a sinner. He was convinced that it would be right in God to cast him off forever, and it would seem to him that God's law required it; and yet his proud spirit would not submit to be saved by Christ. . . . Then I said to him, "Brother S——, there never was a happier spot to hold communion with God than this, where we are now standing, and there can never be a better time to begin than the present. Here in this grove we are secluded from human view, and there is nothing about us but the works of God, and no eye upon us but that of our Maker. What hinders that you should stop here, where you now are, and before you go another step, kneel down by the side of this pine, and give yourself to Christ, and plead for mercy?"

This Spaulding did, and this he always acknowledged was the moment of his redemption.

Revivals seem to have little inhibited the more playful eruptions of animal spirits. One of the first of the so-called nocturnal visitations took place in the early 1780's, when students demolished "the first sprout of the College," Eleazar Wheelock's aging log cabin. The cows that local farmers long pastured on the Green were perennial provokers. One night late in the 1790's students drove the whole offending herd three or four miles up the Connecticut, then into the river and across into Vermont. At another time they herded them into the cellar of Dartmouth Hall, barricaded the doors and held them as hostages in exchange for promises from the farmers that in the future they would pasture them elsewhere. On one occasion students smashed the window of a local merchant (the complainant against them for the herding of cows) and painted his horse white with the words "two dollars" on his sides. Eventually the College removed the Green's ancient pine stumps and erected around it a cordon of wooden rails and granite posts, a few of which survive as the Senior Fence.

Early students, particularly during sporadic outbreaks of warfare over food in Commons, pilfered turkeys and chickens from neighboring barnyards and roasted them in the fireplaces of their rooms. Much more reprehensible was the practice, familiar also to the students of other medical schools, of body-snatching from the local graveyards to provide specimens for the dissecting room.

One of the more spirited incidents of the College's first five decades involved an old cannon and the rising temperature of politics prior to the War of 1812. The students, three-fourths of whom were Federalists, were greatly inflamed when a party of Norwich Republicans (also then known as Democrats) abducted the treasured cannon and hid it on the Vermont side of the river. Tracing it to a house not far from Norwich,

the students procured a search warrant with the aid of a Hanover lawyer, but could find no sheriff or constable in Republican Norwich to
serve it on the owner of the suspected house. The students and townspeople next sent a delegation to the Vermont lieutenant-governor, a resident of Norwich, with a petition for his help. He advised his townspeople that they had better return the cannon, but the suspect who had
hidden it in his house instead dragged it out under the cover of darkness
and buried it in a turnip patch.

When friendly informants showed the Federalist students the cannon's grave, one contingent dug it up and another secured some ropes
with which to drag it back to the College. Reaching the Hanover side
of the bridge, they fired several resounding discharges. Upon hearing
the echoes, an exuberant Federalist officer of the College began ringing
the campus bell, which angered students of the Republican minority.

"Is it possible," they asked, "that our faculty are taking sides in this party row?" In the tumult that followed, the students pulled the cannon up the hill, shouting lustily with every step, while a cluster of Republicans who had gathered on the Green countered with a formidable outcry. The Federalists' retort was a drum to drown the shouts of their adversaries. The monarchists of England were never more zealous protectors of the Stone of Scone than the Dartmouth students were of their precious cannon through the years.

Such upheavals relieved the tedium of a heavy classical curriculum and a calendar unmarked by organized athletic contests or social activities in Hanover or out. Other than during their very proper and infrequent appearances at tea in the house of a professor, the few eligible girls in town were almost inaccessible. Masculine companionship, however, was afforded in the two literary clubs, the Social Friends, founded in 1783, and the United Fraternity, in 1786, whose members vied to pledge, not brawn, but brains, in order to excel in weekly debates and Commencement orations. The fourth Phi Beta Kappa chapter in the country (1787) and the Handel and Religious Societies were the only other noteworthy organizations.

All decorum was cast to the winds when the campus was split in two during the Dartmouth College Case. At first things went smoothly enough, with ninety-five students enrolled in the College and fourteen in the University going their separate ways on the same campus in 1817 and '18. But friction arose from an attempt of the officers of the College to get undergraduates of voting age to the polls in order to bolster the cause of the College at the state capitol in Concord. If students were old enough to vote they were, in the opinion of the opposition, old enough to perform military duty, and the University Party saw to it that the young voters were mustered for training. By pretending to misunderstand orders and making the drills a farce, the College students forced the abandonment of this tactic. When the University Party declared that they would have to work out their taxes by laboring on the roads, each College voter brought five friends and reduced his twelve-hour work period to two.

Since both the University and the College had designs on the Meeting House for Commencement ceremonies at the same hour of the same day in 1817, students of the College, hearing that the University was going to call out the militia to seize the building by force, occupied it the previous day with an arsenal of stones and clubs, and won an easy victory. A sharper test came later when in November the United Fraternity and Social Friends (who feared that the precious libraries they had taxed themselves to collect and maintain were in danger of being appropriated or socialized by the state) tried to pack up their two thousand volumes, then in a building controlled by the University, and move them to safer quarters. Hearing of this, the University appeared with a posse at the library door of the Social Friends and, finding it bolted and too strong to be knocked down, chopped it through with an axe. Upon entering they discovered most of the books gone and the remainder packed for removal. The aroused members of the United Fraternity, holding a meeting in a nearby room, raced out of the building shouting: "Turn out, Social Friends! Your library is broken open!"

A swarm of students armed with sticks of cordwood and spoiling for a fight soon filled the corridor outside the room of the Social Friends. The only escape for the University posse was through the hole in the door. Following the sage counsel of one of their number, a shoemaker, who was heard to say: "I had rather be in a nest of hornets than among these college boys when they get mad and roused up," the University war party surrendered — overcome as its chiefs were destined to be two years later in Washington before the Supreme Court.

2

No glimpse more disarming than that of the English traveler, Anne Royall (*The Black Book,* Vol. 11, 1828), is to be found of the Dartmouth student of the 1820's, or indeed, of any decade prior to the Civil War. She wrote that she came to the College strongly prejudiced against it during the lowering aftermath of the Dartmouth College Case, and expected, upon arrival, "no less than a tornado in Hanover." She had with her a letter

to one of the students, Goveneur [sic] Morris, Esq., a nephew of the celebrated man of that name. It being late when I arrived in Hanover, I made no attempt to deliver the letter that night.

Next morning, being shewn the house where Mr. Morris was said to board — which was but a few steps from the tavern, I walked over to see him. The front door of the house was open and seeing a door to the left I knocked at it, expecting to find some student within who could tell me how to find Mr. M. Some person speaking inside, I opened the door and there sat a great awkward slooney at a small table, from which he never offered to rise. . . . I asked him to "have the goodness to inform me how to find Mr. Morris, I was told he boarded at the house." He "knew nothing about such a man." He spoke quite as rough as he looked. "Such a gentleman is a student here — you appear to be one of the students and not know your fellow student." "No he did not know such a man." I began to tremble for Dartmouth and told him "if he was a specimen it was in a pitiable state indeed." He gazed at me in astonishment, and said he "wished I would go out and shut the door." A gentleman would have shut it himself. He was one of the medical students — I should think he was too lazy for a physician. . . . I turned into another part of the building where I found some of the academic students, who told me Mr. Morris did not board there, but they knew where he boarded and would send him to the tavern, and after laughing at the poor medical student we parted. These medical students are much ridiculed by the other students, who call them by their right name, *Quacks*.

> It is even more a responsibility of higher education in the liberal college to elevate the mind of man than to enlarge or sharpen it. – Ernest Martin Hopkins, 1931.

I had hardly time to return before a number of the students called to pay their respects and to say that Mr. Morris would wait on me directly. My old acquaintance and fellow traveller, Mr. Converse . . . was a student at this college, and hearing of my arrival sent me a polite message that he also would wait on me in a few minutes. But guess my astonishment to find those students accomplished, modest and possessed of all the ease and grace of the first erudite gentlemen. I was thunderstruck! The most accomplished youths, by a long way, of any students I have seen in the United States. In short there is no comparison between them and the students of Cambridge. I was dumb with amazement to see so much ease and grace — covered with blushes they kept their faces toward me till they reached the door; the most finished courtier could not have made a more graceful exit. It appeared to be a dream. It was some time before I dare think it reality. The very small boys, such as in other places stalk into a room like posts — every one walked slowly to the door and there made a bow, such a bow as would have done honor to Chesterfield.

I had not time to recover from my astonishment till Mr. Converse and Mr. Morris came, with a number of other students, all the same, the same modest and respectful deportment. . . . they spent the last moment with me before recitation; some of them came again at one o'clock, and in the evening the whole college turned out, and my parlor exhibited a levee! Had this been in any of the great cities, I should not have been surprised. But, unfortunately, none of our cities can boast of so much worth and innocence. These students are a century before any I have seen, in modesty, innocence and accomplished manners. . . .

Upon the whole, though my pursuits did not leave me time enough to bestow that observation necessary to form a nice judgment, were I even qualified, I would say Dartmouth College is amongst the first literary institutions in our country, and the appearance of the students in those accomplishments which are to render men useful to themselves and others, by a great deal the first.

So unqualified are Miss Royall's tributes that a Dartmouth student generation less chivalrous than the one she depicts might well entertain some doubts as to the accuracy of her reporting. She added that the students she had seen were largely from New Hampshire and Vermont, though there were others from many states, and went on to say, still confident in her power of diagnosis, that their intellectual competence arose from their intensive reading, and their demeanor as gentlemen from the physical location of Hanover, "which is free from those allurements to vice where the population is greater."

*   *   *   *   *

The military exercises that preoccupied the students during the decades prior to the Civil War seem to have arisen both from a taste for adventure and the rising passions of the antislavery crusade.

As early as 1828 William Lloyd Garrison was editing a Vermont paper in Bennington which he later declared to have been almost his first effort in the cause of emancipation. Horace Greeley took up the cudgels across the mountains in Poultney, and in the New Hampshire capital, Nathaniel Peabody Rogers, an associate of Garrison, brought forth *The Herald of Freedom*. While Dartmouth was not in the eye of the hurricane, it was certainly not far removed from it, as the flurry over President Lord's anti-Abolitionist views and his resignation have demonstrated.

Intelligence is understanding and understanding is the beginning of wisdom. – Ernest Martin Hopkins, 1931.

In 1824 Edward Mitchell, a Negro native of Martinique, applied for admission, was examined and approved by the faculty, but was turned down by the Board of Trustees. The students, greatly agitated, held class meetings and appointed a committee to intercede in Mitchell's behalf, one dark-skinned member arguing that he himself should not be at Dartmouth if Mitchell should not. The Trustees reconsidered and Mitchell entered and graduated without further contention.

A great commotion on the Dartmouth campus followed the an-

nouncement in 1855 that the student literary societies had invited the fiery Abolitionist, Wendell Phillips, to speak at Commencement. In *A Dartmouth Reminiscence of 1855* Samuel R. Bond wrote:

I was made chairman of the joint committee appointed by these societies to select and invite the orator, as usual, and arrange for his attendance. I conducted the correspondence . . . and recall that among those who were successively invited were Ralph Waldo Emerson, William H. Seward, Charles Sumner, Oliver Wendell Holmes and George S. Hilliard, all of whom declined. . . . Almost in despair, it was decided to extend the invitation to Wendell Phillips. This was done and a prompt acceptance received, but students sometimes propose and faculties dispose. In fact, when it became known who had been invited as "our orator", I was requested to put in an appearance at President Lord's house at a designated time, and, construing such a request as a command I did accordingly. Professor Sanborn let me in the ante-room, informed me that the faculty was in session, and, as its spokesman, said they had learned that the "United Societies" had invited Wendell Phillips as their orator for Commencement day. I said yes, and that the invitation had been accepted, to which he replied that President Lord's consent had not been obtained. I asked if it had ever been required, or obtained on previously like occasions, and he replied perhaps not, but that he had the right of veto, and would not consent to Mr. Phillips delivering the proposed address; that instead, it had been arranged for Professor Brown to address the alumni at the time and place usually occupied by the orator of the "United Societies". Somewhat incensed and excited I said, "Mr. Phillips has been invited, has accepted the invitation, and is going to speak." "But," he said, "we own the key to the Church" (where Commencement exercises were then held). At this, overcome by my indignation, I arose from my chair and exclaimed, "But you haven't the key to the common . . . and we will have Mr. Phillips speak there at the same time that Professor Brown addresses the alumni, and see which will draw the larger audience". Thereupon he said he hoped there would be no trouble which could be avoided, and asked me to sit down and wait until he had conferred with the faculty. In the course of some ten minutes he returned and said that, under the circumstances, Professor Brown declined to address the alumni, and we might proceed with our arrangements as to Mr. Phillips. . . .

But our troubles were not yet over. While the outer bulwarks of opposition had given away, no cordial welcome by the faculty was to greet Mr. Phillips' entrance to the conservative precincts of the college. . . . If I broached the subject of his entertainment to almost any member of the faculty I would be given a cold shoulder, so, as a last resort, I went to Professor Peaslee of the medical department, with whom I was best acquainted among the professors, and stated my dilemma. He came at once to my rescue, declaring that, while he differed as widely as any of the faculty from Mr. Phillips' views, he considered him one of the finest gentlemen of the land, and that it would be a reproach to Dartmouth College to ignore, or treat him with "scant courtesy" and that if there were room in his own house which had not already been allotted to invited guests Mr. Phillips should have it. . . .

At length Mr. Phillips was lodged in the house of Professor Young. No further impediments blocked the noted agitator's way to the rostrum; his address appears to have gratified the students, if not President Lord and his conservative adherents on the faculty.

Because of its relationship to the great issues of the times a footnote occasionally assumes a place of importance — and the drowning of the son of Harriet Beecher Stowe is a sad footnote in Dartmouth undergraduate history. A sophomore in 1856, Henry Beecher Stowe was accustomed to swim in the Connecticut with his roommate, and on the day of his death he was picking berries on the Vermont side. The farmer whose field the students were in chased them over the fence and into the river. The Vermonter, apparently a disreputable and malevolent character, could easily have rescued Stowe from the spot where he was floundering near the west bank, but made no move to do so, ostensibly because of the affront to his several daughters of the scanty clothing in which students customarily appeared.

"Certainly" as an adverb has been largely displaced by "perhaps." – Ernest Martin Hopkins, 1934.

As soon as he was able to recover the body and transport it to the College in a wagon, Stowe's roommate, Jedediah K. Hayward, telegraphed Mrs. Stowe in Andover, Massachusetts. Receiving no reply, he and several other students accompanied Stowe's body to Andover on the train. Upon their arrival they learned from the telegrapher that, although the Stowes had been away, they were due to return shortly. Hayward wrote that he never knew how he managed to tell Mrs. Stowe of the tragedy.

(Returning to Hanover after the funeral, Hayward stopped at the Eagle Hotel in Concord, where he planned to eat alone in the far end of the dining room, but instead sat down with another solitary figure, a friend and former neighbor of his family, Franklin Pierce, President of the United States. The President's wife had died and he had lost his only son in a train wreck, but his "broken, crushed and downcast appearance," according to Hayward's account of his dark experience, was really caused by charges that Mr. Pierce had bargained with Jefferson Davis to sign a repeal of the Missouri Compromise as the price of his election to the presidency. Hayward remarked that people of a later day could never have any conception of the "frenzied excitement" of the times, deriving from the strength, even in New England, of the opposition to the Abolitionist movement.)

The origin of the Dartmouth Phalanx, the first and most famous of the student military companies, was rooted in state politics, which had grown the prickly thorn of suffrage for all students over twenty-one.* In 1832 Captain Ebenezer Symmes, Hanover tavernkeeper and a member of a state legislature composed largely of elements unfriendly to the College, succeeded in sponsoring an act to make all students (and other youths over eighteen) perform military duty. The faculty strenuously opposed the statute but the students were delighted, and upon its passage enrolled in the ranks of that part of the local state militia known as the "Floodwood" or "Stringbean" Company. Using a stratagem of earlier student trainees, they turned out dressed, or half-dressed, in every conceivable article of clothing. When their captain, an East Hanover farmer named Ulysses Dow, issued an order they crowded around him to ask what he meant. They misconstrued his every command and stepped on each other's feet, all the while complaining loudly. On one occasion they appeared with a flag bearing a crude portrait of Tavernkeeper Symmes, with the devil holding him by the nose and prodding him with a pitchfork. After two years Captain Dow gave up, and the legislature added an amendment to the training act to allow the students to form a separate college company independent of that of the town.

Organized in July 1834, as a unit of the 23rd New Hampshire regiment, and equipped with arms by the state, the Dartmouth Phalanx thrived for eleven years, despite the later alterations in the student

* "In 1836, 1837 and 1839 [the students] outvoted the citizens of the village at the school meeting and took possession of the district . . . though . . . they used their power with discretion and managed the schools well. . . . A bill to exclude them from the Hanover polls was introduced into the Senate in 1838, and became law in 1839. . . . The students . . . hung in effigy the author of the measure. . . . The law . . . provided that 'in all cases where individuals shall leave their home to attend an Academy, College or other literary institution in this State for the purpose of obtaining an education, that absence for such purpose shall not constitute a change of residence so as to cause them to be liable to be taxed or do military duty or to be entitled to vote where such academy &c is situated.' . . . The law remained substantially the same until . . . 1856 when it was repealed, leaving students on the same footing as others. The General Statutes of 1867 undertook to reenact the provisions of the Act of 1839, but . . . limited the measure to the matter of taxation. The Act of July 14, 1871 restored the old law by adding the restriction to the right of voting, the next year . . . the whole was again repealed. It was reenacted in 1874 and in 1876 repealed again." John King Lord, *History of Hanover.*

suffrage and militia statutes which rendered it no longer compulsory. The Phalanx uniform consisted of a black dress coat, trousers (white in summer, dark in autumn) strapped down over the boots; a beaver hat with cockade, and white gloves. Commissioned officers were decked out in dark-green coats trimmed with gold lace and epaulets, and with ostrich plumes on their beaver hats. But that which gave charm and a widespread reputation to the company's appearance on parade, remembered Josiah W. Barstow, 1846 (in a series of reminiscing articles in *The Dartmouth*), "was the perfection of its drill, the precision of its manual, the dignity of bearing, the ready intelligence which characterized every movement of the eye and hand and foot." The pride of the students in the reputation of Dartmouth's crack company found expression in their gift of a silver-fringed and tasseled flag of heavy blue silk, bearing the richly colored coat-of-arms of the Earl of Dartmouth.

Fifty years after the October muster of 1844, there were still some surviving veterans, wrote Barstow:

whose elderly blood warms, as they recall the fife and drum resounding through North Building and Dartmouth Hall at 4 a.m. . . . murdering sleep, and calling the Phalanx to arms for the "muster up to Lyme." Breakfast was eaten on the run or not at all. Ira Allen's stage coaches, previously engaged for transportation, drove up through the fog and gathered in the College rear. The officers were on hand, in full uniform and cloaks, (no ulsters then) the boys sleepy but resolute. The roll call of each section and platoon followed, with inspection of arms and equipment and extra coats, which the early start made necessary. All being ready, the word is given to mount the coaches. A scramble for the best seats ensues, and in spite of mist and darkness, no time is lost in the start for Lyme, where we are due at nine to meet the Colonel.

The officer's carriage, with the band, heads the procession. The well loaded sutler's wagon follows, presided over by the dusky "Bill Wentworth," the ever smiling college barber (himself a load) now puffed up with special pride at his position as cook and steward for the day. . . .

For the students, for the farmers from the hinterlands gathered for the year's most splendidly martial day, the hours raced by in a blend of color and rhythm, of patriotic declamations, songs and cheers. "At the muster up to Lyme — I was there all the time. . . ." Then, much too soon, came the drowsy return to Hanover, and once around the Green in the starlight.

The most memorable muster was that in November, 1843, in honor of Colonel Richard M. Johnson, slayer of the Indian chief, Tecumseh, and a candidate for president of the United States. Word of Johnson's acceptance of an invitation to visit Hanover and Norwich (he was traveling by stagecoach to Montreal by way of White River) reached the students only the night before his arrival. "Every democratic bosom throbbed with enthusiasm," recalled Barstow, as the Phalanx, the Norwich Cadets and the citizens of both towns struggled with hasty preparations for a local holiday. Among these was the agreement of Ira Allen, the stage driver, to furnish his barouche with four gray horses to carry the hero into Hanover.

The program was carried out as faithfully as the deep mud would allow. Colonel Johnson appeared in a "faded army coat and dull red waistcoat which had seen its best days." The whole procession, Barstow remembered,

reached the Dartmouth Hotel covered with mud, but also covered with glory. The hero quickly landed at the front door; the band played *See the Conquering Hero Comes,* and Colonel Johnson, being promptly lifted by the committee to the upper balcony facing the Common, was for a few moments exhibited to the cheering crowd.

The introductory speech was made by Mr. Duncan, who was mounted on a trusty barrel to be the better seen and heard. . . . Of the hero's reply . . . I can remember only his opening words: "Yes, gentlemen, Tecumseh

[218]

was killed, and this (slapping the red waistcoat) was the man that killed him." He then detailed the circumstances of the killing to his half frozen auditors, (the committee holding his military cloak meanwhile) thanked the students . . . complimented the Phalanx . . . and concluded with the fervent hope — "that each member might ever be *semper parata* [sic] to meet an invading foe and drive him from the soil of the republic." The Colonel's Latin was of course employed in deference to his classic surroundings, and was received with tremendous applause, not undiluted with criticism. One Hanover lady, I remember, remarked that "a military man, however distinguished, should be very careful of his genders — in a college town."

The effusive exchange of compliments ending, the procession started down the muddy gulch to Norwich, halting when it reached the bridge, while Marshal-of-the-day Brewster, with his prominent lisp, ordered the band and marchers to be "silent and break step in crossing the bridge lest with marching step we imperil the safety of the structure."

The Norwich cadets, standing at a faultless present-arms on the Vermont side of the bridge, led the procession to the front of their barracks, where a half-cooked ox, "spitted on a hemlock sapling, legs absent, but horns and tail profusely decorated with evergreens and patriotic emblems," was presided over by the white-coated Hanover butcher, his face even redder than usual. The ox was washed down the throats of the hungry multitude with pails of sweet malmsey, the air ringing with eulogies of Johnson, until at last, with a parting salute, the hero was escorted to the hotel. The Phalanx, well-warmed with the spirits that the democratic Captain Partridge deemed vital to such an occasion, but which the proper Whigs of the Dartmouth faculty disdained, returned to Hanover in as good order as circumstances would permit.

It was in 1845, after another parade at Norwich and apparently more sweet malmsey, that the Phalanx was ordered by the faculty to disband. Protesting that they had conducted themselves with propriety, the students countered with angry arguments and with mourning emblems in their windows, but the College remained unmoved. The precious company was mustered out for one final parade in the October sun. Gathering in the Dartmouth Hall chapel to hear an eloquent benediction by their captain, the members marched

without music with reversed arms to the common. . . . . Captain Tilton, in a few well chosen words, bade farewell to the Phalanx, to his comrades and to the flag as it stood in front of the line, and pointing to its motto reminded each soldier that "the true test of manly vigor and dignity is quiet submission in the face of unequal contest." No cheer was heard for every heart was full. The

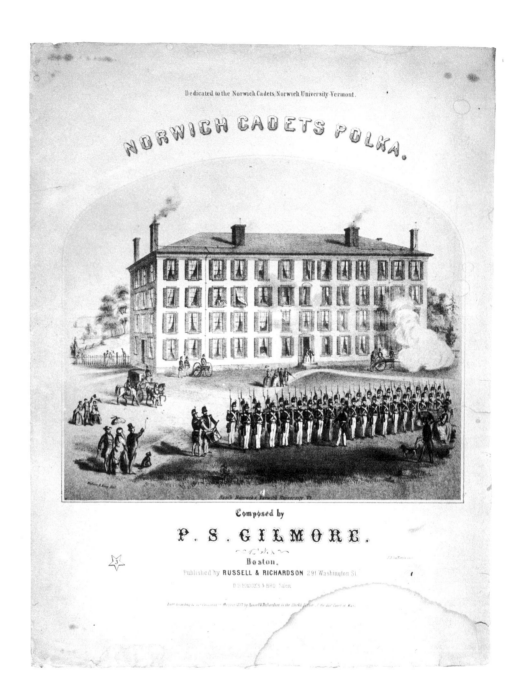

flag was lifted and reverently escorted to its resting place in Reed Hall. Each member saluted it in turn and it was left as a sacred relic in the custody of the College. The guns were then deposited in a vacant room in Dartmouth Hall, the boys separated in silence and the curtain fell. . . .

The Phalanx returned briefly in 1848, only to expire within six months. Another company called the Dartmouth Grays appeared eight years later, proudly carrying a blue silk banner presented by the "Sherman Nuns," the untouchables of Mrs. Sherman's Hanover boarding school. The Grays failed to survive the Class of 1859.

The parades were almost over. The fighting was about to begin. In 1861 Charles Douglass Lee of Hanover became the first enlisted College student in the North. He was followed a year later by the College Cavaliers, a company also containing students from Norwich, Bowdoin, and Union. The exodus then began in earnest. Six hundred and fifty-two volunteers, said to have been the largest number in proportion to enrollment of any college in the North, exchanged tranquil Hanover for the bloody fields of the South. There they confronted the Dartmouth Grays — their forty-four classmates who had joined the army of Robert E. Lee.

3

Students writing home and alumni recalling their undergraduate days made their own literature and wrote their own history of nineteenth-century Dartmouth. They wrote of what aroused and amused them and of the sights, sounds, and tastes of a North Country village. Because times have so incredibly changed, their observations have become meaningful and important in an era that increasingly differs more from theirs than theirs did from that which preceded them. Except for a few more buildings, for the modest physical improvements of a settled community, and for the growing measure of leisure afforded by the age of steam, life in the town and College of the 1870's was much as it had always been.

So that his brother might seek an education at Dartmouth, Samuel L. Powers of the Class of 1874 concealed a similar ambition and remained on the farm (as had seven generations before him) until he could contain himself no longer. His preparation at Exeter was constantly interrupted and he despaired of ever getting to Dartmouth until he learned from friends that President Smith was running a race with President Stearns of Amherst to see who could secure the larger entrance class.

When I made known to President Smith that I was an applicant for admission,

[221]

he wrote down my name and home address, and turning to me said: "Are you a relative of Erastus B. Powers, the preëminent scholar of the class of 1865?"

I replied, "I am his brother."

"Then," said he, "the gates of Dartmouth stand wide open to receive another great scholar from the Powers family."

It was then that I longed to be back in the old dormitory at Exeter, or even on the Cornish farm, but he followed his last remark with one that for the moment brought great comfort to my troubled mind. It was this: "Of course in your case no entrance examination is necessary." My hopes, however, were dashed to atoms when he added, "But the rules of the college require each applicant to be examined before he can be admitted."

> Gigantic forces are at work within the world, the effects of which cannot be foretold but the power of which must be got under control and given direction if we are to avoid new dark ages. – Ernest Martin Hopkins, 1938.

He then gave me three cards, each containing my name, one addressed to Professor Parker for examination in Latin, one to Professor Proctor in Greek, and the other to Professor Quimby in mathematics. He instructed me to call upon these gentlemen, who would examine me, and mark the result on the cards, which I was to return to him, and receive my certificate of admission. . . . About the only questions I answered correctly were those to which I gave the answer, "I don't know." Each professor marked his card with a Greek letter, and as I had already learned the Greek alphabet I observed that these letters were near the bottom . . . which gave them an ominous meaning. On my way back to the President's house my disposition was to tear up those cards and throw the pieces into the hedge, and start back for Exeter, but when I reflected that the cards were college property, and their destruction might constitute a crime which would forever bar me from entering any college, I forebore, and proceeded on my way to see Dr. Smith.

When I arrived at his study the sun had gone down behind the Vermont hills, and the President was sitting in the twilight, near the western window, reading a book. I presented the cards, and he arose from his chair, held them up to the light which came through the window, and a troubled, perplexed expression came over his face. He turned around, secured a match, lighted the large kerosene lamp standing on the centre table, and carefully examined the cards.

He then turned to me, and in a rather severe tone of voice said: "Where did you prepare for college?"

I replied, "I never prepared."

"You will please be good enough to explain your answer."

This I did in a very frank manner, mitigating as far as possible my offense by saying I acted against my own judgment in yielding to the pressure of my friends in the freshman class. The genial, kindly smile returned to his face, and he stepped over to the southerly window and stood for a moment as though in deep meditation, looking down the valley through which the Connecticut river flows to the south passing Amherst College on its way to the sea. Then he stepped over to a desk, filled out a certificate of admission, and passing it over to me he said:

"I congratulate you; you are now a member of the freshman class of Dartmouth College, and I trust your college career will be both pleasant and profitable."

Concerning the faculty, Powers agreed that Professor Young, the astronomer, was the most distinguished during the 1870's. In accordance with an old custom, the Class of '74 ordered the local cabinet-maker to build a twelve-by-four-foot coffin in which to bury all their mathematics books. Professor Young chanced to be in the cabinet-maker's shop one day and, upon being advised of the purpose of the partially constructed casket, asked: "Why so large? A six-quart tin pail would hold all the mathematics there are in that class."

> No man is qualified to be dogmatic about life until he has reckoned the extent to which he would be willing to forego self-indulgence physically or in intellectual exhibitionism, for the sake of helpfulness to others or to the end of creative or constructive accomplishment. – Ernest Martin Hopkins, 1940.

About half of the students roomed in the college halls and the other half in private houses. Those living in the halls furnished their rooms and cared for them but hardly in a manner that would have satisfied the taste of a good housekeeper. The only method of heating was by the stove, and the fuel was wood which the boys bought of farmers who drew it into Hanover on sleds and wheels. The wood was in four-foot lengths and was sawed by the students and carried up to the rooms. The only method of lighting was the kerosene lamp and the candle, with now and then a German study lamp, which made use of lard oil. . . . The water system of that day was the old fashioned well to which was attached a wooden pump which in the coldest weather refused to work until it was thawed out. . . . The boys carried the water to their

[223]

rooms in large earthen pitchers which held about three gallons. There were no bathrooms in the halls and, so far as I know, none in the village. The method of taking a bath in Hanover in my time was by a large tin tub, which when not in use hung on a fixture on a wall in the sleeping rooms, and a large kettle in which the water was heated upon the stove. The rooms in private houses were furnished by the owner, but care, heating and lighting were provided by the students. The charge for rent at the college was entirely reasonable, varying from $7.50 to $18.00 per annum for each student and in private houses about double that amount.

Table board, the most important item in connection with living expense, was furnished by . . . the formation of a voluntary association of some thirty members, who elected one of their number to fill the important office of "Commissary," and he acted as agent for the association, arranging with the landlady to provide dining room, service, and the preparing and cooking of the food, her compensation being fifty cents a week for each boarder. The Commissary furnished all the supplies, and the landlady was entitled to use such part of the supplies provided by the Commissary as were necessary for the support of herself and her family. These landladies usually had large families, and frequently entertained numerous visiting relatives for rather long visits during the winter months. When the club was once under way the Commissary presented a tentative bill of fare, which was discussed in a parliamentary session and amended in such form as to receive a majority vote of the members. . . .

Powers emphasized that Dartmouth during the 1870's was still Yankee in character, with New Hampshire and Vermont supplying sixty per cent of the students, and the other New England states, an additional eleven per cent.

A large [number] were sons of farmers, familiar with labor on the land and in the forests. They were seeking a college training largely on their own initiative, aided by the unselfish and sympathetic sacrifice of hard-working parents of limited means. These boys had carefully thought out the course they were to pursue in life, and entered college with a serious purpose in view. . . . Now and then one disappeared from the college without saying goodbye to his most intimate friends, and the conclusion was quickly arrived at that his funds had become exhausted. One of the best students in my class disappeared early in the junior year, without saying a word even to his own roommate. Some months later two of his classmates were in Boston, and on boarding a street car of the Metropolitan Railway Company they saw their lost member clad in a blue uniform, with brass buttons, serving as conductor and collecting fares. When he came in front of them to take their fares, they exclaimed, with the usual college enthusiam, "How are you, Dan!" He made no reply, but gave them a stony stare and went about his business of collecting nickels. He was forever through with college and all its associations.

A few months after Powers graduated, Clifford H. Smith arrived and dutifully reported his experiences as a freshman to his mother and sister:

Sept. 1 '75 — I arrived here safely, bag and baggage, with nothing broken but my slate. . . . It was *dreadfully* hot and dusty on the cars. . . . I paid out a little over nine dollars yesterday. Bought a wash bowl and pitcher, slop pail, lamp and a few little things. . . .

Sept. 19 — . . . We held our first class prayer meeting this noon, about thirty being present, and eight or ten took part. I never attended meetings that I enjoyed more than I do here. The singing is very fine with so many clear powerful voices, and those who take part seem to be such good and straightforward men. The Sabbath School makes me homesick. Our teacher who does *all* the talking unless some one wants to ask a question talks mostly of the evidence of the truth of the Bible from the fact that none of the miracles were disproved at the time or have been since.

Sept. 25 — . . . You will see that my wash isn't quite as large as we expected, but one shirt does quite well enough for a week and I don't wear cuffs only when I feel like it. . . .

Oct. 2 — . . . We have begun to read Latin so I have to study a great deal more than I did, and the days fly away very fast. Last Saturday night I was initiated with about forty others of my class into the Delta Kappa society, which is solely for doing things like . . . speaking, essays, a paper, of which I am one of the editors a week after next, and other literary exercises. I have got to write an essay for our Christian Fraternity meeting, that comes every Monday evening, in a week or two, and with the necessary amount of play my time is about used up. This afternoon one of my classmates, Rollins by name, and I went down the river a little while. It is the first time I have seen the river since the last day of August. I roll at ten pins some, and kick foot ball most every day.

Oct. 3 — . . . President Smith gave all our class a lecture yesterday suited to our circumstances, and invited all the Christians [Christian Fraternity members] to meet him this afternoon, and twenty six were present to whom he spoke an hour, in a profitable and pleasant way.

. . . My health is comfortable now, although I haven't great strength and my bowels are not just right, but my appetite is good and I hope to get used to Hanover sometime.

Oct. 16 — Wednesday *p.m.* we were on the campus, witnessing the sports, when I heard it passed along that Ohio had gone Republican, and I came near giving three cheers, but concluded it would be prudent to refrain.

It is very muddy and disagreeable when it rains, the ground all around being something like the clay we used to make bricks of. . . . I have written an essay of six pages to read at the Christian Fraternity meeting next Monday evening. . . . I get up generally about half past six in the morning. . . . I have to build my fire and sweep and make my bed, and often do more or less mending, so am busy until breakfast. . . .

Oct. 25 — If the number of meetings one attends Sunday is an index of his goodness I ought to be a pretty religious young man, for I went to six meetings yesterday. First our usual forenoon meeting at half past ten, and we had an excellent meeting, then our class prayer meeting which was fuller and more interesting than any we have had before, there being about thirty-five present. That was out at half-past twelve, then I ate dinner and at 12:45 started with two others for Norwich. As their service begins at one, we were a little late, but had a good sermon. Then at four went to the Sabbath school, then chapel at five, and finally, to the evening service at seven o'clock. . . .

March 4 (1876) . . . May be you would like to know how I spend the ordinary day. Yesterday morning I got up at 6:45 and did my house work till 7:00, and then studied geometry till 7:30. Ate breakfast and went to chapel till 8:10 and then recited geometry till 9. Studied Greek till 11, and recited till 12. Then prayer meeting till 12:30 and dinner till 1. Played till 2 and studied Latin till 2:30. Gymnastics till 3, and studied Latin till 5 and recited till 6. Supper till 6:30 and geometry till 8:30. Then a classmate came and visited me a little while and I wrote a letter and went to bed at 10.

March 10 — . . . Last eve I attended a lecture by Gen. Kilpatrick. I had fully resolved not to go, when an old lady who is at Mr. Andrews wanted to go so bad that she said she would pay .25 of my fare if I would go with her. As the whole fare was only .35 I thought I had better do it and was very glad I did.

I went to quite an extravagance the other day. A man was around selling books and he had a very pretty copy of all the poems of Milton for a dollar and as it was just what I wanted I purchased it.

I have found a man to room with me next year though we haven't decided upon the place yet. His name is George H. Rockwood. He is a very nice fellow, a hard student, a *very* quiet man, a Christian and withal as economical, and poor as I am. . . . He is twenty-two years old, though not as large as I am by considerable. . . . The only fault that I find with him is that he is a democrat. . . .

April 21 — I think you would have liked last night to hear some of the college songs. . . . A large number of the students gathered at the corner of the campus and sang . . . for almost an hour. There is nothing much more pleasant here than to hear these songs just as evening is coming on. . . .

Professor Edwin J. (Bubby) Bartlett, 1872, claimed he discovered the diary of Cuthbert Payson in a pile of trash in the garret of "the old Winthrop dwelling house when it was torn down to make way for the Trumbull Block." Since Payson fails to appear on the roster of students it is obvious that he was selected as a medium to transmit the Professor's own reminiscences. That Cuthbert was nevertheless a flesh-and-blood Dartmouth man, though of an entirely different breed than those quoted above, there is no question. A few of his entries will suffice:

Feb. 6, 18XX . . . I never thought I'd be thankful to come back to this dead place in the winter, with half the fellows out teaching, but I am. Had to go to the hotel for supper. Hod Frary was cross. Said he'd be damned if he'd have students coming for just one meal. If Mrs. Frary wasn't so solemn I'd think she winked at me. And then she said, "You got to take just what we got; this ain't the Parker House or the Fifth Avenoo Hotel." I filled up all right on fish and cream, hot biscuits and apple sauce. Fell on the icy steps of Reed going to the well, broke two pitchers, bruised my face and cut my hand.

Feb. 11. Sunday. The gas fixtures in the church look like spiders.

Feb. 24. . . . Prof. Phussey got screwed into his recitation room this morning and all his class with him. They got out of the window. Three well-placed gimlets did the business. They say the faculty have already got the fellow that did it. If they have they have got the wrong fellow.

March 9. . . . Prof. Young got one on me in Physics this morning. He gave me a problem to do on the blackboard, and I guess I would have got it, but he called on me too soon. He just glanced at it and then explained a better way to do it than I had. He's quicker than a toad's tongue and that is all we've got against him. When he got done talking he said, "You see the point? You see the point?" Well, I didn't, but I said "Yes, sir," just the way we always do. "Well, what is it?" he asked. While I was stuttering around and all the fellows were laughing, the bell rang and he laughed and said, "Never mind: we'll hear about it tomorrow." Hang it! He'll remember it too. He never forgets anything. . . .

March 26. A big open sleigh load of us went down to Leb to see Darling Daisy's Dazzling Dancers. Bum. It took lots of saw-dust to make them look even human, and some of them didn't have any teeth. A big gang of Lebanon "dirties" snowballed us on the way home, and some of the snowballs smelled like bad eggs. Some of the fellows wanted to stop and fight but Hen who drove said they would have to walk home if they did, as he wasn't going to risk the team in any row. They were three or four to one anyway with more coming. Smoked another cigar. I'm getting tough.

April 20. Bought a stove-pipe hat.

April 21. Wore my stove-pipe hat to church.

May 9. I am working all the time that I can get on *The Dartmouth*. . . . What's the use in keeping a diary, anyway! It's baseball time.

That the conjuring-up of impractical jokes reached its zenith in the late nineteenth century is a conclusion that a reader of diaries and reminiscences of the period can scarcely escape. The favorite scene was the old Dartmouth Hall chapel, the one place (other than the Meeting House) where preacher or mischief-maker could gain the attention of the whole student body. In Professor Bartlett's time "a melodeon with the heaves" was replaced with a used pipe organ, "an ungodly kist of whistles" which could be made even more strident by placing a wedge in one of the high pipes so that "a continuous and pervasive wail came forth until the air was gone." One esteemed student organist was accustomed to play medleys of popular songs before chapel until the very moment the President entered, when he would modulate to a slow and dignified selection.

Occasionally the members of one class greased the chapel seats of another, and more than once a corpse from the medical school was ghoulishly propped up in the freshman section to shock those fresh from guileless homes. Once a week the students became unwilling auditors of from one to four seniors speaking original pieces. Bartlett asserted that "anyone who could hold that crowd for twelve minutes could preach a sermon in a boiler factory to an intoxicated gang of cannibals who knew no English."

On one occasion, when "the President had risen to conduct the service, suddenly a huge sheet of paper loosened itself from the wall back of the faculty, gently opened and unrolled, displaying a bitter attack upon one of the classes present by another. For a period a great noise prevailed. . . . It was especially trying for the President, as he was compelled to go through the service without any knowledge of the attraction behind him." The resourceful inventor revealed his identity to Professor Bartlett long after his diploma was safely in hand.

The activities of "Bedbug Alley," dividing the top floor dormitory of Dartmouth Hall, were less susceptible to surveillance and discipline than those of the chapel downstairs. "There I was," confessed one gentle professor, "walking up and down Bedbug Alley and saying to myself, 'Damn! damn! damn!' " The doors to the rooms made suitable sleds for navigating the long stairs, and the wire bedsprings were challenging subjects for electrical experiments. The most inviting of all were those plunderers of sleep, the six successors of the original bell which clanged the College awake during the nineteenth century. The lot of the bellman, a junior who obtained free rent of the third-floor room into which the rope descended, was not often a happy one. Francis Childs has related the exploit of a sophomore who managed to climb the lightning rod ground wire to the belfry after the faculty had nailed up the usual approach and padlocked the bellman's room to forestall the customary all-night Fourth of July serenade. The sophomore had providently tied a rope to the cupola so that he could descend quickly to the ground if he were discovered — which he was. A professor saw the rope and cut it off just below the eaves. The student's descent was much more rapid than he intended. He survived, miraculously, with only two sprained ankles, and the faculty remained ignorant of his identity until years after his graduation.

Francis Clark of the Class of 1873 observed that there were "rough and tough men in the college classes of those days, men who drank and swore and whose virtue was not immaculate." He was convinced, however, that these were a minority and that the students as a whole were serious and upright. An inducement to rectitude was an old-fashioned revival of the early 1870's, during which many class leaders were converted. The vision of troublemakers who could not see the light was improved by warrants to spend from three to six weeks in some clergyman's family.

For years the students enjoyed stealing quietly through the shadows until they were directly under the open window of President Smith's study, there to glean what they could from a special faculty committee on discipline holding court on malefactors in serious trouble. Expulsion from College was often the issue, and since the committee usually divided itself into offense and defense, as in any court, the eavesdroppers gained important clues on how the offender would fare.

Every administration has suffered periods when an atmosphere of uneasy truce has prevailed between the students and their disciplinarians; the interests of the latter were little served by the advent of the student press. Of the many "literary" publications which flared briefly and subsided into oblivion, *The Magnet* in 1835 was the first. *The Hawk* (1844), *The Northern Light* and *Old Grimes* (1848), *The Waif* (1854), and *The Oestrus* (1854-56) were often given to bad taste and bad humor, scarcely a line of which stands the test of time. The yearbook *Aegis* dates from 1875. *The Anvil* (1873), a journal of local, state, and national news, first published as a weekly, became a daily during Commencement, the first college paper to do so in America. It earned a brilliant reputation, and its editors all achieved prominence in later life.

The claim of *The Dartmouth* that it is the oldest college newspaper in America is based upon the tenuous assumption that it was the successor to the *Dartmouth Gazette,* which Daniel Webster edited briefly at the beginning of the nineteenth century. *The Dartmouth* as such began as a literary periodical in 1839 and continued until 1844 when it ceased publication for twenty-three years. In 1875 it became a weekly devoted generally to news, and unequivocally to the principle of freedom of the press. The first of the perennial engagements testing whether that principle should endure (engagements from which every administration wrongly considers it has emerged with the most scars) transpired almost immediately.

The Agricultural School had no more than taken root under the careful husbandry of President Smith than the editors of *The Dartmouth* determined to attack the award of a degree of bachelor of science to

Ho! Verdants!

Whereas, through the inscrutable will of Providence, and the imprudence of their parents, the members of the Freshman class have been prematurely deprived of the privileges of the nursery, and it has been thought by competent medical authority that some simple stimulus adapted to their feeble intellects would be beneficial,

Therefore, We, the members of the Sophomore class, as their guardians, do hereby unanimously resolve to allow said Freshmen to amuse themselves, at all proper hours, with either of the following toys: Rattle, small Horn, or Plug Hat, selection to be left to their own discretion.

Signed,

CLASS OF '77.

agricultural students for three years of bucolic work, while the scientific department conferred the same hard-earned degree for four. The mildly critical article, ostensibly a report of the Agricultural School's Commencement exercises of 1876, was scheduled to appear the next morning. In the meantime, someone smuggled a proof to President Smith and the editor was summoned to his study. Failing to receive any assurance that the article would not be published, the President followed up the interview with a formal communication in the name of the faculty forbidding its publication.

Hastily summoned to a conference, the editors decided to ignore this directive; the article was published, and before the day was over they were permanently suspended. This severe action was not approved by some of the faculty and at least one member of the Board of Trustees, and as a result of a flurry of meetings the editors were informed that if they signed a statement agreeing to faculty control over the columns of *The Dartmouth,* their suspension would not be permanent. The editors refused to sign and retired to the shores of Lake Mascoma, where they camped out for several days pondering their future. At length they drew up a compromise in which they acknowledged the power of the faculty to discipline the editors in case they disregarded any order concerning the conduct of the paper, and their suspension was revoked. However, with the shadow of censorship still hanging over the language of the compromise, the editors decided to suspend publication with this ironic thrust: "Now, that a paper représenting the Faculty would be much more valuable than one representing the students, and very much more valuable than one representing ourselves, we do not deny; but we are not the ones to edit it. . . ." *The Dartmouth* presently returned to its battered fieldpieces, whose volleys have become a permanent broadside of the Hanover scene.

The custom of "horning" was another Sword of Damocles hanging over members of the faculty and administration. It seems to have evolved from the distant past when there was no bell to call the students together. *The Dartmouth* of October 17, 1879, quotes Judge George Washington Nesmith, a Trustee, as recalling a conversation with Reverend Dr. Samuel Wood of Boscawen, a graduate in 1779, during which the latter spoke of a student tax of thirty-three cents a head each term to pay for horn blowing. The task was delegated to the Indian students, who were required to blow on three occasions each weekday for recitations and prayers, and four on Sunday for not less than five minutes each. Since calculating the passage of time proved difficult for the Indians, a walk was devised on which a prescribed number of turns could be made in the allotted minutes.

One of the most memorable horn blows, after the instrument became one of protest, followed the Fourth of July (1851) speech of a Vermont congressman in St. Johnsbury. Though the Passumpsic Railroad had just entered that village the townspeople could not have anticipated the volume of response to their invitation: "Let us have a celebration on the Fourth of July and invite all the world and the rest of mankind to attend it." The horde of Dartmouth students who descended upon St. Johnsbury, finding nothing to eat after the "rest of mankind" had consumed what the citizens had inadequately prepared, advertised their empty stomachs and their opinion of the Congressman's address by blowing their horns.

Occasionally an entire class gathered at a midnight "Shirt-Tail" to serenade an unpopular professor; if the ringleaders could be caught they were sentenced to "rustication" in a country parsonage. The last horning was that of Professor Herbert D. Foster, whose history courses the students considered too rigid. Robed in white, the Class of '97 cremated

their history textbooks in a bonfire, and the sophomores, not to be out-
done, appeared at Foster's study blowing a hundred horns. Because he
ignored them they cut the electric wires to his house, and while he tried
to light a kerosene lamp they raised an even more frightful din.

When the news reached President Tucker, who was out of town on
an alumni trip, he returned at once. In the ensuing investigation each
student was asked only what his part in the outbreak had been; the
leaders confessed and were separated from College. When, after a series
of mass meetings, the students agreed to abandon their barbaric practice, the penalty was removed. In Dr. Tucker's view this was a decisive
step forward in the social progress of the College; its effect was permanent and cumulative in that it resulted in the establishment of the
student governing society, *Palaeopitus*.

The problem was that of the advancing prosperity of the country
manifesting itself in growing numbers of students armed with a new and
potentially dangerous weapon: leisure. Many still lived a hand-to-
mouth existence, but not on the terms of the early nineteenth century.
In his Convocation address of 1905 the President noted that prosperity
was not only enabling many more families to send their sons to college,
but was awakening in them corresponding social ambitions.

The college man of this type is not necessarily aimless, but he is not usually possessed of the tastes of the scholar, nor the ambitions of the man of affairs. What he wants is college life, not college work. . . .

One condition, then, which is comparatively new to American colleges, greatly affecting their office in the training of a gentleman, is the organization of leisure to the degree of very marked encroachment upon work. . . .

Leisure had been creating a vacuum even before Dr. Tucker's time, and the students had begun to fill it with extracurricular activities. Far from having a baneful effect, some of these would appear to have been salutary by present standards, if not those of the early Spartan college. By 1869 a glee club was supplementing the activities of the old Handel Society, which had long supplied church and chapel music even outside the state. The chess players had organized, and there were a number of telegraph clubs, which strung wires to one another's rooms. By 1856 the first of the fraternities, successors of the old literary societies, were holding weekly meetings. (Psi Upsilon and Kappa Kappa Kappa had resulted from the disunited United Fraternity in 1841.*)

The feudal initiations of Kappa Sigma Epsilon and Delta Kappa, the freshman fraternities, ended when the fraternities of the upper classes decided in 1883 to pledge freshmen. That same year the violent annual Cane Rush, which left the Campus looking like a ragpicker's yard, was given up. In 1886 and 1887 Sphinx and Casque and Gauntlet, the secret senior societies, were organized with less than the approval of the whole student body. A band and orchestra, a Banjo and Mandolin Club and some sixty-six other active and semiactive student organizations had entered the field by 1901.

If John Ledyard's eighteenth-century productions were bona fide, the history of dramatics is as old as the College. In 1869 some juniors assaulted the Victorian prejudice against student actors by giving a dramatic performance in the hall of the old Medical School. It was

---

* Alpha Chi Alpha, 1963 (formerly Alpha Chi Rho, 1919, revived, 1956); Alpha Delta Phi, 1847 (formerly Gamma Sigma Society); Alpha Theta, 1952 (formerly Theta Chi, 1921); Beta Theta Pi, 1889 (formerly Sigma Delta Pi, 1858, and Vitruvian, 1871); Bones Gate, 1960 (formerly Delta Tau Delta, 1901); Chi Phi, 1902 (formerly Alpha Alpha Omega, 1898); Delta Kappa Epsilon, 1853; Delta Upsilon, 1926 (formerly Epsilon Kappa Phi, 1920); Gamma Delta Chi, 1935 (formerly Alpha Chi Rho, 1919 and Phi Kappa Sigma, 1928); Kappa Kappa Kappa, 1842; Kappa Sigma, 1905; Phi Delta Alpha, 1960 (formerly Phi Delta Theta, 1884); Phi Gamma Delta, 1901; Phi Kappa Psi, 1896 (absorbed Beta Psi, 1895); Phi Tau, 1956 (formerly Phi Sigma Kappa, 1905); Pi Lambda Phi, 1924; Psi Upsilon, 1841; Sigma Alpha Epsilon, 1908 (formerly Chi Tau Kappa, 1903); Sigma Nu Delta, 1960 (formerly Pukwana, 1901, and Sigma Nu, 1907); Sigma Psi Epsilon, 1909 (formerly Omicron Pi Sigma, 1908); The Tabard, 1960 (formerly Phi Zeta Mu, 1857, and Sigma Chi, 1893); Tau Epsilon Phi, 1950; Theta Delta Chi, 1869; Zeta Psi, 1853 (revived, 1920).

thronged, according to John A. Bellows of the Class of 1870, "by all the elite and fashion of Hanover and . . . applauded to the echo. How ferocious was Farmer as Sally Brass! How captivating and rollicking Brown as Dick Swiveller! How hungry, and cunning, in more senses than one, Mr. George Smith as the Marchioness!"

Despite this bravely successful sortie, news of nineteenth-century student drama is sparse; production problems were aggravated by the refusal of Hanover ladies to perform on the stage, so that students had to take all the female parts. Thus the entertainment of the long winter evening was typically the musicale by faculty and students at Bartlett Hall, followed by cake and coffee in the candlelight of the social rooms downstairs.

Attendance at the performances of professional road companies was more permissible, especially if they were operas. *The Dartmouth* of June 17, 1898, reported the production of *Uncle Tom's Cabin* in a tent on the high-school playground. "The students lined the bleachers around the edge of the tent, while some of the more courageous of the faculty and their wives occupied reserved seats in the arena. . . . While the play was in progress the players were often interrupted by side remarks from the students, one of the most notable coming at the afflicting scene of Eva's deathbed." The remark, alas, has not survived.

Dr. Tucker was not editing *The Dartmouth;* had he been doing so its announcement of the first Carnival, which little resembled its winter successors, would surely have been different. "Only a few days now remain before Hanover will be plunged into a period of gaiety and mirth second only to the great annual carnival in Rome. . . ." Held in May, 1899, the Carnival consisted of a street parade of floats and marchers from all the organizations in and about the College, a bicycle parade, a twilight hum of the Glee and Mandolin Clubs on the upper piazza of the Wheelock Hotel, an open-air band concert, debate and baseball game with Williams, a three-hundred-dollar display of fireworks, a minstrel and dramatic show, and the first Junior prom. All went well except the bicycle parade which, according to *The Dartmouth,* might have succeeded grandly if so many students who had merely watched had taken part in it. "Several of the riders rode artistically decorated wheels, A. B. Leavitt, Class of 1899, especially attracting attention, wearing colored tights and riding a wheel encased in green and white, while in a basket on the front of the handle bars was a sweet little girl with her flowery locks tied with colored ribbons and with her dress also adorned. He drew first prize." As for the minstrel show, *The Dartmouth* reported a "scene suggested by the Moorish palace of the late King Henry the Eighth with Turkish sycophants at his feet and lackeys of the reign of Louis XIV surrounded by the African embassy. . . ."

The century expired with the inglorious but exciting bang of the Spanish-American War, and with the arrival of Admiral George Dewey in West Lebanon on a special train. "You know I can't make a speech," responded the hero of Manila Bay to the cheering students, "but I will introduce Governor Rollins who can. But before he begins I want to say a few words to you. I am very glad to see you boys. You are going to own the country some day."

*   *   *   *   *

Not many years ago Morris Bishop wrote in *The New Yorker* of Dartmouth's good fortune as the possessor of a garland of songs no other college could attempt to match. An inquiry brings the investigator

irrevocably to the unique traditions of Place, and of the out-of-doors and the four seasons.

For generations the symbol of the College was, and indeed still is, the Old Pine that for a century and a half stood in the winds on the ridge overlooking the Green. It may have been first growth; it was certainly there before the Revolution. During the 1850's graduating classes adopted the custom of gathering around it to smoke a pipe, which was passed from one to the other. The Rev. S. Lewis B. Spear, 1854, wrote that at that time a fine wreath of cedar with red berries was woven around the tree and that on Class Day the seniors gathered about it to read their chronicles and prophecies, to smoke their pipe, to sing *When Shall We* [All] *Meet Again?* and finally to rush forward toward the tree to secure pieces of the wreath as mementos.

Lightning struck the tree in 1887 and a whirlwind in 1892, after which it failed steadily. When it was cut down in 1895, Henry P. Rolfe, 1848, gathered its history in a sketch published in the *Concord Evening Monitor.* Further speculation upon the origin of the old song, *The Three Indians,* or *When Shall We Three Meet Again?* was presented in *The Dartmouth* on February 12, 1897, which quoted Rolfe as follows:

My father, who was born in Boscawen, and always lived there until 1840, was four years younger than Dartmouth College, the College having had birth in 1769 and my father in 1773. He was a very fine tenor singer and among the songs he was accustomed to sing were *Burgoyne's Lamentation, Perry's Victory* . . . and . . . *When Shall We Three Meet Again?*

He told me that when he and Chellis Shepard were young men they attended Commencement at Hanover several years, and when at Commencement he learned the song and the tune of *The Three Indians;* and before I was ten years old I knew both the song and tune very well. He told me that the song was composed by one of the native Indians and it was sung around the young pine at the time they left and separated. He said there was a young pine in the College grounds around which they built a wigwam, which was called "The Bower" where they stayed much of their time. When I went home at my vacation in the fall of 1844 he inquired of me about the pine and was surprised that it was no larger than I represented it to be. . . .

Dismissing the tradition of the Indian composer, Fred Lewis Pattee, 1888, proved English authorship of the strongest part of the song, but did not think this diminished its importance in the Dartmouth repertory. "It is a Dartmouth song . . . taken over early by Dartmouth men, given Dartmouth color and persistently for a century promulgated as a Dartmouth fact."

[237]

When shall we THREE meet again ?

Meeting of the Three Friends.

The parting of the Three Indians.

Composed and Sung by three Indians, who were educated at Dartmouth College, at their last interview beneath an encanting bower, whither they frequently resorted, in the midst of which grew a " Youthful Pine."

WHEN shall we three meet again ?
When shall we three meet again?
Oft shall glowing hope expire,
Oft shall wearied hope retire,
Oft shall death and sorrow reign,
Ere we three meet again.

Though in distant land we sigh,
Parch'd beneath a hostile sky ;
Though the deep between us rolls,
Friendship shall unite our souls,
Still in Fancy's wide domain,
Oft shall we three meet again.

When our burnish'd locks are grey,
Thined by many a toil-spent day ;
When around the youthful Pine,
Moss shall creep and ivy twine,
Long may this lov'd bower remain,
Here may we three meet again.

When the dreams of life are fled,
When its wasted lamp is dead,
When in cold oblivion's shade,
Beauty, wealth and power are laid,
Where immortal spirits reign,
There may we three meet again.

There shall we forever rest,
Leaning on our Saviour's breast,
There shall we forever be,
Gazing on the Eternal Thee ;
There shall we all Him adore,
There shall we three part no more.

The Meeting of the Three Friends.

Once more welcome dearest friends,
Now at least our wandering ends,
And though hope did oft depart,
Oft though sorrow sped its dart,
Let our griefs no more remain,
Since we Three now meet again.

Though remote we long have been,
Many a toilsom day have seen ;
Tho' the burning zone we've trac'd,
Or the polar Earth embrac'd,
We've sweets from friendship sought,
Often of each other thought.

Let us seek that cool retreat,
Where we three oft us'd to meet ;
Where beneath the spreading shade,
We have oft together stray'd,
And where at last with anguish'd heart
We did tear ourselves apart.

Ah! how altered is this bower,[power
Where first we felt sweet friendship's
How has time with ruthless blow,
Laid its vigorous beauties low,
Nought but this lone Pine remains,
And its naked arms sustains.

Are we then that youthful three,
who reclin'd beneath this tree ?
Then with verdant foilage crown'd,
Now with moss and ivy bound,
Not more alter'd is this Pine,
Than our looks with wasting time.

Every feature then was fair,
Nor was grief depicted there,
Then our sparkling eyes did glow ;
Then our cheeks with health did flow,
Then the lamps of life were bright.
Now they spread their glimering light

Though our mortal strength decay,
Though our beauties waste away ;
Though the lamps of life grow blear,
And the frost of age appear,
Yet our friendship bright shall bloom
Far beyond the closing tomb.

It is the geography of this oldest song — and of the illustrious lyrics of Richard Hovey and Franklin McDuffee — that has, in the words of Robert Frost, "made all the difference."

> For the wolf-wind is wailing at the doorways
> And the snow drifts deep along the road,
> And the ice-gnomes are marching from their Norways,
> And the great white cold walks abroad.

". . . her sharp and misty mornings / the long cool shadows floating on the campus / the crunch of feet on snow / the long white afternoons / . . . the hill winds / . . . the still North. . . ." So the burden of remoteness was not a blight at all but a virtue, and the vigorous climate, the builder of institutional and personal character.

The eternity of challenge and response for student and institution alike again became painfully apparent when, at the moment of Dartmouth's greatest enrollment of 1,500 students in all branches of the College at the opening of the fall term of 1916, battalions of khaki appeared on the Common. The death, on Christmas of 1915, of Richard N. Hall, 1915, a volunteer ambulance driver in France, reportedly the first American college graduate to lose his life in the War, profoundly disturbed a campus not yet prepared for war. Indeed in January of 1916 the editor of the *Jack O Lantern* wrote to *The Dartmouth* from the Ford peace ship that, although he had always seen the desirability of international peace and arbitration, he had not been clear on the question of preparedness before; he was now glad to take his stand on the side of absolute disarmament. When the *Jacko* published in May an editorial chiding the faculty for granting three hours' credit for summer training at Plattsburg ("Soon we will have one hour given for a walk to Moose Mountain, and three hours for the Mount Washington trip. Then will come credit for keg parties and honorable mention for steady attendance at Junction dances. . . .") the editor was permanently suspended from College, despite a petition of one thousand names appealing for his reinstatement.

To one who was in college in the winter and spring of 1898 when the Spanish War broke [observed the *Alumni Magazine*] the contrast of then with now is growingly impressive. . . . It was somewhere in the blizzardy fag end of winter that news came of the sinking of the *Maine*. It was on a Wednesday night, . . . and with the exciting word there was an immediate rush for broomsticks. . . . The declaration of war . . . found Dartmouth students busily drilling on the campus. Then came enlistment and a Dartmouth Company enrolled in the New Hampshire Guard and went to Chickamauga Park and typhoid fever.

But their going was a thrilling thing. They all marched into the chapel for vespers on the Sunday just preceding (for everyone went to chapel then) and President Tucker spoke to and of them. Probably no one of them remembers now what he said. But every man who sat in that crowded chapel, hushed and tense, remembers the solemnity of the service, the throb that went with the President's words, the lump in his own throat, the brimming of his eyes that he tried to ignore; the almost groping slowness and silence of the crowd as it dispersed after the exercise.

Presently, on a great day, the whole College escorted the volunteers to the station and saw them off to the war. The band played, noisily at least, the crowd cheered, and frenzied Dartmouth yells . . . rent the air. . . .

This time there have been no heroics, no cheering, no swelling excitement. Silently, one by one, or in little groups, slipping away by night trains, so as to avoid something of the struggle of goodbyes, the men have gone. And thus the College has dwindled, — wasted, one might almost say; for the steady exodus has left great empty spaces in its life and brought a singular quietness on what remains. Whoso would find activity must seek the athletic field where khaki clad youths are building elaborate trenches; or, just before evening, he may stand at the head of the campus to see the regiment march and counter march and, at length, draw up facing the soaring flagpole with its blowing stars and stripes at the top.

In September, 1918, the enrollment was down to 750 men, over half of whom were freshmen. Through President Hopkins's untiring exertions Army and Navy corps were established at the College in October, with all undergraduates over eighteen as members. The fraternities were closed, the dormitories became barracks, the Commons, an army mess hall. Then, unbelievably, came news of the armistice.

4

The College and the country, having girded themselves for the supreme effort, suddenly emerged into the prosperous, undisciplined, and strangely anticlimactic 'twenties. Immediately after the War the freshmen could not take their cues from upperclassmen, because there were not many of the latter, and what there were could not find themselves. Movies seemed to claim more attention than study, or even athletics. The pendulum was swinging back into the postwar trauma that Dartmouth had first known after the Revolution; actually it was more like the return of the outer convolution of a series of concentric circles to the same area, but not the same place, for the circumstances this time were quite different.

> . . . if I were a young man trying to decide where I would go to college,
> I would find out of what college Dr. Hopkins was President and go there.
> – John D. Rockefeller, Jr., 1950.

We are in the froth of the post-war wave [*The Dartmouth* asserted in 1925]. . . . This generation of ours has been painted a gin drinking, thrill seeking group. As a matter of fact, the pennywise novelists have not produced accurate pictures. They have portrayed the minority who seek extremes. They have painted us as carousing with Bacchus and toying with Venus. But we do none of these as a generation. The weak among us have thus fallen victims to the freedom brought by the war. But our generation has not taken liberty for license as a unit.

This generation of ours, instead, has taken freedom to mean freedom from the duty of application. We have abused freedom until we are victims of laziness. We talk and dance and cultivate languor, but we do not work.

The editors spelled out this hypercritical evaluation of themselves and their fellows. They were irreverent, they respected nothing that transcended them, they had lost their humility, they were intolerant, they were blind to the beauties of simplicity, they scorned the virtues exalted by their elders, they confused individualism with eccentricity, they were smug, self-centered and without ambition and they were ignorant. They were "fish outside the water of life."

Since usually the younger generation is defending itself against the disparagement of the older, it is refreshing to find an antidote to the students' sharp self-deprecation in the defense of the Rev. Frank L. Janeway, (h) '22, who left Hanover in 1912 and did not return until ten years later. In an address before the Secretaries Association in 1923 he declared that, although he did not find the atmosphere charged with a quest for scholarship, he felt that the new students were not only doing far more thinking than their World War predecessors, but more independent, frank, and critical thinking. The "decline of authority" that was currently affecting the intellectual life of the students was not, he declared, a Dartmouth phenomenon, but one shared by the other colleges, one which the War hastened but did not cause.

He noticed a definite improvement in the appearance and deportment of the students. Ten years earlier, and for many decades prior to that, they seemed to place a premium on "hardness" that had derived from provincialism and isolation — the "tenor of life of some of the ways of the woodsman. . . ." He found it greatly satisfying to note the change in attitude

that if a man is not hard, he must be soft. That is not true. If a man is not hard, he may be gentle, and the gentleman is a man of strength, not softness. Don't think for a minute the modern Dartmouth man is soft. The granite of New Hampshire . . . suffers nothing for being polished . . . and if this granite is to be used as pillars of court houses, of halls of government and churches, we prefer it polished.

Professor William K. Stewart, writing in *The Dartmouth* in November, 1924, further dispelled the widely accepted concept of the Dartmouth man as a "roughneck," who in his most extreme form was "thought to have combined a maximum of brawn with a minimum of brain, to have terrorized instructors and defied discipline, to have been impervious to culture. . . ." Despite the externals, the sweaters and the hobnailed boots that formerly prevailed on the campus, the legendary roughneck, declared Professor Stewart, was foreign to his long experience on the faculty. The larger and wealthier student body had inevitably become diversified, and something of that close-knit democracy of the old days, when every student greeted every other on the Campus, had passed. As in other institutions, intellectual interests had been in decline during the War and for a year or two afterward, and since then there had been a "pronounced turn for the better that has received the grandiose name of 'intellectual renaissance.'" In sum, the professor found current undergraduates as amenable to reason, as decent and gentlemanly as their predecessors.

There was, as *The Dartmouth* testified, a minority given to excesses — there always is — and Professor Harry R. Wellman, in a series of

outspoken essays in the *Alumni Magazine* and elsewhere, laid the actions of these students to examples set in their homes. They acquired attitudes naturally distasteful to them, he asserted, because the times decreed that these were popular attitudes. "The colleges do not originate these customs; they are the direct product of the home town smart set."

In the heat of the debate about what was wrong with the younger generation, and who was responsible, *The Dartmouth,* on November 20, 1923, printed the reply of an English instructor to the inquiry of a parent whose son had failed. The case was in no sense typical, the editors said (nor was it characteristic only of the 'twenties), but did demonstrate a complacency in the home which needed to be dispelled if the College were to do its most effective work.

Has your son ever heard you express a broadly rational conception, ever joined with you in any fine sport of the mind? . . . Did you ever take him to an orchestral concert, or to a really good play? Your son's face and actions and speech have already answered these questions for me. You have stuffed his mind with dull platitudes, have done everything you could to convince him of the impiety of original thought. You have crammed his soul with ugly chromos, jazz, movies, yellow journals, and sensational magazines. You have addressed your son every day, for eighteen years, in ungrammatical, ill-chosen, and fumbling words. Yet you do not blush to toss him to me with a "Here! Make a scholar of him."

Concerning the "intellectual renaissance" that had developed at Dartmouth during the 1920's, the students differed as to whether it was real or spurious. *The Dartmouth* in 1923 thought that the newly vaunted practice of drinking tea each afternoon was affectation; that the burgeoning membership of the new "literary society" and attendance at the concerts of world-famous artists was

ostentatiousness . . . governed by mob spirit. Each year a few literary lights pick some pet author and he is read by all the lesser lights for the rest of the year. Year before last it was Cabell, last year it was Mencken, this year . . . who knows? . . .

But the worst evil of all is that the Newly Born are attempting to gather all the Great Unwashed into the fold. . . . When a minority group, which has for a length of time been in disfavor, at last gains tolerance, it will invariably attempt to force its views upon former opponents and will abuse such as will not be converted. And this is the attitude of the average Dartmouth intellectual. We have fought so long against the evil of outward uniformity and the lack of courage to be "different" that we are bound to the evil of intellectual uniformity.

The controversy was still raging in 1925 when W. H. Cowley, 1924, in the *Vox Populi* column of *The Dartmouth,* which he had edited the preceding year, put the aesthetes in proper perspective, if not in their place.

. . . may we go back to the early rumblings of these changes — three years. . . . The athlete reigned in Big Green glory with the strutting manager running a close second. Lecturers came to Hanover to talk to vacant seats or were openly ridiculed if their meetings were compulsory. Rallies were religious ceremonies from which no one stayed away. And everybody wah-hoo-wahed for Dartmouth as the greatest college in the country because *he* happened to be a Dartmouth man. It was the day of the Rah Rah, and it was a great day.

Against all this, a growing few protested. And their numbers grew and continued to grow until last year one woke up to discover that styles had changed and that to talk of books was the thing to do — and to go to lectures. Even athletes meekly sat on the floor in a crowded hall to hear Bertrand Russell and others talk over their heads. Rallies died out, the wah-hoo-wah got just a bit rusty. It was the style. This year it has become apparently fashionable to go even further. It used to be proper for one to be two-fisted and hammer-chinned, evidently it's now in form to be lily-fingered and pretty-pretty. Instead of glorifying the athlete and backing the team, Hanover now lauds the poet and backs the visiting speaker. And instead of long wah-hoo-wahs, one hears short sips of tea while the college sits about and shakes its head at those old barbarian Rah Rah days. It's the day of the aesthete, and it's a great day — a great day for the *New* Rah Rah.

> There is a lot of difference between a college presidency as a profession and as a mission. – Ernest Martin Hopkins, 1964.

And now you in turn arise to denounce this New Rah Rah. The reigning Rah Rah doesn't please you any more than the brand that flourished two years ago pleased me. And you protest. Were I turning out editorials in Hanover again I should protest too . . . every time the Rah Rah poked up its head too persistently in any form, I should take a poke at it. Any kind of over-emphasized, disproportionate Rah Rah — at any time! . . .

The cyclical character of student enthusiasms overwhelmed the new rah rah, even as it had the old. Perhaps the only certainties of undergraduate life were the annual epidemic of "pinkeye" and compulsory chapel; even the latter became optional in the early 'twenties after long and fervent debate. With the passing of the ancient institution of required daily chapel attendance there also passed, even among men not noted for their piety, according to the *Alumni Magazine,* "a certain glory from the earth."

About thirty seconds before the stroke of eight o'clock [remembered Harold Braman, 1921,] . . . bell number three started to toll twenty times. This had the same effect as the "eight count" of a boxing referee, and immediately reduced the number of potential worshipers to those either inside the edifice or those within about a 200-yard radius — provided they were fleet of foot and long of breath. If you were in front of the Bookstore or just emerging from

College Hall you didn't have a chance, but if you had started across the diagonal duckboards you might make it.

As the last doleful toll sounded, the chapel monitors slammed the three front doors in your face, and your humble entreaties and vigorous poundings were unheard through the two-inch-thick oak and iron-bound portals.

Congregationalism had long since ceased to dominate the Hanover Plain, as had the College the temporal life of the students. The Class of 1925 contained 149 Congregationalists, 109 Episcopalians, 72 Presbyterians, 53 Methodists, 47 Roman Catholics, 37 Baptists, 20 Unitarians, 19 Christian Scientists, 10 Universalists, 10 Jewish and 2 Reformed Jewish, 7 Lutherans, and various other faiths including 21 with no church preference.

The College's new Selective System of admission, later adopted by many of the great universities in the country, was furnishing the sociologists with useful material. Approximately seventeen hundred reasons for choosing Dartmouth were listed by the Class of 1926. The foremost had to do with location and among these the most poetic was: "The ideal spot for either work or vacation is the place where the hand of God still reigns supreme over nature." Hanover's distance from the city, its unique winter sports, and even its "liability" as a place where no girls were close at hand were listed as attributes. Many were attracted by the College's facilities, both educational and physical; some because of the heralded democracy of student life, and some inevitably because, as one student put it: "for seventeen years, last August, I have been the son of a Dartmouth alumnus."

A time study of the student day revealed pointed changes from the era when the sharp northern air was inhaled only on the way from dormitory to chapel to eating club to recitation; when whist was a general indulgence and girls appeared only at Commencement, and then heavily chaperoned. Winter Carnival and other houseparties and proms were changing that. But on the average day the student was working nine hours, sleeping a little over eight hours, and spending the remainder under the broad heading of recreation such as sports, conversation, the movies, extracurricular reading, and thinking about girls.

In 1926 *The Dartmouth* asserted that the vitality and morale of the students had never been lower, nor the custom of "weekending" out of town ever so widespread. This statement must be considered within the context of the times: in 1928 only thirty-nine students had permission

to drive cars in Hanover. Roads were poor, the railroad too often led only vaguely toward one's destination, and classes started again early Monday morning.

The attitudes of any generation, most of all the 'twenties, are too various and transient to be synthesized. An incipient railroad strike found the students out of sympathy with the unions. "Foreseeing the conditions which must ensue if the strike orders are carried out," asserted *The Dartmouth* in 1921, "the undergraduate body stands ready to don overalls, wield pick and shovel if necessary, to do their small part in seeing to it that the necessities of life are carried to those who are unable, in a crisis of this kind, to help themselves." William Jennings Bryan, arriving in a blizzard in 1923 to speak on "Science versus Evolution" proved merely entertaining. The students were greatly taken with concerts by Hofmann, Heifetz, Schuman-Heink, Flagstad, and Rachmaninoff. In 1924 they voted two-to-one for Edward Bok's peace plan, thus favoring international cooperation and repudiating isolationism. Their overwhelming presidential favorite (and that of the faculty) was Calvin Coolidge. In the dreary aftermath of the flood of 1927 nine hundred students rallied to the leadership of Professors Lewis Stilwell and Herbert West to dig West Hartford and White River Junction out of the mud.

Perhaps the most tangible hallmark of the students of any generation is their dress, which in the 'twenties consisted of aging white flannels or knickers, brown leather jackets, flopping galoshes, and crushed soft felt hats perched forward on the head — a dramatic contrast to the uniform of a century before. In 1825 a black single-breasted coat with rolling collar (having on the left breast a sprigged diamond and on the left sleeve half a sprigged diamond for freshmen, two halves placed one above the other for sophomores, three for juniors, and four for seniors), vest, cravat, and black or white pantaloons comprised the recommended but not compulsory attire. During the 1870's the tall silk hat was considered *de rigueur* for the gentleman, and therefore the student, together with a string tie, long black coat, and gray trousers. Those who could grow beards or side whiskers did so. The rugged, unkempt look accompanying the rise of athletics brought the sweater and the sweat shirt, squeaking corduroys, and hob-nailed boots. In June, 1930, metropolitan photographers and newsreel cameramen came to Hanover to photograph some six-hundred Dartmouth pioneers in shorts. These gave way successively to suits or odd jackets and slacks, then to leftover army twill and eventually to the epoch of severely "pegged" chinos and blue jeans.

> Some of us studied hard and learned a great deal; some of us, mentally gifted, learned a great deal without studying hard; some learned as much as they thought they needed and devoted much time to other than scholastic activities, often of distinct value; some sat and talked; some sat and meditated, and some just sat. – Leon Burr Richardson, 1950.

New Englanders no longer comprised even half of the enrollment of the 1930's; nearly every state in the Union and many foreign countries were represented. Students tended increasingly to come from families with professional or business backgrounds. Richardson thought highly of their manners and poise; they were easy to manage in the classroom, they were neat and attentive. They perhaps lacked "dogged perseverance in doing difficult tasks, which is not easy of attainment by those who have never been confronted by the necessity of doing such work and who have always lived sheltered lives." This background, together with the aching aftermath of the great depression, produced subtle changes of attitude.

Few students had escaped the shock that accompanied the loss of financial security to their parents. While the sons of those with no resources to lose were working their way through College just as they would have been obliged to do had there been no depression, the greater number were now coming from earlier moderately affluent families who found themselves in straitened circumstances. As on all other campuses the "depression theory" of radicalism was soon manifest in the pronouncements of a vocal minority, whose short-lived publication, *Steeplejack,* asserted in 1934 that "the most striking and incontrovertible event is the failure of capitalism. In its literature as in its religion, our culture has shown increasingly unmistakable decay." Also ". . . until an international communal order is achieved, the worth of the College will be tested by the number of radicals it contributes to society." What the Junto, the Dartmouth chapter of the American Student Union and, for a few years, even *The Dartmouth* (a daily since 1920) were saying was enough to induce alumni nightmares that the Campus had become a rank Marxian breeding ground. *The Dartmouth* was investigating the conditions of workers in the granite quarries of Barre; there were Youth Congresses and Student Strikes against War.

But these were symptoms only of those susceptible to the allergy of the times. In the presidential straw vote of 1932 Herbert Hoover received 1,120 votes from the students and 38 from the faculty. Norman Thomas, Franklin Roosevelt, and W. Z. Foster received 274, 255, and 12 student votes, respectively, and 31, 23, and 1 from the faculty. In the presidential poll of 1936 more than half of the students voted Republican. The Democrats ranked second and the other parties trailed far behind.

Perhaps the foremost compensation of the threadbare 'thirties to the students was their discovery that money was not the only tender of a rewarding life. A reaction against the leftists, a newly objective outlook on business and politics, enthusiasm for the creative professions and, among freshmen, a revival of interest in religion and a moral earnestness were apparent toward the end of the decade.

. . . I think they have grown more studious with time [affirmed "Ma" Smalley, proprietor of Dartmouth's most memorable eating club.] Leastwise they discuss classroom work a lot while taking their meals nowadays. Another thing, they blush now when I roll into the midst of an off-color story. Why in the old days they used to rush me with any new joke or strange happening

bumped into while away from school. I got so I could usually go 'em one better on the recount. However, I don't know whether their current silence is because the boys have changed or in deference to my *getting older*. Perhaps it's a little of both.

It was, it seems, the students who were getting older. The benevolent but proprietary dictatorship of the minister-presidents of past generations had yielded, under President Hopkins, to a policy of granting the students all the responsibility they could rise to. During the mid-1930's supervision of their conduct in dormitories and fraternities was transferred to their own councils. In 1934 for the first time, rigid rules, self-imposed by the students and governed by *Palaeopitus,* were substituted for administration police at Winter Carnival. In 1938 a system of a prescribed number of classes that could be cut with impunity each semester was annulled. With the establishment of the Undergraduate Council and then the adoption of the honor system at examinations over two decades later during the administration of President Dickey, student government became a full reality.

Even the perplexing question of supervision of a student press sporadically given to irresponsible pronouncements was resolved, or at least settled, in 1939 with control of *The Dartmouth* vested in a board of eleven proprietors, seven from the editorial and business staffs, and four from *Palaeopitus,* the faculty, the administration, and alumni. At Dartmouth, unlike many other colleges and universities, editorial decisions in the columns of the undergraduate daily remain with the students, thus guaranteeing their access to what President Dickey has called "the raw material of freedom." The risks in the present system of various kinds of unwarranted abuse are considered less dangerous than those inherent in administrative censorship.

In contrast to large-city universities where fraternity life is sought out of a diffusion of interests on scattered campuses, fraternities at Dartmouth have had a long history of striving to justify themselves against criticism that they have been indifferent elements in a village whose life is largely that of the College itself. President Hopkins personally abolished the rushing of freshmen in 1924 and during the 1930's tried to help fraternities rid themselves of the onus of being largely social. Their uplift through self-government and an increasing preoccupation with the purposes of the College have been gradual but positive.

Among the proliferating student organizations of the 1930's the Dartmouth Players (successor of the Dartmouth Dramatic Association) gained a central role both in the College and the community. Since the mid-'twenties (when Hanover ladies and girls at last assented to become actresses depending upon the nature of the plays and the attitude of the undergraduate body) student productions had outgrown their excessively amateur status of previous years. In 1936 the Players selected in advance a complete season's program that ran the gamut of ancient Roman comedy through Shakespeare and the first nonprofessional performances of *Merrily We Roll Along* by George S. Kaufman and Moss Hart. At the same time the Experimental Theater was presenting original and often volatile student one-acts under the ebullient direction of the Messrs. Bradlee Watson and Henry Williams. Even the fraternities, in their annual play contest, took wholeheartedly to the stage.

No less an impact upon the extracurricular scene in and far outside Hanover during the 'twenties and 'thirties was being made by the six musical organizations: the Glee Club, Instrumental Club, the Band, Orchestra, the Barbary Coast, and a community group resuming the name of the Handel Society. Despite the relentless turnover of its members the Barbary Coast, the descendant of an informal post-World War I jazz combine, was esteemed by Glen Gray during the 'thirties as the best college band he had ever heard, and by Fletcher Henderson, the celebrated arranger, as ready "for big stuff, if they want it." The ancient wail against Hanover's isolation was becoming less apt. At its eighth spring-houseparty dance in 1938 Green Key (the junior society organized in 1921 to afford students of other colleges hospitality on their visits to Hanover), contracted with both Tommy Dorsey and Artie Shaw, who set up simultaneously at opposite ends of the gymnasium to engage in a battle of swing, whose equal, for financial if for no other reason, will never again be heard in Hanover or anyplace else.

The best-known social institution of Dartmouth students in the 'twenties and 'thirties was, of course, the Nugget, the village movie palace. Its unique reputation had evolved from a not-too-distant past of lantern slides and flickering travelogues. (On December 4, 1914, Lyman H. Howe conducted his student audience into Vesuvius "through a canopy of steam, vapor and smoke down inside the sheer lava walls of the abyss.") The theater as such was the conception of the late sports writer, Bill Cunningham, 1919, who needed more money for his tuition and prevailed upon F. W. Davidson, a Hanover businessman, to build a theater. Davidson obliged in 1916 with a structure whose walls were wisely constructed of galvanized tin and whose seats were of wood and iron, strongly bolted to the cement floor. Cunningham became manager and piano player and the first target of the Nugget's historic missile of protest, the unhusked peanut.

While the movies were silent the audiences were not. The students, delightedly mocking the shallowness of the films of the day, shouted advice to the performers who happily were beyond the reach of their

threats. One of the liveliest of such occasions, Bill Cunningham recalled to George O'Connell, was *Tiger Rose,* in which the film's

plot turned on the heroine's decision. She could save the hero's life by entering the villain's cabin unchaperoned. She approached the cabin and the audience cheered. Overcome with revulsion she hesitated. "Stick, stick!" the crowd implored. "You can't quit now!" The heroine gathered her courage again (cheers), hesitated (groans), then walked in to her fate. She was rewarded with a thunderous "Wah Hoo Wah!" . . .

Years later when Anne Boleyn's head fell during the showing of an epic production of *Henry The Eighth,* a quartet of students in the front row stood up and sang *Annie Doesn't Live Here Any More.* Fires have produced two succeeding Nuggets, each more comfortable and dignified than its predecessor. Though, given sufficient provocation, audience participation still flares up occasionally, it has become far less common as both students and films have matured.

Don't join too many gangs. Join few if any. Join the United States and join the family — but not much in between unless a college. – Robert Frost, Hanover, 1943.

The 'thirties were the last of what might be called the traditional years of the College. Most classes were relatively small and seminars intimate and unhurried. Many of the professors had been reared in the nineteenth century, many were properly and distinctively of the "old school." A five-piece student orchestra played at dinner in the College Hall Commons; a dining room in the new Thayer Hall was set aside for seniors who wished to be waited on. The far-away rumblings of Hitler and Mussolini could occasionally be heard, but was it not a fact that the Italian railroads were running on schedule for the first time in history? The only evil winds were those which had blown from the Caribbean and laid the Green half bare of elms in September, 1938. For a few days Hanover looked less like a College than a lumber camp, with students out clearing the streets with crosscut saws. The era of lantern and candlelight returned briefly as *The Dartmouth* hand-set a one-page hurricane edition.

Among other extraordinary phenomena, natural and unnatural, none created more stir than the arrival in 1939 of the disenchanted F. Scott Fitzgerald, together with a Hollywood crew to film Winter Carnival as

[253]

part of a movie about college life, or at least Hollywood's conception of it.

Nothing written during these years seems in retrospect to have been as portentous as a quatrain about the atom which appeared in a collection of undergraduate verse:

> The shape of them was never known,
> Nor was the color either;
> In fact, that they are all a myth,
> I am a firm believer.

*   *   *   *   *

During the nationwide Peace Mobilization of 500,000 students in April, 1936, 1,100 Dartmouth undergraduates voted for the abandonment of compulsory military training, although in May of the same year Palaeopitus asked the administration for a course on war. Responding to a poll conducted by *The Dartmouth* in 1939 the students favored permanent neutrality by a ratio of more than 92 to 1.

Now the older generation has a chance to see what it has taught us [*The Dartmouth* asserted in 1940] and it is dissatisfied with its work. The same teachers who told us that we should avoid involvement in a European war at any cost are now telling us that we are cowards, or pro-Nazis, because we listened to what they taught us about forming independent judgments, independent belief. The parents and teachers who wanted to give us a solid foundation on which to rest their responsibilities are now saying that we are weak, because we do not accept the easy responsibility they wish us to accept.

Quite the same sentiment prevailed on every campus. It was unfairly attributed to the propaganda of extremists, and it was a little harsh of *The Dartmouth* to ascribe it to the teachings of the faculty, for the outlook of the World War I generation had been the same before the United States involvement. In each case, the nation once committed, debate ceased.

Over five thousand men, most of them lieutenants in the Naval Reserve, passed through Dartmouth's six-weeks training school between July, 1942, and June of the following year. Other thousands were enrolled in a V-5 course for aviation cadets. In July, 1943, Dartmouth received the largest V-12 naval training unit of any college in the country. On August 5, the conversion complete, Secretary of the Navy Frank Knox arrived to review the massed ranks of the trainees, to be followed two weeks later by Under Secretary James E. Forrestal, 1915.

A service flag of all the Dartmouth men who served in the Second World War would have to be large enough to carry a constellation of nearly nine thousand stars, all too many of them of gold. " 'Round the girdled earth they roamed" as never before; and the durability of the College's spell stood the test. Col. Corey Ford wrote of Dartmouth men among the prisoners held by Japanese in the Philippines in December 1942:

It was hard even to think of Christmas in that atmosphere of barbed wire and bayonets, they said. They were sick and starved and lonely and forgotten. There were no Christmas letters, no packages, no tree; no hope even. They tried to put Christmas out of their minds. But very early on that Christmas morning, before it was light, the camp wakened to the unaccustomed sound of singing. A handful of men had gathered in the dark outside the barracks, and as their fellow prisoners listened they sang, very softly, the *Dartmouth Winter Song.* The homesick Americans lay on the bare filthy boards and listened to that universal song of the north wind and snow and the great white cold, the beechwood and the bellows and the pledge of fellowship, and it brought some things close that had been very far away. They listened in silence, and the only sound in the dark was when a man began to cry.

*   *   *   *   *

History did not repeat itself when they came back in 1945. An atomic bomb had fallen and time did not seem to permit a postwar trauma. Outside Hanover was a world of new realities. Inside, the oldest-looking fellow in College was a freshman and the youngest-looking a senior.

Most of the contrasts between veterans of desperate years in far places and those, too young to go, who had gained their knowledge of the War in the periodical room of Baker Library, were less obvious. An English professor observed that despite the veterans' lack of literary experience they possessed an uncanny ability to think things out clearly and with exactness. A corollary, perhaps, was their higher sense of values. The innocent and pleasant illusions of traditional college life were forever lost to them. They could agree that their maturity gave them a better understanding of many things but denied them the tender responses to the College environment that they might have enjoyed at eighteen. They sought the marrow of education and were in a sweat to consume it. Their impatience was understandable, even admirable, but was hard to deal with. In their search for objectives they would consult for hours on their programs, cross-examining their advisers.

Many were married, and the lingerie on the clotheslines behind the Fayerweathers was indeed something new to behold in Hanover. "In place of the rows of pinball machines that were once the main attraction in Fletcher's basement," noted the undergraduate editor of the *Alumni Magazine* in 1946, "one now stumbles over parked perambulators lined up neatly like half-tons at a surplus war materiel market."

Time ministered to the student body's split personality; in 1947 the fur-lined Air Force jackets, the combat boots, the fatigues, began to disappear. Presently the veterans were gone, but vestiges of their anxiety, their preoccupation with the curriculum, their industry, their search for meanings, remained.

In the nostalgic hearts of alumni the College is the last place that should be subject, in John Dickey's words, to the "accelerating ob-

solescence" afflicting most human institutions today, yet the contrasts between the environment of the present Dartmouth undergraduate and that of the pre-World War II student become daily more evident. Not wholly without foundation is the suspicion of many pre-World War II alumni that if they applied for admission today they could not get in, and if they got in they could not pass. It is true that the competition is infinitely keener than in their time, but since the proposition is incapable of disproof let it be asserted that if they had had to meet it most of them would likely have done so. If one is aware of the crush of applicants to Ivy League colleges he is not surprised that so many of the aptitude scores of entering freshmen today are in the seven hundred percentile range. Nor should one be astonished that the overall average of Dartmouth fraternity men in 1962 was 3.3 (on a scale of five points). "These are not averages to be viewed lightly," wrote the undergraduate editor of the *Alumni Magazine,* "nor do they indicate an atmosphere pervaded by wine, women, song and TV." The student is preoccupied with his studies; he is headed for graduate school and must also meet mounting competition there.

As for its enrollment Dartmouth is no longer even largely a New England college. Over forty per cent of the Class of 1960 came from the Middle Atlantic states and only twenty-three from New England. Students from the Far West comprised nine per cent that year and those from the South, five. One fourth of the members of the same class enjoyed partial or total scholarships amounting to $760,000. A worthy student's inability to pay is fortunately becoming less of a roadblock to Hanover.

A perennial complaint issuing from the gymnasium and from Robinson Hall is that the professors are encroaching more and more upon athletics and upon extracurricular activities. Granting the amount of "booking" that is going on these days, the complaint seems strangely unjustified, for the number of extracurricular activities has become so large and various as to defy a brief summary. Approximately one student out of six is engaged in the task of governing the community of undergraduates through an extensive structure of dormitory and fraternity officers and committees, with the Undergraduate Council, founded in 1947, the ultimate authority. Discrimination in fraternities, one of the most sensitive issues with which student government has dealt, has been formally abolished by Trustee action based on a deliberate process of Campus referendum and enforcement; its vestigial remnants in isolated cases are disappearing.

The professional, thousand-watt radio station, WDCR, established in 1941, requires the energies of a staff of about 130 and claims to be the nation's first and only AM station operated entirely by students. Various small singing groups have added new hues to the already broad musical spectrum. The Forensic Union's Debating Team has won national acclaim. There are French, Spanish, Italian, German, and Russian language clubs; press, photography, film society, bicycle, sports car, flying, chess, judo, pre-law, Young Republican, Young Democrat, international relations, psychological, and geological clubs. Voluntary Reserve Officers Training Corps units of the Army, Navy, Air Force, and Marine Corps consume other thousands of foot-pounds of extracurricular energy.

Professor Benfield Pressey has written of the decline of such traditionally distinct student types as the woodsman, the aesthete, the earner-of-his-own-way, the rah-rah boy, the burly inarticulate athlete, the politician; and of the regrettable demise of regional accents of speech. Today's freshman has often traveled more widely than his teachers. An eclectic interest in classical music, poetry, in ballet and opera seems permanently to have replaced the almost total indifference of earlier students. Following the Second World War there was a good deal of talk about an above-all preoccupation with Security. Now one learns of a pervading interest (perhaps arising out of the current inclination toward graduate study) in making serious and constructive contributions to society.

The once-vaunted maleness of the College, somewhat vitiated by the married students, continues to generate debate, although with busloads of girls arriving on weekends the plea for coeducation seems at least temporarily academic. In a forum on this and other subjects some years ago, one student said he did not know how many other places there are in this country where one could find three thousand normally functioning males who voluntarily confine themselves to a hilltop. Another thought that making Dartmouth coeducational would spoil it, that life in Hanover has a certain cleansing effect and that it permits the student a certain amount of irresponsibility. This aged debate seems destined to grow older before Dartmouth ceases to be a college for men.

It is their ready assumption of responsibility and their sound decisions when the chips are down, according to Dean Thaddeus Seymour, that set Dartmouth students apart. The reasons may be the close-knit environment of the town, the tendency of the College to be "self-selective" in the students it attracts, and its policy of granting them choices that elsewhere are either less available or completely lacking. Since responsibilities have been offered recent classes of Dartmouth students, and they have accepted them, they may be considered more mature, in many respects, than their predecessors.

And yet the more the present student is said to differ the more he remains the same. His basic anxieties change very little. Homesickness has, for example, prevailed for nearly two centuries — that dreaded freshman disease, wrote Dean Gordon Bill,

which is often laughed at by inexperienced laymen, which is often not appreciated by the average doctor and which, in its initial effects on a college course, is about as serious as those of infantile paralysis. As far as its effects on his nervous system, his digestion and his mentality are concerned, I would about as soon see a matriculant enter my office with smallpox all over him as to see him enter with that haunted look in his eyes and with the beads of perspiration on his brow which are always present in such cases.

The January Syndrome, another historic hazard, continues to follow the exhilaration of the holidays. It is then, according to the Dean of Freshmen, Albert I. Dickerson, 1930, in his letter to parents, that their sons

come in to say they think they should quit college or transfer; go to work, or join the army, or travel. They talk about their health, their sinuses, the climate; about your health or business problems, or the illness of aunts or grandparents; they yearn for the life of the big city (whether or not they have ever lived in one), they have suddenly discovered that a local college (where possibly a particular girl happens to be attending or planning to enroll) offers courses especially well adapted to their suddenly discovered needs. . . .

It is, one may finally conclude, not so much the students but the backdrop that is changing. In an era of superhighways it seems scarcely credible that within the span of a single lifetime it took one hour for the student stage to travel the five miles to Lebanon; and that one of the dark concerns of President-Emeritus Hopkins was the Hamp Howe livery stable on Allen Street. In 1912 horses were still hauling their heavy loads of students and baggage up the hill from the river. As late as the 1930's special trains destined for Boston, New York, and Chicago were lined up at the Norwich station before the Christmas holidays. Now the station is closed. Only thirty years ago Joe D'Esopo's fledgling travel bureau accomplished the then remarkable feat of dispatching a student hurriedly to his home in the Caribbean via Pullman to New York, Pullman to Florida, and a Pan American seaplane to Cuba.

A traffic light at Main and Wheelock has replaced the authoritative red face and ample paunch of Dennis J. Hallisey. It has been years since Deans Craven Laycock, Lloyd Neidlinger, Robert Strong, and Joseph McDonald gave counsel in Parkhurst Hall, or the durable Spud Bray (and his assistant, Nelson Wormwood) tracked some misdemeanor to its source; or that the town character, Nat Woodward, last shuffled up the street, or the quick-talking Fletcher negotiated a deal outside his smoke shop, or John Spagett unloaded one of his plaster of Paris atrocities on an innocent freshman. Old buildings have departed and new ones have appeared. Yet the white row on the hill presides over the Green, as it has for many thousand sunsets, foursquare against the changing times.

It is said that nothing that is not true can be great. No alumnus, however long he has been absent, can doubt the lasting integrity of this Place, nor fail to identify his own associations with those of the current harvest of students. Nor can he mistake these sharp and misty mornings, these long white afternoons, these clanging bells, for those anywhere else on earth. The wolf-wind is still wailing at the doorways. The steps of Dartmouth Hall are still for singing.

Wearers of the Green

F. WILLIAM ANDRES and ERNEST ROBERTS

. . . whereby the channel of their diversions may be turned from that which is puerile, such as playing with balls, bowls, and other ways of diversion, as have necessarily been gone into by students in other places for want of an opportunity to exercise themselves in that which is more useful, and better calculated to answer all the great and good ends proposed, . . . it is therefore earnestly recommended to the students . . . that they turn the course of their diversions, and exercises for their health, to the practice of some manual arts, or cultivation of gardens, and other lands, at the proper hours of leisure. . . .

THUS did Eleazar Wheelock begin the "regulation" of sports at Dartmouth. He later recorded his success in a letter to his son-in-law, William Patten, written in May, 1771:

The Youth are all to a man, since I have expell'd one, well pleased with my plan of improving the vacancies in cultivation of their lands — this is now the 2nd week of Vacation — & they are all as busy as bees in making their Gardens, and a surprising alteration they have made in the face of things. . . .

Presumably the first Dartmouth student to distinguish himself by athletic prowess, other than that demonstrated with a hoe, was Dartmouth's celebrated runaway, John Ledyard, the companion of Captain Cook and solitary wanderer through Russia, Siberia, and Africa, whose brief undergraduate career has already been described. Surely his daring voyage down the Connecticut in a dugout required both the dexterity and fortitude of the natural athlete.

The chronicle of Dartmouth athletics is as lusty as that of the College itself. The location that Dr. Wheelock chose so carefully has had an incalculable influence both upon Dartmouth and her sons. Its frontier isolation bred a mixture of independence and fellowship; its country setting and social simplicities fostered the adventurous course, the exercise of resourcefulness, and the acceptance of another's talents and his use of them as the true measure in the evaluation of his contribution and his rank. The compactness of the College's social organization seems peculiarly suited to the expression of natural enthusiasm and the unabashed adoption and declaration of enduring loyalties. From these forces and attitudes sprang what has been termed the Dartmouth spirit — better to be felt and shared than defined. A visitor to the College who seems to have felt it and shared it was Christopher Morley. After he had spoken to the undergraduates in 1922, he affirmed that spirit exists in direct proportion to the degree to which it is morally and spiritually uplifting, and observed that the

affection that men feel for their colleges is not wholly disinterested; they love the memory of their own youth. But we have never seen any college yet where we did not catch some distant glimpse of the essential spirit for which its graduates love it. And as for Dartmouth, perhaps we shall longest remember a little bronze tablet in the shower room of the gymnasium. It tells that shower baths were erected in the memory of Stanley Hill, who was fatally wounded at Rheims in 1918, and that the room is "dedicated in his name to the brave and clean young manhood of his beloved Dartmouth." The inscription concludes with the quotation (is it from Browning?), "That Life is long which answers Life's great end."

Athletic sports, whether the running, leaping, and swimming of Dr. Wheelock's first Indian youths or the highly organized and disciplined football or crew of today's undergraduates, have made an irreplaceable contribution to the students' achievement of what President Dickey has termed their "own independence while coming to at least tentative terms with one community after another," as creative men who may "one day leave behind them a sum greater than the total of [their] inherited qualities and fortuitous fortunes."

In larger part than generally acknowledged, the textbook, the teacher and the midnight oil are supplemented by the desire for, the commitment to, and the grace of athletic sports. Each of these components of the educational system is highly competitive and equally harsh and uncompromising in the inevitability of its judgments. In both the test in the classroom and the contest on the playing field the undergraduate is stripped down to his bare self and his measure is taken competitively and with unrelenting honesty; thus he is helped along the way toward knowing himself, and in the process, his fellows.

No one has stated the case for athletics more perceptively and persuasively than President Tucker, who found that the adjustment of college life to intercollegiate athletics was difficult and at some points a most vexatious problem. Still, he accepted athletics as a legitimate part of the life of the College, recognizing that recreation is no substitute for

A front View of DARTMOUTH COLLEGE, with the CHAPEL, & HALL.

a contest. In a survey of his administration after his retirement he stated his creed:

. . . I held fast to my educational belief in athletics during a somewhat stormy period of discussion, substantially for the moral possibilities rather than the physical results to be gained. I have always been doubtful of the value of the physical results, especially to the most highly trained athletes.

Among these moral advantages Dr. Tucker emphasized the potential for leadership growing out of competitive sports and the beneficial character of their democracy. He recognized that the one and only inexorable test, whether in scholarship or competitive sports, is the attainment of excellence. In either case the man relying solely on his own talent and effort is placed on a level with the man who has some inherited advantage. He considered that competitive sports give the student who is not of the highest scholarly aptitude self respect and courage by reason of being able to do well something of recognized value, and he felt that the loss of this privilege would on the whole lower the tone of college life. He found further value in students facing up to the moral issues inherent in the management of intercollegiate athletics, citing as an example the action of the Dartmouth Athletic Council with the acquiescence of the undergraduates in barring ten baseball squad members from further intercollegiate contests for having played professional engagements during the summer of 1906.

Save for Dr. Wheelock's initial admonition Dartmouth has never been an apologist for athletic sports. Quite to the contrary she has believed in them and made significant contributions to their development, regulation and administration, especially at the intercollegiate level. In the early days when "foot-ball" was being played at Dartmouth with excessive zeal, presidents themselves often exercised this regulation by personally wading into the vortex of the maelstrom. Regulation was more easily achieved after athletics attained an organized and recognized status within the life of the College. This was some years in coming, removed by a century from the canoeing, foot-racing, and ball-throwing in which the Indian youths excelled, and the more decorous game of wickets on the College Green as depicted in an engraving of 1793.

Team games developed slowly during the nineteenth century, for students had their fill of exercise in sawing cordwood for the stoves of their rooms and in doing the daily chores that were their lot in the College's relatively modest society. But as early as 1827 students were playing football on the Green during the noon recreation hour, and cricket clubs covered the Green during that summer. Walking, that universal form of exercise that has survived the ages, had its adherents. Strolls of ten or fifteen miles on a Saturday afternoon were common; in 1831 Amos Tuck and a classmate walked from Hanover to Concord in a single day. (Sherman Adams, 1920, and William Fowler, 1921, apparently hold the endurance record with a single all-day hike of 83 miles, on which they visited every cabin owned by the Outing Club.)

The sport that became and remained the most popular of unorganized athletics was Dartmouth's own brand of foot-ball — true football, with kicking the only method by which the ball could be propelled, and with the whole student body at liberty to participate, described by Frederick Chase as ". . . the free, joyous, and exhilarating pursuit of the ball over the green by every student, according to the measure of his inclination and powers." Various methods of choosing sides were followed, the most common being "whole division," pitting the seniors and sophomores against the juniors and freshmen, or the two large literary societies: the Social Friends against the Fraters. John Scales of the Class of 1863 recalled that the game consisted in kicking the ball from the vicinity of the flagstaff eastward across the Green toward Dartmouth Hall and getting it over the fence into College Street; opponents tried to drive it in the opposite direction and over the fence to Main Street on the west side of the Green. Proof that foot-ball found favor with at least one college administration is furnished by President Bartlett's description of how it was played during his undergraduate years in the mid-1830's:

. . . all the college joined in every fair day. And a very picturesque and exciting game they made it, now in long array, now in solid knots, now in scattered groups, and now sweeping like a cyclone, with its runners even more effective than its rushers. And it had its kickers, too. I remember one of them, a senior when I was a freshman, and the stupendous boots he had made on purpose, with soles fully a half-inch thick. I can seem to see him as he stood once on the extreme edge of the surging mass of strugglers, the football far out of sight in the center, but the boots going like a horizontal trip hammer all the same. . . .

If this rough and hearty game was played elsewhere, no other college is known to have competed with Dartmouth. In the spring and summer seasons of these early years students also enjoyed cricket and quoits, the latter described by President Bartlett as "a popular and good exercise". A go-as-you-please style of baseball is mentioned by Judge David Cross as being played occasionally by a dozen or more students as early as 1837. In 1856 it was described by Amos N. Currier as "much played but not organized." In the *Aegis* of 1862 the Dartmouth Baseball Club of twenty members is listed for the first time, but games were evidently confined to contests among members of the club.

A gymnastic apparatus set up by students in 1826 behind Dartmouth Hall was superseded by the "Freshman Gallows," installed near the Bema, consisting simply of two uprights, seven or eight feet apart, with notches in the sides for a bar, and two suspended ropes with rings. Such was the apparatus available for the young gymnasts until the erection in the eighteen-sixties of Bissell Gymnasium with its wealth of equipment.

The great river bounding the College and the town on the west afforded good summer swimming but it was not until the eighteen-fifties that organized rowing or modern boating, as it was then called, became an active undergraduate sport. Interest was stimulated by the construction of a four-oared clinker-built gig by two students, the brothers Church. *The Phoenix* in 1857 describes the "Dartmouth Flotilla" that then enlivened the river as consisting of six boat clubs, one with an eight-oared, three with six-oared, and two with four-oared boat, with a total membership of sixty-five. Misfortune struck Dartmouth oarsmen when an August freshet swept away the floating boathouse with seven boats moored in and around it.

Although the slowly rebuilt flotilla produced no spectacular victories it was, apparently, responsible indirectly for the choice of dark green as the College color. Having attended in 1866 a large regatta where he first saw the Harvard crimson displayed, Alfred A. Thomas, 1867, considered his own Alma Mater deficient without a color. After a discussion in September, 1866 green was adopted for a variety of reasons, perhaps not the least of which was that students and faculty alike

looked out every day over the green hills of Vermont and loved them. As for the rowing flotilla it was again destroyed in the great freshet of 1869.

Dartmouth first appeared in intercollegiate athletic competition in the spring of 1866 when it was defeated by the Nicean Baseball Club of Amherst by a score of 40 to 10 in a game of five innings. The following season, accompanied by twenty-five student rooters, Dartmouth visited Amherst for a return contest and won 30 to 24 in a game described as having commenced at ten in the morning and lasted five hours. Intercollegiate baseball gained sufficient standing by 1871 to induce the faculty to grant the team leave of absence for a trip to play four games with Tufts, Brown, Harvard and Bowdoin. The *Aegis* called "base-ball" a "manifold blessing to the college . . . an absorbing amusement and exciting exercise. . . ." The pitcher, in that early day, recalled Edwin J. Bartlett,

was restricted to a straight arm underhand pitch but he was only 45 feet from the batter and was allowed nine balls. Runners were not allowed to overrun 1st base; fouls counted for nothing unless they were caught in the air or on the first bound. Only babies wore gloves: that is, they were not worn. Catchers had neither mask nor chest protector . . . baseball was somewhat more an heroic venture than at present.

A revival of interest in rowing so interfered with baseball, however, that that sport fell into the doldrums until the winter of 1877 when, in another of a series of catastrophes, the boat house roof collapsed under the pressure of heavy snows and destroyed most of the equipment. The least taxing sport of this period appears to have been croquet, affected by seniors during their last term. It was regarded, according to Professor Bartlett, "as effeminate, but from the language occasionally overheard it may have been a virile game after all."

The College's first gymnasium, named for George H. Bissell, 1845, was completed in 1867. Described in the College catalogue as a "beautiful and commodious structure," it housed six bowling alleys on the first floor and the main gymnasium on the second. Bissell insisted that the bowling alleys be installed, according to Richardson, because of disciplinary action taken against him for indulging in this forbidden sport when he was a student. The expectation that required exercise would have healthful effects at first seemed fully justified to Dr. Dixi Crosby, who noted a decline among students of dyspepsia and other symptoms of a sedentary life. As the novelty subsided, however, their attitude toward enforced calisthenics became less than enthusiastic; by 1873 the weekly newspaper, *The Anvil,* confessed that Bissell Hall was more ornamental than practical.

A challenge in 1875 from the students of Tufts College for a game of Rugby football was declined because there was no Dartmouth team and the undergraduates knew little about the game. In October of the same year the first field meet took place on the Green, a quarter-mile track and a straight-away of 120 yards having been laid out on the grass. Among the events were the wheelbarrow race, the hop, skip and jump, the sack, and three-legged races. The faculty suspended classes for the two-day program, which also featured boat races on the river and which became an annual event of great interest for many years thereafter.

After decades of preliminaries, Dartmouth fielded its first inter-collegiate football eleven in 1881. In uniforms furnished by Princeton the squad practiced throughout the fall of 1880 without being able to schedule a game. Because of a faculty vote against out-of-town contests during the school week a match was finally arranged with Amherst the following November 16 (Wednesday) on the Green in Hanover. The experienced visitors were more polished in their play but Dartmouth was physically the stronger. Captain Clarence Howland, 1884, organ-

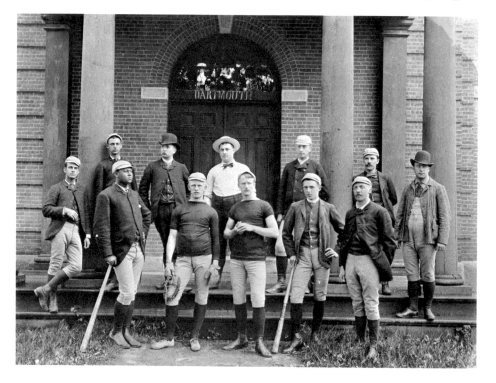

izer of this first team, recalled that there was no scientific system of signals, and Dartmouth's offense consisted mostly of sending the half-backs around the ends. The only touchdown was made by Charles W. Oakes, 1883, who ran almost the length of the field to score. Oakes, later a physician and grandfather of a future Dartmouth hockey coach, glowingly wrote home as follows:

This has been quite an exciting week for Dartmouth. We played a game of foot-ball Wednesday with Amherst, it was the first game we ever played. We beat them one touchdown to nothing. Surprising everyone.

I 'spect I was the hero of the occasion. I made the touchdown and several good runs, and at the end of the game the boys rode me around the campus on their shoulders.

Everyone was nearly crazy during the game. The Professors ran around, clapped their hands, shouted, jumped up and down and fairly went mad. One Professor was overheard to say . . . when I was running the ball, "Go it, Charley! Run right through them, that's good, dodge that man, Charley, do run it in! Hurrah! Hurrah!"

One of the Amherst fellows complimented me on my playing and said I

"CARDIGAN" Snow-Shoe Club.

could play as well as Camp of Yale. Camp is the best player in the country.
. . .

The scoreless return game with Amherst, played after a severe snow storm Thanksgiving Day, was called off after thirty minutes and the two squads adjourned to the old Massasoit House in Springfield for dinner.

Scoring two victories for every defeat for the first eighty-three seasons, Dartmouth enjoyed one stretch of over four decades (1901 to 1943) without a losing football season. The customary formation of the early days was the "flying wedge," designed to gain ground by power alone. The players in V-formation marched in lockstep to the ball which the crouching quarterback tossed into their midst and the play was on.

The origin of the football relationship with Harvard, whom President-emeritus Hopkins considers to have been Dartmouth's best friend in intercollegiate competition, had much to do with the College's subsequent status in that sport. As an early graduate manager of athletics Dr. Hopkins was assigned the major task of re-organizing, regulating, and administering the College's entire intercollegiate sports program.

Repairing a triangular league with Amherst and Williams, upset because of Dartmouth's use of medical students on varsity teams, was his first chore. The second was improvement of the football schedule, which he accomplished by engaging Princeton, Holy Cross and Harvard in 1903. Most important to the subsequent financing of football and all other sports, he arranged with Harvard the same year for a percentage distribution of receipts, replacing the previous small flat guarantee. This was happily consummated just as Harvard was preparing to dedicate its new stadium, a magnificent facility, unique in America at that time. Desiring to christen it with a victory, Harvard substituted Dartmouth for Yale as its dedicatory opponent. The importance of this historic game, which Dartmouth won 11 to 0, was not simply a victory over mighty Harvard, but also the opening it made for Dartmouth competition with the large universities. Prior to this game an undergraduate tax, hopefully but not always successfully levied, had financed Dartmouth teams. The initial fifteen per cent of receipts that Dr. Hopkins had arranged with Harvard yielded the College as many thousands of dollars as it had received hundreds previously. Steadily rising revenue accompanied similar agreements with other intercollegiate rivals until Dartmouth's share of the receipts reached the current forty to fifty per cent.

> It was Hanover's nearest thing to narcotics. If homework got the best of you, two weeks behind with eight contemporary novels to read, a term paper on the construction cycle still to be written, and finals not a week away, you went to the Nugget. – *The Undergraduate Chair,* 1944.

The College's gridiron fortunes rose dramatically under the tutelage of graduate coaches such as Walter McCornack, 1897, Frank Cavanaugh, 1899 (famed later as the Iron Major at Holy Cross, Boston College, and Fordham), and Clarence Spears, 1917, whose conquest of the University of Washington in 1920 at the dedication of its new stadium in Seattle, was notable also as the first game played by Dartmouth on the west coast.

In 1925 the gods threw green thunderbolts across the land when Coach Jess Hawley, 1909, and a squad of outstanding players came together by happy chance. For two seasons their nearest approach to defeat was a tie with Yale in 1924. The following year they scored 340 points in eight games (second only to Washington with 366), while allowing the opposition but 29. Harvard was defeated 32 to 9 before 54,000; Cornell was annihilated 62 to 13, its worst defeat ever. This game was credited with ending the earlier strategy of a team choosing to kick off after being scored upon. Dartmouth led only 14 to 13 at the first quarter, then caught fire as Cornell elected repeatedly to kick off. Arriving at Chicago, Dartmouth was rated a three-to-one underdog against Alonzo Stagg's Big Ten power. With brilliant passing and rugged defense the Indians carried the day 33 to 7 and Dartmouth was awarded the mythical national championship.

But there was one opponent through all the years into the mid-1930's that the College had been unable to conquer: Yale. Beginning with the opening game in the series in 1884, when Yale made its only appearance in Hanover "at great expense" and inflicted upon the home team a calamitous defeat of 113 to 0, Dartmouth had consistently failed to muzzle the New Haven bulldog. Talk of a Yale Jinx abounded on the street and in the newspapers, particularly after the resumption of the Dartmouth-Yale series early in the nineteen-twenties, with such narrow Yale victories as 16-12, 6-0, 14-13, and 7-2. But on the occasion of the memorable 33 to 33 tie in 1931 The Jinx seemed assailable. Yale threw away certain victory when a Dartmouth team, trailing by 23 points late in the third period, achieved the breathtaking deadlock.

> . . . if we faculty have the elemental sense to honor this new earnestness by expecting a great deal from it; if we can be steel to this flint, we can make the era of the returned GI a memorable one in the intellectual history of the College. – Arthur M. Wilson, 1946.

Three years later there appeared in Hanover for the first time a man with a thin face, aquiline nose and tight lips, Coach Earl H. (Red) Blaik, whom President Hopkins brought from West Point where he had been assistant coach. He is vividly remembered as the serious taskmaster who helped return Dartmouth football to respectability by insisting that manners and conduct on and off the field were as essential as athletic skills. He had not only to create a strong team but to work psychologically to break the obsessive Jinx. In his first season Dartmouth again lost to Yale 7 to 2. On the November morning in 1935 when the team left once more for New Haven, Mrs. Blaik gave each player a flower for his buttonhole. Quartered outside of New Haven the night before the game, the players did not go to the Bowl until time to dress, nor leave the dressing room until two minutes before the whistle.

Dartmouth scored first and when Yale ran a punt back for a touchdown in the third period the conversion attempt hit the crossbar and

fell short. By running back a pass interception in the fourth quarter Dartmouth scored again. With their team leading 14 to 6 and only three minutes remaining Dartmouth supporters came charging out of the stands and tore down the goal posts. The reaction was uproarious at Dartmouth Clubs in San Francisco, Atlanta, St. Louis, and Boston, where direct telegraph wires from New Haven and large grid-graphs had been installed to chart each play. In Hanover 500 students who had not been able to make the pilgrimage to New Haven surged onto the Green to build a bonfire; several gained entry to the chapel to ring the bells. Silenced since the fire the previous spring, the Dartmouth Hall bell pealed for four hours. On the motion picture screen in the Nugget Theater, whose doors the manager wisely decided to open wide to all celebrants, Heroine Alice Faye fortuitously triggered pandemonium by uttering the line: "And what about my football player from Dartmouth?" A wooden tombstone, branded "Yale Jinx. Born 1884. Died 1935." was planted on the Common.

The most famous game in Dartmouth's history and certainly one of the most extraordinary in the annals of football was that with Cornell at Hanover in 1940. It was won by Dartmouth after it had ended in defeat. In the emotion-charged final moments of the game, with the visiting team struggling to beat the clock and a 3 to 0 Dartmouth lead, Referee William Friesell became confused and awarded Cornell an extra or "fifth" down. Undefeated Cornell scored on this, the last play of the game, and was declared the winner, 7 to 3. The error, apparent to the multitude of anguished partisans, was soon confirmed by the official movies of the game and was readily admitted by Friesell, who in a telegram to the Dartmouth captain apologized and assumed full responsibility. A second telegram from the Cornell athletic director stated that "in view of the conclusions reached by the officials that the Cornell touchdown was scored on a fifth down, Cornell relinquishes claim to the victory and extends congratulations to Dartmouth."

In his seven seasons in Hanover Blaik captured two Ivy League titles. He then returned to West Point to restore its gridiron fortunes during the succeeding eighteen years. The Second World War disrupted the fourteen-year span of Coach DeOrmand (Tuss) McLaughry's tenure as Blaik's successor. For two seasons, 1943 and 1944, Dartmouth's V-12 Navy enrollment played makeshift schedules. Although post-war squads found themselves arrayed in every contest against major teams, they won twelve and lost only four in 1948 and '49.

In 1955 Denver University Coach Bob Blackman, unknown to eastern football, took command of the Dartmouth squad, soon stamping its action-packed practice sessions with his trademarks of imagination, resourcefulness, and infinite attention to detail. Delighted with his squads of bright, eager students, Blackman piled variation on variation so that they could play an entire game without twice using the same formation. They took pride in learning to operate from 42 defenses, with ingenious stunts and refinements added. Always first or second in Ivy League defense and in the top ten nationally, Dartmouth played several seasons without allowing some opponents (Brown, Columbia and Pennsylvania) to score a single point. By 1957 Blackman had achieved a record of seven victories, one defeat and one tie. He lost the Ivy title that year in a snowy finale at Princeton, 34 to 14, but gained revenge the following season as Dartmouth put on a fourth-period rally against Princeton for a 21 to 12 triumph and the League championship.

The 1962 season produced an undefeated, untied Dartmouth team to match that of the 1925 champions. With the Harvard game shown on eastern television, Dartmouth's swarming defenses held the Crimson to only five first downs, 99 yards by rushing, and a score of 6 to the Green's 24. With 10,000 huddled against a northeaster swirling around the Bowl, Yale could not even penetrate the Green's 44-yard line. The faded specter of The Jinx groaned impotently as a sportswriter commented that never in thirty years of observing football in the Bowl had he seen a Yale eleven so frustrated.

At this moment Dartmouth led the nation in fewest points allowed (nine) and ranked among the top three teams in both rushing and passing defense. But gradual attrition through injury had been working on the tackle posts with the result that the defensive bubble burst in the final two games with Cornell and Princeton. These two teams combined to score 48 points through hard running and pass interceptions. The Green offense, however, assumed the burden by piling up 66 points in the two closing games, and the undefeated record and Ivy title were assured.

> We teachers all seem to fail: what we teach is forgotten, even how we teach is forgotten, and if what we do lasts at all, it lasts by the spirit. And the spirit springs more from what we are and how we live than from what we know or have done. – Benfield Pressey, 1948.

In 1963 Dartmouth lost to both Harvard and Yale, but in a spectacular two-touchdown surge late in the game against Princeton, leading contender for the Ivy throne, the Indians forged ahead to a 22 to 21 victory and to what had seemed an improbable division with Princeton of the Crown. Demonstrated once again was that response to adversity which has often characterized Dartmouth teams and which gives athletic competition its place in the educational process.

*   *   *   *   *

In 1954 the presidents of eight eastern colleges: Brown, Columbia, Cornell, Dartmouth, Harvard, Pennsylvania, Princeton and Yale, which had long been nicknamed "Ivy" by sportswriters, officially adopted the name for their league, while setting up such stringent regulations for football as a round-robin schedule, the banning of spring practice and post-season games, the prohibition of athletic scholarships, and the requirement that financial aid be based on economic need. These were the latest measures to correct long-standing abuses in intercollegiate sports arising from an intemperate desire to win, which in turn had led to professionalism and bitter criticism of a rival's motives and ethics.

As early as the turn of the century intercollegiate athletics had begun to outpace educational evaluation of its place and purpose. Spectators and partisans, perhaps even more than participants, lacked the balanced sense of value and fitness that today tempers the appraisal of what is good and what is excessive. It was often hard to discern any semblance of the ennobling benefits the competition was supposed to yield. Creation of a philosophy as to the place of athletics in the College at this time was, as has been said, a paramount concern of President Tucker.

In 1893, when Dartmouth alumni presented the College with its athletic field of seven acres laid out with facilities of all kinds, arrangements were made to place the control of the athletic organization (with the exception of eligibility of students and excuses for absences from Hanover) in the hands of a committee of the alumni, subject to the ultimate approval of the Board of Trustees. The committee became, in 1900, the Athletic Council, elected by the alumni and composed of three of their number, three members of the faculty, and three undergraduates. Alumni donors produced in succession an elaborate new gymnasium in 1909, the Spaulding swimming pool, tennis courts, grandstands, a varsity house, the Davis hockey rink, a golf course, and the Outing Club House. The most recent additions have been the spectacular Nathaniel Leverone Fieldhouse, enclosing more than two acres unbroken by vertical supports, and within the gymnasium itself a large new swimming pool and a remodeled basketball court with spectator capacities of 1500 and 2100, respectively.

No individual had more to do with the early regulation of Dartmouth athletics and perhaps the entire intercollegiate sports program than Edward K. Hall, 1892, who as an undergraduate played end for Dartmouth football teams and in later years became vice-president of the American Telephone and Telegraph Company. It was he, working with Dr. Hopkins, who finally persuaded the undergraduates to bar graduate students from College teams, to limit athletic participation to four years, to require for eligibility one year of residence after transfer, to restrict contests to the playing fields of the institutions themselves, and to ban freshmen from varsity teams.

Hall was the leader of "rebels" who challenged the domination of the Football Rules Committee by Harvard, Yale and Princeton, and secured a change in the regulations to permit the forward pass. The cloak-and-dagger background of the crucial Committee meeting, which took place in New York in the winter of 1905, has never been told. Much misinformation has indeed gained credence, such as the presumption that pressure from Theodore Roosevelt, who considered football a brutal game, resulted in changing the rules. There is no question that it was then an outlaw sport, unpopular in many quarters and even barred at such universities as Columbia and Stanford.

The Rules Committee had been dominated by Walter Camp. Those

colleges who would not agree to the rules of Camp's committee would play football, but not with Yale, Harvard, or Princeton. Thus, according to Dr. Hopkins, Hall mobilized the other eastern colleges and formed a rump committee, which met the same night in 1905 as Camp's, and forthrightly presented its views. When the old committee just as forthrightly turned them down the insurgents voted to abide by their own rules. Toward midnight it was apparent that some members of the old committee, notably Percy Haughton, were wavering, and when after feverish consultation the Harvard coach decided to join the new group, Camp's committee capitulated.

This is the way I have always thought a college should look. – Dwight D. Eisenhower, 1953.

Upon the formation of a new committee (with the old and new groups equally represented) Camp, at Hall's urging, was elected president, while the latter became secretary. Eventually Hall became president, and as football regained its former favor with the American public, he built a house in Hanover where, until his death in 1932, meetings of the Rules Committee were held and its records maintained.

The Dartmouth College Athletic Council has become the overseer of a wide-ranging sports program to match its considerable portfolio of property and facilities. It is axiomatic that football, with its immense popularity and earning power, dominates other equally or, in some respects, more important sports. One of the principal policies of the "Presidents' Agreement" in 1954 was to restrain this trend; yet one cannot deny that without football's popularity and financial strength the other sports would never have gained their present vitality and stature.

The public image of Dartmouth commonly reflects not football but skiing as the College's most characteristic sport. The millions of enthusiasts and far greater number of dollars currently invested in this burgeoning national pastime make doubly significant the fact that American winter sports grew up at Dartmouth. It is said that the only skis in Hanover in 1911, eight and a half feet long and five and a half inches wide, as fashioned by a local carpenter, belonged to Fred Harris, 1911, the founder that year of the Dartmouth Outing Club. Harris was also the organizer of the first official Dartmouth Winter Carnival, and later of the U. S. Eastern Amateur Ski Association. Professor Edwin Frost wrote that skis were to be seen in Hanover in the late eighteen-eighties, and mention of a Snowshoe and Chowder Club suggests at least some nineteenth century winter sports tradition, however half-hearted. But to Hanover belongs their first earnest advocacy and to Dartmouth the first ski team of any American college. The home-grown competition at the first Winter Carnival in 1911 shortly acquired inter-collegiate status with McGill University and later the University of New Hampshire, Harvard, Williams, Vermont, and Middlebury sending teams. Construction of the country's first motorized tow in Woodstock, Vermont, in 1934 greatly accelerated the phenomenal growth of skiing. Dartmouth's part in the sport, both from the standpoint of the su-premacy of its teams and the contributions of its coaches to technique, is already historic.

Among the first neat impressions of the telemark on American snow were those made by Colonel Anton Diettrich, formerly fencing master at the court of the Hapsburgs, from whom Dartmouth students learned proper defense against an opponent's foil and how to remain on their skis on icy New Hampshire hills. After Diettrich came Gerry Raab and then, in 1930, Otto Schniebs, who brought the Arlberg technique to America and for six years raised future Olympic skiers up from the snowplow, through the "tail-wag," the Arlberg crouch (in three stages), the single-stem, double-stem, lifted-stem christie, the pure christie, the open christie. To the production of proficient teams Schniebs added that of skis and boots of his own design, and a black and sticky wax which he concocted in his garage. Walter Prager from Davos sustained the tradition of European coaches, but the accomplishments of Ameri-cans — of a Dartmouth librarian, Nathaniel Goodrich, and of a Dart-mouth physicist, Charles Proctor, 1900, — must be acknowledged in any account of the origins of American skiing. For seven years Good-rich, whose other enthusiasm was mountain-climbing, devoted himself to collecting material for *The American Ski Annual* and editing it. In 1923 Professor Proctor laid out the first slalom course in the United States on Golf Course Hill. American slalom racing and Charles Proc-tor are inseparable; he became in 1932 chairman of the Olympic or-ganizing committee and served for years as an official at Lake Placid.

These are, of course, but the bare bones of the story; the students who became champions at Dartmouth have themselves spread the gos-pel of skiing westward to the Rockies. The primitive facilities of their undergraduate years have meanwhile become a one-hundred-acre de-velopment with modern ski lifts, several downhill trails, a clubhouse and overnight lodge of pine logs with a capacity of 125. Within the compass

[281]

of three decades the weathered and much remodeled ski jump above the Vale of Tempe's 40-meter hill has become one of the oldest monuments of a young sport.

The chronicle of skiing is but one chapter in the annals of the Outing Club, familiar to many only as the host of February's Carnival with its visiting queen and her court, its athletic contests, its house-parties and dances, its sparkling snow sculptures. In 1913 the Outing Club built its first cabin on wild Moose Mountain and now has 10 altogether, along with rest shelters, on some 100 miles of northern forest trails. It supervises the Bait and Bullet and the Ledyard Canoe Clubs, whose members run the white water of the surrounding rivers. Climbing K-2 in the Himalayas, Tutoko in New Zealand, and Mount Everest; manning one of the coldest and windiest weather stations in the western hemisphere at the crest of Mount Washington, and the Tenth Mountain Division in World War II; rescuing in remote New England forests the frostbitten victims of plane crashes; journeying to the Arctic and Antarctic to unfold the secrets of gacier ice and permafrost — these and less spectacular accomplishments of alumni derive from the interest engendered by the Outing Club during their undergraduate days.

If the director of the Dartmouth College Athletic Council were to report some year that its basketball, hockey, track, baseball, lacrosse, golf, soccer, swimming, tennis, squash, and wrestling teams had won every contest, the ultimate and impossible would have been achieved. Environment and heredity subject college athletics to a process of natural selection; a small college emphasizing one sport is the frequent master of a large university attempting to cover the whole spectrum. Moreover, the hierarchial position of a particular undergraduate sport is an unstable one. Each tends to shift with the times; to wax, to wane, to wax again. It is inevitable that a chronicle such as this will incline to lay greatest emphasis upon those sports which are in the ascendancy at

the moment of writing, and correspondingly devote less attention to others with perhaps even longer or more honorable pasts.

Like those of all other sports, Dartmouth basketball teams have known both triumph and failure in equal and unequal proportions. Their best years were 1927, when they captured the Eastern League championship, and 1936-44, under the tutelage of Coach Osborne Cowles, when they dominated the League for eight consecutive years. Twice they entered the national collegiate tournament only to lose to Stanford in 1942 and to Utah two years later. Decline then set in, and recovery came with three more Ivy League victories in the 'fifties under Alvin Julian.

Erratic temperatures and sudden snowfalls on local ponds characterized the unhappy twenty-five-year upbringing of Dartmouth intercollegiate hockey. Greatly celebrated in 1930 was the dedication of the covered Davis Rink, although it too depended until 1953 upon outdoor temperatures for its presumably superior natural ice. It proved, however, to be frozen long enough and hard enough for Coach Eddie Jeremiah to train Dartmouth teams to win from others with better facilities forty-six consecutive games, seven out of nine Ivy League titles, one mythical national championship and half the international crown.

One of the most dramatic events in the annals of Dartmouth track, since the first meet on the Green in 1875, had nothing to do with the intermittent headlines made by undergraduates, but with the appearance in 1939 of Miler Glenn Cunningham on Hanover's springy board track. Conceived by Coach Harry Hillman and designed by the Thayer School, it was constructed of clear Canadian spruce with the joints pegged down around the inside circumference of Alumni Gymnasium. When Cunningham was invited to Hanover the American indoor record for the mile was 4:06. Coach Hillman expected him to break it but released little advance publicity because he feared something might go wrong. The track was resurveyed to make certain the distances were correct. All runners in the race were registered with the A.A.U. and handicaps were assigned, a normal procedure at the time.

Resting for a week before the race, Cunningham jogged around Hanover for three days but would not set foot on the track until starting time. Despite the lack of publicity and the fact that they could see only about one-sixth of the race at any one point, spectators crowded the gym, ignoring the March air that poured through the opened windows. Cunningham ran the opening 440 in 58 seconds and then, a bit wary of

such speed on a strange track, slowed down in the second quarter, turning the half-mile in 2:02.5. The third quarter also was a bit slow, 61.7 seconds, but then he rallied for a closing 60.2 and an unprecedented clocking of 4:04.4. He was very strong at the end and there was speculation that with more faith in the track he might have achieved the elusive four-minute mile. The next morning the story was on page one of every paper in the country and the Dartmouth board track became almost as famous as Cunningham. The following year John Woodruff arrived to set a half-mile record of 1:47.7, in its way a better performance than Cunningham's. The track survived until 1947 when it was scrapped because of its weakening supports.

Pre-eminence, obscurity, and partial redemption in the hierarchy of college sports has been the lot of baseball. Nearly a century ago Dartmouth was playing thirty games a season. On Memorial Day in 1906 12,000 spectators paid to watch the game with Holy Cross on the latter's new diamond in Worcester. The insistence of Dartmouth upon allowing medical students to play and the difficulty of arranging paying games in Hanover attended the formation and dissolution of triangular and larger leagues. At length in 1925 a league was established with Columbia, Cornell, and Pennsylvania, to be expanded five years later by the current schedule with other Ivy schools and Army and Navy. The revival of baseball was sparked notably by Robert Rolfe, 1931, who later played third base with the Yankees in six World Series, and his Dartmouth coach, Jeff Tesreau, formerly of the New York Giants. Dartmouth won the first title in 1930, and again in 1935. The following year it shared with Navy a tie for the championship and won again in 1938. An ensuing doldrum ended in 1963 with a tie for the eastern crown.

> Without intending to be facetious I might say that asking a retiring teacher to compare the undergraduate of 1961 with his counterpart of a generation ago is actually something like asking an elderly cow for her impression of her latest calf as compared with those she best remembers before the herd was improved by magic ministrations of artificial insemination and improved scientific feeding. – Artemas Packard, 1961.

The construction in 1963 of a second and larger pool in the east wing of Alumni Gymnasium opened the way for greater achievements in Dartmouth swimming. Coached by Karl Michael, 1928, this sport produced twenty-seven All-America swimmers and a series of teams without a losing season prior to 1962-63.

Soccer was introduced at the College in 1914. Dartmouth soccer teams were notably successful during the long regime of Coach Tommy Dent, and yet more triumph attended Dent's coaching of lacrosse beginning in 1926. Undergraduate tennis dates from a single grass court in 1884, and golf from the opening of an eighteen-hole course in 1921, later supplemented by nine additional demanding holes designed by the veteran coach Tommy Keane. The College's golf teams have had their share of success despite the handicap of tardy Hanover springs, an adversity that has also plagued the rowing crews.

It was not until 1934 that Dartmouth rowing rallied from the nineteenth century series of natural calamities, then to be struck again in 1952 when the boathouse roof collapsed under heavy snow and de-

stroyed all the equipment. Since the nineteen-thirties crew has graduated from Lake Mascoma, with an old icehouse as its base, to that
part of the Connecticut River at Hanover known as Wilder Lake, im-
pounded behind the new Wilder power dam. The roof of the new boathouse is unlikely to yield to anything short of nuclear attack. Some 200
undergraduates turn out annually to engage in one of Dartmouth's
oldest and, at the same time, youngest and largest informal sports,
financed and operated partly by the students.

In recent years one of the most engaging developments on Hanover
playing fields was the sudden appearance in 1953 of Rugby, a cross between soccer and football more nearly resembling the free-for-all scrim-
mages on the Green three-quarters of a century ago. Indeed, the free-
swinging behavior of the players and proponents of this informal sport
often proved embarrassing to the Athletic Council. Wearing cast-off
football cleats and donated gear on a field they had hacked out of
Hanover spruces, the new players of an old game coached themselves
and passed the hat for their expenses by walking up and down the side-
lines between the halves of out-of-town games.

Triumphantly, they won, in the fall of 1958, the mythical eastern
title with a total score of 89 to 0, and at the close of the football season
were joined by four of Dartmouth's champion Ivy League eleven. Then

came a timely invitation to the Rugby Club to go to England at the behest of Eddie Eagan, Chairman of the People-to-People Sports Committee. Through the last-minute efforts of Orton Hicks, 1921, Vice-President of the College, the trip was made possible by checks from loyal alumni and Rugby enthusiasts, aided by Pan American Airways, the editors of *Sports Illustrated* and Corey Ford, progenitor and patron of Dartmouth Rugby. The chairman of Young and Rubicam, Sigurd F. Larmon, 1914, agreed to meet the remaining deficit for the first American team to invade England in the 135-year history of the game.

The day after their arrival they were in the thick of their first game or "fixture" against the experienced Halsmere team or "side." The score: Dartmouth 12, Halsmere 0. The Dartmouth players, reported *The Times* (London) "made their entrance with all the bounce and, at the same time, the endearing humility of Pooh's great friend Tiger." *The Daily Telegraph* described their "impressive preliminaries" as comprising "a series of exercises performed in a circle and ranging from press-ups to a painful contortion which the military would be pleased to call 'alternate toe-touching.' These completed, a short conference was held, the group eventually breaking up with a fierce war-cry." Following the match British enthusiasts rallied to their aid, almost as if the Americans had lost. The sportsmanship of a former Cambridge Blue who volunteered to be the Dartmouth coach, would never be forgotten. "They weren't so much interested in winning over there," the Dartmouth captain said later "as they were in helping us to be a better Rugby team."

> From here on, Gentlemen, to the end of the road, the choice of the good, the beautiful, and the true will be made for you only if made by you.
> – John Sloan Dickey, 1949.

Indeed a much better team resulted, so much better, in fact, that Dartmouth defeated the highly esteemed London-Scottish Richmond side 16 to 13. The *Daily Telegraph* exclaimed: "The British are not unused to rude reverses, but this victory of an American Rugby XV must be considered one of the nastiest upsets since Bunker Hill." What made this fixture and indeed all the others most memorable was the camaraderie displayed by the British side who formed a double line and applauded the mud-caked Dartmouth players on their way to the dressing room. The more games the Americans won (the final tally was seven victories and two defeats), the more enthusiastic their op-

ponents, the press, shopkeepers, children, and British statesmen became. Shaking hands with the Dartmouth players Field Marshal Montgomery exclaimed: "Jolly good. Makes us sit up, you know, keeps us from getting too complacent. Jolly good indeed." The Earl of Dartmouth honored the team with his felicitations as did Ambassador John Hay Whitney who observed that the Indians seemed to be painting the town green. A treasured comment for a team from a country where rivalry is sharper-edged was that of an elderly member of the Saville Club who, upon being informed that Rugby was also played in America at Yale and Harvard, paused for a moment and asked: "Harvard? Harvard? Oh yes, isn't that somewhere near Dartmouth?"

Only too soon the clock struck twelve and the Dartmouth Ruggers were back on their homemade playing field in their castoff cleats and borrowed gear, preparing alike for future triumphs and inevitable but, in view of their experience in England, less chafing defeats.

There is this, written by Colonel Franklin A. Haskell, 1854, about the Union troops in his brilliant narrative of the Battle of Gettysburg, that can also be said about all the wearers of the green and their forbears through the years: "They had lost some battles — they had gained some. They knew what defeat was, and what was victory. But here is the greatest praise that I can bestow upon them, or upon any army; with the elation of victory, or the depression of defeat, amidst the hardest toils of the campaign . . . at all times and under all circumstances, they were a reliable army still."

The Modern College

RALPH NADING HILL

THAT Dr. William Jewett Tucker was the spiritual refounder of Dartmouth and that out of his sense of high moral purpose arose the momentum of the next generations is a conviction shared alike by the thinning ranks of those who remember him and by students of the College's history. Of all of Dartmouth's preacher-presidents the record of the first was rivaled only by that of the last. When in 1892 he was urged to accept the presidency, Dr. Tucker was fifty-three years old and had already served the College as a Trustee for a decade and a half. After his graduation from Dartmouth and from Andover Theological Seminary he had spent thirteen years in the ministry in New Hampshire and New York and had then returned to the Seminary as Professor of Sacred Rhetoric, with the intention of spending the rest of his life as a teacher. Entangled at Andover with other alleged heretics in a controversy that had in part arisen from the publication of Darwin's *The Descent of Man,* he had searched for, and eventually found, paths of intellectual freedom for his independent inquiries and did not wish to stray from them. However, when the search for a new president at Dartmouth, after the lapse of a year, still pointed to Dr. Tucker, he yielded to the entreaties of the Trustees in February, 1893.

In *My Generation* he was later to confess that his principal motive in accepting the presidency was the attraction of the institutional life of a college and the need at Dartmouth for regeneration of its spiritual values. Unlike that of the neighboring universities, Harvard and Yale, Dartmouth's mission in Dr. Tucker's view was to "fill to the full the college ideal." It was because of Dartmouth's distinctiveness of object and remoteness of place that its voice in the wilderness had been heard so far off — in the streets of London, in the churches throughout Great Britain, and at the Court of the King. The Indian School, the migration to the wilderness, the great political and legal dramas had stamped upon the history of the College the hallmarks of adventure. The future lay in the infusion of the unifying spirit of these traditions into the life of the College. This end Dr. Tucker sought above all, and this end above all he achieved.

. . . a man does not get very far on his way in the midst of the stern and often disturbing facts of life without feeling the need of drawing upon such resources of the *spirit* as are in him. It is the presence or absence of this deeper sense of things which determines not only a man's personal happiness, but in a large degree, his power over others.

Thus Dr. Tucker counseled the freshman class in the Convocation of 1903 and thus he revealed the secret of the College's awakened sense of purpose during his administration. Manifestly this arose because Dr. Tucker himself was the embodiment of the values he sought for the College. Leon Burr Richardson wrote that the effect of the President's chapel talks could scarcely be conveyed to those not exposed to their influence.

. . . the audience . . . was not inherently sympathetic to religious or moral appeals, [but] as the address began, each member of the student body set himself to listen; as it continued, a silence almost painful in its intensity reigned, broken only by the calm, quiet voice of the speaker. . . . Dr. Tucker . . . had the art of powerfully influencing men in the mass, of making an appeal . . . so intimate in its character that each individual felt that the message was for himself alone . . . each . . . felt himself bound to the president by a tie which he could not explain, but of the reality of which he had no doubt . . . he cherished for him a high sense of personal indebtedness, a high sense of veneration . . . a feeling of intimate personal affection, even of love. . . .

Soon evident were the outward accomplishments of a man full of wisdom and experience, a man of moral force and vitality, of dignity and humility in whose company, wrote Ernest Martin Hopkins, "men outgrew the limitations of their natural dimensions." The year before his accession to the presidency the freshman class numbered 78. Twelve months later it was 120, the largest that had ever been admitted. By the turn of the century the enrollment in the undergraduate college had reached 627; eight years later it had again nearly doubled, with a freshman class of 350. When Dr. Tucker took office there was no Commons,

no central heating, running water, or electricity in any academic building. (Baths for students were first available only in the gymnasium and in Sanborn, which levied upon unfortunate residents of other dormitories a fee of twenty-five cents for each bath.) The dormitories bore the scars of half-a-century and many other buildings were down-at-the-heel. During sixteen industrious years Dartmouth's physical plant was doubled, a performance that might not have been expected of a Congregational minister.

To Hanoverians whose heritage was wells and cisterns, one of the President's most revolutionary contributions was a $99,000 water system with reservoir and watershed, paid for jointly by the College and the precinct. Equally remarkable to a congealed student body dependent in dormitory and classroom upon the exasperating wood stove, was the new central heating plant (1898) with its mile-and-a-half of underground steam pipes and its three electric dynamos, which introduced to the College buildings, however dim and fitful its beam, the incandescent lamp. Few were the daylight hours, except on Sundays, during the Tucker years when saws and hammers were not to be heard. Thirteen dormitories, either new or remodeled from older buildings, appeared between 1894 and 1908 (Sanborn, 1894, Crosby, 1896, Richardson, 1897, Hubbard House, 1899, Fayerweather, 1900, College Hall with its Commons, 1901, Elm House, 1901, Wheeler, 1905, Hubbard, 1906, Fayerweather North and South, 1907, Massachusetts, 1907, New Hampshire, 1908).

Those who consider alumni resistance to change a recent phenomenon must be apprised of the resentment in Dr. Tucker's day of old-timers who thought that easy living in his new dormitories would ruin the students. Among them was Dr. John Ordronaux, who visited Hanover frequently to lecture in medical jurisprudence. "I think," wrote Dr. Tucker in his book, *My Generation,*

that each new dormitory with its sanitary equipment was an offense to him, and evoked the most strenuous denunciation that his unequaled command of Latin derivatives could supply. I never failed to avail myself of the intellectual treat which followed when once he caught sight of the modern Sybarites who dwelt in the modern dormitories. Very generously, but not quite consistently, Dr. Ordronaux left a "good Samaritan fund" to the value of $30,000 for the benefit of professors longest in service, who had experienced the early privations of college life. . . .

Among other structures for which Dr. Tucker was responsible were

[294]

Butterfield (1895), erected for the Biology, Physiology, and Geology departments from funds given late in the administration of Dr. Bartlett, and Webster Hall which was completed in 1907. The Hanover Country Club and Occom Pond date from 1901, the year of the second reconstruction of the Wheelock Hotel and the paving of Main Street. At this time Dr. Tucker began to acquire real estate in the vicinity of the Green, so that at the end of his administration the College owned all the property around the Green except the church and the bank. The President did not think that buildings should be dropped around at random and laid the foundations of the quadrangle plan that has since developed in the grouping of buildings.

> Rules and forms of conduct involving moral consequences do change, and often swiftly, but the bed-rock of underlying moral values builds up and wears down very slowly, almost imperceptibly over the span of one human life. – John Sloan Dickey, 1951.

Midway in his program devoted to the externals of the College the President received a letter from his Dartmouth roommate, Edward Tuck, who had read that the Trustees were urging Dr. Tucker to take a vacation. Assuring him of his lively interest in the College the Paris financier enclosed a check for his holiday and urged the President and Mrs. Tucker to visit him in France. The result of the journey was a gift of securities soon worth $500,000, the income from which was to be used for administrative and faculty salaries and for maintenance of the library. Another Edward Tuck gift of $125,000 resulted in 1901 in the establishment of the first graduate school of administration and finance in the country in a building (now McNutt) on the west side of the campus, named for Amos Tuck of the Class of 1835, father of the financier.

The gift of Daniel B. Fayerweather of New York eventually amounted to $223,000, and that of Tappan Wentworth, left two decades previously to remain untouched until it reached $500,000 through appreciation, was available in 1902. Charles Wilder, of the Vermont village subsequently of the same name, left $184,000 for the building of the physics laboratory. The College's growing financial strength reflected in part the exertions of Dr. Bartlett, in part those of Dr. Tucker and a lion's share to these three substantial benefactions. Without them little, of course, would have been possible. With them (and with annual appropriations from the state legislature for the first time in history)

Dr. Tucker was able to invest some $900,000 in new buildings, which had so increased facilities that an enlarged enrollment was bringing in $120,000 annually, six times the income from tuition fees before the President took office. Expenses, of course, were greater and in the earlier years there were operating deficits, but these were met with funds available for that purpose and were eliminated entirely as the new College gained momentum.

Like his predecessors and successors, Dr. Tucker was much concerned with the perplexing tendency of the College to evolve into a university and in the process to forfeit essential values of the College ideal. Dr. Bartlett had been an avowed foe of associated schools, and during the first year of the Tucker administration the Agricultural School had gone to Durham. Dr. Tucker resolved the problems of the Chandler School, which for years had occupied the position of an unwanted stepchild, by terminating its independent status and making its scientific course a coordinate branch of the academic College. Thayer School at the same time was receiving approval and aid. The Medical School was strengthened in 1902 through the assumption by the College of financial responsibility for its management. Four years previously its course had been extended from three years to four. Beginning in 1908 its candidates were required to attend the academic College for two years as a prerequisite for admission. Leading to the establishment of Tuck School was the growing importance in the country of business and the corresponding decline among graduates in what for generations had been a preoccupation with the professions of law, teaching, medicine, and the ministry. In Dr. Tucker's view "the colleges representing a liberal education were failing to make a responsible connection, through the lack of a proper intervening training, with the world of affairs."

The terrifying truth is that young men learn responsibility by being permitted some opportunity to be irresponsible. – John Sloan Dickey, 1957.

The Indian school was extinct as a separate entity, and in 1893 the last Indian whose tuition was paid by the old Scottish Fund was attending the College. Thenceforth the Fund (the income from which had gradually accumulated until it stood at $9,000 in 1892) ceased its payments. In 1899 President Tucker conferred in Scotland with the still-recalcitrant Trustees, whose secretary two years later reported against

[296]

the feasibility of educating Indians as missionaries at Dartmouth. At length, in 1922, Scotland's highest court granted a petition to allow the Fund, then amounting to over £10,000, to be used for general missionary purposes for the Indians of North America. Thus ended, after fifteen-and-a-half decades, the identification of Dartmouth with its first cause. Among the Indians, always few in number, who attended Dartmouth in the nineteenth century, none became more famous than Charles A. Eastman, a Sioux of the Class of 1887, who was an agent among his people and as a physician and author achieved great prominence.

Anything worth serious thought often seems to involve complexities beyond the very bounds of human bothering and everything of any consequence is found fastened at one end to the past and at the other end to the future. – John Sloan Dickey, 1953.

The most calamitous event of Dr. Tucker's administration was the burning of Dartmouth Hall in February, 1904. Nearly twelve decades had passed since the summer, fifteen years before the death of George Washington, when work had started on the foundation. Like Balch Hill and the Vale of Tempe the great white building had been so long a part of the landscape that it seemed beyond the reach of catastrophe, yet history demonstrates otherwise. In 1798, when Dartmouth Hall (or "The College" as it was then known) was almost new, the cry of fire through the frosty air brought confusion and near panic. President John Wheelock shouted an order to secure "the Great White Fowl" (some say the zebra, which was also part of the museum), while Professor Woodward begged that the air pump, and Professor Smith, that the library be saved. All were removed, and the fire, which had started in a corner room of the second story, was extinguished through the combined efforts of the students with "a vigorous application of snow." In 1802 a twister sweeping across the village from the south stripped many boards and several heavy timbers from the roof and drove them so far into the ground that they could be recovered only with great effort.

Chapel had just begun on that frigid morning of February 18, 1904, when indistinct shouts were heard outside. As the students poured out of Rollins Chapel they could see smoke and then flame coming from the small room under the bell tower of Dartmouth Hall. Almost immediately the cupola was a pyre, and as it crumpled into the roof smoke suddenly curled from under the eaves in many places. By now the fire

department had arrived but was reduced to semi-paralysis as sheets of ice began to cover men and equipment. Eating down into the top story, the flames raced through the corridors, first north, then south, and transformed the whole building into so hot an inferno that it melted the bell soon after it had plummeted through three floors to the cellar. Shocked spectators remembered a few moments when, after all except a chimney and fragment of wall had been consumed, the massive hand-hewn timbers of the frame, outlined in fire, still stood, the last reminder of the energies of the early College. Every spectator, recalled Professor Eric Kelly, shared a feeling that somehow or other the world had come to an end. Only the night before, as on countless occasions beyond memory, Dartmouth Hall had been the scene of a mass meeting. Suddenly all the jokes about "Bedbug Alley" on the third floor no longer seemed funny. When he read of the blackened ruin there was not an alumnus from whose memory a hundred nostalgic images did not spring.

It was Melvin O. Adams, 1871, in a call to Boston alumni, who crystallized the reaction with the words: "This is not an invitation; it is a summons!" Within three months enough subscriptions had been pledged to make possible plans for the laying of the cornerstone of a new Dartmouth Hall. Dr. Tucker's preoccupation with the College's traditions inspired an invitation to the ceremonies to the Sixth Earl of Dartmouth, the great-great-grandson of the benefactor for whom the College was named. Lord Dartmouth had long wished to present to the College manuscripts having to do with its founding that had been retained in the possession of his family.

For the ceremonies October 26, 1904, Hanover was covered with bunting. An electric arch over the site of the fire bore the legend: 1791-Dartmouth-1904." Hearty cheering greeted the arrival of Lord Dartmouth and his party from West Lebanon by carriage on the fair afternoon of the 26th, and from the moment he reached the piazza of the Inn his schedule was an active one. He saw a football game between the first and second teams, dined with the students in Commons (the boys sang songs during an unscheduled interval when the lights went out); he witnessed live tableaux of the College's history by the Dramatic Club, received the honorary degree of Doctor of Laws at the dedicatory services in the church; marched in an academic procession to the grave of Eleazar Wheelock, where Dr. Tucker delivered a tribute, and from there, in the rain, to the site of Dartmouth Hall to lay the cornerstone. The formal ceremonies were concluded at an elaborate banquet attended by President Eliot of Harvard and the Hon. Elihu Root, among other notables. On the evening before Lord Dartmouth's departure the students lit a large bonfire, in the light of which at the Senior Fence he spoke of his great pleasure in becoming a true member of the College.

The somewhat wider building that rose from the ashes of the first Dartmouth Hall was a faithful replica in elevation except for details of the windows, and the cupola. With the help of an old photograph, greatly enlarged, the architect, Charles A. Rich, 1875, was able to reproduce the embellishments of the interior. Designed exclusively for classroom and departmental purposes, his arrangement of the floor plan was quite different, however. A large lecture hall in the center of the first floor only, replacing the two-story chapel, was the most conspicuous change. Considered by architects to be even more impressive than the original, the new Dartmouth Hall cost $101,700 and was dedicated on February 17, 1906, without the cooperation of the weather. The cold was so extreme that as the band led the academic procession through the snow the instruments froze one by one until only the drums were left, much to the hilarity of the students. After Dr. Tucker had pronounced the dedication they cheered loudly as they marched around the building, and the doors were then thrown open.

[299]

In one respect the great fire of 1904 had proved a blessing in disguise. Trustee Henry B. Thayer later wrote that more than any single event it crystallized alumni sentiment and "marked the beginning of that never-failing support of their alma mater that has characterized the alumni body ever since." The earliest concern of the alumni had been to gain a larger voice in the affairs of the College. During the Bartlett administration they had embarked upon an unrelenting and at times bitter campaign for broader representation on the Board of Trustees, with the result that in 1893 the legislature gave permission to the College to change the composition of the Board so that five of its twelve members could be nonresidents of New Hampshire, all of them alumni and all to serve five-year terms. Thus ended, in a manner quite different from that envisioned by the combatants in the Dartmouth College Case, the domination of the College by conservative Congregationalists.

> We all know that we all outgrow a lot of things. For this form of biologic redemption, let the good Lord be thanked. – John Sloan Dickey, 1954.

Unlike his predecessor, Dr. Tucker did not look upon the change in the Board as an invasion by the alumni, but as a milestone on the journey to a better College. The annual celebration of Dartmouth Night, an observance in and outside of Hanover honoring the alumni, began in 1895. In 1901 a spirited celebration of the one-hundredth anniversary of the graduation of Dartmouth's most illustrious alumnus, Daniel Webster, was staged in Hanover with addresses and a torchlight parade of alumni and undergraduates in costume. The building of Webster Hall and the reconstruction of Dartmouth Hall were in essence alumni projects. But the most important development in alumni relations resulted from Dr. Tucker's appointment of Ernest Martin Hopkins, following his graduation in 1901, first as Secretary to the President and then of the College. In 1905 Mr. Hopkins formed the Association of Class Secretaries and established the *Dartmouth Alumni Magazine,* which he served as its first editor. Later he organized the graduate liaison body to the Board of Trustees, the Alumni Council, serving also as its first president.

In 1906 Henry H. Hilton, 1890, proposed that an annual subscription be conducted by the alumni to pay for such necessary projects as the raising of scholarship funds which the College could not afford out of ordinary revenue. The result the first year was the not very impressive amount of $4,758, but it was the precursor not only of the later imposing contributions to the Alumni Fund, but also of similar efforts of the alumni of other universities and colleges.

In the task of bringing the alumni closer to the College Dr. Tucker was so far-sighted and, as in his other many-sided responsibilities, so resourceful and often so daring that the Trustees, in the words of Richardson, "found themselves breathless in the attempt to keep within reaching distance. . . . When his schemes which appeared to them to be extremely hazardous, almost invariably resulted in a successful outcome, they found themselves reduced to the position of rather dazed acquiescence. . . ." Over their determined, even bitter opposition Dr. Tucker had the courage and vision to spend endowment funds for the building of dormitories, a policy which proved both wise and rewarding. The physical and nervous energy that the President expended on all the facets of his work to achieve a threefold growth of the College in fifteen years, were taking an inevitable toll. Toward the end of the winter of 1907 he undertook a strenuous trip among the Alumni Clubs and returned exhausted and ill. When he learned that a weakness of his heart precluded further work and responsibility he tendered his resignation. Urged to remain at least as titular head of the College until his successor could be chosen, he served two more years until 1909, when, in his seventieth year, he retired.

> Nothing within the power of man is more important today than the measure of maturity which Americans can contribute to their national character. – John Sloan Dickey, 1954.

"One sees Dr. Tucker," recalled Robert F. Leavens of the Class of 1901, "as he appeared crossing the Campus or approaching on the sidewalk, erect, alert, his walk that of the army quickstep, his greeting that of an officer — friendly but not effusive, with an almost military salute. One sees him in his trim, horse-drawn single seater, buggy or sleigh, alone or with Mrs. Tucker at his side." Wherever they were now, the two thousand graduates of his seventeen years still heard the echoes of the restrained but earnest voice in chapel appealing to them, perhaps, to choose a life of generous consecration to an ideal.

With his strength partially restored in retirement he lived seventeen years longer, until he was lost to Dartmouth on September 29, 1926. Although he never professed to have been a pioneer in the science of education, the metropolitan newspapers considered that a great educator had died. Certainly Charles Hall, the janitor of Rollins and Web-

ster, who had rung the Dartmouth Hall bell for Dr. Tucker's inauguration and tolled it for his commemorative service, thought so. And the
faculty could agree to a man with Professor George D. Lord, who said:
"In his presence heaviness and meanness vanished: they did not even
show themselves before his nobility." But it remained for *The Dartmouth,* which has never been given to sentimentality, to strike the responsive note: "The spirit of the college, the love which we have for it,
the number of men who bear her name and the things which make us
so proud to be Dartmouth men — we credit joyfully to Dr. Tucker."

*   *   *   *   *

At least once during his administration of seven years Dartmouth's
tenth president, Ernest Fox Nichols, confessed to a friend that he
thought himself woefully miscast in the job. He had been accustomed
to the laboratory where things got done quickly or at least eventually.
As President he found that he left one problem behind on a trip and
came back to eight more. His brilliant successes in the laboratory and
classroom had been responsible for his invitation into the shoal waters
of the administration. In 1898 he had come by way of the Colgate
faculty to Dartmouth's department of physics where, with Professor
Gordon F. Hull, he had conducted the far-reaching experiments on the
pressure of light described elsewhere in this volume. From Dartmouth
he had gone to Columbia University in 1903, and from there back to
Dartmouth.

The laws governing human relations and the writing of speeches on such diverse subjects as educational policy and alumni relations seemed so much more subtle and variable than those governing the pressure of light that in 1916 Nichols resigned the presidency to return to the familiar and reassuring world of physics, this time at Yale. From there he went to a General Electric laboratory and thence to the Massachusetts Institute of Technology as its president in 1921. Forced to resign shortly thereafter because of ill health, he died several years before his elder predecessor at Dartmouth.

While Dr. Nichols's administration cannot be judged to have been momentous, neither can it be said that it was time wasted. In the seven years ending in 1915-16 the enrollment rose almost one-third to 1,422, and the endowment to over four million dollars. The new buildings were the Alumni Gymnasium, Parkhurst, Robinson, North and South Massachusetts, and Hitchcock. The handsome acquisition of forty-five acres west to the river, given by Mrs. Emily Howe Hitchcock in 1912, led two years later to the opening of Tuck Drive. Bissell Hall was remodeled to accommodate Thayer School, and Tuck more than doubled its enrollment. In 1913, however, the Medical School ceased to give a degree and restricted its course to two years. To facilitate the conduct of the College's growingly complex business, the Board of Trustees was divided into committees, and the administration into departments with specific responsibilities. And Dr. Nichols did fortify the end-zone of academic excellence against the onrush of organized athletics and the allure of fraternity life.

The return to the College of Ernest Martin Hopkins as the eleventh president in the Wheelock succession was greeted by statements in the press that never before had the selection of a college president rested so much on trust. As Secretary of the College, Mr. Hopkins had questioned the value of the Ph.D. degree as proper preparation for liberal arts teaching. In a sacrosanct club of clergymen and educators — he being neither — this was not popular doctrine. There has never been an alumni outcry less rational than that which accompanied the selection of Mr. Hopkins as not being "a big enough man for the job."

Born in Dunbarton, New Hampshire, in 1877, President Hopkins had gone from the lamplight of his father's Baptist parsonages in small New Hampshire and Vermont towns to Worcester Academy, there to earn his tuition by carrying the mail eight miles a day on foot. During summer vacations he labored in the Massachusetts granite quarries at North Uxbridge, beginning at a wage of seventy cents a day and eventually rising to the position of derrickman. In college he did well academically and became editor of the *Aegis* and *The Dartmouth*. In view of his early pioneering in the department of alumni relations and his assumption of much other administrative responsibility and planning toward the end of the Tucker regime, his nine-year postgraduate service as Secretary of the College can scarcely be separated from his twenty-nine-year administration as President. The interval between 1910 and 1916 was in effect merely a leave of absence during which, as manager of the educational department of the Western Electric Company and as employment manager of Filene's in Boston and of the Curtis Publishing Company in Philadelphia, he gathered administrative skills vital to the industry of education.

> . . . one of the principal functions of the institution of the college today as never before, is to maintain a climate of purpose and program which will protect the student from immaturely concluding that the facts of life in higher education confront him with a dilemma of damning choice as between professional and liberal studies rather than a difficulty his learning can manage. – John Sloan Dickey, 1962.

Free of cant and jargon, hammered out of conviction born of experience, President Hopkins's inaugural message, like many of his subsequent Convocation and Commencement addresses, was a responsible inquiry into the social and moral health of America, foretelling with startling prescience what some, at least, would diagnose as an even more virulent national distemper nearly half a century later.

We have as a people specialized so completely in recent years on claiming rights, that our senses of obligation and responsibility have become atrophied. Authority has been weakened, not only in state and church but in home and school, until it commands less respect even than obedience. Amid all this, somehow, the conviction has begun to grow that dilettante philosophizing about rights, and claims to opportunities which have not been earned offer too little compensation in constructive accomplishment for what society is called upon to sacrifice in the character of the individuals who compose it. . . .

The ceremonies of President Hopkins's inauguration reached their climax on Dartmouth Night, October 6, 1916, with the gathering of the entire student body on the campus. Lighted torches were distributed and as a skyrocket went up the band played. Nearly two thousand marchers proceeded first to the President's house and then Webster Hall, filling the night with cheers.

(Freshmen who saw the inauguration were fortunate enough to

witness as seniors another memorable fete, the Sesquicentennial celebration. "Some of those," wrote Homer Eaton Keyes in the memorial book,

who gleefully attended the celebration of the one hundred and fiftieth anniversary of the founding of the College, and at that time conducted themselves with becoming joviality and sprightliness of youth, will now hobble into the arena of the two hundredth, to smile toothless response to plaudits of a new generation. . . .)

The problems posed by the entrance of the United States into the First World War were less acute than those of previous wars only because it did not last so long. Of the 1,500 students at Dartmouth before the Commencement of 1917, 500 departed for the service, and by fall over half the undergraduate body had enlisted. Income from the Army Training Corps and the generous support of alumni made up a heavy operating deficit. The President had no more than gripped the reins of administration when he was called to Washington by Secretary of War Newton D. Baker to deal with the problems of manpower in industries producing supplies for the army.

An unprecedented embarrassment of riches in the surge of applications for admission following the war was in a way as vexing as a dearth of students at other times in Dartmouth's history. Of 798 applicants to the freshman class in the fall of 1919, 100 had to be turned away. The following year only 624 out of 1,000 were accepted and in 1921 the pressure was so great that less than half of a potential freshman class of 1,200 could be admitted. Determining to limit the College to 2,000 students, the Trustees in 1921 adopted a pioneering system of selective admission, the prototype of such programs in other colleges and universities. It provided for the weighing of many factors: scholastic, extracurricular and personality, the latter established through interviews and letters. Such intangibles as capacity for leadership, social adaptability, breadth of interests, motivation, fortitude, perseverance, judgment, and emotional stability were taken into account. Everything else being equal, geographical provenience of an entering class was considered with a view to widespread representation. The main features of selective admission, of which the above are an oversimplification, remain today, although the pressures upon the admissions office have of course become immeasurably greater, and the proliferation and refinement of the determining factors correspondingly more complex.

Obviously this larger enrollment filled the buildings to the eaves, so

that President Hopkins, like his immediate predecessors, had to concentrate on an increased endowment which would in turn permit the enlargement of the educational plant. The volume of funds pouring into the College during his stewardship of nearly three decades was without previous parallel. The endowment rose from $4,184,000 to $22,208,-000, and the value of the educational plant from $1,769,000 to $7,688,-000. The scope of the building program which gifts, including the annual Alumni Fund, made possible was the most impressive of any since the founding of the College.*

While large gifts and their transformation into brick and cement are properly the materials of history, even more so are the people behind the gifts and the buildings. The era of the 1920's and '30's was the last before foundations began to replace individuals as the source of large grants; and since many of the individuals were empire-builders of the old school, they imparted to the administrative history of the College a good deal of excitement and human interest.

President Hopkins first met George F. Baker, the omnipotent and enigmatic New York banker, during a Cornell dinner at the Commodore Hotel. As the last speaker of the evening Dr. Hopkins sat at the head table next to Mr. Baker, who was much interested in Cornell. Commenting that his uncle (Fisher Ames Baker, 1859) had gone to Dartmouth, Baker spoke of his interest in a memorial and asked Dr. Hopkins what could be done with $25,000.

A man is known by his best choices. – John Sloan Dickey, 1954.

"Very little," replied the President with calculated frankness. The matter was dropped, and Dr. Hopkins left with the feeling that the College had lost twenty-five thousand dollars. Later, however, Baker sent a check for $100,000. In a grateful letter the President wrote, pressing his luck, that he was handing the check to the Treasurer to place on account. Wherewith Baker went to his friend, Henry Thayer, on whose board he served at the American Telephone and Telegraph Company, and asked: "How much is it going to cost me to buy out of this situation, anyway?" Thayer's long experience in advancing the

---

* Steele, Spaulding Pool, Topliff (1920), Russell Sage, Athletic Field and Stadium (1923), President's House (1924), Davis Field House (1926), Clement Green House, Dick Hall's House, Silsby (1927), Baker Library, Dartmouth Outing Club House, Gile, Sanborn (1928), Carpenter, Davis Hockey Rink, Lord, Streeter (1929), Chase, Ripley, Smith, Tuck School, Woodbury, Woodward (1930), Dartmouth Hall rebuilt (1935), Thayer (1937), Cummings (1939), New Butterfield, Heating Plant addition (1940). In addition McNutt, Reed, Thornton, and Wentworth were rebuilt; Hilton and Chase fields were acquired and nine holes added to the golf course.

College's interest came into play, and Baker's eventual gift was one million dollars.

In this way did the Dartmouth library, originally in Bezaleel Woodward's humble dwelling, then in Dartmouth Hall, then in John Wheelock's house, then back to Dartmouth Hall, then in Reed and subsequently Wilson Hall, find indeed the most imposing sanctuary for books among all contemporary undergraduate libraries in the country. Henry B. Thayer's responsibility was not only that of gaining George F. Baker's sponsorship. As chairman of Dartmouth's Physical Development Committee from 1926 to 1935 he was regularly on the library construction site supervising details. A native of Northfield, Vermont, Thayer had gone directly from College to the Western Electric Company as a shipping clerk in 1881. Twenty-seven years later he became its president, and in 1919, chief officer of the parent company, American Telephone. So engrossed did he become in Baker Library that on occasions he postponed meetings of the Telephone Company so he could remain in Hanover. Handsome returns from his strenuous efforts in endowment work were yielded long after his death.

On September 18, 1928, the aging George Baker, having arrived from New York with his nurse on a special train, was escorted by President Hopkins and Thayer from the Norwich station to the new library, which he pronounced to be "a lot of building for a million dollars." There was soon forthcoming from him a second gift of an equal amount for the operation and maintenance of the vast edifice that Fred Larson had designed.

To generations of Dartmouth men the name of Edward Tuck conjured up the image of a distant patriarch with a handle-bar moustache and almost unlimited resources. It was general knowledge that he was a graduate (1862), for he was long the oldest living alumnus, but he had dwelt so many years in France and had so long outlived his contemporaries that he seemed to many like a proper, unbending figure in Mme. Tussaud's waxworks. A native of Exeter and graduate of Phillips Academy as well as Dartmouth, where he ranked second in his class, he had begun the study of law in his father's office in Exeter but had to abandon it owing to weakness of his eyes. After short terms as vice- and acting-consul at Paris he served for some years as liaison officer between Paris and New York for the banking firm of John Munroe & Company. In twelve years he became its head and in 1881 he retired in Paris as an international financial advisor to kings and prime ministers. For decades Vert-Mont, his estate near Paris, was a forum of history and economics for presidents, generals, senators, and judges. His benefactions to France were many, chief among them an immense gift of art treasures to be lodged in the Tuck Gallery of the Petit Palais in Paris. During the First World War he and his wife, the former Julia Stell, built a military hospital near their estate which they endowed privately. In America he gave the building for the New Hampshire Historical Society in Concord, and at Dartmouth his benefactions had, as we have seen, already begun under the Tucker and Nichols administrations.

> Whatever the origin of the way Dartmouth men feel about the College, it is now a part of their heritage that anything less than extraordinary response to any call from the College would be letting themselves down. – John Sloan Dickey, 1959.

President Hopkins's first meeting with Tuck came as the result of a lively controversy in the Board of Trustees about investment policy. The President was trying to generate interest in common stocks, but many of the older members would hear of nothing but bonds. So often did they raise the question of how Edward Tuck might invest the College's portfolio that the President set sail for Paris to find out. Arriving at the sculptured gardens of Vert-Mont and entering its marble halls he found a short, well-groomed gentleman whose expression could change quickly from twinkling humor to stern determination. Tuck settled the stocks-and-bonds questions in few words: "Never owned a damned bond in my life!"

There was a good deal of pleasant conversation, with news of the College predominating, but rapport was not really established until Tuck asked the President what he would like to do in the evening, expecting no doubt that the Paris opera would be his choice. "As a matter of fact," the President said, "I would rather like to see the Folies Bergère." Tuck was delighted and, ordering his car, instructed the chauffeur to stop at The Opera to pick up two programs on the way to the Folies. On their return to the Tuck residence at the end of the evening the opera programs, studiedly rumpled, were placed on a table in the entrance foyer so that they would be seen by Tuck's nieces, who were also house guests at that time. The next morning at breakfast Tuck seized and held the offensive by expatiating at length to his nieces about the performance at the Opera. President Hopkins did not know what he himself would say if called upon to comment. From this mo-

ment onward he and Tuck were friends, which greatly enhanced the latter's interest in the College. His devotion to it indeed became so strong that his most prized possession was a gold replica of the Wentworth bowl, given to him by the Trustees in gratitude for his benefactions.

By the time of his death in 1938 at the age of 95, Dartmouth had received from Edward Tuck more than $4,500,000. Three-fourths of this huge sum had been for general endowment, and the remainder for construction. In 1925 he financed the building of the President's House and in 1928 the impressive group of buildings for the Business School at the end of Tuck Mall. A clue to the broad outlook of Dartmouth's greatest benefactor was his reaction to an appeal in the early 1930's to support a group of alumni in their charges that liberalism was becoming too strong in the College. Tuck replied that all the money he had given had been to uphold the policies of the College, not to dictate what they should be.

Entirely different was the background of Benjamin A. Kimball and Frank S. Streeter, both benefactors during the Hopkins administration and both hard-working Trustees, whose disagreement on subjects other than the welfare of the College was notorious. As the alter egos of the Concord and Montreal and Boston and Maine railroads, respectively, theirs was an internecine economic and political war waged publicly in the legislative halls of Concord. Kimball indeed became a leading character in Winston Churchill's noted novel, *Coniston,* on the rough-and-tumble activities of a New Hampshire political boss.

Of the service to the College of these two indomitable figures, Streeter's, having begun as early as 1890, was longer concerned with matters of central importance. Only thirty-seven years old at that time he had already cut a wide swath from East Charleston, Vermont, where he was born, from St. Johnsbury Academy and from Hanover, following his graduation in 1874. He very early became recognized as the leader of the bar in New Hampshire and later as a prominent corporation lawyer for Amoskeag Cotton Mills, Western Union, and the Boston and Maine, following its merger with the Concord and Montreal. To his adversaries he was as pontifical and arrogant as his physique was ponderous; to his friends, a quick-witted ally with a winning streak of sentiment.

In 1890 his name was proposed to fill a vacancy on the Board of Trustees occasioned by the death of 89-year-old Judge Nesmith of the Class of 1820. The election of a mere stripling of doubtful piety who had been out of College only sixteen years was unthinkable, and the Trustees summarily elected a less controversial figure. The storm of resentment forced the Board of Trustees to increase alumni representation, and as a result Streeter was elected in 1892. He labored unsparingly for thirty years as the unofficial right bower of three presidents and, according to President Hopkins, became the single most potent sponsor of alumni participation in the affairs of the College. Almost a prototype of the ruthless empire-builder with a soft spot — in his case, Dartmouth — Streeter contributed more than his share of folklore to the administrative history of the College. With one eye at variance in its position with the other, he looked formidable even in his kindliest moments and was delighted, although his wife was not, with an accurate portrait of himself which had been done for the College. "Looks just like me!" he declared. "Some day the students will look up at it and say: 'Who's that old sonavabitch, anyway?'"

. . . only out of commitment is any man fulfilled with his fellows, whether in the embrace of fellowship or loneliness of leadership. – John Sloan Dickey, 1960.

The circumstances of his death in 1922 were so melodramatic as almost to seem designed for an emotional appeal for the Alumni Fund. They are among the most poignant in President Hopkins's memory. In Concord Streeter was dying of cancer, and his nurse telephoned to say that he wanted to see the President. The next morning Dr. Hopkins made the journey:

When I went in the nurse said: "Mr. Streeter is in a coma, but he comes out of it every two or three hours and he wants you to go in and sit beside the bed so that you'll be right there when he comes out, because he has a very limited time that he's conscious." I went in and sat down and I don't think I'd been there more than five minutes when he opened his eyes. He always called me "Boy," and he put his hand on mine and said: "I knew you'd come down, Boy. There's one thing I wanted to say to you. . . . I'm not a religious man. None of the technical qualifications for church or religious membership influenced me very much, but I think every man has to give worship to something bigger than himself, and Dartmouth College is a good enough religion for me." He almost immediately lapsed off again into a coma, and those were the last words he ever said to me.

Sadness and service to the College have often been united in the experience of its leaders. Mr. Hopkins recalls the tragic necessity two years later to inform Mr. and Mrs. Edward K. Hall that Dick, one of their two sons, a sophomore at Dartmouth, was dying.

It was the only case of polio in the College that year. Dr. Gile called me up Monday morning and he asked if I could get hold of Ed Hall, and I said yes. Dick had been down to the Harvard game on Saturday and had come back apparently with a hard cold. Sunday afternoon it began to go bad, and Dr. Gile made up his mind it wasn't a cold. Ed and Sally caught the train that got up here at midnight. When I left the hospital Dr. Gile said he didn't think he would live until they got up there, but he would do everything he could. The minute we arrived Ed went in and Sally sat out in the anteroom and I'll never forget it. It was one of the most emotional periods of my life because Ed came out just as stony-faced as he could be and sat down beside Sally and said: "We haven't got our boy any more." . . . But quite illustrative of him, within three or four days after that he sent for me and said they wanted to build something in the way of a monument. How would the College feel about an infirmary? That was the beginning of Dick's House.

The genesis of the English Department's elaborate Sanborn House was the pot of tea that stood ready for students day and night in Professor Sanborn's white Colonial dwelling on the west side of the Green. Mrs. Sanborn, a niece of Daniel Webster's, had observed this custom as long as her son, Edwin Webster Sanborn, 1878, could remember. When he made a gift to the College of nearly two million dollars for an English Department building and library books, it was appropriate that the gracious Sanborn study be reproduced in the new structure as a memorial to his parents. His father, Professor Edwin D. Sanborn, 1832, had been a member of the Dartmouth faculty for almost half a century. Many other buildings arose from such impulses rooted in warm remembrance of things past.

During the 1920's and '30's management of the rapidly accumulating properties of the College became a prime responsibility. Lewis Parkhurst, 1878, a trustee for over three decades and the donor of the Administration Building, wrote in 1924: "We own blocks of real estate scattered from one end of the country to the other: the remnants of an old plantation in Virginia, stores and tenement houses in Kansas City, vacant lots in Seattle, city property in Chicago, stores and mill property in Lowell. . . . The policy of the trustees in these later years has been to dispose of such property as soon as possible and reinvest the proceeds in such manner as will best serve the interests of the College. . . ."

Not the least of Dartmouth's far-flung possessions were the old land grants in Vermont and New Hampshire, although revenue from the former, once so vital to the College, had long since diminished. Like so many other remote hill townships, Wheelock, Vermont, had been struck by a series of disasters. The best of its youth had been sacrificed to the Civil War, and an outbreak of diphtheria had further depleted its human resources. Through the sale of land the Vermont grant had in a century and a quarter shrunk to one-fourth its former size, and forests were creeping over the stone walls of the remainder. With the rise of the pulp town of Berlin, the College's forty wild and rocky square miles in northeastern New Hampshire had, however, produced unexpected logging bonanzas, first in 1888 through a twenty-year lease to lumber baron George Van Dyke, and later through a transaction with the Brown Paper Company which yielded over a million-and-a-half dollars.

College presidents whose energies are given exclusively to the enlargement of endowment and physical plant are known by their colleagues as "builders," a sobriquet of praise not without a trace of condescension, for walls and glass are not the vivifying stuff of education. It was through his thoughtful and resolute statements on many topics of moment in education and society that President Hopkins became the conscience of the liberal arts college in America.

Among his addresses eliciting nationwide comment, probably that in 1932 entitled *Change Is Opportunity* (amplifying statements made ten years previously in an address entitled *An Aristocracy of Brains*) was the most provocative.

. . . the most serious danger threatening civilization today is the rapid development of a perverted sense of democracy, at home and abroad, which encourages public opinion not only to accept but to idealize mediocrity and which allows public opinion to be ostentatiously arrogant in its indifference to intelligence and antagonistic toward any process of thought in its leaders which rises above its own average mental capacity. The fallacies of interpretation of statements that all men are created equal have become embodied in our thinking until we have ceased to admire either the man richly endowed who has capitalized all available facilities to make himself competent in high degree or the man who has broken down the confining walls of limited opportunity and has emerged from his environment mentally and spiritually capable of great works. Under the spurious standards of our present-day democracy enthusiasm is reserved largely for the common man who remains common rather than for the common man who makes himself uncommon.

In some quarters this was considered a most illiberal statement. In his diverse attitudes, not easily arranged as "liberal" or "conservative," Dr. Hopkins proved the fallibility of such convenient and overworked designations. The measure of his breadth of view is only possible if one notes his disposition of the many explosive packages deposited in his office over a period of years.

During the Red scare of the 'twenties he was pelted with criticism from the alumni and the public at large for his refusal to cancel an invitation from the student Round Table to the Communist leader, William Z. Foster, to speak in Hanover on the subject: *The Left Wing of the American Labor Movement*. "Personally I am opposed to Foster," announced the President. "I think that he has not used his influence and power wisely and has sometimes misled his followers, but the students can hear him in a college hall if they wish, provided they raise the money to bring him to Dartmouth without my cooperation."

Foster came and went, and the students, if the report of the undergraduate editor of the *Alumni Magazine* is an indication, took him in their stride. The controversy waxed hottest in the aftermath of Foster's visit. "Drawing and quartering," Dr. Hopkins recalled, "were among the milder threats that poured in by mail, telegraph, and telephone day after day, amid dire predictions that the good name of the College would be sullied beyond any hope of being cleansed by anything it

might do in later years, in effort to regain standing." The President stood his ground with the statement:

A friend of mine wrote to me some months ago that he would as soon have Lenin and Trotsky speak at Dartmouth as some of the speakers whom we were having there. I replied that if those responsible for a theory of government which now dominates an eighth of the earth's surface and a great host of her people were available for the explanation of their theories to the undergraduate body, I should be glad to have the students hear them and have them form their judgment as to the dangers or merit of Bolshevism on the basis of direct evidence, rather than through the inconsistent and contradictory pronouncements of anti-Bolshevist propaganda.

Largely because of this statement Paul Blanshard, in an article in *The Nation* in 1934, cited Dartmouth as an example of a private institution controlled by businessmen trustees which was nevertheless liberal. Praised by Blanshard for his militant stand in behalf of free speech, the President was quoted as saying: "If turning handsprings on top of the college gymnasium would teach men to think, I would be perfectly willing to do it."

At the same time, however, in a Convocation address, he took severely to task those who were exploiting

in their own interest the field of liberal thought. This professionalized group, arrogating to itself all virtue and good intent, and denying these qualities to all others; patronizing those who will not whittle their conclusions to the exact dimensions of the prescribed code; manipulating intellectual processes and capitalizing dogmatic assertion as preferable to accepting the conclusions of logical thought — this group is doing more to breed suspicion of and hostility to true liberalism than is being done, or could be done, by all available forms of reaction if combined in militant array. Ill-nature, intellectual arrogance, and churlish intolerance are but sorry concomitants of any movement, but they are singularly out of place and tragically harmful in association with any movement which desires to be recognized as liberal.

Dr. Hopkins confirmed no decision which in retrospect turned out more inflammatory, than the invitation of the Art Department in 1932 to Jose Clemente Orozco to paint frescoes on the walls of the Reserve Room in Baker Library. A barrage of complaints asserting that Orozco's avant-garde talent was as dubious as his political background assailed the Administration Building. Orozco's dramatic portrayal of the contending forces in western civilization has survived, although the President long bore the scars of this bitter controversy. As an

[316]

antidote Walter Humphrey was commissioned for the murals on the ground floor of Thayer Hall which depict voluptuous Indian maidens and muscular braves, both with minimum adornment, in a fanciful interpretation of Dartmouth's origin. Quite a different quarter of the alumni body proved as vocal in its displeasure as the critics of Orozco.

One problem which Dr. Hopkins shared with his predecessors and his successor, and about which he had a great deal to say throughout his administration, was the retention of a fast hold on the liberal arts tradition lest, by design or default, it be taken hostage by the university idea. "That transformation," he said in 1925 to the Alumni Council of Amherst College,

which could not be made from the outside may conceivably be made, in the course of time, from the inside if the colleges fall into the necessity of being manned more largely by instructors narrowed in interest by the graduate schools, by men who have not yet seen the vision of the college and who underestimate the social significance of good teaching. Such men of necessity have been brought into college faculties in increasing proportions during the rapid growth of colleges in recent years. Herein the college has suffered in that the only accepted method of training college teachers unfits them to a considerable degree for interest in, appreciation of, or contribution to, the college until the effect of the graduate-school training has worn off and the ideals of professional scholarship requisite for the teacher have been transmuted into ideals of amateur scholarship requisite for the citizen.

On another occasion the President spoke of the scholastic specialist who sacrifices all else to the perfection of final excellence in his chosen field as a "staff officer, informed in regard to a single subject, rather than . . . a principal upon whom the world's responsibilities may be loaded."

> . . . we must at least redouble our efforts to restore the relevancy of moral purpose as an essential companion of intellectual purpose and power in any learning that presumes to liberate a man from a lesser to a larger existence. – John Sloan Dickey, 1960.

He began a searching inquiry into the objectives, achievements, and opportunities of the privately endowed college of liberal arts. Some of these were found to be independence, stability, flexibility in the selection of students, freedom for insistence upon high standards of scholarship, and freedom from restraint, enforced uniformity, and political influence. As the result of a study in 1924, that of the Committee on

Educational Policy, arbitrary course requirements were lessened and replaced by a program comprising a major subject selected by the student, by a set of comprehensive examinations as prerequisite for the degree, and honors courses for students attaining higher grades.

An arresting commentary in the *Alumni Magazine* entitled *Dartmouth From Without,* concerning the changes, external and internal, that were being wrought on the Hanover Plain, came in 1932 from the pen of a University of Chicago professor, James Weber Linn, who had not visited Hanover since 1912. He thought that undergraduate education at Dartmouth had passed through as many phases as at any place in the country, and had become "at long last, as vital."

We used to believe, in the Middle West, that Dartmouth was determinedly, not to say crudely, "athletic". We heard, and circulated, stories of young men who rode the rods to White River Junction . . . of janitors and night-watchmen from Colorado and Montana, exported to Hanover by zealous alumni, there to be turned by Wallie McCornack into All Americans; of other freshmen slaughtered like sheep by ferocious sophomores, because they combed their hair and read French. . . .

Though athletic victories continued to be blazoned on her banners, one began to suspect the existence of laboratories, and even of classrooms, among [Dartmouth's] dormitories and beside her playing fields. She was still more notable for her interest in winter outdoor sports than for the indoor sport of reading; but it was whispered that a considerable group of her undergraduates were concerned with the fine arts, and even painted in the open, their heads bloody no doubt with contumely, but unbowed with shame. And then came Hopkins, one of the great college administrators of America, openly placing emphasis on scholarship and intellectual practice. . . . Could we have been mistaken, all these years? . . .

The outsider sees Princeton become a university, Yale become a university. The outsider sees Amherst, Williams, Knox, Grinnell, and many others remaining small colleges, beautiful, endearing to the spirit, the gift-shops of culture as the universities are its department stores. The outsider sees Dartmouth as the great American college; vivid; the one Rubens in our collection.

It would be difficult to find, during an era which spanned two wars and two depressions, more telling evidence of an institution becoming the lengthened shadow of one man. Had the times not been as harsh the landmarks might have been different, though scarcely less impressive. In the middle of the threadbare thirties Dartmouth Hall burned again and was rebuilt for $200,000. In the same year, 1935, a social survey directed the "attention of local chapters and national fraternities," wrote Leon Burr Richardson severely, "to the question of whether they had any excuse for existence." A consequence of the study was the building of the new Thayer Dining Hall, the latest action emphasizing the centrality of the College. (In 1921 the Trustees had voted that their approval be required of all fraternity-building plans. The number of residents in each fraternity was limited, and none was permitted to have dining facilities.) The spectacle of nine-tenths of the undergraduate body watching one-tenth play intercollegiate sports had been altered with compulsory recreation for freshmen and sophomores and a vigorous program of intramural contests. The annual Alumni Fund had become a real bulwark against hard times. Students from nearly all of the forty-eight states and many foreign countries composed a firm enrollment of 2,500. Dartmouth was a national institution.

There remained for President Hopkins and for Dartmouth the undoing by the Second World War of much that had been done, the sorest of trials for a peaceful enterprise. They were gray years of blue uniforms, of marching and countermarching on the Common, of mounting casualty lists, and of the wrenching of every fiber of the College organism. When it was over, and the patient was discovered to be sound, if somewhat spare, Dr. Hopkins stepped down after his vigil of twenty-nine years.

The powerful and persuasive men who had tried to lure him from Hanover had all been turned away. Not the least of these had been former Secretary of War, Newton D. Baker, who came to Dartmouth with a committee to persuade Dr. Hopkins to go to Johns Hopkins as its president. The President also declined an offer to head the University of Chicago. Whatever obligations he had been able to take on without jeopardizing his responsibilities to Dartmouth, such as the chairmanship of the Woodrow Wilson Foundation, he had assumed, and upon his retirement was covered with degrees and honors.

Most vivid, and possibly most valued because of the confusion attending it, was the award of a degree from Yale. The circumstances were related by Leon Burr Richardson:

The solemn festivities were proceeding as scheduled and the President of Dartmouth was standing before President Angell to receive the distinction. At this moment an aged alumnus of Yale, in the front of the audience, was seized with a fit, with loud vocal accompaniments. In the uproar which he created, the ceremony had to be postponed until the unfortunate victim of the attack had been tenderly borne, all the time protesting loudly, from the hall. In the interim President Hopkins remarked to his brother president, "I am sorry to be the occasion of such irritation to one of your valued alumni." Whereupon President Angell retorted, "Very frequently we receive protests from our alumni at our judgment in the award of these degrees, but never has one come to us so vociferous, so emphatic and so *immediate* as this."

The changing of the guard took place on November 1, 1945, in the solemn faculty room of Parkhurst Hall, with President Hopkins and President-elect John S. Dickey seated on a dais and with Trustee John R. McLane, Dean Gordon Bill, and the Rev. Roy B. Chamberlin before them facing the oak benches filled to the aisles. The room was silent as Executive Officer Albert I. Dickerson and Treasurer Halsey C. Edgerton brought forth the heavy leather case bearing the charter granted by the authority of George the Third. They placed it on the desk next to the gleaming silver bowl given to Eleazar Wheelock and his successors by John Wentworth, the royal governor of New Hampshire.

In his final address President Hopkins recalled the noble figure of Judge David Cross, who in his 97th year in 1914 made one of the most eloquent addresses ever heard in Hanover. It had been the good fortune of Dr. Hopkins to take Judge Cross to the train, and on the way the eminent alumnus had said: "Son, I graduated in 1841. I have known a

member of every class that ever graduated from Dartmouth and it was entirely possible for me to have known every graduate of Dartmouth College. You are young and you are going to be associated with the College for a long time, and I should like to have you in your later years say to men that you had known a man who knew a man in every class that graduated from Dartmouth." Then the judge said: "Son, never forget that origins are important."

> . . . nothing is more important to the vigor and responsiveness of liberal learning in America today than that the undergraduate college with its unique institutional concern for the total fulfillment of both the individual and his society should remain at the heart of things because it is concerned with the heart of things. – John Sloan Dickey, 1961.

With the reading of the inscription on the silver bowl Dr. Hopkins presented it to John S. Dickey, 1929, who thereupon became the twelfth president of the College. His first act was the reading of this citation:

Ernest Martin Hopkins: New Hampshireman by birth and choice; graduate of Dartmouth College, Class of 1901; disciple and collaborator of Tucker; eleventh President of the College in the Wheelock succession. The measure of your devotion and of your doing, like that of other true north-country men, will never be weighed in any man's scales. Your services, both in counsel and in administration, have been often sought in the nation's public and private affairs. You, regardless of the prizes proffered — and some men know how great they were — chose, when choice was necessary, to serve this College. In this thirtieth year of your leadership the College you and Mrs. Hopkins so lovingly served and you in all respects so largely built stands ready to carry forward, in the fore, today's great tasks of the historic college. That, Sir, is your work and your reward. On behalf of the men of Dartmouth, by virtue of the authority vested in me by the Trustees and in grateful and affectionate testimonial of your place in the Dartmouth family as the most beloved of the College's sons I hereby confer upon you the degree of Doctor of Laws.

Following his retirement the President Emeritus embarked upon another eventful career as president and chairman of the National Life Insurance Company and as director and counselor of numerous other enterprises.

In 1958, on the occasion of his eightieth birthday, twenty-two hundred alumni crowded the Waldorf Astoria's grand ballroom, splendidly decorated in green and white, for a testimonial banquet. Just prior to the dessert the lights dimmed and a towering green and white birthday cake was set before Dr. Hopkins, while with military precision the army of red-coated waiters filed in bearing miniature cakes, each with a lighted candle, to the hundreds of other tables. Sherman Adams, 1920, Nelson Rockefeller, 1930, and President Dickey all spoke their greetings to Dr. Hopkins, as did President Eisenhower in a message he had written, Sherman Adams testified, in longhand. And the Dartmouth Glee Club, behind a semitransparent curtain bearing a colored image of Dartmouth Hall, sang Richard Hovey's haunting songs.

* * * * *

In many ways the administration of John Sloan Dickey has reflected a personal background entirely different from that of his predecessors. A magna cum laude, Phi Beta Kappa, and Rufus Choate Scholar at Dartmouth, he graduated from Harvard Law School in 1932, and within a year entered a career of public service which continued, except for one interval (1936-40), until his return to Dartmouth as President. Under Assistant Secretary of State Francis B. Sayre he dealt with legal and economic problems in the State Department. In 1940 he became Special Assistant to Secretary of State Cordell Hull and for five years fulfilled a variety of assignments, the last as the director of the State Department's Office of Public Affairs. As a member also of the State Department's policy and coordinating committees he had much to do with setting up the United Nations Conference at San Francisco in 1945, during which he served as Public Liaison officer of the United States delegation.

He had for four years been a member of the executive committee of the Boston Alumni Association, but his knowledge of the diverse affairs of the College was embarrassingly slight during his first weeks in office. A month or so before beginning his duties he appealed to his predecessor for advice, with small success. Dr. Hopkins at length broke his silence in response to a final urgent plea. "As a matter of fact," he said, "there *is* some advice I would give you. Don't have anything to do with murals."

This counsel has been followed, but there is little else on the Hanover Plain with which the Dickey Administration has had nothing to do. Although historical perspective on that which has not yet become history is difficult, it is quite clear that the manifold accomplishments of the Dickey administration will rank in character with those of Eleazar Wheelock, William Jewett Tucker, and Ernest Martin Hopkins. One need not view with unvarying approval all that is going on (or "on going" as the President likes to put it) to recognize that he has assiduously applied Robert Frost's dictum to "get something up" for Dartmouth. The changes have come thick and fast, though no faster than those in the cosmos of science or the topography of world affairs. In the eyes particularly of pre-World War II graduates, not only the product appears to have been redesigned, but also the tools to make the patterns.

Much that has happened may be traced to the battered door of the Director of Admissions. With a total undergraduate enrollment fixed by the Board of Trustees at about 3,000, Dartmouth is still a small college, at least by comparison with some of the country's vast diploma mills. The ceiling on enrollment has consequently become the immovable object, and the floodtide of applications since the Second World War, the irresistible force. The admissions office has had no choice other than to become ever more selective, and the faculty progressively more responsive to the intellectual capabilities and appetites of the "aristocracy of brains" that Dr. Hopkins visualized in 1932.

There has certainly been no more painful administrative Charley horse than that imparted by the sons of disappointed alumni who have been outdistanced in the footrace for admission. Commenting that "there are tramp intellectuals, just as there are tramp athletes," an alumnus recently questioned a system of selection that places such overriding emphasis on scholarship that the slow-starters, who frequently become more effective citizens, are sacrificed. The response was that there are bound to be inequities until the perfect admissions system is invented, but that few would propose a substitute for high scholarship as the leading indicator, least of all great corporations in their recruitment of college graduates. The most forcible statistic that President Dickey and Director of Admissions Edward Chamberlain have offered in support of emphasis on brains is that nearly eighty per cent of the students at Dartmouth today plan to attend graduate school. A revolution has taken place within a single generation.

Out of President Dickey's own involvement in international affairs grew the conviction that the outlook of the average undergraduate, reflecting a psychology of introspection and self-sufficiency, should be broadened to an awareness of the great forces reshaping the nation and the world. At the same time young veterans in search of a serious and meaningful intellectual experience as intense as the hard transactions of war were returning in overwhelming numbers. The first response of the President was a requirement for seniors, the Great Issues Course. By bringing eminent authorities to lecture in Hanover it seeks to make such liberal studies as the sciences and social sciences, philosophy, and history tributaries to the ground swell of contemporary affairs that the seniors will shortly be breasting. The Great Issues Course was something of a precursor to what President Dickey has called "the strategy of comparative study . . . that is, studying a subject not simply in a sequential or chronological way but also, by using the principle of comparative learning, to reach across cultural and national boundaries in literature, philosophy, the arts, government and economics as a way of keeping breadth and the vitality of cross-fertilization in liberal learning in the future." In 1963 the Ford Foundation granted Dartmouth $675,-000 for a broad experiment by the faculty in comparative studies. It may result in changes of profound importance in the scope and teaching of the liberal arts.

The Great Issues concept of cultural inter-penetrations has joined the railroad, automobile, airplane, radio, and television in dispelling Hanover's once splendid (or not-so-splendid) isolation by gestating such special convocations as Great Issues in the Anglo-Canadian-American community, which in 1957 brought to the campus for a weekend of critical discussions the Prime Minister of Canada, the British Ambassador to the United States, the Master of University College, Oxford, the editors of *The Times* and *The Economist* (both of London), the Assistant to the President of the United States, the U.S. Representative to the United Nations, and the publisher of *The New*

York Times. Convened in Hanover in 1960 to discuss Great Issues of Conscience in Modern Medicine were such international luminaries as Aldous Huxley, C. P. Snow, and the Nobel Prize winning geneticist, H. J. Muller. In quick succession the College also acted as host to two symposia in a series sponsored by the Ford Foundation that has come to be known as "Dartmouth Conferences." The first was between representatives of the USSR and the U.S., and the second between Japanese and Americans.

Judging by its imitators and therefore its admirers, the three-term, three-course curriculum, introduced in 1958, has been the most prominent auxiliary of the quickening academic tempo, although the quickening has proved more the consequence of this change than the cause of it. Three subjects a term for three terms a year obviously reduces by four the total number of courses taken by students in as many years, but the new schedule permits more intensive concentration on each subject. It makes better use of the compounding and recompounding of knowledge and of that shrinking resource of both student and teacher — time. The College is not all of a mind about it, but the consensus is that it is working well, certainly if the greatly increased circulation of Baker Library books is any indication.

Beginning in 1963 a fourth or summer term of instruction was added to fill those drowsy weeks, long the exclusive preserve of caretakers, tourists, and pigeons, but since the 'fifties shared by executives of the American Telephone and Telegraph Company and other groups in pursuit of refresher courses in the liberal arts. No longer can an educational plant afford three months of idleness.

Among custodians of moral values and keepers of the peace it is a common lament that a civilization so abundantly productive in science and technology should be so poor in the manufactures of the spirit. In an academic world where so much emphasis has needfully been placed upon competence, there has likewise been apprehension about what President Dickey, in *The Atlantic Monthly,* of April 1955, has called "the issues of conscience. A concern for the choice of good and the rejection of evil in an institution of liberal learning quickens all humanistic studies and prevents our increasing reliance on the physical and social sciences from smothering those intuitive insights which produce and spring from goodness in a man. . . . To create the power of competence without creating a corresponding sense of moral direction to guide the use of that power is bad education."

A voice from the past, that of Nathan Lord over a century ago, reveals moral rearmament to have been a perennial concern of Dartmouth presidents: "The very cultivation of the mind has frequently a tendency to impair the moral sensibilities, to induce that pride of conscious ability and variety of attainments . . . so they become, surely through insensibility, most pernicious in their influence upon the individuals who cherish them, and contribute to poison those streams, which ought only to carry abroad health and blessing to the world." To advance the moral and spiritual purposes of the College the Trustees established in 1951 the William Jewett Tucker Foundation, in memory of the minister-president who had so eloquently counseled the students to cultivate their consciences as well as their minds. In the vortex of the whirling academic life of the present day the Tucker Foundation, with its own dean, has been concerned not with what men will do but with what they will be.

> It still seems to me that all else in our civilization depends upon making the physical power now possessed by man subject to the moral and political controls of a just international community. – John Sloan Dickey, 1961.

Of all of the developments of the administration of President Dickey that which is bringing the "teacher-scholar" to Dartmouth has come nearest to rekindling one of the memorable altercations of the past. The sharply competitive intellectual society of an era which the President has called one of "the accelerating obsolescence of knowledge" has carried a College once a prime source of baccalaureates for the ministry, later a source chiefly of business and now of the professions, on a collision course with professional preparation on the one hand, and liberal education on the other. That the President does not consider the situation necessarily to constitute a dilemma is discussed in his introduction to this chronicle. It is sufficient here to report the startling metamorphosis of the associated schools, arising at least in part from the contending forces of specialization.

While developing a multi-million dollar program to provide new buildings and integrate the basic sciences and the medical sciences, the Medical School has maintained its traditional two-year course. At the same time seventy-some faculty members in Hanover have been provided with facilities for research, so that they are both teachers and investigators, and their students, while learning the ABC's of medicine, are introduced to serious science in the laboratory with the option ahead of becoming practicing physicians or research men.

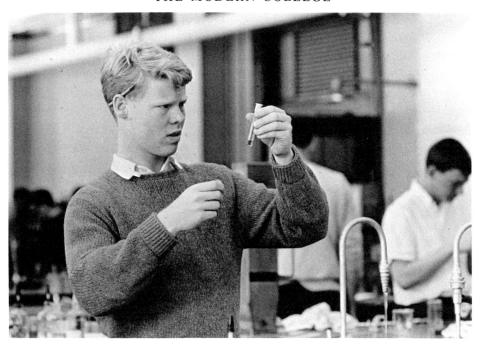

Studies of heart and lung disease, the mechanism of cancerous growth, and the chemical changes responsible for rhythmic functions in single cells headed some forty research projects in 1959. Three years later Charles Gilman and his Dartmouth sons gave one million dollars for a five-story Life Sciences Laboratory to complete a new Biomedical Center consisting of the Medical Science Building, the Dana Biomedical Library, Strasenburgh Hall (a dormitory), and the Kellogg Auditorium. Since 1962 the Medical School and the College faculty have collaborated to offer the Ph.D. program in molecular biology.

Today's Mary Hitchcock Clinic and Hospital little resemble Hiram Hitchcock's thirty-eight-bed "cottage-type hospital" with its staff of five private practitioners four decades ago. The original buff-colored brick building and the adjoining infirmary, Dick Hall's House, have merged with Faulkner House and other interconnected buildings to become the modern counterpart of the "continuous architecture" of the New England farm homestead. An invisible corridor runs across the Connecticut to the 250-bed White River Veterans Hospital, whose supervision is under the Dean's Committee of the Dartmouth Medical School.

Change is also the order of the day at the Thayer School, where Dean Myron Tribus is bent upon an experiment to make engineering attractive to liberal arts students and more responsive to the enlarging horizons of the engineering world. The metamorphosis at Thayer, as in the other associated schools, can be traced to the Trustees' Planning Committee established in 1954, and to a million-dollar gift from the Alfred P. Sloan Foundation to develop a program of graduate work for engineers well educated in the basic sciences and mathematics. Thayer now offers a five-year undergraduate program leading to both the A.B. and the professional degree of Bachelor of Engineering. Graduate courses with a doctoral degree in the same field spread before students wider vistas than those afforded by the earlier specialization in civil, mechanical, or electrical engineering.

Students at Tuck School these days confront the far-reaching problems of American corporation executives. The broadening horizons of the country's pioneer business school rather belie its cloistered setting on the edge of a wood above the Connecticut River. Whether or not a doctoral program is an avowed goal of the Tuck School, Dean Karl Hill, 1938, and his new faculty are developing a demanding curriculum to serve the growing enrollment of graduate students seeking rapport with the far-flung complexities of modern business. At Tuck, as at the Medical School and at Thayer, one senses a reaching out beyond the northern hills.

The U.S. Army Cold Regions Laboratory, a research school with no student enrollment, no courses, and no degrees, is in Hanover partly because of the late Vilhjalmur Stefansson, whose collection helped establish Hanover as a polar outpost in a temperate zone. Since the Cold Regions Laboratory is an agency of the federal government it cannot be claimed for Dartmouth, but it is symbolic of the government money in and around higher education these days. The seven new Choate Road and Wigwam Circle dormitories were all constructed with federal loans under the government's College Housing Program.

Still, the preponderance of support for the College continues to come from alumni and from private charitable foundations. The new Bradley Mathematics Center, and indirectly, its enviable undergraduate and graduate programs are owing to the generosity of Alfred P. Sloan and his lifelong colleague, Albert Bradley, 1915, former president and chairman of General Motors. A million dollars from John D. Rockefeller launched the drive for the ambitious center for the arts named for President Emeritus Hopkins, while a benefaction of half as much again from Nathaniel Leverone, 1906, paid for the great vaulted field house designed by the Italian architect, Pier Luigi Nervi. The temptation always exists to name the spectacular gifts and honors, but the truth is, of course, that the backbone of the endowment consists of the vertebrae of thirty-odd thousand individual alumni.

Not long ago Stanley B. Jones, 1918, made a study of the cavalcade of gifts and givers through the years and of some of the interesting circumstances surrounding them. The first president of the Alumni Association, Judge Joel Parker of the Class of 1811, gave in 1868 fifteen thousand European trees to landscape the College Park. Albert O. Brown, 1878, former governor of New Hampshire and a Trustee until 1931, declared that his lifelong wish was to leave the College a million dollars, a goal which with resourcefulness and frugality he had achieved when he died in 1937. Since then his unrestricted bequest has grown to $3,507,000, the income from which has been responsible for a number of building projects for officers, faculty, and staff.

This I suggest may be the uniqueness of Dartmouth's opportunity now: to demonstrate a revitalization of the historic college purpose in today's terms. – John Sloan Dickey, 1961.

Christian Smith, a Hanover tailor dying at the nadir of the 1930's depression, left all he had, $8,805.50 for the benefit of the faculty. A post-Civil War graduate left $1,500 "to provide the nucleus of a fund which is to grow by compounded income, interest and profit accumulations for one hundred and fifty years during which neither principal nor interest shall be used for any purposes whatsoever other than the cautious and skilful investment as occasion may require." Johnny Johnson, 1866, literally showered the College with parcels of real estate. Every time he returned to Winter Carnival some undergraduate club found itself the beneficiary of his enthusiasm. He left money for "turkey funds" so that students who could not go home for Thanksgiving might enjoy a proper banquet at the Moose Mountain Cabin of the Outing Club. Concerning a small piece of property in Tacoma, Washington, that Johnson acquired by mortgage and gave to the College, President Emeritus Hopkins recalled:

Dr. Blank and I, while on a trip to Tacoma, began inquiring for this address, which (for the benefit of our Tacoma alumni) I shall call '50 Ridge Road'. As we proceeded, the neighborhood deteriorated rapidly, until we found ourselves proceeding along a footpath beside the railroad tracks. Eventually we came upon a large down-at-the-heel house badly in need of paint, which bore the number that we sought. Dr. Blank was obviously ill at ease in such sordid surroundings, so I mounted the steps and knocked. Presently the door was opened by a slatternly woman who bawled: 'Why are you coming around here knocking so loud for? You know the girls is always sleeping in the morning!' We left in some confusion and later, when the house was torn down, the trustees were not exactly overwhelmed with a sense of loss.

Frustrated in his attempt to secure lodging on several postgraduate visits to Hanover, Randolph McNutt, 1871, gave $50,000 in 1923 toward the addition to the Inn of fifty rooms, whose occupancy, it is certain, he was never denied thereafter. Non-alumnus Emil Bommer of Brooklyn, intent upon leaving his money to a college without women, first settled upon Yale. When he saw a headline that Yale was granting degrees to one hundred and fifty nurses, Dartmouth became his beneficiary — for more than half a million. The $2,500,000 bequest of Leon E. Williams, 1915, the largest in the College's history, included a 73,000-acre ranch in northeastern New Mexico, some 35,000 acres of range land in central South Dakota, a large farm in Nebraska, and a fertilizer plant in Colorado.

Probably the College's most unusual bequest was about one hundred acres on and below the summit of Mount Washington, together with a cog railroad composed of tracks and trestles, seven antique steam engines with their cars, and the Summit House, their destination. For twelve years some thirty thousand tourists a season rode to the summit amid clouds of steam and coal smoke under the auspices of the College. In 1962, determining that it really ought not to be in the transportation business, it sold the railroad to the protégé of Colonel Henry N. Teague, 1900, whose bequest it had originally been. In 1964 the College sold Mount Washington's summit to the state for the benefit of all the people. Of course there have been hundreds of gifts more classical in form and both large and small, for the supreme purposes of faculty and scholarship endowment. The largest of these, a million dollars from an anonymous donor, established twenty Daniel Webster Scholarships in 1953.

A capital gifts campaign among the alumni during 1957-59 produced seventeen-and-a-half million dollars. Canvasses for the Alumni Fund in the mid-1960's were yielding around a million-and-a-half dollars annually. In 1963 the College was awarded the grand prize of $5,000 for "sustained performance in alumni support" by the American Alumni Council at its fiftieth anniversary meeting. These phenomena — they are nothing short of that in the view of other institutions — can partly be explained by an effective organization of the alumni classes through class agents and other officers of the alumni clubs and enrollment committees, and of the Alumni Council, which helps the Board of Trustees advance the affairs of the College. The alumni relationship with the campus is strengthened through offerings of opportunities to alumni to share in the intellectual life of the College by returning for special symposia, lectures and other exposures to the academic program. The corporate College recognized in 1921 the broadening geography of its alumni body by raising from five to seven the number of nonresidents of New Hampshire on the Board of Trustees, and in 1961 by increasing the Board from twelve to sixteen members, only five of whom are now required to be residents of New Hampshire.

As a permanent bond between Dartmouth and every living alumnus, graduate or nongraduate, the Alumni Records Office tracks its subjects with bloodhound persistency. Charlotte Ford Morrison, long mistress of the hunt as Alumni Recorder, heard from one alumnus as follows: "So sure as your sins shall find you out, so will Dartmouth College." A plea for information from another alumnus was returned with the message: "John Jones does not live at this address any more. His wife lives here but she does not want his mail, or him!" A letter attempting to locate one of the few "lost" graduates was returned from a state penitentiary marked: "You are not on our accredited list of correspondents." Such alumni, happily, are a tiny minority. The achievements of the 11,091 Dartmouth veterans of World War II would alone produce a volume, to say nothing of the peaceful accomplishments of the whole alumni body in virtually every known endeavor.

For more than a third of a century the *Dartmouth Alumni Magazine,* a consistent prize-winner in its field and the strongest adhesive binding graduates to the College, has been in the hands of Dartmouth's durable Secretary, Sidney C. Hayward, 1926, and Charles E. Widmayer, 1930, who have managed to compress between its covers articles of moment in the educational world in addition to news of the campus and all of the classes.

The foregoing merely describes the mechanism of Dartmouth's vital alumni movement, it does not explain its mysteries. One can organize *dum domum boves redeant,* but the spirit must be willing; and that brings the relationship of Dartmouth men and their Alma Mater back to metaphysics again.

From 1946 through 1963 the endowment of the College jumped from twenty-two to one-hundred-million dollars, a great leap even if inflationary forces are taken into account.* Treasurer John F. Meck, 1933, presides over a payroll of fourteen hundred people and an annual disbursement of over eighteen million dollars in operating expenses, in addition to twenty-seven million in building investment since 1956. Whereas formerly most of the business of the College was conducted personally by the President, the administration today has perforce become similar to that of large industrial corporations with department heads carrying the responsibility for their vast and specialized affairs.

Construction and maintenance have become industries in themselves. With several prominent exceptions the building program during the Dickey regime would not be immediately apparent to a casual visitor, for buildings have a way of dropping into place as if they had always been there.† (It was only in 1953 that Clark School sold its property to the College, yet a whole generation of students is innocent of the knowledge of a former preparatory school within a stone's throw of Baker Library.)

> Just as a fine mind will not take the place of strong, trained legs in the competition of a foot race, nothing can take the place of a prepared intellect as the basic qualification necessary for today's academic pace in our leading colleges. – John Sloan Dickey, 1961.

It is no longer Dartmouth in the village of Hanover but Hanover in the presence of Dartmouth.

Much of the vitality of an institution such as Dartmouth flows from powerful creative forces quietly at work below the surface plane which alone meets the eyes of most observers. Yet the College through its long

---

* In the sixteen years ended June 30, 1962, Dartmouth received over $9,900,000 from fifty-one foundations, trusts, and similar non-governmental sources; and $6,775,799 from government agencies. The National Institute of Health ($3,911,355) and the National Science Foundation ($2,163,603) account for over $6,000,000 of the total.

† Sachem Village (married students), 1946, (relocated in 1958); Clark School: North, Cutter, and Fairbanks Halls, 1953; Thayer Dining Hall (addition), 1956; Brundage Lodge, Dartmouth Skiway, Faculty Housing (10-14 North Park Street), College Hall (remodeled), 1957; dormitories: Bissell, Brown, Cohen, Little, Wigwam (Circle); Wilder (addition), Rivercrest (thirty rental units), 1958; Steele Chemistry (addition), North Fayerweather (remodeled), 1959; Baker Library (addition), Hanover Inn Tavern and Middle Massachusetts (remodeled), 1960; Bradley-Gerry Mathematics and Psychology, Hanover Inn Motor Lodge, Medical Sciences Building, 1961; Hopkins Center, Kellogg Auditorium, Nathaniel Leverone Field House, West Wheelock Street apartments (staff housing), Sachem Village (new units), 1962; Dana Biomedical Library, Crosby Hall (addition), Fairbanks Hall (Dartmouth Films, moved to Sanborn-Lane House), McNutt (remodeled for Management Center), Robinson (remodeled), Strasenburgh (Medical School dormitory), 1963; Gymnasium (remodeled for basketball and new swimming pool), 1962-63; Charles Gilman Life Sciences Building, 1964. In addition one million dollars was expended on the enlargement of the steam distribution system, electric power plant and lines, and sewage system in 1957-58.

history has not been averse to pageantry when summoned by circumstances, such as the presence of the nation's chief executive. Thus President Monroe who in 1817 arrived on horseback was greeted "by the roar of cannon and other demonstration of joy;" and equivalent acclaim met the arrival of President Eisenhower in 1953 for the College's 184th Commencement.

The visit of Dwight D. Eisenhower was different from those of his predecessors, as all things now differ from the days of a simpler nation and a simpler College. Throngs lined the route from the Lebanon airport to Hanover, and at the Commencement exercises 10,000 people sat upon 10,000 folding chairs to form the largest assemblage ever gathered in Hanover. Sixteen special press telephone lines fed the news to the outer world, and dozens of city-clad Secret Service men merged into the College landscape as inconspicuously as a brass band. The Commencement procession was without precedent in length and plumage. Beyond the panoply of the moment two occurrences, at what came to be known as "the Eisenhower Commencement," left enduring marks. The first, born of necessity to accommodate unparalleled numbers of people, was the holding of the exercises for the first time before the main entrance to Baker Library, with unlimited audience capacity stretching south over the Library lawn, across Wentworth Street and into the middle of the Green itself. As has occurred often in the life of the College a "tradition" was born overnight, and simultaneously an established practice — the holding of outdoor Commencement exercises in the Bema — disappeared into history.

A second occurrence left a mark not only on the history of the College but on that of the nation. In an impromptu utterance to the Senior Class the President of the United States said:

Don't join the book burners. Don't think that you're going to conceal faults by concealing evidence that they ever existed. Don't be afraid to go in your library and read every book, as long as any document does not offend our own ideas of decency. That should be the only censorship.

How will we defeat communism unless we know what it is, what it teaches and why does it have such an appeal for men, why are so many people swearing allegiance to it? It's almost a religion, albeit one of the nether regions.

We have got to fight it with something better, not try to conceal the thinking of our own people. They are part of America. And even if they think ideas that are contrary to ours, their right to say them, their right to record them, and their right to have them at places where they're accessible to others is unquestioned, or it's not America.

In due course, time demonstrated that these words, immediately reproduced throughout the land, constituted one of the strongest links in a series of ultimately decisive attacks upon the then prevailing national climate of suspicion, hate, and discord known as McCarthyism.

Perhaps because it anticipated an educational need as much as it has filled one, Dartmouth's pioneering Hopkins Center is foremost among the developments of the Dickey administration. If, as it seems, a vast renaissance of interest in the arts is abroad in the land, modern Agoras on other campuses can only follow where Hopkins Center is leading.

Concerning the values of his College, Eleazar Wheelock wrote: "Our aim may therefore be stated as a stimulation of those gifts of the intellect with which nature has endowed the student so that he becomes . . . a better companion to himself through life. . . ." To this ideal Dartmouth presidents have long paid their homage and bent their energies. The Center arose out of dashed dreams. The new theater that Warner Bentley understood he would soon have when he came to Dartmouth in 1928 as director of The Players fell victim successively to a depression, a war, another war, and inflation. Yet from the postponement a much broader concept evolved: a center for the creative and performing arts with theaters, dressing rooms, rehearsal rooms, lecture halls and classrooms, art galleries, studios for painting, sculpture and graphic arts, music facilities for listening, practicing and broadcasting, metal and woodcraft workshops, a banquet hall and lounges for students, faculty, and alumni.

> . . . the management of time, choice and priority is . . . the most manly extracurricular art of all, — the self-disciplined life. – John Sloan Dickey, 1962.

The dedication in 1962 of the vast eight-million-dollar project, designed by Wallace K. Harrison, inaugurated ten days of musical and dramatic performances and panel discussions, exhibitions of paintings, sculpture, and crafts; and brought to Hanover a constellation of names in music, art, and the theater. At the conclusion of the opening ceremonies on November 8 the 85-year-old patriarch of Dartmouth, whose name the Center bears, remarked:

> . . . If one believes, as I do, that education is not education if it is simply an education of the specialist; if one believes, as I do, that something more is

[335]

necessary than to become technically expert in the sciences; if one believes that beauty and art and all that microcosm that we call culture are as essential to man as anything else, then the significance of this occasion begins to be apparent. This is something more than the addition to the campus of a structure of dignity and grandeur. . . . It is something more than an exhibit of what a college plant can be made. It will in the course of events, I am certain, become the heart and soul of Dartmouth. Man is something more than a chemical compound enclosed in a skin, the mind is something more than a computer, and the soul of man — nobody knows what it is, but it exists. And this Center stands for all those things.

The second climax of the dedication came on the last night, Saturday, November 17. Following a formal reception in the lounge and a banquet in the Center's Alumni Hall, with the President and the President Emeritus as guests of honor, five-hundred alumni and friends of the College dispersed to attend, in different places at the same time in the same great building, a concert by the Dartmouth Community Orchestra, the pipe organ and Glee Club, and a drama by the Dartmouth Players. The art galleries were full. Reflected in the vaulted windows of the Center were the flames of a campus bonfire celebrating the winning that day of the Ivy League football championship. Tomorrow Nervi's soaring field house would be dedicated.

The spirits of all those laborers in learning who have gone before were gathered on the Green that night — a communing of the thousands of men whose heritage is the College on the hill.

Bibliographical Note

SINCE this book is an informal chronicle rather than a formal history we have dispensed with the apparatus expected of a scholarly treatise. This does not mean, of course, that we have not constantly kept in mind the necessity for accuracy. In a great many if not in most cases the sources of our information will be obvious from the text. We have deposited our working notes and the annotated first draft of our manuscripts in the Dartmouth College Archives to which the curious reader and the historical sleuths in doubt about obscure references may have access.

We have relied heavily on the histories of Dartmouth College by Chase (Frederick Chase, *A history of Dartmouth College and the town of Hanover, New Hampshire*. Edited by John K. Lord, Cambridge, [Mass.]: J. Wilson and Son, 1891, vol. 1, and Concord: The Rumford Press, 1913, vol. 2), Smith (Baxter Perry Smith, *The history of Dartmouth College*. Boston: Houghton Osgood and Co., 1878), and Richardson (Leon Burr Richardson, *History of Dartmouth College*. Hanover: Dartmouth College Publications, 1932, 2 vols.)—especially the latter; on the history of the town by Lord (John King Lord, *A history of the town of Hanover, N. H.*, with an appendix on Hanover roads by Professor J. W. Goldthwait. Hanover: The Dartmouth Press, 1928); on the Hanover bicentennial book (Francis Lane Childs, editor, *Hanover, New Hampshire, a bicentennial book, essays in celebration of the town's 200th anniversary*. Hanover: [Hanover Bicentennial Committee] 1961); on the files of *The Dartmouth* and the *Dartmouth Alumni Magazine;* Dr. Tucker's autobiography, *My generation* (Boston: Houghton Mifflin Co., 1919); and on the collection of President Emeritus Hopkins' speeches, *This our purpose.* (Hanover: Dartmouth Publications, 1950.) We have also drawn material from newspaper clippings and letters in the Alumni Records and Faculty Files. The principal additional sources for the various chapters are noted below.

Chapter I. The Historic College

Barstow, Josiah Whitney, "Reminiscences of Professor Shurtleff", *Dartmouth Alumni Magazine,* vol. 4, December 1911, p. 52-54.

Belknap, Jeremy, *Journey to Dartmouth in 1774,* edited by Edward C. Lathem. Hanover: Dartmouth Publications [1950].

Beveridge, Albert Jeremiah, *The life of John Marshall*. Boston: Houghton Mifflin Co., 1916-19, 4 vols.

Caverno, Charles, "Reminiscences of forty years ago", *The Dartmouth*, vol. 17, November 8, 1895, p. 129-130.

Centennial celebration at Dartmouth College, July 21, 1869. Hanover: J. B. Parker, 1870.

Childs, Francis Lane, "Dartmouth Hall, old and new", *Dartmouth Alumni Magazine*, vol. 28, January 1936, p. 7-17.

Choate, Rufus, *A discourse delivered before the faculty, students and alumni of Dartmouth College, on the day preceding commencement, July 27, 1853, commemorative of Daniel Webster*. Boston: J. Munroe and Company, 1853.

Emerson, Ralph Waldo, *An Oration, delivered before the literary societies of Dartmouth College, July 24, 1838*. Boston: C. C. Little and J. Brown, 1838.

Fuess, Claude Moore, *Daniel Webster*. Boston: Little, Brown & Co., 1930, 2 vols.

Hill, William Carroll, comp., *Dartmouth traditions, being a compilation of facts and events connected with the history of Dartmouth College and the lives of its graduates, from the early founding of the College in 1769 to the present day*. Hanover: printed at the Dartmouth Press, 1901.

Lathem, Edward Connery, "Dartmouth and Dartmouth", *Dartmouth Alumni Magazine*, vol. 51, December 1958, p. 30-32.

McCallum, James Dow, *Eleazar Wheelock, founder of Dartmouth College*, Hanover: Dartmouth College Publications, 1939.

McCallum, James Dow, editor, *The letters of Eleazar Wheelock's Indians*. Hanover: Dartmouth College Publications, 1932.

Pattee, Fred Lewis, "Dartmouth jottings of a somewhat desultory reader", *Dartmouth Alumni Magazine*, vol. 16, February 1924, p. 317-321.

The proceedings of the Webster Centennial . . ., edited by Ernest Martin Hopkins . . . and printed under the supervision of Homer Eaton Keyes. [Hanover: printed for the College at the Dartmouth Press, 1902]

Richardson, Leon Burr, "The Dartmouth Indians, 1800-1893", *Dartmouth Alumni Magazine*, vol. 22, June 1930, p. 524-527.

Shirley, John Major, *The Dartmouth College causes and the Supreme Court of the United States*. St. Louis: G. I. Jones and Co., 1879.

Ticknor, George, *Life, letters and journals of George Ticknor*. Boston: James R. Osgood & Co., 1876, 2 vols.

Wheelock, Eleazar, *A brief narrative of the Indian Charity School, in Lebanon in Connecticut, New England. Founded and carried on by that faithful servant of God the Rev. Mr. Eleazar Wheelock*. London: printed by J. and W. Oliver, 1766.

Wheelock, Eleazar, *A continuation of the narrative of the Indian Charity School, begun in Lebanon, in Connecticut, now incorporated with Dartmouth-College, in Hanover, in the Province of New Hampshire*. New Hampshire: printed in the year 1772.

Wheelock, Eleazar, [Reprints of narratives] Rochester, N. Y.: The Genesee Press, 1908?-1910?, 9 vols.

Chapter II. The Place

Bartlett, Edwin Julius, *A Dartmouth book of remembrance, pen and camera sketches of Hanover and the College before the Centennial and after*. Hanover: The Webster Press, 1922.

Belknap, Jeremy, *The history of New Hampshire. . . .* Philadelphia: printed for the author by R. Aitken, 1784-1792, 3 vols.

Henry, James Dodds, *History and romance of the petroleum industry*, illustrated by Philip Pimlott, Eric Swinstead. London: printed by Bradbury, Agnew & Co., ltd. [1914]-, 1 vol.

Powers, Grant, *Historical sketches of the discovery, settlement, and progress of events in the Coos country and vicinity, principally included between the years 1754 and 1785.* Haverhill, N. H.: J. F. C. Hayes, 1841.

Whitman, Walt, *Calamus, a series of letters written during the years 1868-1880 . . . to a young friend (Peter Doyle),* edited with an introduction by Richard Maurice Bucke. . . . Boston: L. Maynard, 1897.

Chapter III. The Faculty

Ames, Adelbert, *The morning notes of Adelbert Ames, Jr., including a correspondence with John Dewey,* edited and with a preface by Hadley Cantril. New Brunswick, N. J.: Rutgers University Press [c1960].

Balsdon, John Percy Vyvian Dacre, *Oxford Life.* London: Eyre & Spottiswoode, 1957.

Brown, Bancroft Huntington, "Mathematics at Dartmouth", 1769-1961. Dedicatory Conference. Albert Bradley Center for Mathematics, Dartmouth College, November 3, 1961. Typewritten copy in the Dartmouth College Archives.

Chapman, George Thomas, *Sketches of the alumni of Dartmouth College, from the first graduation in 1771 to the present time, with a brief history of the institution.* Cambridge: Riverside Press, 1867.

Currier, Amos Noyes, "Dartmouth College fifty years ago", *The Dartmouth Bi-Monthly,* vol. 1, June 1906, p. 244-254.

Dictionary of American Biography, under the auspices of the American Council of Learned Societies. New York: C. Scribner's Sons, 1923-36.

Hardy, Arthur Sherburne, *Things remembered.* Boston: Houghton Mifflin Co., 1923.

James, William, *Memories and studies.* New York: Longmans, Green, and Co., 1912.

LeDuc, Thomas Harold André, *Piety and intellect at Amherst College, 1865-1912.* New York: Columbia University Press, 1946.

Mayo, Lawrence Shaw, *John Wentworth, governor of New Hampshire, 1767-1775.* Cambridge: Harvard University Press, 1921.

Mecklin, John Moffatt, *My quest for freedom.* New York: C. Scribner's Sons, 1945.

Morison, Samuel Eliot, *Three centuries of Harvard, 1636-1936.* Cambridge: Harvard University Press, 1936.

Sanborn, Katherine Abbott, *Memories and anecdotes. . . .* New York: G. P. Putnam's Sons, 1915.

Whitehead, Alfred North, *Dialogues of Alfred North Whitehead,* as recorded by Lucien Price. Boston: Little, Brown & Co. [1954].

Chapter IV. The Students

Bartlett, Edwin Julius, *A Dartmouth book of remembrance, pen and camera sketches of Hanover and the College before the Centennial and after.* Hanover: The Webster Press, 1922.

Bartlett, Edwin Julius, "Faculty meetings", *Dartmouth Alumni Magazine,* vol. 20, December 1927, p. 140-145.

Bartlett, Edwin Julius, "Pen and camera sketches of Hanover and the College before the Centennial, IV. The old chapel", *Dartmouth Alumni Magazine,* vol. 13, May 1921, p. 442-450.

Caverno, Charles, "Reminiscences of forty years ago", *The Dartmouth,* vol. 17, November 8, 1895, p. 129-130.

Clark, Francis Edward, "Dartmouth days, a chapter from an unpublished autobiography". *Dartmouth Alumni Magazine,* vol. 9, May 1917, p. 306-312.

Dartmouth College. Class of 1827, *A memorial of the college life of the Class of 1827, Dartmouth College . . .*, by Alpheus Crosby. Hanover: 1869-70.

Dartmouth College. Committee for Survey of Social Life in Dartmouth College Fraternities. *Report of the Committee for Survey of Social Life in Dartmouth College Fraternities.* Hanover: 1936.

Hapgood, Herbert Jackson and Craven Layock, editors, *Echoes from Dartmouth, a collection of poems, stories, and historical sketches by graduate and undergraduate writers of Dartmouth College.* Hanover and St. Johnsbury: [C. M. Stone & Co., printers], 1895.

Hayward, Jebediah Kilbourn, "A Dartmouth tragedy", *The Dartmouth Magazine,* vol. 15, March 1901, p. 174-182.

Kendall, Amos, *Autobiography of Amos Kendall,* edited by his son-in-law, William Stickney. Boston: Lee and Shepard, 1872.

Lord, John King, *A history of the town of Hanover, N. H.,* with an appendix on Hanover roads by Professor J. W. Goldthwait. Printed for the town of Hanover by the Dartmouth Press, 1928.

McClure, David and Elijah Parish, *Memoirs of the Rev. Eleazar Wheelock, D.D., founder and president of Dartmouth College and Moor's Charity School. . . .* Newburyport: published by Edward Little & Co., and sold at their bookstore, Market Square, C. Norris & Co., printers, 1811.

Nash, Ray, *Navy at Dartmouth.* Hanover: Dartmouth Publications, 1946.

Powers, Samuel Leland, "Dartmouth in the seventies", *Dartmouth Alumni Magazine,* vol. 16, February, March, and May 1924, p. 304-311, 388-396, 575-580.

Powers, Samuel Leland, *Portraits of a half century.* Boston: Little, Brown & Co., 1925.

Smith, Clifford Hayes, "Four years at Dartmouth". [Excerpts from letters written from Dartmouth College, 1875-79.] Typewritten copy in the Dartmouth College Archives.

Spalding, James Alfred, "The school and college life of Judah Dana of the Class of 1795", *Dartmouth Alumni Magazine,* vol. 9, February 1917, p. 155-166.

Chapter VI. The Modern College

Dartmouth College, *Exercises and addresses attending the laying of the cornerstone of the new Dartmouth Hall and the visit of the Earl of Dartmouth to the College October 25 and 26, 1904,* edited by Ernest Martin Hopkins. Hanover: printed for the College, 1905.

Dickey, John Sloan, "Conscience and the undergraduate", *The Atlantic Monthly,* vol. 195, April 1953, p. 31-35.

Dickey, John Sloan, "Dartmouth's ongoing purpose", *Dartmouth Alumni Magazine,* vol. 54, April 1962, p. 18-20.

Dickey, John Sloan, "Education's 'New Frontier' ", *Dartmouth Alumni Magazine,* vol. 53, March 1961, p. 27.

Ford, Charlotte E., "You're a V.I.P. to the A.R.O., the Alumni Records Office keeps an eye on 23,000 Dartmouth men and has fun as well as headaches", *Dartmouth Alumni Magazine,* vol. 41, January 1945, p. 20-22.

Hopkins, Ernest Martin, "The beginnings of Dartmouth's alumni organization", *Dartmouth Alumni Magazine,* vol. 47, March 1955, p. 16-19.

Jones, Stanley Burt, 'I give and bequeath to the Trustees of Dartmouth College . . .', *Dartmouth Alumni Magazine,* vol. 39, January, February, April 1947, p. 28-30, 21-22, 28-29.

Parkhurst, Lewis, "What are the Trustees doing?", *Dartmouth Alumni Magazine,* vol. 16, June 1924, p. 665-672.

Richardson, Charles Francis, "William Jewett Tucker, an appreciation", *Dartmouth Alumni Magazine,* vol. 19, December 1926, p. 140.

BIBLIOGRAPHICAL NOTE

Richardson, Leon Burr, *Dartmouth College, a statement of its objectives, achievements and opportunities*. Hanover: Dartmouth College Alumni Council, 1937.

Richardson, Leon Burr, "Streeter Hall, dormitory name recalls robust Dartmouth figure", *Dartmouth Alumni Magazine,* vol. 36, May 1944, p. 17-18.

Richardson, Leon Burr, "Useless Dartmouth information", *Dartmouth Alumni Magazine,* vol. 34, February 1942, p. 9-12.

Tucker, William Jewett, Personal power, counsels to college men. Boston: Houghton Mifflin Co., 1910.

ACKNOWLEDGMENTS

Our debt to the Dartmouth Library and to the College Librarian, Richard W. Morin, is great. His encouragement and editorial judgment have been invaluable. Edward Connery Lathem, Associate Librarian, has also made important contributions, as have Mr. Kenneth C. Cramer and Mrs. Doreen P. Hanna of the Archives. We are indebted to President Emeritus Ernest Martin Hopkins for the hours spent with him. His wealth of memories, some of them "off the record", has given us a special sense of Dartmouth in the first four decades of the twentieth century.

The following gentlemen have read the manuscript in whole or in part and have been helpful with suggestions and kindly criticism: President John S. Dickey, President Hopkins, Professors Francis Lane Childs and F. Cudworth Flint, Messrs. Morin and Lathem, Messrs. Francis Brown, John F. Meck, Gilbert R. Tanis, Sidney C. Hayward, Charles E. Widmayer and Upton P. Lord. We are grateful also to Ford H. Wheldon, Dana W. Atchley, to Adrian Bouchard and Mrs. Anne Scotford of the Dartmouth Photo Bureau, and to our typists, Mrs. Inez M. Kellam, Mrs. Claire Packard, and Mrs. Laura Twitchell.

Index

DC = Dartmouth College